COMMUNIST AND POSTCOMMUNIST POLITICAL SYSTEMS

Communist and Postcommunist Political Systems
An Introduction

Third Edition

Stephen White
John Gardner
George Schöpflin
Tony Saich

St. Martin's Press　　New York

First and second editions published under the title *Communist Political Systems*

First edition 1982
Reprinted 1984, 1985, 1986
Second edition 1987
Reprinted 1988

This edition first published in the United States of America in 1990

Printed in Great Britain

ISBN 0–312–05019–4 cloth
ISBN 0–312–05020–8 paper

Library of Congress Cataloging-in-Publication Data
Communist and postcommunist political systems : an introduction /
    Stephen White ... [et al.].—3rd ed.
        p.   cm.
    Rev. ed. of: Communist political systems / Stephen White. 2nd ed.
1987.
    Includes bibliographical references and index.
    ISBN 0–312–05019–4.—ISBN 0–312–05020–8 (pbk.)
    1. Communist state. 2. Communist countries—Politics and
government.   I. White, Stephen, 1945–   .   II. White, Stephen,
    1945–   Communist political systems.
JC474.W48   1990
321.9′2—dc20   90–35857
                                                              CIP

Contents

List of Maps, Figures and Tables

Map

Tables

Figures

Preface to the Third Edition

This book appears at a time of unprecedented change in the communist world. In the USSR and China, and most dramatically of all in Eastern Europe in 1989 and 1990, an entire generation of leaders has been replaced and a succession of new governments, many of them largely or entirely non-communist, has been elected to take their place. Entering the 1990s, indeed, it is unclear how useful it remains to speak of a 'communist world', and far from clear how the political systems that are emerging, particularly in Eastern Europe, may best be characterised.

The third edition of this book, accordingly, is a very different one from its predecessors. We have a new title, designed to draw attention to the changing nature of the political systems with which we are concerned – 'postcommunist' (although still strongly influenced by Marxism) as well as 'communist'. We have a new set of authors, Tony Saich having joined us in place of the late John Gardner, whose untimely death has been a serious loss to the world of communist scholarship. And, most important of all, the contents of this book are very different indeed from those of the two preceding editions: a new chapter on the leaderships is one such change, but all the other chapters have been substantially – and in some cases almost entirely – rewritten, and the bibliographies and other parts of the book have been thoroughly revised.

It would be idle to pretend that in a single volume of limited dimensions we can exhaust the subject of communist and postcommunist politics, still less that our approach and conclusions will command universal assent. We do, however, hope that like its predecessors, *Communist and Postcommunist Political Systems* will provide a clear, accurate and up-to-date guide to a set of systems that remain central to world politics in the late twentieth century, and we hope also that it will help to identify (if not in every case resolve) some of the controversies with which the study of these systems has always been associated.

STEPHEN WHITE
GEORGE SCHÖPFLIN
TONY SAICH

Glossary

ASSR	autonomous soviet socialist republic
CCP	Chinese Communist Party
CMEA/Comecon	Council for Mutual Economic Assistance
Cominform	Communist Information Bureau
Comintern	Communist Third International
CPSU	Communist Party of the Soviet Union
GDR	German Democratic Republic
GNP	gross national product
LCY	League of Communists in Yugoslavia
NEM	New Economic Mechanism (Hungary)
NEP	New Economic Policy (USSR)
NKVD	People's Commissariat of Internal Affairs (security police in USSR, later KGB)
NPC	National People's Congress (China)
OECD	Organisation for Economic Co-operation and Development
PLA	People's Liberation Army (China)
PPF	People's Patriotic Front (Hungary)
PRC	People's Republic of China
RSFSR	Russian Republic
USSR	Union of Soviet Socialist Republics
WTO	Warsaw Treaty Organisation

1

The Comparative Study of Communist and Postcommunist States

Communist states are a relatively recent phenomenon. When the First World War broke out in 1914 there were none at all. For many years after the Russian Revolution of 1917 there were only three, the USSR itself and two Asian outposts, Mongolia and Tuva; and as late as the end of the Second World War there were only five such states, located for the most part in Eastern Europe (Albania and Yugoslavia as well as the USSR). Since then communist regimes have come into existence elsewhere in Eastern Europe (Bulgaria, Romania, Poland, Czechoslovakia, Hungary and the German Democratic Republic), in Latin America (Cuba), and also in Asia (China, North Korea and most recently Laos and Kampuchea). As a result of these changes there were sixteen states which, in the 1980s, could reasonably be classified as communist. Far-reaching changes in Eastern Europe at the end of the decade meant that this was, in the early 1990s, a classification that was less easy to defend, and we have accordingly identified the states concerned as 'communist and postcommunist' in Table 1.1. All of these states remained profoundly influenced by Marxism–Leninism; some of them, however, had formed largely non-communist governments and were adopting economic and other policies that were likely to take them outside even a 'postcommunist' world in the later 1990s.

Beyond the 'communist and postcommunist' world, with which we are principally concerned in this volume, a number of other regimes, particularly in the developing countries,

TABLE 1.1

Communist and postcommunist states, 1990

Name of state	Date established	Area (000km²)	Population mid-1987 (millions)	Level of development
Union of Soviet Socialist Republics	1917	22 402	283	(Non-market economy)
Mongolian People's Republic	1924	1 565	2	Lower middle-income
People's Republic of Albania	1944	29	3	(Non-market economy)
Socialist Federal Republic of Yugoslavia	1945	256	23	Upper middle-income
Socialist Republic of Vietnam	1945/76	330	65	Low income
People's Republic of Bulgaria	1946	111	9	(Non-market economy)
Republic of Romania	1947	238	23	Upper middle-income
Republic of Poland	1947	313	38	Lower middle-income
Democratic People's Republic of Korea	1948	121	21	Lower middle-income
Czechoslovak Republic	1948	128	16	(Non-market economy)
Republic of Hungary	1949	93	11	Upper middle-income
German Democratic Republic	1949	108	17	(Non-market economy)
People's Republic of China	1949	9 561	1 069	Low income
Republic of Cuba	1959	115	10	Lower middle-income
People's Democratic Republic of Laos	1975	237	4	Low income
People's Republic of Kampuchea	1975	181	7	Low income

Source: Based upon the World Bank, *World Development Report 1989* (New York, 1989).

were guided to various degrees by Marxism–Leninism in the 1980s and early 1990s. There was, first of all, a group of states that professed a commitment to Marxist policies and had close economic and political relations with the USSR, and which were governed by 'vanguard revolutionary-democratic parties' (as they were known in Soviet terminology). In the late 1980s this group included Afghanistan, Angola, Congo (Brazzaville), Mozambique, Ethiopia, Madagascar and the People's Democratic Republic of Yemen. Beyond this, a rather larger group of states had adopted some of the features of communist rule, such as a single-party system and large-scale public ownership, and were publicly committed to Marxist policies. These states, guided by what Soviet sources termed 'national liberation' or 'revolutionary-democratic' movements, included, for instance, Nicaragua under the Sandinistas, Zimbabwe, Benin, and Grenada (until its ruling New Jewel Movement was overthrown by US military action in 1983). The sixteen ruling parties, taken together, were known as the 'world socialist system', based around a 'socialist community' of the USSR's closest allies. More broadly, all the ruling and non-ruling parties, about 100 of which were acknowledged in Soviet sources with about 80 million members, constituted what was called the world communist movement.

Communist states, however broadly defined, are thus a small minority of the 150 or so states that are members of the United Nations. Their importance, however, is much greater than these limited numbers might suggest. The communist states, for instance, account for about a third of the world's population, and for more than 40 per cent of the world's industrial production. The communist states include the world's largest state, the USSR; the world's most populous state, China; one of the world's main trading blocs, the Council for Mutual Economic Assistance or Comecon; and one of the world's two major military alliances, the Warsaw Treaty Organisation. Above all, from the point of view of the political scientist, the communist states collectively constitute one of the world's main models or types of political system, one which is not simply different from but fundamentally opposed to the Western liberal-democratic or capitalist system. To official spokesmen in the communist countries the difference is one between 'socialist democracy', which, whatever its imperfections, embodies the real interests of working people, and the 'bourgeois democracy' of the capitalist West, serving the interests of a small minority of exploiters. In the Western countries, on the other hand, the difference is seen as one between 'democracy', based upon the freely expressed will of the people, and the 'dictatorship' or 'totalitarianism' of the communist East, based upon the power of a self-appointed minority of party functionaries. Although greater emphasis was being placed, in the late 1980s, upon the need for a cooperative approach to world problems, the differences that existed between these two types of government was still seen by both sides as the most fundamental of all those that existed in world politics.

Most political scientists would consider four main differences between communist and Western liberal-democratic systems to be of particular importance, and together these features may be regarded as the defining characteristics of a communist system. In the first place, all the communist states in the 1980s based themselves upon an official ideology, Marxism–Leninism, which was derived from the theories of Marx, Engels, Lenin and (in China) Mao Zedong, and which provided the vocabulary of politics in these states as well as the basis upon which their rulers claimed to exercise authority. (This was not, of course, to say that all the rulers and populations of the communist states were necessarily wholly committed to Marxist values, which is a separate and empirical question.) The economy in the communist states, secondly, was largely or almost entirely in public rather than in private ownership, and production was typically organised through a central planning apparatus and conducted by means of national economic plans. The communist states, in other words, had what were normally referred to as 'command' or 'administered economies', rather than the 'market economies' of the capitalist West.

The third distinguishing feature of the communist states in the 1980s is that they were ruled, in all but exceptional circumstances, by a single or at least a dominant communist party, within which power was typically highly centralised.

This was ensured by the application of the principle of 'democratic centralism', by which each level in the hierarchy had to submit to the decisions of the level immediately above it, and by the 'ban on factions', which forbade any attempt to organise an opposition within these parties (this did not, of course, mean that there were no differences of opinion or even informal groupings within them). And finally, the range of institutions which in Western societies were more or less independent of the political authorities, such as the press, the trade unions and the courts, were in the communist states effectively under the direct control of the party hierarchy. This wide-ranging control over virtually all areas of society was known as the party's 'leading role', and for the communist authorities themselves it was of particular importance: it was, for instance, to recover this 'leading role' for the communist party in Czechoslovakia that the Warsaw Pact powers justified their intervention in that country in 1968.

These features of the political system are all important, and they all apply, or have at least applied until very recently, to the communist and postcommunist states we shall be considering in this volume. It does not necessarily follow, however, that the differences between one communist state and another are thereby reduced to insignificance. On the contrary it has become apparent, particularly over the last decade or two, that the label 'communism' may conceal almost as much as it may reveal, and that there is a greater degree of variety between the communist states in terms of their political processes – influenced as these are by the different histories, cultures and social structures of these countries – than their common institutional framework might at first suggest. Indeed even here the differences between one communist state and another are by no means negligible. In most communist states, for instance, virtually all productive resources are in the hands of the state, but in others, such as Poland, most agricultural land has been left in private ownership. In most of the communist states, similarly, a single communist party holds power, while in others, such as China, Vietnam and North Korea, a variety of nominally independent parties are permitted to exist, and in still others, such as Poland and Hungary, a form of competitive multiparty politics had become established by the early 1990s. There are also important social and cultural differences between one communist state and another. Some of the communist states, for instance Poland and Cuba, are traditionally Roman Catholic, while others are Eastern Orthodox or Buddhist, and one (Albania) is officially atheist. And there are wide disparities between them in terms of their levels of economic and social development.

Indeed so considerable are the differences between one communist state and another and so great are the similarities between them and some other countries, particularly in the developing world, that some have gone so far as to suggest that the notion of a communist political system is nowadays of little analytical utility. One of the most influential statements of this view is that of John H. Kautsky. The communist states, Kautsky has argued in an article provocatively entitled 'Comparative communism versus comparative politics' (1973), do not have in fact any particular distinguishing characteristics apart from the symbols they employ, and most of the features supposedly distinctive to these systems can in fact be found elsewhere. Like a number of other political scientists Kautsky prefers to emphasise the distinction between developing or 'mobilised' regimes, some of which are communist, and developed or 'adaptation' regimes, a category which includes the economically more developed communist states as well as the Western liberal democracies. Although the changes that took place in many communist-ruled countries in the late 1980s certainly reduced their distinctiveness, for most political scientists communist political systems did nonetheless retain a number of distinguishing features, such as their official ideology, their largely nationalised economies and the leading role that was played within them by their single or dominant ruling parties, and these features, taken together, were widely agreed to mark out a sub-set of political systems which it was reasonable to consider as a group and instructive to compare with each other. This, however, in no way precluded their comparison with political systems in other countries, either in the developing or developed world. Comparative communist politics, seen in this light, was best seen as a sub-field within comparative politics, not, as Kautsky appeared to suggest, as an alternative to it.

The development of the communist state system

The Russian revolution of November 1917 was carried through on the assumption that Russia, though a backward country and not itself 'ready' for a revolution in the Marxist sense, could be used to break the economic links that held together the major capitalist powers and thus to bring about a European and eventually a world-wide communist revolution. At the time these perspectives did not seem entirely unrealistic. Immediately after the First World War ended, in 1918–19, there were revolutionary uprisings in many parts of the world, and in Europe Soviet republics were established in Bavaria and Hungary. In 1920 factories were occupied in Italy, and Councils of Action were set up in Great Britain to oppose government policy towards Russia. The following year there was a communist-led rising in central Germany, and in 1923 there were more serious attempts at insurrection in northern Germany and in Bulgaria. In 1926 there was a general strike in Britain, and by about the same date a powerful communist presence had begun to establish itself in China and elsewhere in the colonial world. Soviet influence over this developing movement was exercised through the Communist International, founded in 1919, which was based in Moscow and whose executive committee was largely dominated by Russians. The Comintern, as it was known, saw its task as the provision of revolutionary leadership for the workers and peasants of the developed and colonial countries; these were only held back from more decisive action, it was believed, by the caution and indecision of their reformist leaders.

The Soviet republics in Bavaria and Hungary, however, soon collapsed, the risings in Germany and Bulgaria were ignominiously defeated, and the later 1920s saw authoritarian governments come into power throughout much of Europe which began to repress their domestic communist and trade union movements with a good deal of energy and efficiency. In China, in 1927, what had been the most promising colonial revolutionary movement was bloodily repressed by Chiang Kai-shek, and elsewhere in the colonial world communist parties were enjoying little success. The USSR, as a result, was left almost entirely isolated as the world's first communist state for most of the period up to the Second World War, participating in international conferences and attempting to win popular support in the West while at the same time developing its military and industrial strength and wondering how long it could safely survive in the 'capitalist encirclement' in which it found itself. The only important respect in which Soviet isolation became less during this period was with the establishment of People's Republics in the small Siberian region of Tannu Tuva in 1921 (absorbed into the USSR as an autonomous province in 1944) and in Mongolia in 1924, after Chinese occupying forces had been defeated with substantial Soviet assistance. In all essentials, however, the USSR remained an isolated outpost of communism in international politics, an isolation whose dangers became steadily more apparent as the Western powers continued to fail to offer serious resistance to the rise of Hitler, above all at Munich in 1938. A Nazi–Soviet non-aggression pact was signed in 1939, but in 1941 Hitler abruptly broke it off and invaded the western USSR. In the four years that followed the USSR lost over 20 million dead and suffered material damage on an unimaginable scale. There must have seemed every reason, as the end of the war approached, for Soviet negotiators to try to strengthen the security of their frontiers, above all in the west, and to try in this connection so far as possible to retain control over the parts of Eastern and Central Europe that they had liberated from the Nazis.

At the Moscow, Yalta and Potsdam conferences of 1944 and 1945 these objectives were substantially achieved, in large part with the acceptance of the USSR's Western allies, and the establishment of a system of communist states in Eastern Europe under Soviet control is essentially a product of the division of Europe into rival spheres of influence which was the outcome of these agreements. In some cases there was little domestic support for communist policies and the new government was effectively installed by the Red Army (the German Democratic Republic, North Korea, Poland and Romania). In Bulgaria, similarly, the communist party had previously enjoyed a considerable degree of popular support, but the country had supported the Axis Powers during the

Second World War and it was occupied by the Red Army in 1944, with whose assistance a communist government came into being a few years later. In Czechoslovakia and Hungary, on the other hand, the communist party did enjoy a substantial degree of popular support and the Red Army, despite occasional excesses, was seen by many as the agency by which these countries had been liberated from the Nazis. In Czechoslovakia the communist party in fact secured 38 per cent of the vote, the largest for any party, in the relatively free elections of 1946, while in Hungary the communists became the largest single party after the rather less freely held elections of 1947. In both cases coalition governments were established within which communists swiftly assumed a dominant position.

In Yugoslavia, Albania, North Vietnam and China a rather different path was followed. The communist party in these countries rose to power through its leadership of a popular resistance movement against either Axis or (in the case of North Vietnam and China) Japanese occupation, and had little or no Soviet assistance in doing so. This tended to give these regimes a greater degree of at least initial popular support than the other communist regimes possessed, and it may have encouraged them to take a more independent attitude towards Moscow than the communist governments that were simply imported (as the phrase had it) 'in the baggage train of the Red Army'. In the case of China, and to some extent elsewhere, there was even some doubt about whether the local communists had the backing of the Soviet government in attempting to proceed directly to the establishment of a communist state. Soviet representatives urged a truce with the Chinese Nationalists (the Kuomintang) until the last possible moment, and the Soviet ambassador was reportedly the last to leave the Nationalist government immediately before its downfall. The USSR none the less recognised the Chinese People's Republic on 2 October 1949, the day after its foundation, and in February 1950 the two countries concluded a friendship treaty with a thirty-year period of validity.

The next extension of communist rule was in Cuba, where Fidel Castro assumed power in 1959 with the overthrow of the Batista dictatorship. His programme was initially of a broadly democratic character, but in 1961 he publicly declared his allegiance to Marxism–Leninism, and the country moved subsequently into an increasingly close association with the other communist states. Finally in 1975, following the conclusion of the Vietnam war, North and South Vietnam were merged into a single state with the name of the Socialist Republic of Vietnam (its constitution was formally approved after nation-wide elections had taken place the following year); a People's Democratic Republic was established in Laos following the abdication of King Sayang Vatthana and the abolition of the monarchy; and in Cambodia (subsequently known as Kampuchea) the Khmer Rouge defeated the pro-Western regime of Lon Nol and adopted a new constitution of an essentially communist type. The Khmer Rouge were in turn ousted by a government sympathetic to the Vietnamese military forces which invaded the country at the end of 1978, but this new regime, headed by the People's Revolutionary Party of Kampuchea, has still to win a wide degree of international recognition and is not yet in undisputed control of the entire national territory.

Relations between the communist states have been by no means as stable as a common dedication to working-class interests might ordinarily have suggested. The first split occurred as early as 1948 when Yugoslavia was denounced by the Soviet Union and by Cominform (the Communist Information Bureau, established in 1947) for supposedly giving too much favour to the peasants at the expense of the workers and for exercising the leadership of the communist party (the Yugoslav League of Communists) in an insufficiently decisive manner. In fact there appears no doubt that Stalin simply resented the independence that the Yugoslav leaders were displaying and believed that they could be brought to heel as national communist leaders had been elsewhere in Eastern Europe. If so, he miscalculated badly; the Yugoslavs arrested Soviet supporters within the Yugoslav League of Communists, placed Soviet representatives in Yugoslavia under the surveillance of the secret police and weathered the storm with a largely united people behind them, not least by emphasising the threat to the country from abroad. In 1955 Khrushchev and Bulganin visited Belgrade, and in 1956 a joint Soviet–

Yugoslav communiqué was signed in Moscow which effectively brought the dispute to an end. In the same year there were serious disturbances in Poland, where the workers of Poznań revolted and popular pressures led to the election of a new party leadership headed by Władysław Gomułka, and in Hungary, where a more far-reaching experiment in 'liberal communism' was terminated by the intervention of the Red Army. Some years later, in 1968, an attempt to introduce what was described as 'socialism with a human face' in Czechoslovakia under Alexander Dubček was brought to an end by the intervention of five Warsaw Pact powers led by the USSR.

Relations between the Soviet Union and China, meanwhile, were steadily deteriorating. The Chinese leaders appear to have been dissatisfied with a number of aspects of the Sino-Soviet friendship treaty of 1950, and at the 20th Congress of the Communist Party of the Soviet Union in 1956 they were reportedly unhappy about the manner in which the Stalin question had been handled. The Chinese, as late as 1957, still accepted Soviet leadership of the world communist movement (China, Mao conceded, could not be such a leader because it had 'not even a quarter of a sputnik, whereas the Soviet Union has two'). Soviet support for the Chinese atomic programme, however, was withdrawn in 1958, the USSR was neutral during the Sino-Indian war of 1959, and in 1960 the dispute between the USSR and China came into the open. Khrushchev, speaking at the Romanian Communist Party Congress in June of that year, attacked the Chinese leadership by name. All Soviet technicians were withdrawn; trade between the two countries dropped off sharply; and a series of hostile open letters were exchanged, the Chinese accusing the Russians of 'revisionism' (or lack of commitment to Marxist principles) while the Russians accused the Chinese of 'dogmatism' and 'splittism' (or of attempting to break up the world communist movement). In 1966 both sides recalled their ambassadors and in 1969 matters reached the point of military hostilities along the Soviet–Chinese border in Siberia. Since then relations have improved considerably: the ambassadors returned to their posts in 1970, trade increased substantially, and in 1989, following extended diplomatic overtures, the Soviet General Secretary, Mikhail Gorbachev, made an official visit to the Chinese capital, the first of its kind for thirty years. Both sides committed themselves to 'Chinese–Soviet relations of a new type'; it was unlikely, however, given their historical rivalries and often divergent interests, that the unity of earlier years would ever be restored.

The main institutions which Soviet control is maintained over the other countries of the bloc are the Council for Mutual Economic Assistance (CMEA or Comecon), a multilateral economic and trading association, and the Warsaw Treaty Organisation, a military pact. Comecon, the first of these, was set up in 1949 by the Soviet Union and the East European states largely as a response to the establishment of the Organisation for Economic Co-operation and Development (OECD) by the major Western countries in 1948. Its membership in 1990 included Cuba, Mongolia and Vietnam as well as Bulgaria, Hungary, the GDR, Poland, Romania, Czechoslovakia, and the USSR. Yugoslavia, though not a member, takes part in the work of Comecon in matters of mutual interest, and Afghanistan, Angola, Ethiopia, Laos, Mozambique, Nicaragua and South Yemen are represented on a number of its institutions. Albania ceased to be a member in 1961. Comecon is regulated by a statute which came into force in 1960, by an agreement on the 'basic principles of the international socialist division of labour' of 1962, and by a 'complex programme for the further deepening and improvement of the co-operation and development of the socialist economic integration of the member countries of Comecon', signed in 1971, whose ultimate objective is the complete economic integration of the economies of member countries. The indications are that this programme of integration is regarded with more enthusiasm in Moscow, where Comecon's central institutions are located, than in the countries of Eastern Europe, whose economies are often more advanced than that of the Soviet Union and which have traditionally enjoyed close trading links with the West. This notwithstanding, the economic plans of Comecon's member countries all make specific provision for the furthering of these programmes, and the existence of Comecon serves to bind the economies of its member countries more closely together than would otherwise be the case.

The military side of the alliance is the Warsaw Treaty Organisation, founded in 1955 by a treaty between the governments of Bulgaria, Hungary, the GDR, Poland, Romania, the USSR, Czechoslovakia and Albania (which took no part in the organisation after 1962 and formally announced its withdrawal in 1968). The main policy-making body of the Warsaw Treaty Organisation is its Political Consultative Committee, composed of the party leaders and principal government ministers of member countries, but a number of other institutions work within its framework, such as a Committee of Defence Ministers (established in 1969), a Committee of Foreign Ministers (established in 1976) and a Joint Secretariat (established in 1956 and reorganised in 1976). There is also a Joint High Command, invariably headed by a senior member of the Soviet armed forces, which is responsible for the direction of operational military matters. Efforts have been made in recent years to increase the level of activities and the integration of member countries, though this has not prevented the Romanian government, since about 1964, from playing a somewhat independent role (Romanian forces, for instance, did not take part in the intervention of Czechoslovakia in 1968, and no Soviet forces are presently stationed in that country). The Treaty provides for consultation and mutual assistance in the event of an armed attack upon any of its members; most of the states concerned have also concluded bilateral defence treaties with other members of the pact.

Soviet efforts to retain control over the world communist movement have been less successful, if only because most of the communist parties concerned are in countries militarily beyond their reach. Since the dissolution of the Communist International in 1943 and of Cominform in 1956 the main organised form the movement has assumed has been international conferences of communist and workers' parties, three of which have so far been held in 1957, 1960 and 1969. One indication of the declining measure of Soviet control is the fact that at the last of these conferences in 1969 several ruling parties (the Yugoslav, Albanian, Chinese, Vietnamese and North Korean) did not attend; and of the 75 parties that were present only 61 could be persuaded to sign the final communiqué without conditions (five refused to do so altogether), although it made no reference to Soviet leadership of the movement and contained no specific criticism of the Chinese. Since then there have been a number of regional gatherings of communist parties, such as the meeting of Latin American parties in Havana in 1975 and of European parties in East Berlin in 1976; but many parties have refused to attend these meetings, basically because they refuse to accept even the appearance of external intervention in their domestic policy-making. A number, the so-called 'Eurocommunist' parties, have gone further; they have repudiated many accepted communist doctrines, such as the dictatorship of the proletariat and the need for a single-party system, and have freely criticised what they regard as undemocratic features of the political systems of the communist countries. Although some parties have been persuaded to reconsider their views in recent years a number of others, such as the Spanish and Italian parties, have persisted in their criticisms, and there is some evidence that their arguments have not been without influence upon dissident opinion in Eastern Europe as well as within their own countries.

The communist world: from the 1980s to the 1990s

It was, in fact, in Eastern Europe that the most dramatic changes of all took place in the late 1980s with the overthrow of established leaderships and the formation of wholly or largely non-communist administrations (for a fuller discussion see below. pp. 277–90). The exercise of 'people's power' began in Poland, where a crisis of political authority in 1980–81 between the communist authorities and a self-governing trade union, Solidarity, had led to the imposition of martial law in December 1981. Although martial law had been suspended a year later, Solidarity was still, in January 1989, an outlawed organisation. Round-table talks between government and opposition representatives, however, led to an agreement in April which provided (among other things) that Solidarity would be allowed to contest new and at least partly competitive elections in June 1989. Under the arrangements, elections to the upper house of the Polish Parliament, the Senate, were to be entirely unrestricted, while in the lower house, the Sejm, only 35 per cent of the seats were to be freely chosen, the others being reserved for the Polish United Workers' (or Communist) Party, its two allied parties and several official Catholic organisations. In this way, it was thought, a communist-dominated administration would be preserved.

In the event, the tactic badly misfired. At the elections, which took place in June 1989, Solidarity candidates won all of the 161 seats available to them in the Sejm and 99 of the 100 Senate seats. There was still further embarrassment for the authorities in that all but two of the candidates on a separate non-competitive list of national politicians failed to secure the 50 per cent vote that was necessary for their election. The former Communist leader, Wojciech Jaruzelski, was elected by a single vote to the newly created executive presidency, but attempts to form a communist-led administration were unsuccessful and a coalition headed by Tadeusz Mazowiecki, the former editor of Solidarity's weekly paper who had been imprisoned under martial law, was eventually approved in August 1989. Mazowiecki was Eastern Europe's first non-communist prime minister in forty years; remarkably, in the light of earlier relations between the two countries, the change appeared to occasion no particular concern in Moscow, where official spokesmen congratulated the new prime minister on his appointment and simply noted his willingness to respect Poland's international alliances. At the end of 1989 a parliamentary vote removed the 'leading role' of the communist party from the Polish constitution, and changed the name of the country from a 'People's Republic' to the 'Republic of Poland'. The Polish party, demoralised and declining in membership, duly renamed itself the 'Social Democracy of the Republic of Poland' in January 1990.

In Hungary the ruling Socialist Workers' Party had in fact been the first in Eastern Europe to renounce its leading role, early in 1989. At a party congress the following October the party formally dissolved itself and took the name of the Hungarian Socialist Party, under the mildly reformist leadership of Renzö Nyers. More radical reformist ideas emanated from Imre Pozsgay, a former minister of culture who became head of the Patriotic People's Front (a party-dominated umbrella organisation) in the early 1980s and then a minister of state responsible for social and political reform in the latter part of the decade. Poszgay openly embraced the idea of pluralist politics, including competitive elections and a governmental role for the variety of informal groups that were beginning to emerge in the later 1980s, the most important of which was the Hungarian Democratic Forum. Despite the more accommodating position adopted by the party authorities popular discontent continued to grow, focussing particularly on the treatment of the Hungarian minority in Romania and the environmental consequences of a planned dam on the Danube as well as on economic difficulties of a kind that were familiar elsewhere in the communist world.

In January 1989 the National Assembly adopted a new law on associations which legalised political groups of various kinds, including (it appeared) independent political parties. In February the Socialist Workers' Party went still further and committed itself to the reintroduction of multiparty politics. Discussions between the party authorities, the trade unions and the main informal groupings began in June 1989 with a view to agreeing the constitutional changes that would be necessary to convert Hungary into a functioning democracy. By the end of the year it had been agreed that there would be a new executive presidency, elected directly by the National Assembly, and that in advance of this there would be open elections in which all political forces would be able to compete. It was also agreed that Hungary should be a 'Republic', not a 'Socialist Republic', and a constitutional commitment was made to an 'independent, democratic, legal state in which the values of bourgeois democracy and democratic socialism prevail in equal measure'. In the elections, which took place in March–April 1990, the conservative Democratic Forum secured 42.7 per cent of the vote and formed a non-communist coalition government.

The process of political change took still more dramatic forms in East Germany, Romania, Czechoslovakia and Bulgaria. The collapse of communist rule in the GDR followed an astonishing mass exodus of East Germans, many of them young professionals and skilled workers, to West Germany through Hungary. In May 1989 the Hungarians had begun to demolish their section of the Iron Curtain along the border with Austria. First a few, and then thousands of East Germans took the opportunity to travel to Hungary, and thence to Austria and West Germany, where they enjoyed the automatic right of citizenship. The Hungarians, despite considerable pressure from the East Germany authorities, announced in September 1989 that for humanitarian reasons the border would remain open. Some 12,000 East Germans passed through in the first three days. Pressures for change in East Germany itself began to mount, encouraged by the Lutheran Church and by opposition groups which had formed a pressure group for change, New Forum. Attempts to restrict the flow of emigrants led to a rising tide of popular resistance during October 1989, culminating in the resignation of Erich Honecker, party leader since 1971, and his replacement by the long-standing 'crown prince', Egon Krenz. Honecker was later placed under house arrest amid revelations of the corruption with which the former party leadership had been associated.

The demonstrations continued – in Leipzig, for instance, half a million protestors took to the streets – and a series of rapid concessions, including the reopening of the border with Czechoslovakia, proved insufficient to halt the movement for change. In November 1989, in an act with enormous symbolic significance for Eastern Europe as a whole, the Berlin Wall began to be demolished, allowing direct movement between the two Germanys for the first time since 1962. Despite these concessions Krenz was unable to establish his authority and a rising tide of discontent within and against the ruling Socialist Unity Party led to an emergency congress in December 1989 at which a new leader, Gregor Gysi, was chosen and the party changed its name to include the words 'the Party of Democratic Socialism'. Gysi was a lawyer of liberal credentials who had previously sought to legalise New Forum; another reform-minded Communist, the Dresden party secretary Hans Modrow, became prime minister. As elsewhere, the new leadership announced that competitive, multiparty elections would take place in 1990; in those elections, in March 1990, the conservative Christian Democratic Union won 40.9 per cent of the vote and began to move rapidly towards union with the Federal Republic.

The process of change in Czechoslovakia was also largely

peaceful, although it began with police attacks on huge public demonstrations in November 1989. The demonstrations, the largest for twenty years, were led initially by students and increasingly involved the population as a whole. Just a week after the demonstrations had started, on 24 November, the communist leader Miloš Jakeš and the whole of the Politburo resigned; four days later a parliamentary vote removed the party's leading role from the Czech constitution. The Czech government resigned on 7 December, and on 10 December a largely non-communist administration was formed, the first of its kind for forty years. At the end of the month Alexander Dubček, leader of the 1968 reform movement, was elected chairman of the Czech parliament; the following day the popular playwright, Václav Havel, was sworn in as President. Havel's work had been banned for twenty years and the playwright himself, a leader of the oppositional Civic Forum group, had been arrested earlier in the year. There were, as elsewhere, to be competitive elections in 1990 at which all organised groupings would be free to compete; the communist party, it was clear, would secure a very small minority of seats. Once again these changes appeared to be acceptable to the USSR, unlike the attempt to promote much more limited changes that had been suppressed in 1968.

Very few of the communist-ruled nations, in fact, escaped the wave of political reform. In November 1989 there were mass demonstrations in Bulgaria led by an oppositional group, Eco-Glasnost, which led to the resignation of Todor Zhivkov, party leader since 1954. His successor, Petur Mladenov, renounced the communist monopoly of power and promised to hold free, multiparty elections in 1990. As in most of the other countries, a variety of factors contributed to the change of regime: mistreatment of the Turkish minority within Bulgaria, economic difficulties, and increasing public concern with environmental issues. The Yugoslav party, the League of Communists, agreed similarly at an emergency congress in January 1990 to renounce its constitutionally guaranteed leading role and to prepare the way for multiparty politics. The Albanian leader, Ramiz Alia, addressing his party's Central Committee in January 1990, ruled out the abandonment of socialist principles but accepted the need for some decentralisation of economic management and a limited degree of electoral choice. Similar modest moves towards political and economic reform were apparent in most of the other communist-ruled nations, including Mongolia and Vietnam, but excluding Cuba (where Castro continued to insist on communist orthodoxy) and China (after a widely supported protest movement had been brutally crushed in 1989).

Most spectacular of all, perhaps, was the overthrow of Nicolae Ceauşescu, party leader and virtual dictator of Romania since 1965. The fall of the regime began with demonstrations in the western (largely Hungarian) city of Timişoara on 17 December, which were crushed with exceptional ferocity; an estimated 4000 may have died. The protest, nonetheless, spread to other towns and cities and to the capital Bucharest, where Ceauşescu, addressing a public rally on 21 December, found himself shouted down and almost entirely without public support. The following day Ceauşescu fled the capital but was arrested and brought to trial after fierce fighting had claimed many more lives. On 25 December Ceauşescu and his wife were sentenced to death and executed; reports began to circulate at the same time of the extraordinary opulence in which the former dictator had lived, including a house crammed with art treasures and featuring a nuclear bunker lined with marble. The functions of government were carried on, after Ceauşescu's overthrow, by the National Salvation Council, a loose coalition within which there appeared to be a substantial communist influence. Judicial processes continued against remaining members of the Ceauşescu family and governing circle; arrangements were also made for competitive elections in 1990 which, as elsewhere, would determine the future shape of the political system.

Developments of this kind were possible, to a very large extent, because the Soviet leadership under Mikhail Gorbachev appeared willing to replace the 'Brezhnev doctrine' of limited sovereignty by what was humorously called the 'Sinatra doctrine', meaning that individual East European states would be free to construct their political future in their own way. The Soviet leadership, indeed, appeared to regard the process of change in a broadly positive light, as corresponding with their own policies of *glasnost'* (openness) and *perestroika* (restructuring). Gorbachev, on his election as party leader in 1985, had pledged himself to continue the strategy of his predecessors, which he defined as 'acceleration of socio-economic development and the perfection of all aspects of social life'. These relatively limited objectives soon gave way to a much more widely conceived process of reform, embracing the political system and the economy as well as history, social life, the Soviet federation and international affairs (for a fuller discussion see below, pp. 184–94). The early emphasis was upon economic reform, normally the first concern of Soviet and other communist leaders. A strategy was mapped out at Central Committee meetings in 1986 and 1987 involving 'radical reform' of the economy, including some decentralisation of management decisions, a variety of forms of ownership and moves towards a 'socialist market'. At the same time the media, and cultural life generally, began to experience a greater degree of openness in the treatment of social issues such as drugs and prostitution as well as in the discussion of the Soviet past and the crimes of the Stalin period.

Political reform more particularly was launched at a Central Committee meeting in January 1987 at which the slogan of 'democratisation' was officially adopted. The electoral system, first of all, was reformed so as to permit a choice of candidates. Local elections, in 1987, saw a limited experiment along these lines, and then national elections, in 1989, saw three-quarters of all the seats available being competed for by party and non-party candidates. A working parliament was established, elected by a new national representative body, the Congress of People's Deputies (these and other changes are discussed more fully later in this book). The Communist Party held an extraordinary Conference in the summer of 1988 at which it agreed to democratise its own operations, including secret and competitive ballots for leading positions, which were themselves to be held for a limited period of time. More broadly, a vision began to be developed of a model of socialism that would be democratic and humanist, which would avoid the excesses of the past and allow the creative energies of ordinary people to express themselves much more freely than ever before. This would, it emerged, be a form of socialism that drew upon the experience of other nations, including capitalist ones, in its forms of political organisation and economic life; and it would seek a solution to global issues through joint action with other members of the world community. This was certainly a distinctive vision, although it was far from clear, by the early 1990s, that it was a workable one. Its success or otherwise was in turn likely to determine whether the political changes that were taking place in the communist world led back to capitalism or to a society that combined economic efficiency and political democracy within a recognisably socialist framework.

Models of communist politics

There has been no shortage of models or interpretations seeking to categorise the communist states in a single all-inclusive phrase or label. If the study of comparative communist politics has taught us anything over the years, it is perhaps that the search for labels of this kind is likely to be a vain one and that there is no single model or theory which can adequately accommodate all important aspects of a changing and often contradictory social reality. But an imperfect guide is better than no guide at all, and if we are to make sense of a political system there is really no alternative to making some attempt to identify its most distinctive features and to classify it on that basis. Provided it is understood that models and interpretations of this kind are neither 'right' nor 'wrong', but simply more or less helpful or illuminating in highlighting key features of a political system while necessarily neglecting others, there is no reason why we should not employ them. At least three approaches to the study of communist political systems have enjoyed a particular degree of popularity over the years (a number of others, such as the political culture and group politics approaches, will be considered in subsequent chapters).

The first, the *totalitarian model*, came into widespread use at the time of the cold war, when it was customary to make an extremely sharp distinction between the virtues of democracy, exemplified by the countries of Western Europe and North America, and the evils of communism, which was equated with the tyranny and dictatorship of Eastern Europe. The key feature of the communist systems to which the totalitarian model drew attention was the broad extent of state power, in contrast to the liberal-democratic states of the West in which the power of the state was limited and the rights and liberties of the individual were carefully protected. The leading version of the totalitarian model was put forward by Carl Friedrich and Zbigniew Brzezinski in the mid-1950s. It consisted of six essential traits or features: an official ideology, binding upon all members of the society; a single mass party typically led by one man; a system of terroristic police control; a near-monopoly by the state of all means of effective armed combat; and central control and direction of the entire economy. Some years later Friedrich added two more features to this list: territorial expansion and administrative control of the courts. These features were held to characterise not only all existing communist systems but also the political systems of Nazi Germany and Fascist Italy, and for many years this model was widely accepted as perhaps the single most useful categorisation of the communist states, particularly by those who were impressed by their more illiberal or authoritarian features.

The totalitarian model has subsequently come under criticism for at least two kinds of shortcomings. It has been argued, in the first place, that many of Friedrich and Brzezinski's six or eight points apply not only to the communist states but to many others as well, particularly in the developing countries (whose numbers have of course increased considerably since Friedrich and Brzezinski first put forward their theory). Central control and direction of the economy, for instance, is a common feature of many third world states, few of which could readily be classified as totalitarian, and so also is a single-party system, although this does not necessarily mean that no legal opposition is permitted. A near monopoly of the means of effective armed combat in the hands of the state is indeed a characteristic of virtually all modern states. Conversely, many of Friedrich and Brzezinski's list of characteristics can hardly be said any longer to apply to the communist states, not, at least, without a great deal of qualification. A system of terroristic police control, for instance, typically directed 'not only against demonstrable "enemies" of the regime, but against more or less arbitrarily selected classes of the population', has not been a normal feature of political life in the major communist states since at least the early 1950s. The role of the official ideology has arguably become less restrictive, and the parties tend now to be ruled by groups of oligarchs rather than the 'dictators' specified in Friedrich and Brzezinski's definition. Some have suggested, in the light of these criticisms, that totalitarianism should no longer be regarded as a model but as an ideal type, that is to say a system logically conceivable in theory but most unlikely to be encountered in real life; others have suggested more limited modifications to the model, such as re-designating it 'partialitarianism' or 'totalitarianism without terror'. Few, however, now find the totalitarian model in its original form a useful framework for analysing the communist systems, though some communist states (as well as others) may exemplify a number of its features at different times.

Dissatisfaction with the totalitarian approach, combined with an awareness that some limited forms of politics did indeed continue within the communist monolith, led to a renewed interest in what may be called the *'bureaucratic politics'* model. Those who adopt this approach focus upon three key features of politics in the communist states: first, the dominant position within them of the communist party, and within the party of its top leadership; secondly, the absence of competitive elections or of other effective instruments of democratic control, leaving the party, in effect, in a position of permanent government; and thirdly, the wide scope of the powers that are exercised by the communist parties in these states, as a sort of 'super bureaucracy' superior to and intertwined with the government and social institutions such as the trade unions, the press, industry and the courts. Unlike the theorists of totalitarianism, who also emphasise these points, writers in the bureaucratic politics school do not argue that this means there can be virtually no politics, or competition for influence, within these states (they also place less emphasis upon the role of ideology and coercion). Politics, however, takes place not between the communist party and other contenders for power, as in a Western pluralist system, but within the party and the other bureaucratic organisations that collectively administer the state. The system is conceived as a 'mono-hierarchical' or 'mono-organisational' one, with the top political leadership standing in relation to other parts of the political system much as the board of directors of a large Western corporation stand in relation to their administrative subordinates, and politics takes the form that the struggle for resources and influence typically assumes in a large bureaucratic organisation of this kind.

Perhaps the best known exponent of this approach is Alfred Meyer. Meyer's views were first set out in an article entitled 'USSR, Incorporated', published in 1961, and were then elaborated in a volume entitled *The Soviet Political System: An Interpretation*, which was published in 1965. Meyer summed up his thesis as follows:

> The USSR is best understood as a large, complex bureaucracy comparable in its structure and functioning to giant corporations, armies, government agencies, and similar institutions – some people might wish to add various churches – of the West. It shares with such bureaucracies many principles of organisation and patterns of management. It is similar to them also in its typical successes and inefficiencies, in the gratifications and frustrations it offers its constituents, in its socialisation and recruitment policies, communications problems, and many other features. The Soviet Union shares with giant corporations everywhere the urge to organise all human activities rationally, from professional life to consumption patterns and leisure activities. It has in common with them a thoroughly authoritarian political structure, in which the élite is independent of control by the lower-ranking member of the organisation, even though all or most giant bureaucracies in the modern world insist that their rank-and-file constitutents participate in the organisation's public life.

Like modern bureaucracy, Meyer suggested, communist rule was 'essentially an attempt to impose rational management over social life by means of complex organisations', and the Soviet Union, the largest such state, could 'best be understood as a giant bureaucracy, something like a modern corporation extended over the entire society'. The political system in the communist states was in effect 'bureaucracy writ large'.

Meyer himself devoted relatively little attention to the manner in which policies were formulated and implemented in political systems of this kind. Other writers, however, have identified some of the forms of what T. H. Rigby has called the 'crypto-politics' that are involved. Major institutional interests, for instance, bargain informally for scarce resources; local party officials and ministries press the claims of central political authorities; ministries attempt to become as large and as self-sufficient as possible ('empire-building' or 'narrow departmentalism'); and little attention is paid to external opinion on matters that impose no cost upon the organisation itself, such as traffic and environmental pollution. Writers such as Jerry Hough and Darrell Hammer have been so impressed by the autonomy in practice enjoyed by the major interests in communist societies that they have proposed terms such as 'bureaucratic' or 'institutional pluralism' to characterise their political systems as a whole. More recently, writers such as Valerie Bunce have pointed to the analogies between Soviet-type polities and 'corporatist' systems in other developed and developing countries, in which the central authorities enjoy a close and mutually advantageous relationship with the major functional interests that are represented within the society. Interests of this kind (such as business and labour) are typically granted an institutionalised role in central decision-making and a 'representational monopoly' in return for accepting some controls upon their selection of leaders and their articulation of demands.

Valuable though such perspectives are, it must be said that many studies have tended to assume too readily that bureaucratic behaviour in the West and in the communist states must necessarily be comparable, and relatively few studies have been able to demonstrate empirically the similarities in bureaucratic functioning and motivation in the East and West or that the heads of leading institutions do indeed represent and promote the interests of 'their' institutions against those of other bodies in the policy-making process. John Armstrong, for instance, in a comparative study of the sources of administrative behaviour in the Soviet Union and the West, found many similarities: hierarchical command principles were frequently ignored, informal relationships were important,

and motivation tended to be performance rather than ideologically oriented. There were more differences than similarities between the two systems, however, particularly where
matters such as welfare, communications and career contacts
were concerned. Dmitri K. Simes, who worked as a research
associate at the Institute of the World Economy and International Relations of the USSR Academy of Sciences between
1967 and 1972 and in that capacity prepared a number of
informational bulletins on foreign policy issues for the top
political leaders, found similarly that 'in the Soviet political
system, bureaucratic loyalties and ... affiliations, as a rule,
play only a marginal role'. The supreme loyalty of the
Politburo members was to the Politburo itself, and members
usually considered themselves Politburo representatives in
their respective bureaucracies rather than representatives of
these bureaucracies in the Politburo.

More generally, a closer examination of major institutional
interests has found them by no means so united in defence of a
supposed common interest as the bureaucratic politics
approach assumes. Institutions like the military, for instance,
contain rivalries between the various services, and personal
links, such as those between the 'Stalingrad group' (who took
part in the battle of Stalingrad in 1942), frequently cut across
more functional or sectoral divisions. The party apparatus,
similarly, contains internal differences based upon age, ethnic
background and career patterns, and is not necessarily united
behind a conservative political position, particularly when
departures from official guidelines are necessary to improve
the economic performance of the area or industry for which
they are responsible. Writers, to take another example, are not
necessarily united in favour of an extension of the boundaries
of literary self-expression; many would not survive without
them, particularly the less talented writers typically associated with the literary bureaucracies, and bodies such as these
may often take a more conservative political position than the
party authorites themselves.

Parallels in administrative behaviour, moreover, do not in
themselves justify conceptualising the political system as a
whole as a giant bureaucracy. This neglects, for instance, the
distinctive role of the communist parties, particularly their

monopoly over appointments to key positions in the hierar-
chies that are subordinate to them, and also the role of
ideology. And even if the bureaucratic politics model is taken
to represent a reasonable approximation of the political system
as a whole, it may still be open to criticism in terms of its relative
neglect of the sources of development and change within such
systems. It has been the party bureaucracies, after all, that
have initiated the rapid and often coercive transformation of
their societies, scarcely the policy to expect from bodies that
are supposed to respond passively to institutional pressures
and to respect established legal and bureacratic procedures.
The bureaucratic politics model also makes little attempt to
specify the various and perhaps conflicting social interests of
the different groups with which it deals. Party and state
officials, generals and trade union officials differ not simply in
their bureaucratic roles that they perform; they differ also in
their social backgrounds, status, earnings and relationships
with their constituents, and their behaviour may often make
little sense abstracted from a broader political sociology of
Soviet-type systems and of the relationship between rulers and
ruled in the society as a whole. A concern of this kind, to
specify the social rather than bureaucratic origins of political
development and change, has lain behind the renewed interest
in *Marxist approaches* to communist politics in recent years.

At least two major variants of a Marxist approach to
communist politics may be identified. In the first place there is
what may be called the official Marxist approach, that
favoured by the regimes themselves, in terms of which the
expropriation of the capitalist class in these countries has led
to the inauguration of a period of socialist development which
will lead ultimately to full communism. An approach of this
kind is exemplified, for instance, in the revised Programme of
the Communist Party of the Soviet Union which was adopted
in 1986. The 1917 Russian revolution, according to the
Programme, brought into being the first workers' and
peasants' state and began a new era in world history, an era
of the transition from capitalism to socialism and ultimately to
full communism. A socialist society, such as that constructed
in the USSR and the countries with which it is associated, is
held to put an end forever to the exploitation of man by man

based upon the private ownership of the means of production. It provides, rather, for the planned and dynamic growth of productive forces for the benefit of all citizens, for the widest possible access to social benefits and cultural resources, and for a genuine rather than spurious democracy based upon the broad and equal participation of all citizens in the management of public affairs. A society of this kind is expected to extend itself internationally as more and more peoples seek to take advantage of 'general laws of socialist development' such as the dominant role of the working class and its party, social ownership of the means of production in the interests of the people as a whole, socialist democracy and the friendship of all nations and nationalities on a basis of peace, equality and social progress.

An approach of this kind, its rhetoric apart, does at least serve to identify some of the principal features of the communist systems presently in existence. Within such countries it is indeed the case that private ownership of the means of production has (with minor exceptions) been abolished. There is (again with minor exceptions) no unemployment, and the basic necessities of life such as transport and housing are available at very modest cost to all citizens. Educational and cultural resources are widely accessible, and ordinary working people are well represented in institutions of government at all levels. There is admittedly only one party, or at least one ruling party, but workers and peasants form a very large proportion (usually more than half) of its members, and for them it serves as an instrument of rule, a means of ensuring that the policies promoted by the state are those that they themselves favour. According to this view there can be no 'democracy' in the abstract but only 'bourgeois' or 'proletarian democracy', depending upon which class owns the productive wealth of the society and thereby holds political power. In capitalist societies, it is argued, a small minority of exploiters own this productive wealth and political power is exercised in their narrow class interests; in socialist societies, on the other hand, the means of production are nationalised and the policies followed are those that reflect the interests of the working people as a whole.

Official Marxist perspectives of this kind have not been very influential outside the communist countries themselves, and for good and obvious reasons. In the first place, while it is indeed true that productive wealth is owned by the population as a whole and that working people are well represented in party and state institutions, it has widely been noticed that ordinary workers and peasants become steadily less well represented the closer one comes to bodies of real executive or decision-making power. Among the parties' mass memberships and in local institutions of government, for instance, workers and peasants, as well as women, young people and members of minority nationalities, are indeed represented in proportions that correspond closely to their proportions in the population as a whole. In parliaments and central committees, however, their numbers drop sharply, and in governments and politburos the representation of these less favoured groups drops almost to zero. The communist countries, in other words, are 'workers' states' in a purely formal sense: ordinary working people are indeed well represented within the parties' mass memberships and in local institutions of government, but they do not predominate in higher-level bodies where national policies are actually formulated.

This would matter less if executive and decision-making bodies were genuinely and not just formally accountable to the institutions which elect them, and in which ordinary workers and peasants are typically well represented. A second major reservation about official Marxist theory, however, concerns the reality of 'socialist democracy' in the countries that claim to practise it. Despite reforms in some of these countries, for instance, elections, until recently, have not provided for a genuine exercise of popular choice, and both party and state institutions are centrally dominated and based upon principles such as democratic centralism and the ban on factions which effectively insulate their leaderships from any challenge from below. Associational groups such as trade unions, sports clubs and women's organisations are permitted to come into legal existence only if they agree to support official policies, and their activities are closely regulated and their leading personnel selected by the party and state authorities. The central authorities also control the mass media through the censorship system and in other ways, and there are no independent courts which here as elsewhere might serve as an ultimate guarantee of individual liberties (all of these points are considered more fully in Chapter 7). An authoritarian system of this kind diverges not simply from the official communist self-image; it diverges also, in the view of many scholars, from the democratic traditions of the socialist movement and of classical Marxism itself.

A third objection to official Marxist theory is that it takes no serious account of the substantial material privileges, not simply political powers, which are in practice available to party, state and other officials. In communist countries, which are generally characterised by shortages of various kinds, administered benefits have a greater degree of importance than they would have elsewhere. The existence of such benefits, on a broad and sometimes extravagant scale, has by now been extensively documented in almost all of the countries concerned. Privileges of this kind typically embrace, for instance, an official car and more spacious housing. They also include special shops where a wider range of goods is stocked at lower prices than those that obtain in the state retail network, special hospitals, special sporting and recreational facilities and a variety of other benefits. Well-placed officials can make further use of their connections to secure, for instance, tickets to pop concerts given by visiting Western musicians or access for their children to the most prestigious educational institutions. In some cases official privilege has extended even further. A villa occupied by the former Polish party first secretary Edward Gierek, for instance, was reported by Solidarity to be situated in 4000 acres of parkland, with a dining-room to seat forty, a billiard-room and a private cinema. One of Gierek's closest associates, the former head of Polish television Maciej Szczepański, was reported to have possessed a fleet of luxury yachts and villas, a private harem of prostitutes, and a foreign bank account which he made use of when taking safari holidays in Africa. Soviet, Chinese and other leading communist officials have been reported to enjoy comparable if less spectacular advantages.

The degree of privilege enjoyed by ruling circles in the communist countries is indeed such that a number of scholars have been persuaded they may best be analysed within a 'critical Marxist' framework, in terms of which the ruling group in these countries is conceptualised as an equivalent to the exploitative ruling class of capitalist societies. The most influential statement of this approach is still that of Leon Trotsky, particularly in his book *The Revolution Betrayed* (1937). In this work Trotsky argued that the USSR was still a proletarian or socialist state because it was one in which land, industry and the other means of production had been taken into public ownership. The productive resources of the society, however, were not being used for the benefit of all its members because the bureaucracy, the 'sole privileged and commanding stratum in Soviet society', had taken control over the state machinery and was using that control to further its own selfish interests. The means of the production belonged to the state; the state, however, 'belonged' to the bureaucracy, who had 'expropriated the proletariat politically'. If the bureaucracy succeeded in making its position a more permanent and legally-based one, particularly through the creation of special forms of private property, the gains of the October revolution would eventually be liquidated. The revolution, however, had been betrayed but not yet overthrown, and it might still be redeemed by a 'supplementary revolution' in which the working class could seize political power back from the bureaucracy. More contemporary critical Marxists have developed this into a model of 'transitional society', midway between capitalism and socialism, which is capable of reverting to its capitalist origins but which may also be restored to a state of authentic socialism by a political revolution supported by the working class of other countries.

Critical Marxist theories of this kind have little difficulty in accommodating the existence of privilege such as that enjoyed by ruling circles in the communist countries (which they typically define as 'deformed workers' states'). They are also more willing to confront issues such as political and social inequalities in the communist countries, on which official theory is notably reticent. Critical Marxist interpretations are none the less themselves open to a number of serious objections. In the first place, they are generally rather vague about the nature and composition of the 'bureaucracy' which is so central to their accounts. Should it be defined, for instance, in terms of income (but then many writers, musicians, ballerinas and others should be included), or in terms of position (but many who enjoy a substantial degree of political power may not necessarily enjoy a comparable degree of material advantage)? How large is it, and how does it cohere as a social group in the absence of special 'ruling class' educational and other institutions? Secondly, and perhaps more important, how does 'the bureaucracy' reproduce itself? Given the absence of private ownership of productive wealth, a ruling group in the communist countries, however defined, cannot transfer a position of guaranteed material advantage to its descendants, as a ruling group can do in capitalist countries. Certainly, something may be achieved through personal connections, and particularly through privileged access to higher education. It is none the less striking how few senior members of this 'sole privileged and commanding stratum' have been succeeded to their positions of political power as well as social advantage by their children or close relatives.

Material inequalities, such as special shops and hospital facilities, are in any case not in themselves evidence of exploitation in a properly Marxist sense. For this to apply, it would be necessary to show that one class regularly appropriated the surplus value produced by another, the exploited or subordinate class. Marx, however, defined classes in terms of their relationship to the means of production, and there is no private ownership of such resources in the communist countries which could provide a basis for the appropriation of surplus value in the manner he had indicated. Nor is it appropriate to speak of a working class producing 'surplus value' when individual workers have security of employment and guaranteed wages and do not trade their labour upon the market. The fact that workers may produce more than they directly consume is in itself no evidence of exploitation, given the need for reinvestment and defence and for the redistribution of resources towards the old, the sick and the very young. Nor are even substantial differences in earnings. Indeed it is by no means clear that Marxist terms of any kind provide an adequate basis for the analysis of a form of society that Marx himself did not experience and which he refused to discuss in detail. Some writers in the Marxist tradition, such as Fehér, Heller and Márkus (1983), have argued that Soviet-type societies are in fact best conceptualised in a manner which employs the vocabulary of neither capitalism nor socialism but instead accepts that these are historically unprecedented social formations which require analysis in their own quite specific terms. In such a 'dictatorship over needs' it is political power which confers economic advantage, not vice versa as orthodox Marxism would suggest, and it is forms of political control rather than economic ownership which must be central to any adequate analysis.

If this examination of models of communist politics has served any useful purpose it is perhaps to suggest the inadequacy of any single explanatory formula and the need to employ a more variegated, multi-mode form of analysis. Models, by their very nature, tend to oversimplify and ignore many aspects of a political system in order to call attention to other features which are regarded as of primary importance. The totalitarian model, for instance, rightly emphasises the wide-ranging nature of state power in the communist states but exaggerates the extent to which they are nowadays sustained by terror. The bureaucratic politics model gives due weight to the centrality of the party-state bureaucracy in such systems but tends to ignore important respects in which a communist system is not simply 'bureaucracy writ large'. Official and critical Marxist approaches, for their part, rightly focus attention upon forms of property and the different interests of the various social groups concerned, but neither provides an entirely convincing account of the politics of such societies and critical Marxism in particular tends to counterpose 'actually existing' communist societies to alternative forms of genuine socialism which have never existed and which (for some) are hardly likely to be achieved in the real world. Nor does any of these models provide an adequate guide to the rapid and unprecedented process of change that swept through the communist world, particularly in Eastern Europe, in the late 1980s. It is perhaps safest to conclude, with Archie Brown, that a 'discriminating methodological eclecticism' is the best policy in present circumstances. All of the models of communist and post-communist politics we have considered have their merits and their shortcomings, the areas they illuminate and the areas they neglect; it would be premature to abandon the variety of insights that they provide in favour of a single all-embracing formula.

Further reading

A reliable introduction to the development of the communist states system is available in Seton-Watson (1960). This may be supplemented, in most cases for particulr periods, by Hammond (1975), Fetjö (1974), Brzezinski (1967), McCauley (1977), Deakin, Shukman and Willetts (1975), Seton-Watson (1985), Narkiewicz (1981), Szajkowski (1983) and Westoby (1989). Developments over the 1960s and 1970s are reviewed in Seton-Watson (1980). More recent events may be followed in Ash (1990) and in the *Annual Register* (London) and the *Yearbook on International Communist Affairs* (Stanford, Calif.) A selection of relevant documentary sources is presented in Bogdan Szajkowski (ed.), *Documents in Communist Affairs*, which has been published since 1977 (for the period 1982–4 it appeared in the form of a journal, *Communist Affairs* (Guildford, Surrey, quarterly)). The vexed question of the definition of a communist system is considered further in Kautsky (1973), Waller and Szajkowski (1981), White (1983a), and Furtak (1986, ch. 1). Von Beyme (1982), Wiles (1983) and Holmes (1986) are also helpful.

A number of important older articles on the interpretation of communist politics are collected in Fleron (1969) and Kanet (1971). These may be supplemented by Johnson (1970), Ionescu (1972), Brown (1974), Cohen and Shapiro (1974), Tarschys (1977), Hough (1977), Solomon (1983) and most recently White and Nelson (1986). The standard treatment of totalitarianism is still Friedrich and Brzezinski (1965). See also Friedrich (1969), Schapiro (1972), and Curtis (1979). On modernisation theory, see Kautsky (1973), Nelson (1977) and (1978), and White (1978a) and (1979, ch. 8). On the bureaucratic model, see Meyer (1961) and (1965), and for further discussion Armstrong (1965), Simes (1975), Dawisha (1980), which is followed by a useful discussion, Bunce and Echols (1980) and Solomon (1983), the last two of which review more recent corporatist approaches. On Marxist approaches, see the general accounts in Kolakowski (1978) and McLellan (1979) and (1983), and more specifically Bellis (1979), Nove (1975) and (1983), Nuti (1979) and Fehér, Heller and Márkus (1983).

Basic details about all Marxist-Leninist regimes presently in existence may be found in Szajkowski (1981) and Furtak (1986) and in a 36-volume series of studies under the general title 'Marxist Regimes' (Szajkowski, 1985ff). The Soviet Union and Eastern Europe more particularly are fully covered in Shoup (1981) and Schöpflin (1986). These may be updated by reference to annual publications such as the *Statesman's Yearbook* (London), *Whitaker's Almanack* (London) and the *Europa Yearbook* (London). Periodicals of particular interest to the student of comparative communist politics include *Soviet Studies* (Glasgow, quarterly), *Slavic Review* (Stanford, Calif., quarterly), *Survey* (London, quarterly), *Soviet Union* (Irvine, Calif., quarterly), *China Quarterly* (London, quarterly), *Problems of Communism* (Washington, DC, bi-monthly), *Studies in Comparative Communism* (Guildford, Surrey, quarterly), *East European Politics and Societies* (Berkeley, Calif., quarterly) and the *Journal of Communist Studies* (London, quarterly).

2

History, Societies and Political Cultures

Political culture may be defined as the way in which a social group behaves politically and the nature of the political beliefs and values of its members. Political scientists have usually employed the term as a means of identifying what is unique or distinctive about the politics of a country's population and likely to be of continuing significance in the evolution of their political beliefs and behaviour patterns. This is not, of course, to imply that a country's previous political experience is the only factor that needs to be taken into account in explaining how its political system operates at the present time, or that it will necessarily be the decisive factor in determining its future political development. A country's political culture, for instance, will certainly be affected by its level of social and economic development, by changes in the nature of its political institutions, and perhaps also by the programme of political socialisation which communist governments in particular have sponsored since they have come to power. Most scholars, none the less, take the view that a nation's political experience over the centuries is likely to impart at least a certain bias to the manner in which its political system will subsequently evolve, and students of the communist states in particular have usually been agreed upon the continuing importance of the distinctive national heritages of these countries despite the great similarities between them in terms of institutions, economy and ideology. In this chapter we shall look in turn at the political cultures of the Soviet Union, Eastern Europe and China, identifying in each case a number of aspects of their distinctive historical experience and assessing the extent to which they have exerted an influence upon subsequent political developments.

The USSR: the heritage of autocracy

Both the dangers as well as the opportunities of a political cultural approach are evident in the study of the largest of the communist states, the USSR. In such an enormous territorial expanse, for instance, extending over one-sixth of the world's land surface, there will always be a danger of neglecting local variations as well as the difficulties of the central authorities in making their rule effective in the face of poor communications and the corruption and apathy of their local officials. (Nikolai Gogol's *The Government Inspector* (1836) is an amusing illustration of this phenomenon.) It is also important to be aware of variations over time, particularly over the last decade or so of Tsarist rule when a limited kind of constitutional government was temporarily established; and of the complex and many-sided nature of popular political beliefs and behaviour patterns, in which, for instance, a naive faith in the Tsar could coexist quite happily with the belief that if the Tsar's instructions did not coincide with the people's own immediate interests, particularly in relation to the land, this meant that the Tsar must have been misled or misinformed and need not necessarily be obeyed. Yet for all the reservations and qualifications, one central tendency is clear: 'If there is one single factor which dominates the course of Russian history, at any rate since the Tatar conquest', as Hugh Seton-Watson has put it, 'it is the principle of autocracy' (1967, p. 10).

A central element in this autocratic inheritance was the weakness of representative institutions in pre-revolutionary Russia. There were, it is true, a number of bodies in medieval times with which the Tsar periodically took counsel upon various matters of state. But these bodies – the Boyar Duma and the Zemskii Sobor (Assembly of the Land) – had little independent authority and established no permanent existence, and the first institution of an even remotely parliamentary character to make its appearance in Russia was the State Duma, established in the aftermath of the revolutionary

events of 1905–6. Formally speaking the powers of the new
State Duma were very extensive. It had the right, for instance,
to enact and amend legislation; it could put questions to
government ministers; and it had the right to consider the
national and ministerial budgets. Without the Duma's consent, the Tsar's manifesto of 17 October 1905 promised, 'no
law can come into force'. Ministers, however, remained
responsible to the Tsar not to the Duma, and subsequent
legislation made it clear that all expenditure connected with
the armed forces and the imperial household (amounting to
some two-thirds of state spending) would be outside the
Duma's control. The Tsar, moreover, appointed more than
half of the members of the upper house, the State Council,
which could veto any proposals that the Duma might submit
to it, and he could promulgate decrees on his own authority
which had the force of law. Under the terms of the Basic Laws
of the Russian Empire, which he alone could modify, the Tsar
remained an 'autocratic and unlimited monarch' whose
powers were conferred by 'God Himself'.

It has sometimes been suggested that the Duma's powers,
however limited, were gradually increasing, and that if the
First World War and then the revolution had not occurred
they would gradually have developed into the forms of
constitutional government familiar elsewhere in Europe. The
Duma, certainly, acquired an increasing amount of authority
as time went by, and in 1915 Duma pressure led to the
resignation of four government ministers, the most considerable success that it had yet achieved. The experience of
countries such as Germany and Japan, and more recently of
Spain and Portugal, suggests that there is little to prevent
autocracy from being transformed into a more limited form of
constitutional government if suitable circumstances are present. Yet there were many observers at the time who thought
that such a development was unlikely, and certainly in
comparative perspective it is the weaknesses and limitations
rather than the strengths and potentialities of representative
institutions in Russia that are more immediately apparent (see
Table 2.1). The representative institutions which had been
established had very limited powers, they developed at a very
late stage by the standards of the time, and in some respects

TABLE 2.1

Patterns of political development in selected countries

	First constitutional régime	First parliamentary régime	First extension of suffrage	% of population enfranchised c. 1910
Russia	1905	1917	1905	2.4
Great Britain	1689	1741	1832	17.9
USA	1787	1789	c. 1840	26.3
France	1789	1792	1789	28.9
Prussia/Germany	1848	1918	1824	22.2
Italy	1848	1876	1848	23.4

Sources: Peter Gerlich, 'The Institutionalization of European Parliaments', in Allan Kornberg (ed.), *Legislatures in Comparative Perspective* (New York, 1973), pp. 100 and 106; Dieter Nohlen, *Wahlsysteme der Welt* (Munich, 1978), p. 37; and standard reference works.

they were actually losing rather than gaining powers over the period we have been considering, particularly at the local level. So far as the facts are concerned, at any rate, it is clear that Russia was still governed, as late as the early twentieth century, by a scarcely modified autocracy, and it was the only major European country of which this could still be said (even Turkey had established a form of constitutional government a generation earlier).

The weaknesses of representative institutions in Russia were not simply those of formal powers. Perhaps more crucially, they drew upon a very restricted range of public acceptance and support. This was partly a matter of the franchise, which was extremely limited in comparison with other European nations at this time (see Table 2.1). Only about 3 million citizens had the right to vote in the years before the First World War, a proportion of the total population about the same as had been admitted to the franchise in Great Britain a century earlier, and the system of elections was indirect and heavily biased in favour of landowners and the urban classes at the expense of workers and peasants, who constituted the overwhelming majority of the population. There were further restrictions upon the activities of political parties, upon the reporting of Duma proceedings and upon the holding of public meetings, which could be closed by the police at any time if they appeared likely to 'incite hostility between one section of the population and another'. Patterns of representation in the Duma were also heavily weighted in favour of the landowning classes, and Russia's merchants and manufacturers, a smaller and less influential section of the population than in other European countries at this time, were particularly poorly represented.

Not surprisingly perhaps, the new institutions of representative government appear to have been regarded with no great interest or commitment by the population in whose name they operated. For instance, when the First Duma was arbitrarily dissolved by the Tsar in 1906, after it had met for less than three months, there was no serious attempt to defend it despite an appeal from a number of deputies to that effect, and there was scarcely any greater resistance to the dissolution of the Constituent Assembly by the Bolsheviks in January 1918. Many citizens appear to have been unaware of the existence of the Duma, or at least uninterested in its proceedings, and a knowledge of the relevant democratic procedures seems to have been rather imperfectly founded. Peasants, for instance, appear often to have deliberated together and then cast their votes as a group, and even in the towns electors asked to be told for whom to vote and put letters, petitions, bad verse and insurance policies into the ballot boxes rather than the voting slips they were supposed to have brought with them. Indeed there appear to have been few members of the Russian public at this time who conceived of their political objectives in terms of gaining influence through institutions of this kind. 'The people have a need for potatoes, but not in the least for a constitution', as the radical literary critic Vissarion Belinsky put it, and even liberals were often doubtful of the wisdom of strengthening the Duma and other representative bodies, believing that this would simply transfer power from the hands of the Tsar to those of the landowning nobility where it might not necessarily be exercised more equitably.

One consequence of the weak development of representative institutions in pre-revolutionary Russia was the tendency to conceive of political authority in highly personalised terms, as a link between Tsar and people unmediated by parties, the rule of law or elected bodies of any kind. This 'naive monarch-ism', as it had been called, may have been discreetly encour-aged by the Tsars themselves, and it was certainly in decline by the late nineteenth century and particularly after 'Bloody Sunday', 22 January 1905, when the St Petersburg police fired upon a crowd of unarmed demonstrators who were approaching the Winter Palace with icons and the Tsar's portrait to beg for help and the redress of grievances. Yet it is still a remarkable fact that in Russia, unlike Western Europe, the large-scale peasant revolts which swept across the country in the seventeenth and eighteenth centuries were generally directed not against the Tsar himself but against the aristocracy, who were typically supposed to have removed the Tsar from effective control of the nation's destinies and to which the rebels generally proposed to restore him. The same centuries also saw a large number of imposters who claimed to be the rightful Tsar and who appear to have been able to secure substantial popular support upon this basis, even when (as in the case of the peasant leader Emel'yan Pugachev) they were illiterate. The popular image of the Tsar as recorded in folk-song, literature and proverb provides further evidence of these attitudes. 'Without the Tsar, the land is widowed'; 'God in the sky, the Tsar on earth'; 'No one is against God or against the Tsar'; these were some of the proverbs collected by the lexico-grapher Dahl in the mid-nineteenth century, for instance, and folk-songs spoke similarly of rulers such as Ivan the Terrible and Peter the Great as friends of the people but ruthless enemies of aristocratic or ecclesiastical intrigue. If popular wishes were not respected it must be because the Tsar was an impostor or because he was being opposed by the nobility ('the Tsar is willing but the boyars resist'); between the real Tsar and his people no such conflict of interest appears to have been conceivable.

These patterns of thought and behaviour, admittedly, were more typical of central Russia than of the outlying parts of the Empire, and they appear to have applied more to national and urban politics than to politics at the level of the local village community. In some areas, such as Finland and the Baltic, there was a greater experience of and attachment to the forms of representative democracy, and in Siberia, the north and the

Cossack lands of the south-west, where serfdom had been less firmly established and with which communications in any case were often difficult, a different and more independent-minded set of attitudes towards government appears to have prevailed. Even in central Russia the rising incidence of rural unrest in the nineteenth century, and rather later the estab-lishment of soviets, suggests that deference might not be without its limits. The life of the local community, moreover, went on with little reference to national political developments and was based upon an institution that was at least formally self-governing in character, the village commune or *mir*, within which each adult householder had a vote. Robert Tucker has described the disjunction between these two social worlds as the phenomenon of 'dual Russia', consisting of 'official Russia' (the court, the bureaucracy and state affairs in general) on the one hand and 'society' (the mass of ordinary people and their immediate and largely local concerns) on the other (see Tucker, 1972, pp. 121–42). Popular orientations towards government, the first of these, appear to have been highly personalised, largely supportive of the Tsar as the means by which the country was preserved from anarchy and destruc-tion, and little concerned with procedures and institutions by which he might periodically be held to account. They co-existed, however, with a rich and democratic community life with which all but the political elite identified more closely.

One further aspect of the pre-revolutionary political culture requires some emphasis: the unusually broad scope of govern-ment, whether at the local or the national level, extending not simply into matters such as the preservation of public order and the raising of taxation but also into religious affairs, the detailed administration of justice and public morals. The state was a major participant in the economic life of the nation, for instance, as the owner of extensive collieries, oilfields, forests, industrial enterprises and railways, and in addition it exer-cised close control over other sectors of the economy through the provisions of contracts, the regulation of tariffs, the supervision of company affairs and the operation of a factory inspectorate. Independent bodies, such as trade unions or associations of any kind, could not legally be formed until 1905, and even thereafter they functioned under a variety of restrictions of a formal or informal character. Moreover, it was difficult to defend such civil liberties as did exist through the courts: for despite a major legal reform in 1864, involving the introduction of a jury system for criminal cases, the government retained extensive powers of administrative arrest and, if necessary, the power to suspend the operation of most laws. In political cases – which were defined unusually broadly – trial by jury had in any case been suspended in 1878 after a young woman revolutionary had been acquitted of an attempt on the life of the police chief of St Petersburg. There was also an unusually restrictive censorship system under which, as today, it was permissible to criticise the performance of individual bureaucrats but not to challenge the principles of the regime itself.

Perhaps most important of all was the fact that the religious faith of the overwhelming majority of the population, Russian Orthodoxy, was never as independent of the state as was generally the case elsewhere in Europe. Orthodoxy derived from the Eastern branch of Christianity, the Byzantine, under which spiritual and temporal powers were united in the person of the ruler than separated as in the West, and Orthodoxy in Russia functioned similarly as more or less an official state religion. Church affairs were regulated by the Holy Synod, whose members were chosen by the Tsar and which operated effectively as a department of state. The Church was in turn represented within the government and upon local councils in the provinces; it received financial support from the state; and it enjoyed a monopoly of religious propaganda, including the right to carry out religious education within the schools and to conduct missionary work. There was little suggestion in any of this that religious values were different from and perhaps superior to those of the state; on the contrary they seemed so closely related as to be almost identical. The same, admittedly, could not be said of the numerous schismatic groups which rejected the authority of the state and of the Orthodox Church and saw them both as instruments of Antichrist. The most important of these were the 'Old Believers', so called because they opposed a seventeenth-century liturgical reform, and their presence is a reminder that the Russian theological tradition contains a strong element of non-conformity as well as perhaps a greater tendency towards collectivism and support for official doctrines.

From traditional to Soviet political culture

There are obvious parallels between many of these features of the pre-revolutionary political culture and that of modern times, though it is difficult and perhaps impossible to demonstrate the direct continuity between them. What should at least be clear is that ideas such as that the state should concern itself with the morals and wellbeing of the citizen as well as with his behaviour towards others, that it should take a central role in the ownership and management of the economy, and that it should exercise wide-ranging powers for the citizen's benefit with few restrictions imposed upon it by parliament, the press or political parties, were firmly rooted before the October revolution of 1917 and did not necessarily come into existence subsequently because the Bolsheviks were in favour of them. The new Soviet government, however, set itself a series of further tasks which went beyond or conflicted with the political culture it had inherited, such as eliminating the influence of religion, mobilising the population into higher levels of social and political activity, and replacing values based on private property with values based upon Marxism–Leninism, and it has sought to bring about these changes over more than two generations by a deliberate programme of political socialisation. The political culture of the contemporary USSR, accordingly, still bears the marks of its pre-revolutionary origin, passed on through the family, organised religion, literature and social custom, but it also reflects the impact of Soviet rule since 1917 as well as of the socioeconomic and other changes that have occurred over the same period, such as industrialisation and urbanisation.

It is probably not very helpful to consider the degree of 'continuity' versus 'change' any further in such general terms; let us therefore look more closely at nationalism, a value which appears to have persisted throughout the pre-revolutionary and Soviet periods, and at the changes in the political culture which appear to have stemmed from the experience of Soviet rule more directly.

Nationalism in the USSR is perhaps most immediately associated with the nationalism of the non-Russian nationalities. It is less often realised that nationalism in various forms has always been and still remains a central element in the political culture of the Russian people themselves. In part this was a matter of official doctrine, summed up in the celebrated formula 'Autocracy, Orthodoxy and Nationality' which was propounded by S. S. Uvarov, later Minister of Education, in 1832, and which was taken as the basis of official political doctrine until the revolution of 1905, if not beyond. The formula was intended to imply support for the principle of autocracy, and thus opposition to liberal reforms; for Orthodoxy, or the teaching and ritual of the Russian Orthodox Church; and devotion to the Russian national heritage, together with a reluctance to take Western European thought and institutions as suitable models for developments in Russia. In fact neither Uvarov himself nor some of the later emperors appear to have adhered entirely faithfully to these precepts, and there is some evidence that official nationalism was used, as in other countries, as a means of bolstering popular political support for the regime. At the same time there is no doubt that a popular identification with the strength and territorial integrity of the Russian nation did not have to be invented by the authorities; it emerged particularly strongly in times of war, such as during the Napoleonic war of 1812 and at the beginning of the First World War, and it was also evident in the amorphous but real belief that Russia, as the only major Orthodox power, had to some extent a special destiny as well as a certain superiority to her perhaps more prosperous European neighbours. The less attractive face of popular and official nationalism was apparent in the policy of Russification, carried out with particular vigour in the later nineteenth century, and anti-Semitism.

The Soviet government in its early years took a hostile attitude towards the capitalist and reactionary past that had preceded it and repudiated these elements of continuity, but from the 1930s onwards a revived form of Russian nationalism (called 'socialist patriotism') began to receive a greater degree of official favour. Peter I became 'the Great' again; military leaders of the past, such as Kutuzov and Suvorov, became models for the Red Army; and the expansion of the Russian Empire began to be regarded as more of a civilising than a colonialising enterprise. To some extent, as before, official doctrines of this kind were used by the party leadership in an attempt to manipulate popular political opinion to their advantage. This was particularly the case during the Second World War, when Russian and Slavic patriotism reached an unusual pitch of intensity in part as a result of the deliberate encouragement of the authorities. 'We shall never rouse the people to war with Marxism–Leninism alone', as Stalin is reported to have remarked at this time. And yet popular nationalism, once again, does not seem to have been simply the creation of the party leadership. Soviet soldiers in the field quite spontaneously took up the cry of 'For the Motherland, for Stalin!', and the Orthodox Church immediately identified itself with the defence of the nation as it had done at crucial periods throughout its history. Even emigres found it possible to support the Soviet government, at this time as at others, since although they were hostile to socialism it was at least defending the national territory and accomplishing many necessary social and economic reforms. Many Russians appear to take a comparable pride today in Soviet achievements in sport, science and outer space as well as in the more prominent role the Soviet Union now occupies in international affairs, and it is a source of support for the authorities that it would be unwise to minimise.

The Soviet government appears to have been less successful in developing a comparable commitment to Marxism–Leninism among the population over whom they rule. Despite a considerable effort over more than two generations there appears to be very little interest in or knowledge of the ideology to which the authorities are officially committed, and certainly not enough to be sufficient in itself to legitimate their rule. The main impact of Soviet government appears rather to have been to reinforce the feelings of remoteness of ordinary people from high-level politics and their belief that it would be unprofitable and probably unwise for them to intervene directly in such matters. Working people, as Gorbachev told the 19th Party Conference in 1988, had been 'removed from real participation' in state and public affairs, and some had been 'alienated' from the society at large. This lack of political trust or efficacy had some foundations in the pre-revolutionary period when the government maintained a network of spies and it had a generally deplorable record in relation to civil liberties, but it has increased still further in the Soviet period as a result of the behaviour of the authorities and particularly of the experience of Stalinism. This was a period, still within the memory of older Soviet citizens, when political opponents were executed after show trials, or perhaps after no trial at all; when many millions of people were imprisoned by the secret police on the flimsiest of pretexts; and when an atmosphere of suspicion poisoned relations not only at the workplace but also within the family itself.

'Any adult inhabitant of this country, from a collective farmer up to a member of the Politburo, always knew that it would take only one careless word or gesture and he would fly off irrevocably into the abyss', as Alexander Solzhenitsyn has commented on this period in his *Gulag Archipelago* (1973–5). Perhaps 20 million people lost their lives as a result of the political repression of those years, according to the best Western estimates, and there were still 15 million Soviet citizens in prison camps at the time of Stalin's death in 1953. Many of those who profited from their lack of principle during these years still occupy prominent positions in Soviet life, and it would not be surprising if this period, with the lives and careers it made and unmade, continued to influence Soviet political culture for many years to come. At the same time a number of Soviet citizens, particularly those now in leading positions, may have drawn the rather different conclusion from these years that the substantial achievements they recorded, such as industrialisation, the elimination of illiteracy and the defeat of Hitler, could not have been attained without a high degree of central discipline. And many appear to have believed that Stalin, like the Tsars in pre-revolutionary times, was unaware of the repression that was taking place in his name and that he would put matters right as soon as he was informed of it.

It is perhaps best to end this section by pointing once again to the enormous variety of political attitudes and experiences that are concealed by any generalisations of this kind. There were and still are, for instance, considerable differences of political belief and behaviour between Soviet men and women, between the generations, between the social classes, and between town and country. Perhaps most important of

TABLE 2.2

The major Soviet nationalities

	Census population, 1989 (millions)	% of total	Linguistic group	Traditional religion
The Slavs:				
Russians	145.1	50.8	East Slavic	Russian Orthodox
Ukrainians	44.1	15.5	East Slavic	Russian Orthodox*
Belorussians	10.0	3.5	East Slavic	Russian Orthodox
The Balts:				
Latvians	1.5	0.5	Baltic	Protestant
Lithuanians	3.1	1.1	Baltic	Roman Catholic
Estonians	1.0	0.4	Finno-Ugrian	Protestant
The Caucasian Peoples:				
Georgians	4.0	1.4	Kartvelian	Georgian Orthodox
Armenians	4.6	1.6	Indo-European	Armenian Orthodox
Azerbaidzhanis	6.8	2.4	Turkic	Muslim (Shi'ite)
The Central Asians				
Uzbeks	16.7	5.8	Turkic	Muslim (Sunni)
Kazakhs	10.0	2.9	Turkic	Muslim (Sunni)
Tadzhiks	4.2	1.5	Iranian	Muslim (Sunni)
Turkmenis	2.7	1.0	Turkic	Muslim (Sunni)
Kirgiz	2.5	0.9	Turkic	Muslim (Sunni)
Others:				
Moldavians	3.4	1.2	Romance	Romanian Orthodox

*There is a substantial Roman Catholic (Uniate) minority in the Western Ukraine.
Source: Adapted from *Report on the USSR*, 20 October 1989, pp. 2–3, and standard reference works.

all, there are considerable differences between the political cultures of the various nationalities or ethnic groups of which the Soviet population is composed, the largest fifteen of which have their own union republics with a substantial range of devolved powers. These nationalities are set out schematically in Table 2.2. Russians, it will be seen, account for no more than half of the total population (a proportion which has been slowly declining over the years). Taken together, Slavs (Russians, Ukrainians and Belorussians) account for nearly three-quarters of the total, but there are major differences of language, history and culture between them and most other nationalities in the USSR, as well as long-standing animosities among themselves, particularly between Russians and Ukrainians, which the passage of time appears to have done little to alleviate.

Of the major non-Slavic groups, the Baltic nations have a rather different history, having come under strong German, Polish and Swedish influences at different times. They are generally Protestant or Roman Catholic in religion, not Russian Orthodox; they have been under Soviet rule for a rather shorter period of time than most other nationalities, since about 1940 rather than since the revolution; and even today their way of life remains demonstrably more 'Western' than that of most of the other Soviet nations. The Caucasian peoples – Georgians, Armenians and Azerbaidzhanis – have also a very different history, religion and culture to that of the Slavic majority, and they are perhaps even more conscious of these differences than the Baltic nations (for instance, there were mass riots in Tbilisi, the capital of Georgia, in 1978 when it was rumoured that Georgian was about to be dropped as one of the official languages of the republic). The Caucasian nationalities are renowned for their Mediterranean climate, their fruit and wine, their paternalistic attitude towards women, their feuds and their corruption, but also (particularly the Georgians) for their high levels of education and cultural achievement. Both Georgians and Armenians have their own independent churches and have been Christian since about the fourth century, some six centuries earlier than the Russians (a difference to which they are generally not slow to draw attention).

The greatest cultural division of all, however, is between the Slavs and other European peoples and the predominantly Muslim nationalities of Central Asia. The peoples of these republics are the descendants of the great Mongol empire of medieval times, and they have generally been under Russian rule for no more than the last hundred years or so. The peoples of these republics – Uzbeks, Kazakhs, Kirgiz, Tadzhiks and Turkmenis – speak languages that are generally of Turkic origin; they are predominantly Muslim in religion; and their traditional culture and values, with which their religion is inextricably bound up, appear to have been altered very little by the experience of Russian and now of Soviet rule.

The Central Asians, for instance, are generally reluctant to permit the employment and education of women, and even today the proportion of women members of the communist party and of local soviets in these republics is a good deal lower than it is elsewhere in the USSR. Fewer pigs are kept in these republics (pork being an unclean meat for Muslims, as it is for Jews), and traditional customs such as the charging of bride money, elaborate wedding feasts and pilgrimages to the graves of local holy men are still practised (very few Soviet Muslims are permitted to make a pilgrimage to Mecca), sometimes with the covert support of local party members and officials. There is generally little intermarriage between the Central Asians and non-Muslim nationalities, particularly Slavs, and a knowledge of Russian is much less common than it is among the other peoples of the USSR. Perhaps most alarming of all from a Russian point of view, the population of these republics has been increasing much more rapidly than the all-union average and on some projections may account for 25–30 per cent of the total Soviet population by the end of the century.

Soviet official policy had traditionally maintained that national differences of this kind would eventually disappear as socio-economic conditions became more uniform throughout the USSR, as a knowledge of Russian became more widespread, and as younger generations brought up under wholly Soviet conditions displaced those that had acquired their formative experiences under capitalism. Under Brezhnev it was claimed that a 'new historical collectivity of people – the Soviet people' had come into existence, based upon common economic interests and cultural and political values. Gorbachev, in his early speeches, appeared to accept this complacent view. Addressing the Party Congress in 1986, for instance, he referred to Soviet nationalities policy as an 'outstanding achievement of socialism' which had 'done away for ever' with national oppression and inequalities of all kinds. An indissoluble friendship among the Soviet nations had been established, and a Soviet people, a 'qualitatively new social and interethnic community', had come into being, 'cemented by the same economic interests, ideology and political goals'. The speech, however, also acknowledged that there were tendencies towards 'national isolation' and 'localism', and as nationality relations steadily deteriorated over the following period his speeches became increasingly sombre and realistic.

The nationality issues of the Gorbachev years were very different in character, reflecting the variety of cultures, histories and levels of development of the peoples that made up the USSR. There were, however, some general concerns. One of them was the excessive centralisation of economic management. According to press reports, for example, fully 57 per cent of industrial output was the responsibility of central ministries in Moscow. A further 37 per cent was jointly administered by central ministries and the republics, and only 6 per cent was run by the republics alone. The Estonian party leader, addressing the 19th Party Conference in 1988, complained that 90 per cent of the republican economy was run by central ministries; the Latvian party secretary, addressing the same meeting, added that until a short time previously, pastry cooks in Riga had to obtain the permission of Moscow ministries if they wanted to change the recipe for the tarts they baked. This led to unbalanced development in each of the republics, and sometimes to the wasteful and dangerous development of raw materials and nuclear power. Equally, there were cultural concerns. The Baltic nations, for instance, were worried about immigration. Low local birthrates and high rates of inward population movement, particularly of Russians, had left Estonians just 62 per cent of the population of their republic (compared with 90 per cent in 1940), and Latvians a bare 52 per cent (and a minority in their capital city). There were anxieties about the survival of the local languages, and of local customs.

Influenced by considerations such as these, movements of national self-assertion developed throughout the USSR in the late 1980s, from Russia and the Ukraine to the Bashkir and Tatar republics and the 'small peoples' of the Far North. The strongest pressure for full self-determination came from the Baltic peoples, the first clear sign of which was the demonstrations that took place in August 1987 on the anniversary of the Nazi–Soviet pact which had led to the incorporation of these republics into the USSR. Encouraged by this wave of civic activism, popular fronts came into existence in all three republics during 1988. Nominally 'in defence of *perestroika*', the fronts soon began to press for a 'pluralist society' with no single organisation 'usurping' political power, for a partly privatised economy, and for the demilitarisation of the republican territories. The pre-Soviet national flags and anthems were restored in the autumn of 1988; old street names returned; and traditional festivals such as Christmas day were declared public holidays. Under strong pressure from the republics, a form of economic decentralisation was approved by the Supreme Soviet, to take effect from January 1990. Public opinion, however, had moved still further, to a position of support for full independence; and despite the warnings of Moscow, the local authorites began to develop their own currencies, tax regimes and pricing systems. Most alarmingly of all, from the point of view of the centre, the local communist parties (first of all the Lithuanian, in December 1989) began to sever their links with the CPSU as a whole.

The other nationalist tensions that emerged in the late 1980s were for the most part 'communal' in character, in that they took the form of inter-ethnic clashes rather than pressures for formal separation from the USSR. The most serious was in the Caucasus, where what became virtually a civil war developed between Armenians and Azerbaidzhanis over Nagorno-Karabakh, a small enclave within Azerbaidzhan which was overwhelmingly populated by Armenians. Originally a part of Armenia, the district had been transferred to the jurisdiction of traditionally Muslim Azerbaidzhan in 1923. There had been periodic protests against what was regarded as cultural discrimination, and in February 1988 the local soviet in Nagorno-Karabakh voted in favour of the reintegration of the area with Armenia. This precipitated massive demonstrations in Armenia itself, and a parliamentary vote in favour of the reincorporation of Nagorno-Karabakh. The Azerbaidzhani Supreme Soviet, for its part, insisted upon Article 78 of the Soviet Constitution, which provided that the territory of a union republic could not be changed without its consent. Eventually, after continuing communal violence had claimed at least a hundred lives, the Central Committee resolved in January 1989 to place the region under a 'special form of administration' (in effect, direct rule from Moscow). This was brought to an end in November 1989, after which the area reverted to Azerbaidzhani rule; but there were further riots and demonstrations, which claimed more than a hundred lives in January 1990 alone. The Kremlin's special representative in the area spoke openly about the prospect of a 'Soviet Lebanon' if the violence continued.

After several postponements, a Central Committee plenum on the national question finally met in September 1989. It approved an elaborate 'platform', which acknowledged the damage that had been done to national relations by the repression of the Stalin years and by later attempts to accelerate the process of integration on the basis of the premature conclusion that the national question had been definitively 'solved'. In its place the platform offered a 're-newed federation' with greater devolved powers for the union republics, including their transfer to a cost-accounting basis within what would continue to be a single state and a unitary domestic market. The Russian Republic, in particular, was to be given greater rights, including its own party organisation (which was established, in the form of a 'Bureau', in December 1989). The Communist Party as a whole, however, was to remain a united, 'consolidating and directing force of social development', based on democratic centralism, with a single statute and programme. National languages were to be encouraged, but Russian remained the language of inter-ethnic communication, and all languages must have equality of status. Gorbachev, addressing the meeting, emphasised the economic links that bound the republics and regions together; a powerful federal state, in his view, 'corresponded to the interests of all the people that made up the USSR'.

The plenum certainly marked an advance in the seriousness with which the national question was regarded by the Soviet leadership; but it was less clear that it represented a 'solution' to what was not a single problem but a whole complex of related issues. How, for instance, could republican self-sufficiency be 'organically combined' with a single plan and budget? And how could an integrated economy accommodate a variety of currencies, tax regimes and forms of property? It was difficult, equally, to see a ready solution to the pressure of the various national groups for a greater degree of cultural self-expression, given the ethnically mixed com-

position of each of the republics as well as of the USSR as a
whole. More than 60 million Soviet citizens lived outside their
'own' republic, and very often they had little knowledge of the
language of the majority population in the republic in which
they lived. How could the local language be given an additional status without disadvantaging those who had no knowledge of it? And how could the Soviet system, including its
armed forces, function if there was no widely understood
common language? Nor was it easy to envisage a political
form that would accommodate the interests of the various
nationalities and yet maintain the existence of the USSR itself.
Entering the 1990s, it was the Soviet state in its existing form,
rather than the aspirations of the various nationalities, that
appeared more likely to be sacrificed.

Eastern Europe: political traditions old and new

The pre-communist political cultures of Eastern Europe were
characterised by backwardness. This backwardness manifested itself in a variety of ways, some of which have survived
the communist revolution largely untouched. In other ways,
however, the communist revolution has brought about a far-
reaching transformation. To understand how the existing
political cultures of Eastern Europe may be assessed, one
must look at the pre-revolutionary culture, at the communist
political culture of the post-revolutionary period and at the
state of affairs a generation after the revolution.

The traditional political culture

In the political arena, the most striking aspect of the East
European political cultures was the dominance of the state
and the weakness of society. The principle of reciprocity of
rights between ruler and ruled was much weaker than in the
West, if it existed at all. With considerable variations from
polity to polity, going roughly from Central Europe to the
Balkans, the state was the primary political actor and principal entrepreneur and exercised something close to hegemony
vis-à-vis society, both in regulation and in initiative. In

particular, although nowhere in Eastern Europe did a Russian-type patrimonial state develop, the dominance of the state was guaranteed by the absence of popular control over the money-raising powers of the ruler (taxation) and over the means of coercion (army and police). The position of the ruler, which by the twentieth century had become the bureaucracy, was based on the doctrine of the discretionary power of the state, derived from the royal prerogative, whereby the state had the right to take action untrammelled by constraints from below. In other words, the discretionary power of the state inherently excluded the doctrine of parliamentary sovereignty and resulted in the transformation of legislatures into façades. In the entire pre-communist period there was only one instance of a ruling government losing power through elections (Bulgaria 1931); rather, a new prime minister would be appointed by the managers from the power elite and he would 'make elections' by using the coercive apparatus of the state or other illegal and semi-legal methods. This was the reverse of the order in which governments were changed in genuinely democratic societies, where the concept of popular sovereignty had meaning.

The power élite itself varied in composition, but it was invariably constituted by an alliance of the bureaucracy and other elites. In Poland and Hungary the alliance included the magnates and large landowners, the gentry (*szlachta* in Poland), finance capital and large-scale commerce, the military and the church or churches. The bureaucracy was recruited from these elites and it successfully co-opted the bulk of the intelligentsia (similarly recruited) to carry out the various tasks requiring technical knowledge. The small working class and the peasantry tended to be excluded from this alliance. But consonant with the hegemonial and façade quality of the system, social democratic and peasant parties could and did function – uninfluentially. The bourgeoisie (understood as the entrepreneurial class) was politically weak and deferred to the gentry-bureaucratic alliance. In the Czech lands there was no native aristocracy to speak of and the political elite was more broadly based on the bourgeoisie, finance capital and other sectional interests; peasant and working class interests also secured some representation in this system. Nevertheless in inter-war Czechoslovakia, as in the other Eastern European countries, politics rested on the power of the bureaucracy, which mirrored the permanent coalition of five political parties in power, the *pĕtka*, and which ruled through a series of interpenetrating elites – the trade unions, the press, the military, to some extent the churches, and the judiciary. In all these states, therefore, there was no full political integration, in which state and society were co-terminous and where all the subjects of the state were genuinely citizens with equal rights. In Poland and Czechoslovakia the fabric of the state was further weakened by an absence of national integration – large national minorities remained in some form or another outside official favour by reason of their nationality. In systems of this kind there could be no single public opinion, because society was divided into several social and/or national fragments with limited or nonexistent communication between them.

Much of this was true of the Balkans, but there were also differences. The traditional native aristocracies had been swept away (Bulgaria, Serbia, Greece, Slovenia) or else they had been co-opted into the state (Romania, Croatia, Bosnia, Albania). In the Balkans a merchant–patrician elite and the military were also of importance. The most striking factor, however, was the overwhelmingly peasant character of these societies, up to 90 per cent of the total population. The states were run in the interests of the bureaucracy; the peasantry were excluded and viewed the bureaucracy with hostility as an alien and exploitative agency. The failure of national integration was as much of an issue as in Central Europe, afflicting Yugoslavia and Romania with particular problems.

As far as religion was concerned, Eastern Europe was an area of enormous diversity. Poles and Croats were overwhelmingly Roman Catholic and Czechs, Slovaks, Hungarians, and Slovenes largely so. There were significant Protestant minorities in Hungary (Calvinist and Lutheran) and among the Czechs and Slovaks; and the area that eventually became the German Democratic Republic was four-fifths Lutheran. In the Balkans there was a closer link between religion and nationhood, and Christians belonged to the various Orthodox churches. Islam was represented by the Bosnians, who spoke Serbo-Croat, by the Albanians and by the Turkish minorities, the remnants of the erstwhile Ottoman empire. There were sizeable Jewish communities at various stages of assimilation in Central Europe.

In all these states, the instruments of coercion were freely used to ensure the unchallenged hegemony of the elite, whether these challenges derived from social or national grounds. However, it is worth noting that where there was no conflict of interests the state did not necessarily interfere and did not necessarily seek a monopoly position. The objectives of the elites did not, on the whole, go much beyond securing their own positions; there was a rhetorical commitment to modernisation, which could be jettisoned as soon as conflict arose. At the same time it was noteworthy that during the 1914–45 period (i.e. including the accelerated growth of the two world wars) some development did take place, such as improvements in communications and education. Modernisation was seen primarily as a means of extending the power of the state (by creating a greater tax base and an increase in the size of the armed forces) rather than of increasing the welfare of society; this was a pattern inherited from the military-bureaucratic empires of the nineteenth century.

Thus by 1945, the political cultures of the Eastern European societies included acceptance of the power of the state to regulate society over a wide area of life, a habituation to arbitrary methods and authoritarianism which could be offset by corruption, hostility towards the state on the part of the majority coupled with a messianic concept of political change, and a feeling among a minority of the intelligentsia that change could only be effected from above through the agency of massive state action. Among both the intelligentsia and the peasantry there were strong elements of messianism, and change was generally viewed as a radical transformation rather than as a series of orderly steps towards reform, albeit in different forms. In general, the radical intelligentsia took various intellectual models as their utopia (Marxism, Fascism, neo-Catholicism or populism), whereas peasant messianism derived from the restricted world-view of the East European peasant (bounded by highly conservative, traditional peasant communities and drawing on religion as the source of the myth values which formed the benchmark of desired change).

The peasant challenge to the established order and the ruling elites, both in 1917–21 and in the 1930s (when it emerged as right-wing radicalism), was defeated throughout Eastern Europe because the peasantry lacked a tradition of sustained, organised action and was weakened by its antagonism towards politics. Both these shortcomings could be traced to the limited political experience of the peasantry, its political illiteracy, in polities where the contact between the peasant and the state was limited to the gendarme, the tax-gatherer and the recruiting sergeant. Not surprisingly, the peasant tended to regard politics and the seat of politics, the city, as alien and parasitical. Finally, the capriciousness and inexperience of peasant leaders likewise contributed to the failure of the first challenge of mass politics in Eastern Europe. The acute economic crisis of the 1930s and the dislocation of the war intensified the frustration and resentments of the peasants and made them susceptible to political sloganeering promising immediate transformation.

On the other hand, it should be stressed that in these polities the élites exercised a hegemony and not a monopoly. Thus some political pluralism – the autonomous functioning of social institutions capable of articulating political alternatives and representing particular interests – could and did coexist with the discretionary power of the state. Institutional and social autonomy was often circumscribed and might be confined to the upper echelons, the privileged sections of society. If the state wished to extend control over them it could do so, although it might have to pay a political price. The areas in which such nascent pluralism did exist included the educational system, the press, the trade unions and some other social organisations. Even the courts were not necessarily under strict control, unless power interests were threatened, and the same applied to local interests. The right to autonomous economic initiative, i.e. private enterprise, likewise existed. This had the important result that national and social minorities could find some protection against discrimination by the agencies of the state controlled by the majority nationality. Overall, the hegemonistic and authoritarian political cultures of pre-war Eastern Europe were moderated to some degree by incipient pluralistic values and practices of this kind.

The cement binding rulers and ruled together in an at least partially consensual framework was nationalism. In all the states of Eastern Europe, the newly emergent elites of the nineteenth century took power against the ruling empires by the propagation of nationalist ideologies. These ideologies were, of course, received from the West, although they were significantly modified in their reception by the different political context of Eastern Europe. But the mobilising element of nationalism was highly successful, in that it brought to political awareness increasing numbers of individuals who had until then had next to no political self-identity and a largely static one at that.

Nationalism proved effective in creating a new political identity *vis-à-vis* the state and towards other polities, especially when the nation could be presented as being under threat. But it offered no answers whatever to the challenge of mass politics, to the problem of creating social institutions to mediate between the individual and state; indeed, if anything, it promoted an unmediated concept of mass politics, in which the utopian ideal was one where all national awareness was identical and where conflicts of interest did not arise. This was exacerbated by the manipulative qualities inherent in nationalism and the use made of them before 1945, while urgent socio-political problems were neglected. Hence by 1945 the system associated with nationalism was widely discredited and there was something of a revulsion against nationalism as such. Nevertheless, that did not signify that national identity ceased to be of relevance. All or almost all East Europeans when they considered their relationship to the state of which they were subjects identified themselves in national terms, and that identity, based on factors of shared culture and language (and in the Balkans of religion as well), and on a concept of the 'ideal territory' of the nation-state, retained its power of attraction.

The communist tradition

The communist tradition and political culture of East European parties developed against this background. The communists' interpretation of their experience, however, differed from that of the majority, and they learned different lessons

from it. Driven by an ideology with a claim to a total transformation of society, the communists had initially had high
hopes of achieving objectives during the revolutionary upsurge
that gripped Eastern Europe in 1917–21. The upsurge had its
origins in war weariness and dislocation, in the radical expectations of massive change promoted by war and the example of
the Russian Revolution. On the face of it the communists, who
had their antecedents in the left of Social Democracy and were
reinforced by prisoners-of-war returning from Russia (where
many had taken an active part in the revolution), should have
been well placed to profit from the radical upsurge.

Their record, however, was one of failure. In Yugoslavia,
the communists emerged as the third largest party in the
elections to the Constituent Assembly in 1921, and in Montenegro they polled an absolute majority of votes. In Poland,
where the leaders of the reconstituted state were able to draw
on massive popular support in the defence of the country
against the Soviet Union, a solid core of communists retained
their beliefs. In Czechoslovakia, when the socialists split, the
communists emerged more numerous and better organised
than the social democrats. Yet despite these gains and the
radical groundswell that made them possible, the communists
were nowhere able to translate their support into long-term
political strength. They misunderstood or overestimated the
nature of the upsurge, which was based on the discontent of
the peasants, who generally distrusted and despised the urban
intellectuals and workers who led the communist parties. The
experience and ability of the established political elites,
moreover, proved more than a match for the messianic
radicals, who had expected that the 'bourgeois state' would
collapse after one determined push; and the communists'
messianism and radicalism alienated many potential supporters who might have wanted change but not in the direction
insisted on by the communists. Thus the lesson drawn by
communist leaders from the 1917–21 experience was to
distrust mass politics as unreliable, to seek no allies except for
tactical ends and to opt for conspiratorial methods of organisation. In this they were assisted by the ruling elites which
banned the communist parties (except in Czechoslovakia) and
helped to drive them into a political ghetto.

The second formative process undergone by East European parties was Sovietisation. This might be seen as a kind of intellectual, ideological, political and organisational colonisation of East European institutions by Soviet ones. Whatever autonomous traditions, aims, concepts, experience or roots these parties might have had, they were forced to abandon them and to subordinate themselves absolutely to Soviet experience (this applied to West European parties as well, of course). Those who refused to submit were expelled or liquidated. The imposition of this Soviet-type political system may have weakened or eliminated local Marxist traditions, but it had the result of welding together disparate, often disputatious individuals into an effective political force. By the 1930s obedience to Moscow was unconditional and Soviet instructions were carried out even when these clearly ran counter to a party's local interests. The Romanian Communist Party, for instance, was obliged to proclaim a policy of self-determination for Romania's national minorities 'up to and including secession'; this ensured that the party would be shunned by ethnic Romanians and would attract support almost exclusively from the country's ethnic minorities.

The membership of all the East European parties was therefore seriously depleted by their own actions, by Soviet colonisation and by police persecution, but those who remained or were recruited in the 1930s were steeled in a tough school of 'conspiratorial politics' and ruthlessness, the underground, infiltration of other legal bodies (like trade unions), and obedience to Moscow. This experience bred contempt for other political forces, especially the social democrats (which was reciprocated), for the established institutions of the state and the political system generally, and an attitude which regarded one's political opponents as enemies to be liquidated. Political change was not to be the result of debate and compromise, the aggregation of competing interests, but of ruthlessness and force; and criticism was not legitimate comment but hostile attack. All in all, the communists brought a rather simple, black-and-white view of the world with them into the post-war era.

The third formative experience was to some extent the practice of the first two lessons, the application of the conspiratorial principle and organisational efficiency in the resistance during the war. Their resistance role and the prestige of the Soviet Union as liberator proved to be the factor that brought the communists out of the political ghetto. Noncommunist parties or groups co-operated with the communists against the enemy, found that collaboration in some areas was possible (although not without problems) and assumed that wartime co-operation could be extended into a post-war era of radical reform. For the communists, on the other hand, the equation had not really changed – they had been too deeply marked by their local and Soviet experiences. Imbued by an intransigent sense of their own infallibility, they acted decisively and with the assumption that 'history was on their side'. Above all, in the initial post-war period, they persuaded or bludgeoned non-communist reformers (social democrats or peasant parties) into co-operation by raising the spectre of 'reaction' and by insisting that only two positions were possible in the political constellation of the time – wholehearted co-operation (i.e. subordination) or wholehearted opposition. This black-and-white worldview and the dynamism that accompanied it – a certainty that the communists had all the answers – carried the communists into the early post-war era.

The political cultures that evolved from a conflation of the communist, revolutionary value system and the original precommunist tradition had all the marks of the difficulties of combining two such disparate elements, despite the points of similarity between them. On the one hand, the communists were clearly able to make use of much of the pre-existing tradition of deference to authoritarianism and acceptance of the dominance of the state over society. The wartime radicalisation and, for that matter, actual radical change, like the sweeping away of the old order, coupled with a widespread expectation of change (if not necessarily in the direction taken by the communists), were likewise put to good use by the new communist administrations.

Their historic achievement of concentrating energies to begin the initial push towards industrialisation, which had eluded their predecessors, at the same time resolved the most acute socio-economic problem besetting Eastern Europe:

the peasant question. (In Czechoslovakia and the GDR an industrial base had already been created and the agrarian question lacked the same degree of urgency.) With industrialisation came an end to rural over-population, hunger in the countryside, limited opportunities, and the exclusion of the majority of the population from the ambit of the state. The communist revolutions also brought improved health and welfare, education, transport and communications, and administrative techniques. For the first time ever the whole of Eastern Europe was exposed to equal standards of administration, whether in towns or in the countryside. The promotion of a generation of individuals of working-class and peasant origins, who came to form the new class, brought untapped talents into politics and the intelligentsia. The concentration of power in the hands of the state, broadly speaking, was not as such out of line with East European political traditions and has continued to receive conditional backing from the bulk of the population throughout both periods.

Since the transformation

The communist value system, as already suggested, was never deeply internalised except by relatively small sections of the population. Nevertheless, the impact of four decades of the superimposition of this system was profound and far-reaching. At the very least, this was the system, and its accompanying set of values, against which people were reacting. Towards the end of communism in Central and Eastern Europe, the system sought to base its survival on a strategy of selecting social groups and offering them special deals. This has given rise to a set of values that are complex and contradictory, but undoubtedly influential in responses to the past and the present.

There was a widespread revulsion against the communist system, a rhetorical rejection of everything that it stood for, but coupled with attachment to some of the ideas and institutions that it had constructed. On the whole, the populations of these states are suspicious of entrepreneurialism, competitive markets and politics, but are at the same time committed to freedom, or at any rate an abstract concept of the elimination of restrictions on the individual, and have very high expectations. The high levels of dependence on the state and the correspondingly low levels of individual initiative are paralleled by unrealistic beliefs about the early economic effects of democracy and pessimism about the future. In effect, the last forty years have created extensive confusion, and this applies to both groups and individuals.

The rejection of communism by society as a whole is often very radical and thoroughgoing at the surface level. Yet this can also be coupled with suspicion of politics as such and an inability or unwillingness to accept the significance of democratic mechanisms. Thus in *Poland* in the elections of June 1989, the electorate completely rejected the communist party in a near absolute fashion. This was contrary to the communist party's own calculations and came as a surprise. Yet this should not be taken to mean that the system of welfare benefits and subsidies has been rejected as well. Rather, it appeared as if Polish society wanted to be rid of communism, understandably after the previous forty years for which they properly held the communist party responsible, but to be able to select which bits of communism they could keep and which would be governed by the market. In the event, the Solidarity government introduced a very radical free market strategy, which did attract support in the initial phases.

However, the elections of 1989 in Poland produced a number of other surprises. In addition to the rejection of the communist party, the Church also fared rather badly. In three constituencies, candidates were run against Solidarity with the support of the local hierarchy on a Christian Democratic ticket. All three performed badly. The implication is that the Solidarity movement had been invested with enormous political significance as the emancipator of Polish society and the political role of the Roman Catholic church, which had sought to appear as the representative of society during the martial law period, was not acceptable in competition with Solidarity. The longer term inference to be drawn from this evidence was that the political function of religion as a *de facto* opposition was declining in importance and that eventually Roman

Catholicism in Poland was likely to acquire a moral and culture saliency only.

Another result of the elections with broader relevance was the relatively high rate of abstentions. Only 62 per cent of the electorate actually voted, a strikingly high abstention rate in a situation that was seemingly so politicised. The explanation for this figure suggests that around half of those who abstained are the standard abstainers, the political neutrals and apathetic voters who exist in every country. The other half, around a fifth of the electorate, on the other hand, are the 'passive radicals'. This section of the population is fully aware of the political struggle but wants to have nothing to do with politics at all, regarding Wałęsa as no different from Jaruzelski. Their aspirations are for a Western standard of living at once, with which they are familiar from hearsay, television or actual experience, and their impatience prompts them to demand everything straightaway.

The failure by the Polish party to enforce collectivisation has, furthermore, conserved a fairly traditional peasantry, which remains sizeable – still some 30 per cent of the population, although this is bound to decline as the oldest generation dies out and is not replaced. For the time being, however, the countryside remains qualitatively different from urban areas, in that the peasantry remains deeply religious, it looks to the preservation of its traditional way of life which is only partly supportive of the market, and it is suspicious of urban areas.

Overall, the picture in Poland is of a somewhat fractured political culture, with various currents that are less than clear in their view of politics, in their expectations and in their likely behaviour. All this is held together by a strong, well developed and clearly articulated sense of nationhood, to some extent religion as a badge of identity and the symbolic and real authority of Solidarity. How deep and well established the patterns in the political culture required to support democracy may be cannot be determined. Above all, the balance between authoritarian and democratic currents has still to be determined.

The situation in *Hungary* had some analogies with that in Poland, but the differences are probably more important.

While the social structure of the two countries shows some similarities, their experiences under communism have pushed them in different directions. The lessons from the Polish experience were that political activism could bring dividends, whereas what the Hungarians learned after the suppression of 1956 about participation in politics was overwhelmingly negative. The subsequent broadening of its limits by the Kádár régime was coupled with an encouragement to divert energies into economic activism. The other leg of this strategy was depoliticisation, whereby all political activity and initiative were reserved by the party to itself and so was actual political thought. Essentially, politics was banished from Hungary for a generation and the rituals of the system, like the quinquennial elections, were nothing like sufficient to offset this.

In consequence, when the communist system disappeared in 1989, the popular reaction to this was muted. In the various by-elections to parliament, it proved difficult to generate enough support to make the 50 per cent turnout needed to validate the poll. At the same time, the emergence of the new system would have been an excellent opportunity for the population to begin the process of building its own institutions, notably trade unions, and to become politically active through the various new parties. On the whole, this did not happen. There were no effective new trade unions and the bulk of the population viewed political activity with indifference verging on suspicion.

Various explanations were advanced to account for this, some of them relevant to understanding the emerging political culture. In the first place, between a tenth and a fifth of the population were thought to be not equipped to deal with politics in the sense needed for a competitive system, by reason of being underprivileged intellectually, economically or socially. The country's sizeable gypsy minority fell largely into this category. Historically, the Hungarian peasantry had been excluded from politics and were subsequently sucked off the land by industrialisation.

However, their values had not undergone any major shifts as a result and some of this was transmitted through the family to the next generation, leaving a fair proportion of society ill-fitted to deal with politics and for whom Kádárist depoliticisation was ideal. A further section, particularly in parts of the working class, had enjoyed certain benefits from the old system – levels of pay higher than justified by their contribution to the economy – and were in any case comfortable with hierarchical, authoritarian relations. To these could be added the employees of the myriad bureaucracies, often performing monotonous and irrelevant work, but in employment and reluctant to face the rigours of a labour market.

Finally, unlike Poland, Hungarian nationalism was a much weaker force and so, therefore, was the cement binding society together. The communist period had consistently, and to an extent successfully, sought to play down the meaning of nationhood in Hungary, through education and the media, for example. This had the result, as evidenced by numerous surveys, that only a relatively low level of popular interest existed in the future of Hungary as a state and in the Hungarian nation. The populist intellectual current made major efforts to offset this and to promote a stronger, more active consciousness of nationhood, but this was only partly effective.

There was considerable evidence that the part of the industrial working class vulnerable to authoritarianism was relatively strong in *Czechoslovakia*. It was noteworthy that in the general strike called by Civic Forum, participation was just over 60 per cent. The implication of this figure is that while a clear majority rejected the communist system, a noteworthy minority had other views. Some would obviously have been motivated by fear, but others would have been expressing their support, qualified or otherwise, for the old system. The argument here is that the extraordinary stability of Czechoslovakia in the 1970s and 1980s was explained by the relative satisfaction of the industrial working class with a system that offered it a tolerable standard of living, the chance of upward promotion and at least rhetorical participation. Crucially, they were ready to accept hierarchical relations as an authentic and fruitful way of social organisation and, hence, rejected the prospect of an open political system and economic competition.

The impact of the transformation on the *German Demo-*

cratic Republic (GDR) was contradictory and destructive, indicating that the foundations of the state had been far less well established than assumed previously. The first indication that the level of acceptance of the authoritarianism and efficient welfare state provided by the GDR was lower than assumed came in the summer of 1989, when large numbers of East Germans tried to take advantage of the gap in the Iron Curtain provided by Hungary's open frontier policy. The motivation of these emigrants was overwhelmingly political, rather than economic, and sociologically they were in the very categories on which the state relied heavily – relatively young, articulate, educated and skilled. Evidently, the internalisation of official values was unsuccessful in this case.

However, the impact of this large wave of emigration was highly unsettling in the GDR itself and led to widespread demonstrations against the restrictive foreign travel policy of the state. Again, this indicated that the circle of those with a negative or strongly negative view of the system was large enough to launch a process that eventually destabilised the state. The possibility of travelling to the West brought it home to East Germans that their German identity was more authentic than they had been led to believe and the comparisons which they then made with West Germany were highly damaging to the GDR. This set off a wide-ranging dissatisfaction with the status quo. Whereas the reform process might at first have culminated in a reformed but still socialist system, within a matter of months the dominant tide of opinion had shifted towards pushing for reunification, again underlining the strength of a German identity and reinforced by the expectation of access to a higher standard of living.

The situation in *Romania* was very difficult to assess. The Ceauşescu régime had effectively gone a very long way towards destroying the factors that make for a community. Even the sense of nationhood had been devalued by Ceauşescu's exaggerated use of it as an instrument of legitimation. Thus in the aftermath of the transformation, the single most important factor was probably the sense that a revolution had taken place – the first in Romanian history – and that as a result, the country's despotic régime had been ended by the will of the people. But what other communal values remained was hard to assess. Virtually everything else was negative – the rejection of everything that Ceauşescuism had stood for. There was no easy agreement on the form of government, on the extent of accountability for the past or on the structure of the future. The destruction of values under Ceauşescu created a state of affairs where the population was prey to manipulation, arousal on an affective basis and a sense of continual crisis.

Overall the transformation in Central and Eastern Europe brought about an extraordinary fluidity of values, which would take some time to crystallise. The rejection of communism as a set of ideas and as a system of symbols appeared to be complete, but otherwise there was little agreement on what should replace them.

The political culture of China

The dangers of generalisation inherent in the political culture approach, noted earlier in this chapter, apply with special force to China. The tendency to think in terms of a single culture is reinforced by the fact that the Chinese state has existed for over two millennia, except for relatively brief periods of disintegration. The dominant view as outlined below is of an insular state governed by a well-refined hierarchical system of government presided over by the Emperor. The insularity was reflected in the name of the country itself *Zhongguo*: literally meaning the middle or 'central' kingdom.

Obviously, this view does provide a starting point for explaining much of China's dominant political culture; but equally, it clouds other important parts of China's political heritage. China has witnessed periods of extensive dealings with foreigners such as in the Han (205 BC–AD 220) and the Tang (AD 618–907) dynasties. These were periods of extensive trading when foreign products were well received in China and when Chinese goods reached far-flung corners of the globe. This trade was even accompanied by the influx of foreign systems of thought. Most noticeable was the increasing influence of Buddhism, which arrived from India from the late

Han period onwards. The later Qing periods, despite some attempts to keep the foreigners out (AD 1644–1911), and the Republican period (1911–49), were both influenced by foreign trade and the influx of new ideas. The Taiping Rebellion (1850–64) with its strange mix of half-baked Christianity, iconoclasm and traditional notions of peasant rebellion, mounted a major challenge to the Confucian orthodoxy. The May Fourth Movement (1915–19) also witnessed a major attack on the Confucian tradition and revealed an intellectual fascination with a whole host of foreign ideas ranging from liberalism to Marxism to anarchism.

Indeed, during the 1980s reformers in the CCP tried to make use of the more cosmopolitan, trading culture of China's coastal regions as a key element in their economic programmes. In particular, Zhao Ziyang, who was dismissed in June 1989 as party General Secretary for his alleged support of the student demonstrations, favoured a development strategy that relied heavily on coastal trade and investment by revitalising historic links with the overseas Chinese communities in Southeast Asia.

Other factors also warn against the dangers of generalisation. Although less than half the size of the USSR, China's land area is vast and is criss-crossed with mountain ranges. Communications are relatively poor and regional differences are therefore fairly marked. Moreover, while most of the country lies in the temperate zone, there are wide variations of climate. The forces of nature have not been tamed as fully as in more advanced countries, and these impose different sets of problems in different provinces. The severity and diversity of these problems may be illustrated by the fact that in 1981 millions of people in north-central China faced quite severe food shortages because of extensive drought; in the western province of Sichuan, 1.5 million people lost their homes because of floods.

There is also the sheer size of the population. At the time of the Roman Empire the Han dynasty was already ruling over a state of 60 million people. The population today exceeds 1100 million. Some 94 per cent of the population is Han (as the Chinese call themselves) and the ethnic question does not loom so large as in the USSR. Nevertheless the minority nationalities, which are ethnically, culturally, religiously and/

or linguistically distinct from the Han, exceed the total population of the United Kingdom.

Despite these warnings, the attempt to encapsulate China's history in the space of a few pages involves making some sweeping statements. Nevertheless it is essential that the attempt be made as distinctive features of the political culture can only be understood in terms of its sheer continuity.

The origins of Chinese political culture

When a bronze culture and a writing system developed in north China in the second millennium BC the civilisations of Mesopotamia and Egypt were already old. Unlike them, however, Chinese civilisation was never 'lost', but has continued to develop and expand up to the present day. The characters used in *People's Daily* derive from inscriptions used for divination over 3000 years ago and a few of the archaic forms are still recognisable to any literate Chinese. The weight of the Chinese tradition was already apparent in the days of Confucius (551–479 BC). Far from claiming to innovate, the sage and his disciples merely claimed to look back to an earlier Golden Age and urged rulers to revert to 'the ways of antiquity'. Confucius's teachings provided the ideological cement for imperial China, although subject to reinterpretation to produce a doctrine appropriate to the interests of the state. Until the collapse of the Qing dynasty in 1911 Confucius was revered as the greatest teacher and philosopher that had ever lived, and no man was considered educated unless he was steeped in the classics.

This easy familiarity with their own history which Chinese enjoy persisted into the communist era, although of course radically different lessons were then drawn from the 'feudal' past. Thus in the 1970s rival leaders cloaked their disagreement over politics and personalities under a mass campaign to 'criticise Confucius' in general and Confucians in particular. They did so on the reasonable assumption that 'the masses' would not be unduly surprised to find their newspapers filled with discussion of events which had occurred perhaps 2000 years previously, but which were deemed to be relevant to contemporary affairs. There is simply no exact parallel to this

in the European tradition. To invent one it would be necessary to imagine that Graeco-Roman civilisation had
flourished without a break from Homer onwards. One would
also have to assume that the Roman Empire, despite occasional difficulties, had continued to regenerate itself in its full
glory until in the twentieth century it had been destroyed by a
revolt of the Roman *plebs*. For Chinese civilisation contributed
to, and was in turn preserved by, political unification.

The word 'China' derives from the state of Qin whose ruler
hammered rival states into submission and so became the
'first emperor' in 220 BC. His tyrannical reign was marked by
the building of the Great Wall, although his dynasty was
short-lived. For more than 2000 years thereafter, however, the
norm was for China to be unified into a large and powerful
state, the eras of imperial greatness being identified by the
names of the major dynasties: Han, Tang, Song, Yuan, Ming
and Qing. Two of these were alien in origin, having been
imposed by conquest from the north. The Yuan dynasty was
established by the Mongols in the thirteenth century. China's
last dynasty, the Qing, was set up by the Manchus in 1644.
But in neither case did the fundamental nature of the Chinese
state change significantly. China was vast, its population
numerous, its economy rich and its political institutions
highly developed. The conquerors were 'barbarians' whose
temporary superiority rested mainly on military prowess.
They found it easier to govern along traditional Chinese lines,
and very quickly succumbed to sinification.

The physical and cultural superiority which China generally
enjoyed in East Asia had major consequences for China's view
of her place in the world. Whereas western states co-existed
with others of roughly comparable strength and a similar level
of economic and cultural development, China enjoyed a
splendid isolation. To the north there were nomads, to the
east the Koreans and Japanese and to the south the peoples of
what is now Vietnam. Where relations existed these 'lesser'
peoples were regarded as 'barbarians' who, in return for
accepting tributary status, were permitted to enjoy the benefits of Confucian civilisation. But China considered that they
had little to offer in return.

Despite periods of extensive trading and even exploration,

China possessed a remarkable lack of awareness of the outside world. This persisted even at the end of the eighteenth century when, in 1793, George III sent Lord Macartney to Peking to press for greater trade links and the establishment of diplomatic relations. Macartney took as gifts for the emperor a number of examples of the products of industrialising Britain, including a hot-air balloon, clocks and watches, and scientific instruments. On arrival he was expected to kowtow like any other 'barbarian' and considerable time elapsed before a satisfactory compromise was eventually reached. Even then, the mission was unsuccessful. The emperor presented Macartney with a letter to George III which illustrated vividly China's ignorance of what was happening elsewhere. This informed the king that 'we have never valued ingenious articles, nor do we have the slightest need of your country's manufactures'. The monarch was also instructed to 'simply act in conformity with our wishes by strengthening your loyalty and swearing perpetual obedience so as to ensure that your country may share the blessings of peace'. Such an attitude was to cost China dear, and was to make her eventual exposure to modernisation a particularly traumatic experience.

Turning to internal arrangements, state, society and family were organised on strictly hierarchical principles. Confucianism stressed the importance of maintaining harmony and, in its official version, this meant that the lower orders were taught to 'know their place' and to subordinate themselves to their superiors. At the pinnacle of the system stood the emperor, an awesome figure with divine attributes. He was an absolute ruler entrusted with power through the 'Mandate of Heaven'. Some emperors were great scholars, warriors and active in state affairs, carrying out tours of their domains. Others rarely left their palaces and were heavily dependent on information given to them by the most senior imperial advisers.

The state was actually governed by a sophisticated salaried bureaucracy which, as early as the first century BC, is said to have been composed of 130,000 officials. At the centre the bureaucracy was divided into a number of specialised departments, but at lower levels imperial 'magistrates' exercised a wide range of administrative and judicial functions. Although large in absolute terms, China was not 'over-governed'. The imperial administration stopped at the seats of government of approximately 2000 countries ito which China was divided.

The official elite was unusual in that from Han times it was recruited primarily from men of education. This practice became institutionalised in the famous 'examination system'. With the exception of a few 'dishonourable' groups, males of all classes of society were free to compete, and only rarely was it possible to buy success or to acquire an official post by means of 'connections'. The belief that this method of selection was both fair and rational contributed enormously to the legitimacy of the elite, and the manifest link between educational achievement and political power encouraged a reverence for the former. It also resulted in a reasonable degree of social mobility in that families blessed with a succession of bright offspring could achieve a degree of eminence while the latter held official positions but tended to revert to their original obscurity as soon as nature showed its preference for regression to the norm.

China was, however, a limited meritocracy. The examinations tested candidates' ability to master officially prescribed interpretations of the Confucian classics and to reproduce them in appropriately stylised forms. This in turn required that candidates had a formal, lengthy and orthodox education, and the state provided little of this. There were many instances of poor boys being sponsored by a wealthy relative or kinship organisation, but as a general rule education was restricted to children of the well-to-do who could afford to pay. Those who successfully passed the gruelling series of examinations joined the ranks of officialdom and occupied themselves with the usual governmental tasks of an agrarian society. They collected taxes, raised forced labour and conscripts as required, saw that irrigation systems were repaired and extended, and settled disputes. In general they acted in conjunction with, and in the interests of, the local landlords.

This was due partly to the fact that they were drawn from the same strata of society, and local landlords who had failed to obtain official positions for themselves tended to constitute the 'natural' leaders of rural China on whom the magistrates relied. It was also a result of corruption; for official stipends were small. Some officials were content to retire 'with only wind in their sleeves'. Many, however, resembled the man who was so rapacious that 'even an egg was smaller when it passed through his hands'. Therefore they sold 'favours' to the local gentry, who could afford them and saw to it that exactions fell most harshly on the peasantry.

The landlord class was, then, in a favoured position, just below the ranks of officialdom in the hierarchy. Chinese landlords rarely owned vast estates, and landholdings were extremely modest compared with those in Tsarist Russia. But landlords were a leisured class nevertheless. One of the less attractive features of Confucian culture was the widespread belief that a gentleman should not engage in manual work, and landlords left the actual farming to others. They themselves pursued interests appropriate to persons of education: they wrote poetry, painted, practised calligraphy and, of course, studied antiquity.

It was the peasants who did the work. The bulk of the population, they ranged from persons who hired labour to assist them to landless labourers who lived by selling their labour power. In terms of Confucian ideology they enjoyed an honourable position. So, too, did artisans. This still left a number of groups in society who were officially regarded with contempt, among whom were merchants. Merchants lacked education and, unlike peasants, did not actually 'produce' anything, but managed nevertheless to create wealth for themselves. They were often regarded as parasites, an attitude which was ultimately to marry nicely with Marxist theories of capitalist exploitation. Commerce did flourish but it was subject to official regulation and, if an activity were particularly profitable, would then be made an official monopoly. Consequently, it was not until the middle of the nineteenth century that a bourgeoisie of any real significance began to appear and that came about only as a result of foreign penetration.

Soldiers, too, found little favour. Dynasties were founded by force of arms, and martial emperors and great generals were accorded respect. But this did not extend to the common soldiery. The contempt of the scholar-officials for them was epitomised in the saying, 'One does not use good iron to make a nail, nor a good man for a soldier.' There were also the *déclassé* elements. These included common criminals, those like fortune-tellers and prostitutes who earned their living by dubious means, and itinerant fishermen, boatmen and coolies. There were also the secret societies. These existed throughout Chinese history and were to be found in both secular and religious varieties. They were a refuge for the unwanted and the disaffected, providing the lowly members of society with what has been termed a 'surrogate kinship organisation'. With heterodox beliefs and esoteric rituals, the societies were outside the law. Their activities ranged from operating as Chinese Robin Hoods to mounting full-scale rebellions, and they participated in the overthrow of several dynasties. Generally, however, their influence was limited.

Finally, there was the family. This, too, was meticulously structured and children were brought up to recognise their own place and that of their relatives within a framework which stressed male dominance and, above all, the utmost respect for the aged. Within the home given names were rarely used; instead family members addressed each other in terms of rank: 'elder brother', 'younger sister', and so on. The stress was on duties rather than rights and, in the event of disputes, the young were expected to subordinate themselves to their elders and to 'swallow bitterness' and endure their lot without complaint. Self-assertiveness was actively discouraged and the interests of the group took priority over those of the individual.

The masses expected their government to administer efficiently thus allowing them to get on with their business. This would ensure legitimacy for the regime. Thus, the Chinese peasant preferred a distant relationship with government and so long as it got on with its job, they would support it. Should a government fail to meet its obligations, it could lose the 'mandate of heaven' thus making rebellion legitimate. Loss of the mandate was indicated by such natural disasters as floods and droughts. In practice, however, the only indication of the correctness of the rebellion was whether it succeeded. A rebel leader would establish a new dynasty and the process of rewriting history would begin. Reforms would be reinstituted, including a more equitable distribution of land, and the new dynasty would embark on an era of greatness before succumbing, eventually, to decay and overthrow.

The Chinese state was expansive in terms of its view of its role. Unchallenged by other organisations (there was no organised church as in the West), the state assumed an all-embracing role that included defining correct ethical values. The state defined these values on the basis of the prevailing interpretation of Confucianism. The local official was to embody and proselytise Confucian values and the masses were expected to simply follow the examples provided for them. The recurrent campaigns launched by the CCP in the 1980s to combat 'spiritual pollution' and to 'build a spiritual socialist civilisation' are just the latest manifestations of this phenomenon.

The state thus assumed the role of educator. In the same way that couplets hung in public places in imperial times extalling Confucian values, so huge billboards in the PRC beam out messages for the people to love the party, the army and the nation. This approach is strengthened by the traditional view that people possess innate goodness, and that the proper education would enable them to achieve their full potential. In practice, however, 'goodness' was equated with those attributes which the imperial authorities deemed desirable for the maintenance of the existing social order, and the use of education to inculcate 'correct' ideas was fully accepted as part of government policy. Under the Ming and Qing dynasties particularly, great efforts were made to promote official orthodoxy. Those who received a lengthy formal education in order to compete in the imperial examinations were, of course, taught to value conformity. But the imperial authorities were not content to leave matters there. The Qing dynasty, especially, tried to indoctrinate the masses also by establishing a lecture system. In every district lecturers were appointed on the basis of their scholarship, age and good character, and were required to expound imperial maxims twice a month. Edicts of a morally uplifting nature were provided by the emperors themselves for the edification of their subjects and attendance at the lectures was compulsory. An interesting feture of the system was that lecturers were required to use examples of virtuous behaviour for purposes of emulation. Equally, those deemed guilty of anti-social behaviour were criticised, their names were posted in public places and remained there until they showed contrition for their acts. Thus the communist glorification of moral exemplars and vilification of 'negative examples' has an imperial past.

This kind of thinking clearly leaves little room for participation in politics. Indeed, ordinary Chinese did not consider they had any right to participate in government and, being fully conscious of the fact that government meant demands, tended to minimise their contacts with it. Nevertheless there was a widespread acceptance of the 'rightness' of the state's institutional arrangements, and Confucianism was the basis for the value system to which most subscribed. For much of the time the bulk of the population was passive, and foreign visitors commented on the 'easy governability' of the Chinese people.

One last consequence of this heritage is that the concept of 'Loyal Opposition' was unknown. The state did not acknowledge the legitimacy of an opposition that was a necessary part of the political system. This sharply defined the role of intellectuals within traditional society, with political control of literature and other such pursuits being widely perceived as legitimate. The scholar-officials who were the product of this system often possessed great political power and social stature. In turn, because most scholars were officials, it worked against the striving for intellectual autonomy. Intellectual autonomy was dangerous and would most probably end up in loss of position or even moral and social exile. In the same way as the dynasties built up their armies of scholars to write up their official histories and to provide arguments for their legitimacy, so too has the CCP built up its coterie of 'establishment intellectuals'.

The harsh authoritarianism of the imperial system was somewhat mitigated by the officials themselves. The lengthy education they had undergone laid emphasis on moral virtue and, just as the good subject and the 'filial son' were inseparable, officials were supposed to act as the 'fathers and mothers' of the people, strict but fundamentally benevolent.

This led to another role for the scholar-official. When higher level officials, up to and including the Emperor, were seen to be engaging in venal, corrupt practices, the scholar-official assumed the role of moral critic and guardian of the nation's higher ethical values. Many did criticise such practices even at the risk of exile or death for themselves and their families. Thus in 1959, when Peng Dehuai remonstrated with Mao for the hardship inflicted by the Great Leap Forward and suffered disgrace for his pains, he was acting in a noble tradition. Wu Han, a playwright, promptly drew attention to this by writing a play entitled 'Hai Rui Dismissed from Office'. This dealt with the life of a Ming dynasty official who had similarly spoken up on behalf of an oppressed peasantry and had been dismissed by the emperor for so doing. 'Emperor Mao' was among those who recognised the analogy, and in 1965 Wu Han became the first target in the Cultural Revolution and paid the price.

Similarly, the student demonstrators of mid-1989 attacked the corruption of the top CCP leadership and called for greater regime liberalisation. In launching their criticisms, they linked themselves with previous patriotic movements that had attacked a corrupt regime or one that was seen as betraying the nation's heritage.

In the first decade of the nineteenth century China was shaken from her isolation by Russian expansion towards the Pacific and the power of the 'barbarians' was clearly demonstrated with China's humiliation in the Opium Wars (1839–42 and 1856–60). Defeat in these wars led to a series of unequal treaties in favour of the imperial powers. The powers were able to open up 'treaty ports', areas which eventually totalled 4 million square miles. The unrestricted commercial and industrial activities of the foreign powers, permitted by the treaties, hampered native enterprises. Domestic products lost their market as imports flooded in. In the face of military defeat and economic subordination, to ignore the 'barbarians' was no longer a feasible option.

Some recognised the power of the West and felt that a form of accommodation was necessary. Initial reforms in the mid-nineteenth century consisted of a mechanical borrowing of certain features of Western progress, particularly military ones, and were not intended to introduce new cultural values. This approach is best summed up in the phrase of the reformer Zhang Zhidong, 'Chinese learning for the fundamental principles, Western learning for the practical application'. The policy of selective adaptation proved short-sighted. It did not comprehend the interrelated nature of Western societies and failed to see that their technology could not easily be disentangled from the social and cultural matrix in which it was embedded. However, this kind of thinking has found an echo in the reform period of the 1980s. China's premier leader Deng Xiaoping has pursued a similar strategy designed to import the high technology needed for China's modernisation programme without bringing in 'bourgeois ideas'. Deng's policy has run into precisely the same problems as the nineteenth century reformers, with catastrophic results.

The second reaction was to fall back on China's xenophobic traditions and try to shut out the foreigners altogether. Indeed, the late Qing officially acknowledged no role at all for foreign trade within economic development. At its most extreme, this view led to violent attacks on the foreign presence in China as witnessed in the Boxer Movement (1899–1900) with its slogan of 'wipe out the foreigners'. Xenophobia has found resonances in the contemporary PRC. For example, in the mid-1970s, Deng Xiaoping's opponents, the 'Gang of Four', proposed a development strategy based on the principles of self-reliance. At best, foreign trade would play a residual role and all efforts were to be made to restrict the impact of bourgeois ideas. In particular, the group attacked Deng's plans to import technology on a large scale and to pay for it through the export of China's minerals. They accused Deng of being a traitor and of turning China into a 'appendage of imperialism'. Similarly, following the student demonstrations of mid-1989, it was clear that one faction in the leadership blamed the West for the disturbances because of the influx of new ideas. Their solution was to launch a political campaign to combat 'bourgeois liberalisation'. In criticising the influx of bourgeois ideas, their attacks fell heavily on the USA and it seems that there is one faction in the leadership, albeit a minority, that would like to see all American influence out of China. It would seek to revive stronger economic ties with the Soviet Union and Eastern Europe, and derive its high technology from the ideologically less troublesome Japan and the politically less powerful smaller West European nations.

The third reaction was to propose all-out Westernisation as a solution to China's ills. The defeat of China in the Sino-Japanese War (1894–5) caused many intellectuals to become profoundly disillusioned with their heritage and to seek solutions outside of China. Increasingly Confucianism was seen as the centre from which all China's failures radiated. In their search, Chinese intellectuals began to go to Japan, Europe, the USA and latterly Soviet Russia for the ideas that might save the Chinese nation. However sinified Marxism–Leninism may have become under Mao Zedong, it must be remembered that it was introduced into China by a generation of intellectuals who were profoundly disenchanted with their intellectual heritage and who sought in a foreign ideology a salvation for China. In the 1980s, with a rising crisis of confidence in the CCP's legitimacy to rule, individuals such as the scientist Fang Lizhi again rejected their heritage and proposed the adoption of a Western political system based on the ideas of universal suffrage, a multiparty system and a division of powers.

The inadequacies of Confucianism created a gap in the intellectual sphere which other thought systems sought to fill. A period of intellectual ferment and discussion resulted in the May Fourth Movement (1915–19), a movement that entailed a wide-ranging cultural and nationalistic renaissance. By the time of this movement, the imperial system had been swept away and replaced by a nascent republican system (1911–12).

The Republic lasted until 1949 on mainland China (and continues to claim to be the rightful government from its island stronghold of Taiwan). However, in many respects it is best regarded as a watershed between two eras. Its early years were characterised by warlord rule in which power was fragmented and was exercised by men offering diverse solutions to China's problems. Eventually Chiang Kai-shek succeeded in imposing a new unity. However, because of the Sino-Japanese war of 1937–45 and the rise of Chinese communism, Chiang's regime could do little to forge lasting institutions and distinctive values. It represented an uneasy amalgam of Western ideals, attempts to revive Confucian principles and a strong element of dictatorial practice. Reforms rarely got further than the statute book, and the mass of the population remained deprived of any effective voice. It was left to the Chinese communists to try to lead China into the modern world and to attempt to provide new institutions and values.

Chinese political culture in the postrevolutionary period

The tradition outlined above was added to by the political culture of a Leninist political party and its Stalinist variant as well as the CCP's own experiences in the revolutionary struggle. Although socialist ideas were entering China from the late nineteenth century, knowledge of Marxism began to make a significant impact only after the First World War. At a time when the victors were demonstrating that their concern for nationalism and democracy was largely confined to Europe, the Bolsheviks' success in seizing power, their superb organisational capability in subsequently defending their state, and their promises that they were quite different from the 'imperialists' exerted a powerful influence. In its early days Sun Yat-sen's Nationalist Party sought Soviet assistance, and in 1921 the Chinese Communist Party (CCP) was established.

Initially communist successes were minimal as the party attempted to follow slavishly ideas and practices formed in a European context. But Mao Zedong succeeded in 'sinifying' Marxism by tying it to the criticism of specific features of the traditional Chinese culture. What Mao did, in essence, was to exploit the dissatisfaction with Confucian values and institutions which had become widespread during the decline of the Qing dynasty. In part he did so by making use of the 'counterculture' of peasant rebels and secret societies which had always existed alongside the dominant orthodoxy of the Confucian élite. Of rich peasant stock himself, Mao came to emphasise the revolutionary potential of the peasant masses when he investigated their opposition to the traditional political and economic power structure in his home province. His 1927 'Report on an Investigation of the Peasant Movement in

Hunan' concluded that in the last analysis the peasants were the best judges of those placed in power over them. He held that peasant violence was greatest in those areas where the local gentry and landlords had been most oppressive and that the masses could be trusted to distinguish between their various exploiters. He wrote:

The peasants are clear-sighted. Who is bad and who is not, who is the worst and who is not quite so vicious, who deserves severe punishment and who deserves to be let off lightly – the peasant keeps clear accounts and very seldom has the punishment exceeded the crime.

Mao's appreciation of peasant consciousness convinced him of the value of political participation as an instrument for attitudinal change. He was impressed by the speed with which traditional attitudes of passivity could be cast aside and how peasants were able, more or less spontaneously, to establish their own political organisations. He was also quick to note the value of violence in facilitating changes, and argued that it was essential to go beyond polite debate:

To put it bluntly, it is necessary to create terror for a while in every rural area, or otherwise it would be impossible to suppress the activities of the counter-revolutionaries ... Proper limits have to be exceeded in order to right a wrong or else the wrong cannot be righted.

Thus in contrast to old ideas of hierarchy, Mao put forward a populist faith in the ability of ordinary people. He saw the masses as China's greatest asset in building the revolution, an enormous reservoir of creative power. Whereas Confucian China had insisted that the educated should rule, Mao made a virtue out of the very backwardness of much of China's population. Thus he was to write in 1958:

China's 600 million people have two remarkable peculiarities: they are first of all poor, and secondly, blank. That may sound like a bad thing, but it is really a good thing. Poor people want to change, want to do things, want revolution.

Mao's respect for the peasantry in particular and for the

masses in general was further strengthened by the circumstances by which the communists came to power in China. In contrast to the Bolsheviks, the CCP had to fight a protracted war and had to do so in the villages of the rural hinterland. There, desperately short of labour power and material, the party could only survive by developing techniques of 'people's war'. To gain support guerrillas must offer a better deal than their enemies are able to do. Hence in the rural areas, and particularly in the great base area centred on Yan'an in the years 1937–45, Mao concentrated on creating a political and military machine which had a genuinely popular base. This was embodied in a style of leadership and participation designed to ensure that leaders and masses remained united, the famous 'mass line'. In his most celebrated statement on the subject, Mao in 1943 defined the 'mass line' when he instructed that:

> In all practical work of our party, all correct leadership is necessarily 'from the masses to the masses'. This means: take the ideas of the masses (scattered and unsystematic ideas) and concentrate them (thorough study turn them into concentrated and systematic ideas); then go to the masses and propagate and explain these ideas until the masses embrace them as their own, hold fast to them and translate them into action, and test the correctness of these ideas in such action . . . Such is the Marxist theory of knowledge.

This approach, with its rejection of bureaucratic practices, gave the party a distinctive political style which did much to bring it to power in 1949. Thereafter it helped it to consolidate that power by mobilising the populace in a host of mass campaigns. These were directed at human targets such as 'counter-revolutionaries' and landlords, but also natural ones: pest and diseases and the Chinese earth itself. The intention was that through involvement many Chinese would undergo attitudinal change and learn to 'take the attitude of being the masters', whether by attacking former 'exploiters' or by learning, through participation in water conservancy campaigns, that the forces of nature could be tamed.

In theory, the 'mass line' was about consultation, education, persuasion and eliciting an enthusiastic response. It was not, however, necessarily concerned overmuch with democracy. Through the 'mass line' it was hoped to combine the benefits derived from consultation with those at the lower levels and those of a tight centralised control over policy formulation. Mao and his colleagues were Leninists and the party was the revolutionary 'vanguard', not simply an agency for implementing the wishes of the people. The weakness of the 'mass line', was, ironically, that it reflected in part a traditional view that the masses would accept the leadership's interpretation of their true interests if only these were properly explained.

Chinese communist theory did acknowledge that differences of interest could exist; but, in practice, Mao and his supporters were unwilling to accept the existence of different, competing groups in Chinese society. Mao's speeches to the Yan'an Forum on Art and Literature in 1942 made it perfectly clear that he rejected a plurality of views in favour of conformity to the revolutionary tasks prescribed by the party at a given time. Although, in the Cultural Revolution, Mao was to launch an assault on the party as an institution, he was still unwilling to accept a plurality of views among the masses who were expected to display loyalty towards him.

From the late 1950s to Mao's death in September 1976 acute difficulties arose, especially in the Great Leap Forward and the Cultural Revolution, when Mao's attempts to impose a particularly utopian interpretation of socialism conflicted with the view of their best material interests held by the masses and, increasingly, large sections of the party leadership also. In place of persuasion the 'mass line' degenerated into hectoring, bullying and resort to purges. In the face of widespread opposition to his radical policies in virtually every area, Mao blamed everyone and everything but his beloved 'masses' and the policies themselves, and attacked not only individuals but the institutions of the People's Republic also. The immediate result was widespread violence, near-anarchy in many places, and the reappearance of many of the more unpleasant aspects of traditional patterns of thought and behaviour. Mao himself sought to bolster his position by permitting, and probably encouraging, a personality cult which bestowed upon him the awesome attributes of a traditional emperor. Other political leaders banded into highly polarised factions which brought to Beijing an era of palace intrigue reminiscent of imperial dynasties in their days of decline. In an uncertain world ordinary citizens sought a measure of security by resorting to particularist loyalties based on 'connections'.

Apart from this reliance on mobilisation, the role of the military is an important legacy of the pre-1949 struggle and the CCP in power exhibits some traits of a military political culture. The military experience meant that CCP leaders have a positive view of the role to be played by the army, not only in the sphere of military policy formulation but also in the whole sphere of domestic politics. Before 1949 party and military leaders were often interchangeable and since 1949 many leaders have concurrently held party and military positions. Many others in important party posts were military commanders during the pre-liberation years. In some respects, the CCP was forced to behave like other warlord regimes in China to defend its territory. Mao recognised that any solution to China's problems was essentially a military one. This has had a lasting legacy in terms of the simplistic, militaristic thinking that is a feature of the approach of the veteran revolutionaries. The vocabulary of war and struggle still abound in the political rhetoric of the PRC.

Further, the army itself, particularly at times of stress, has been often held up as an example of revolutionary purity to be studied by the whole of society. For the veteran revolutionaries who were still ruling China in 1990, the army represented selfless action and simple, plain living. It represented a time when decisions were easy and when it was clear who the enemy was. This contrasts enormously with the complex urban environment over which they had to rule after 1949. Individual soldiers have, on occasion, been put forward as models for emulation because of their embodiment of the communist spirit. This tendency to extol the military and praise its simple life style was apparent after the crushing of the student movement in mid-1989. In the leadership's eyes, the urban folk had yet again shown their unreliability with their 'counter-revolutionary' attacks on the party's right to rule. Again it was the peasant army that had intervened to save the resolution.

Faced with a damaged economy and widespread demoralisation, the leaders who have ruled China since Mao's death in September 1976 have, by voluntary or imposed choice, dismantled most of his policies and have, tacitly at least, rejected many of the principles underlying his desire to produce a thorough and irreversible transformation of traditional attitudes. The new emphasis on economic development with a greater role for market forces was not well served by a highly rigid centralised political structure staffed by bureaucrats who were adept at hiding behind administrative rules and regulations. In its place was to come a more responsive political system staffed by professionals who could provide the necessary advice to devise and implement the more technocratic policy programme. However, the attacks on the core values of a Leninist political structure have been severely resisted in some quarters.

The reformers sought to revert to alternative traditions of Chinese entrepreneurship to pull China out of its relative economic backwardness. In the countryside, the 'production responsibility system' leaves agriculture collectivised in theory but in practice has restored individual household farming. In both town and country private commerce was allowed to flourish. Even Confucianism was harnessed to the cause of economic development, with Chinese historians producing articles on how Confucian scholars of the late Song dynasty had much to say of direct relevance to China's modernisation.

The pro-reform former General Secretary, Zhao Ziyang, recognised that many of China's problems derived from its feudal heritage as well as its own revolutionary experiences. At the party's Thirteenth Congress in 1987, Zhao noted that

> China's existing political structure was born out of the war years, basically established in the period of socialist transformation and developed in the course of large-scale mass movements and incessantly intensifying mandatory planning ... It fails to suit economic, political and cultural modernisation under peacetime conditions or the development of a socialist commodity economy.

Some of China's intellectuals have gone further and launched a major attack on Chinese traditional culture as the source of many of the system's ills. They draw parallels between Mao Zedong, and even Deng Xiaoping, and the Emperors of old, and argue openly that the tendency of a Leninist party to concentrate power in the hands of a few is exaggerated by the lingering influences of a feudal political culture.

The implications of such an attack for continued CCP rule have not gone unnoticed and the return to power of the veteran revolutionaries in mid-June 1989 after the student demonstrations shows how much attraction the ethical values of communism such as collectivism, egalitarianism and class struggle still hold for this group of older revolutionaries and their supporters in the party-state apparatus. However, it is unlikely that they will retain power for more than a few years at most and then China will have to resume its search for a modern political culture that can sit easily with its own traditions.

Further reading

The classic study of political culture is Pye and Verba (1965), which contains a chapter on Soviet Russia by Frederick Barghoorn as well as further more analytic discussions. There are shorter introductions to the concept in Kavanagh (1972) and Rosenbaum (1975). The political cultures of a number of communist states are surveyed in Brown and Gray (1979); a further more methodological discussion, focusing particularly upon the USSR and Czechoslovakia, is available in Brown (1985).

The fullest available study of the political culture of the USSR is White (1979). Glazov (1985) is a stimulating emigre account. See also the classic study by Inkeles and Bauer (1959) based upon interviews with post-Second World War emigres; the results of interviews with more recent emigres are presented in Gitelman (1977), White (1978b) and Millar (1987). On patterns of Soviet historical development, Tucker (1977), Bialer (1980), Cohen (1985) and Hosking (1985) are particularly helpful. White and Pravda (1988) deals with developments in the official ideology. On the national question in the USSR, see Katz (1975), Carrère d'Encausse (1979), Lapidus (1984), Connor (1984), which deals with Marxist regimes generally, Akiner (1985), which deals with Soviet Muslims, and Karklins (1986). On religious and nationalist movements, see Dunlop (1983) and (1985), and Ellis (1986). Memoirs which may particularly be recommended include Ginzburg (1967) and (1981), Yevtushenko (1963), Etkind (1978) and Khrushchev (1971–74).

Two classic accounts of the inter-war period in Eastern Europe are Seton-Watson (1986) and Rothschild (1974; see also Rothschild, 1989). There is no one synoptic work on the political cultures of the post-war period, but a number of country studies are useful. Among them are Ulč (1974) on Czechoslovakia, Toma and Volgyes (1977) on Hungary, Pavlowitch (1971) on Yugoslavia, Zukin (1975) and Doder (1978), also about Yugoslavia, Mićunović (1980), which is primarily about foreign policy but which also contains valuable insights on Yugoslav attitudes, Oren (1973) on Bulgaria, and the relevant sections of Jowitt (1971) on Romania. Shafir (1985) and Heinrich (1986) provide more recent surveys on Romania and Hungary respectively, with a first chapter in each dealing with history and political traditions. Memoir literature and novels which should be noted include Kohout (1972), Illyés (1967), a brilliant account of the pre-war Hungarian peasantry, Brandys (1981), which offers an analysis of Polishness, and Mlynár (1980), which is interesting on the Czechoslovak leadership's perceptions of the Soviet Union in 1968.

An immensely detailed and valuable study of Chinese political culture is Solomon (1971). A study that places China in its Asian context is Pye (1985). A fascinating account of the interrelationship between traditional culture and communist practice can be found in Beaufort (1978) and the effects of China's tradition on the PRC's foreign policy is covered by Hunt (1984). On patterns of Chinese historical development and contemporary trends, see Schram (1973, ch. 1). For studies of Mao see Schram's biography (1970), his assessment of Mao's thought up until 1949 (1986), and Starr (1979). On recent doctrinal developments, see Schram (1984) and Brugger (1985). The influences of neo-traditionalism in the urban workplace are interestingly handled by Walder (1986). A solid overview of change in the 1980s is provided by Harding (1987) and essays on most facets of the reform programme are in Benewick and Wingrove (1988). Watson (1984) deals with social stratification, Gold (1985) considers personal relationships since the Cultural Revolution. Schell (1988) chronicles changes in values under the reform programme.

3

Structures of Government

The formal structures of government – constitutions, legislatures and executives – have not normally been accorded much attention in the study of communist political systems. There are good reasons for this. In the first place, the electoral system has until recently been closely controlled in these countries and, although there is sometimes a choice of candidate or even of party in local or national elections, the whole process is closely controlled by the communist party and no candidates openly opposed to Marxist–Leninist principles have normally been allowed to stand. The legislatures to which the deputies are elected meet infrequently, their votes are normally unanimous, their legislative output is fairly meagre, and no direct challenge (again with some recent exceptions) is ever issued to the governments which are nominally responsible to them. The communist or ruling party normally provides a majority of deputies in these assemblies, its members constitute a party group or caucus which is expected to take a leading part in their proceedings, and party members, all of them subject to party discipline, dominate the key positions at all levels. Although there is some variety among them in terms of institutional form (see Table 3.1) and, as we shall see, in organisational effectiveness, it has been conventional, for reasons such as these, to regard communist legislatures as mere 'rubber stamps' and formal government structures more generally as of little consequence for the domestic political process.

Valid though these criticisms are, it has become apparent in recent years that they equally be taken too far. Communist legislatures, certainly do not normally challenge the governments they nominally elect, still less the communist party

91

TABLE 3.1

Legislatures in the communist states

Country	Name of legislature	No. of chambers	No. of deputies	No. of parties	Electoral choice
Albania	People's Assembly	1	250	1	No
Bulgaria	National Assembly	1	400	2	No
China	National People's Congress	1	2978	9	Yes*
Cuba	National Assembly	1	499	1	Yes*
Czechoslovakia	Federal Assembly	2	350	5	No
GDR	People's Chamber	1	500	5	No
Hungary	National Assembly	1	352	1	Yes
Kampuchea	National Assembly	1	117	1	Yes
Korea	Supreme People's Assembly	1	615	3	No
Laos	People's Congress	1	45	1	No
Mongolia	Great People's Khural	1	370	1	No
Poland	Sejm	1	460	3	Yes
Romania	Grand National Assembly	1	369	1	Yes
USSR	Congress of People's Deputies	2	2250	1	Yes
Vietnam	National Assembly	1	496	3	Yes
Yugoslavia	Federal Assembly	2	308	1	Yes*

*Elections to legislatures in these countries are indirect and a degree of choice is permitted at the preliminary stage only.
Sources: International Centre for Parliamentary Documentation of the Inter-Parliamentary Union, *Parliaments of the World*, 2nd ed. (Aldershot, Hants, 1986); *Ezhegodnik Bol'shoi Entsiklopedii 1988g.* (Moscow, 1989); and press reports. It should be noted that important institutional changes are currently in progress in a number of these countries.

authorities; and they accept the official doctrine by which the party rules, or decides 'political' questions, leaving state institutions the task of governing or of carrying out the decisions that the party has approved. Communist legislatures, however, are not thereby condemned to an entirely negligible role in the political system. They help to legitimate the system, by providing it with at least an appearance of electoral endorsement by the people to whom all power theoretically belongs; they provide a 'school of government' for a substantial proportion of the population, particularly at the local level where the rate of turnover of deputies is most rapid; and they provide a useful means by which the party authorities can give at least the impression that the issues that concern the population are being seriously discussed at a policy-making level. Above all, through their developing committee structures they provide a means of investigating matters of public concern as well as of checking upon the performance of government and discussing the annual economic plan and state budget. It is difficult to establish empirically the extent to which representative institutions in the communist states now dispose of a substantial measure of independent authority; in Poland, Hungary and Yugoslavia, at least, they would appear to do so, and in the other states the influence of representative institutions is by no means negligible. The changes of the late 1980s in the USSR, in particular, suggested something of a general trend towards more professional and influential legislatures throughout the communist world.

The USSR: constitution, legislature and government

The largest of the communist states, the USSR, is officially a federation consisting of a voluntary union of fifteen nominally sovereign union republics (the RSFSR or Russian Republic, the Ukraine, Belorussia, Latvia, Lithuania, Estonia, Moldavia, Georgia, Armenia, Azerbaidzhan, Kirgizia, Kazakhstan, Uzbekistan, Turkmenia and Tadzhikistan). The RSFSR is by far the largest of these republics, accounting for about 76 per cent of the total area and for about 51 per cent of the total population. All the other republics are far smaller and most of them have a population of no more than a few million. The union republics are described in the present Constitution, adopted in 1977, as 'sovereign Soviet socialist states', and they have a considerable range of formal powers, including the right to secede and to establish diplomatic relations with foreign powers. (Two of them, the Ukraine and Belorussia, have in fact been members of the United Nations since its foundation.) The laws of the USSR as a whole, however, take precedence over those of the union republics, the decisions of the national government are binding throughout the USSR, and the state as well as the party is officially committed to the doctrine of democratic centralism by which the decisions of higher bodies of state authority are binding upon lower ones. The union republics, accordingly, are rather less than sovereign states; but they do provide a formal expression of the multi-national character of the state (in each of them a particular nationality is supposed to be predominant), and, as we shall see, they exercise a substantial number of devolved powers of government.

The principle of democratic centralism applies not simply to relations between the federal government and the union republics, but also to relations between the union republics and the lower levels of government that are subordinate to them. The most important of these sub-divisions are the regions (*oblesti*) into which the eight largest republics are divided, and the districts (*raiony*) into which the regions, larger cities and the other union republics are divided. A simplified representation of these divisions is set out in Figure 3.1. A number of nationalities which are not sufficiently numerous to have their own union republics exercise a more limited range of powers within an autonomous soviet socialist republic (ASSR), an autonomous region or an autonomous area. There were 114 regions in the USSR in 1990, which together with the twenty ASSRs, eight autonomous regions, ten autonomous areas and six territories (*kraya*) form the 'provincial' level of government in the USSR. Below them

FIGURE 3.1 The state structure of the USSR (simplified)

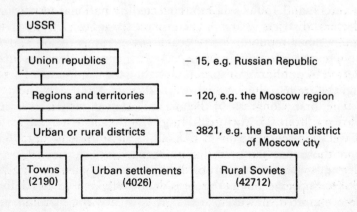

come the urban and rural districts (628 and 3193 respectively in 1990), and then the towns, urban settlements and villages which constitute the lowest level of state authority, or local government proper. At all levels of this system soviets or councils are elected, since 1989 for five years at a time. In 1990 more than 2.3 million citizens were serving on elected bodies of this kind at various levels, and more than 30 million citizens were associated with their work, usually by unpaid activity on a voluntary commission of some sort. The soviets in turn elect executive committees or (at the union or autonomous republican level) councils of ministers to carry on the day-to-day work of government.

From 1937 until 1988 the representative system was headed by the Supreme Soviet of the USSR, which was elected every five years and met twice a year for a couple of days to approve government proposals. Following an extended discussion the Constitution was amended in December 1988 so as to provide for an entirely new representative body, the USSR Congress of People's Deputies. The Congress was to meet in regular session once a year and would elect a standing parliament, the Supreme Soviet, from among its members. The Congress is exclusively empowered to adopt and amend the Constitution and to determine the national and state structure of the USSR; it also establishes the 'guidelines of the domestic and foreign policies of the USSR', including long-term state plans and programmes. The Congress consists of 2250 deputies, 750 of whom are elected by territorial electoral districts with equal numbers of voters, and 750 of whom are elected by national-territorial electoral districts (32 from each union republic, 11 from each autonomous republic, 5 from each autonomous region and 1 from each autonomous area). A further 750 deputies are elected by public organisations including the Communist Party and the trade unions, which were allocated 100 seats each.

The first Congress of People's Deputies, which met in Moscow from 25 May to 9 June 1989, soon emerged as a Soviet representative institution of a rather different character from those that had preceded it. Gorbachev, as expected, was elected to the newly-established post of Chairman of the USSR Supreme Soviet, or president. What could not have been expected, however, was that two candidates would be nominated to stand against him, and that he would secure election, after a series of searching questions from the deputies, by a less than unanimous vote (2123 in favour but 87 against). Anatolii Lukyanov, who was elected First Vice-Chairman of the Supreme Soviet four days later, faced a still more extended inquisition from deputies, including questions about his responsibility, while working in the central party apparatus, for the increase in reported crime that had taken place over the same period. Gorbachev addressed the Congress on 30 May, and prime minister Nikolai Ryzhkov addressed it on 7 June; most of the remainder of the session was given over to speeches from deputies – initially on procedural matters, but latterly on all aspects of party and state policy and often of a sharply critical character.

The head of the Soviet women's committee, for instance, Zoya Pukhova, complained that the USSR was lagging behind many developing, not to speak of developed countries in its attention to women's rights, and called for 'more profundity' in the speeches of Gorbachev and other leaders on these

FIGURE 3.2
The USSR Congress of People's Deputies and Supreme Soviet

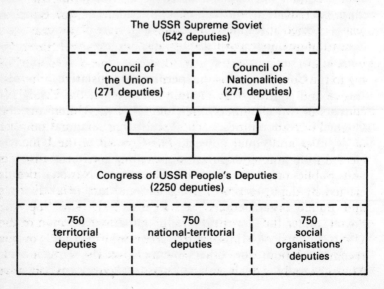

matters. The former Moscow party secretary, Boris Yeltsin, complained that power was still monopolised by the party and state apparatus and warned that the head of state had accumulated so much authority that a 'new dictatorship' was possible. Another target was the KGB. Yuri Vlasov, a former Olympic weightlifter, in an astonishing speech, listed the sites in which the KGB had buried its victims and accused it of crimes 'unknown in the history of humanity'. He went on to describe the contemporary KGB as an 'underground empire', all-powerful and largely uncontrolled, and called for its head-quarters to be moved from central Moscow and for its activities to be directly supervised by the Congress and Supreme Soviet. Andrei Sakharov, the physicist and former dissident who became the country's most popular parliamen-tarian before his death in December 1989, read out an alternative programme which included the removal of the Communist Party and its leading role from the Constitution. All these developments were followed on Soviet television, so avidly indeed that there was a fall of about 20 per cent in labour productivity over the same period. Later sessions of the Congress were transmitted, in shortened form, after working hours.

One of the Congress's first acts was to set up the new-style Supreme Soviet, a much smaller body of 542 deputies which was expected to remain in session for most of the year (the Constitution suggested it would normally have two three- or four-month sessions every year). The Supreme Soviet, accord-ing to the Constitution, is the 'permanent legislative, adminis-trative and control body of state authority of the USSR'. It consists of two chambers, the Council of the Union and the Council of Nationalities, each of which has an equal number of deputies and equal powers. The Council of the Union is elected from among deputies representing territorial districts and public organisations; the Council of Nationalities is elected by deputies representing national-territorial districts and public organisations (see Figure 3.2). The Supreme Soviet, under the Constitution, appoints the chairman of the USSR Council of Ministers (or prime minister) and, on his recommendation, the other members of the government. More generally, it deals with national-level policy on economic,

financial, social and cultural questions; it approves the
state plan and budget, regulates the conduct of foreign policy
and determines the use of Soviet armed forces domestically
and internationally.

Despite the charge of an outspoken historian, Yuri Afanasyev,
that it was a 'Stalinist–Brezhnevite' body with an 'aggressively
obedient majority', the new Supreme Soviet, when it met for
the first time on 3 June 1989, soon showed that it was a very
different institution from its docile predecessors. One sign of
this was the elaborate committee system that was set up,
including committees of the Supreme Soviet as a whole as well
as commissions attached to each of its two chambers. One of
the Supreme Soviet's new committees dealt with defence and
state security; another dealt with *glasnost'* and the rights of
citizens. Some 928 deputies, about half of whom were members of the Supreme Soviet itself, were elected to serve on the
new committees and commissions, and about two-thirds of the
work of the new parliament was expected to take place under
their auspices. Another promising sign was the establishment
of an organisational base for the Supreme Soviet in central
Moscow, with a library and electronic services. Yet another,
potentially more significant difference was the formation of an
inter-regional deputies' group, in effect a radical caucus,
under the leadership of Boris Yeltsin and others. The group,
which had its own funds and a newspaper, represented at least
the embryo of a form of parliamentary opposition that had no
obvious precedent in the Soviet period.

Much of the business of the first session of the new Supreme
Soviet was concerned with the consideration of prime minister
Nikolai Ryzhkov's nominations to the new Council of Ministers.
It was a very different team, at least in terms of personnel.
Only ten of Ryzhkov's nominees had served in the Soviet
government elected in 1984, and fewer than half had served in
the outgoing administration. Nearly a third were entirely new
to government service, six were members or candidate members of the Academy of Sciences, and the average age was a
modest 55 (the final list included the Soviet Union's first non-
party minister, a biology professor who became head of the
Committee on Nature Conservation). The structure of the new
government was also a different one. There were no more than

57 ministries and state committees altogether; some 25 ministries were to be wound up, and those that remained were to be 'ministries of a new type', exercising general rather than detailed supervision within their area of competence. What was certainly new was the attention with which Ryzhkov's proposals were received: all the candidates were closely questioned both in committee and later in the Supreme Soviet itself, and at least six of the original nominations were rejected. This 'parliamentary marathon' took about three weeks; Rhyzhkov later suggested it had been the most unusual process of government formation in Soviet history.

Formally speaking the Council of Ministers is responsible both to the Congress of People's Deputies and to the Supreme Soviet, and it must report to the Supreme Soviet on its work at least once a year. The Council of Ministers is empowered to deal with all matters of state administration which do not fall within the competence of other bodies; in practice this includes the conduct of a wide variety of government business, including economic management, foreign relations, defence and social welfare. Under legislation approved in June 1989 the Council of Ministers contained 26 'all-union' ministries, based in Moscow and for the most part responsible for heavy industry, and 11 'union-republican' ministries, based in Moscow and also in the republics, and including foreign affairs, finance, justice, culture and internal affairs. There were four all-union state committees, including science and technology, and 15 union-republican committees, including the State Planning Committee (*Gosplan*), the State Committee on Material-Technical Supply (*Gossnab*), the State Committee on Labour and Social Questions, the State Prices Committee, the State Education Committee and the Committee of State Security (KGB). Some other minor state functions, including utilities and inland water transport, are wholly regulated at the republican level.

A further body, the Presidium, is formed on an *ex officio* basis and is also accountable to the Supreme Soviet. Broadly equivalent to a collective presidency, it consists of a chairman, a first vice-chairman, 15 vice-chairmen (one from each of the union republics) and the chairmen of the two chambers of the Supreme Soviet, the chairman of the Committee of Public

Inspection (a supervisory agency) and the chairmen of the committees and commissions of the Supreme Soviet. In March 1990, after a brief public debate, the third Congress of People's Deputies approved a still more significant constitutional change: the institution of a powerful executive Presidency, the first in Soviet history. The new Presidency – to which Gorbachev was elected on 15 March – disposed of formidable powers. He could nominate the Prime Minister and leading government officials, veto legislation, propose the resignation of the government and rule by decree. He also headed a powerful Presidential Council with responsibility for Soviet foreign and domestic affairs. Soviet liberals complained that these extensive powers could open the way to a new dictatorship; in reply, its supporters argued that the President would in future be elected by a national and competitive ballot and for a limited period of office (two five-year terms at the most). Either way, it represented a potentially decisive shift of authority from a single ruling party to a nationally elected head of state.

Elections and voters in the USSR

Elections in the USSR, since virtually the outset of Soviet rule, had been 'elections without choice'. At the national level there was no choice of candidate, still less of party. It was theoretically possible to vote against the single candidate, but to do so required the use of a booth at the side of the polling station, as a vote in favour required no mark at all: the ballot paper could simply be dropped, unmarked and even unread, into the box. A vote against the single list of candidates was hardly encouraged by such procedures and at the national level the vote in favour, and the turnout, were never less than 99 per cent. At the 1984 elections, the last under the unreformed system, the turnout was a record 99.99 per cent and the vote in favour of the list of candidates for each of the two chambers of the Supreme Soviet was 99.94 and 99.95 per cent respectively. Voters could, if they wished, make use of an 'absentee certificate' allowing them to cast their vote elsewhere, but removing them from the electoral roll unless they presented themselves in another constituency. Many of those concerned simply refrained from voting; there was also a significant level of electoral abuse, with fathers voting for their families, friends for their neighbours, and electoral officials for those that failed to put in a personal appearance. Not surprisingly an exercise of this kind commanded little public confidence, and there was some evidence of a decline, in the 1970s and 1980s, of the numbers that were willing to attend voters' meetings and other electoral activities.

A further disincentive was that the composition of each group of deputies, at local and at national level, was normally settled in advance by the party authorities. Quite detailed regulations were issued as to the proportion of candidates that were to be women, young people, party members and so forth; local officials were left to find individuals that satisfied the criteria they had been given. In one remarkable case, reported by an emigre source, a notorious prostitute was nominated by a local soviet as she was the only one in the constituency that met the relevant criteria: female, single, with two children, aged between 35 and 40, and a factory worker. The whole process was based upon an effective electoral monopoly on the part of the CPSU, which either nominated candidates directly or arranged for their nomination by other bodies, such as the trade unions, over which it had a controlling influence. The Constitution reserved the right of nomination to such bodies, and attempts that were made by *ad hoc* groups of citizens to challenge this monopoly proved unsuccessful. Not surprisingly, survey results found that there was little popular identification with an electoral mechanism of this kind: a poll in October 1988, for instance, found that no more than 5 per cent of those taking part in a by-election could even name the candidate.

Gorbachev, in his speech to the 27th Party Congress in 1986, referred briefly to the need to make 'corrections' to the Soviet electoral system, and in 1987 a limited experiment was announced by which a choice of candidates would be nominated in a small number of enlarged multimember constituencies. In the end just over 1 per cent of the constituencies were formed in this way, and they returned no more than 4 per cent of the deputies that were elected to local soviets in June 1987. Press reports made it clear that this was nonetheless a there were greater difficulties than usual in securing nomination, and in the election itself there were some notable casualties, including party and state officials, factory directors and collective farm chairmen. For many officials the whole experience was evidently a novel and rather distressing one; at the popular level, however, the response was much more favourable. There was a 'real feeling that people were choosing', according to press reports, and surveys found that while only 55 per cent of those asked took a positive view of the new arrangements before they had been put into effect, fully 77 per cent supported them afterwards.

A new electoral law, adopted in December 1988, extended these practices more broadly. The right to nominate was extended to voters' meetings of 500 or more (in practice, a considerable restriction), and an unlimited number of candidates could be put forward. Deputies were not allowed to hold governmental posts at the same time as they exercised their representative duties (how, it was asked, could ministerial deputies be expected to hold themselves to account?), and they were normally required to live or work in the area for which they had been nominated. Candidates, moreover, were required to present 'programmes' to their electorate, and they had the right to appoint up to ten campaign staff to assist them. Voters, for their part, were required to pass through a booth or room before casting their vote, and to make a positive indication of their preference unless (exceptionally) only a single candidate was standing. The new law was to apply to all future elections, beginning with the national elections in March 1989; these, the Central Committee promised in November 1988, would be 'unlike all those that had preceded them'.

Exactly how different they would be became apparent over the months that followed, as preparations were made for the election itself on 26 March 1989. Under the new law the campaign was to proceed in two stages. In the first, nominations were to be made and then approved by a selection conference in the constituency or social organisation for which the candidate was seeking election. In the second, candidates that had been 'registered' in this way were to compete for the support of their respective electorates: in the ordinary constituencies up to polling day, and in the social organisations up to an election meeting at some point during the previous fortnight. These were new, eleaborate and sometimes unpopular provisions. The representation that had been given to social organisations, in particular, appeared to violate the principle of 'one person, one vote'; and the holding of selection conferences was also challenged. Who really needed such 'elections before elections', asked a number of letters to the papers? And why should bodies such as stamp collectors have the right to return parliamentary representatives? It was pointed out, in reply, that selection conferences were necessary in order to reduce the number of nominations to manageable proportions, and in any case this stage of the proceedings was bypassed in many of the Baltic and Moscow constituencies precisely so as to leave such choices to the electorate.

Voting in the social organisations began on 11 March 1989. The most important of all the organisations concerned, the CPSU, had agreed to register no more than 100 candidates for the 100 seats it had available; all of them were duly elected, 52 of them unanimously, but there were 12 votes against Gorbachev (hadn't he, after all, been a member of the now discredited Brezhnev administration, asked some party members?) and 59 against his liberal ally, Alexander Yakovlev. The largest number of negative votes (78) was cast against the prominent hardliner, Yegor Ligachev. This allowed Boris Yeltsin one of his standard campaign jokes: what would have happened if the CPSU had put forward 101, not just 100, candidates for the seats it had available? Few of the social organisations followed the CPSU's example and registered no more candidates than seats available, and in some of them, notably the Academy of Sciences, there was a genuine electoral struggle. The Academy, very controversially, had decided not to nominate Andrei Sakharov and some other reformers for the 20 seats it had available. In the event only eight of the 23 nominees secured the necessary majority when the ballot took place; further elections had to be held a month later to fill the vacant places, and at these Sakharov (who died the following December), the space scientist Roald Sagdeev and several other reformers were successful.

Some 2884 candidates had been selected to fight the 1500

ordinary constituencies. In 384 of them, despite the intentions of the new electoral law, there was just a single nomination, but elsewhere there was a choice and in one Moscow constituency as many as 12 candidates were competing for the support of voters. In the event, 271 constituencies failed to declare a result because none of the candidates had secured a majority; in many of them there had been no more than a single candidate and the voters had evidently refused this attempt to avoid a competitive process. Still more unexpected were the defeats suffered by party and state leaders at all levels. The prime minister of Latvia was defeated, and the president and prime minister of Lithuania; so too were 38 regional or district party secretaries throughout the country. In Moscow the runaway success of Boris Yeltsin, with 89.4 per cent of the vote, was a snub for the central party apparatus, which had taken every opportunity to impede his campaign. The most spectacular defeats, however, took place in Leningrad, where the casualties included the regional first secretary (a junior Politburo member), the regional second secretary, the chairman of the city soviet and his deputy, the chairman of the regional soviet and the city party secretary. It was understandably some time before the full dimensions of this rebuff reached the columns of the Soviet daily press.

Who were the new deputies? They were certainly different, as a group, from those that had preceded them (see Table 3.2). There were, in fact, more party members than ever before: 87.6 per cent of the total, well above the previous level. There were also more officials than ever before, particularly from lower levels of the administration, although this was hardly the intention of those who had promoted the new law. The scientific and cultural intelligentsia, however, was much better represented than in any previous Soviet parliament: economists and writers, actors and directors, sociologists and journalists had been returned in considerable number. There were five church leaders, the first ever elected to a Soviet legislative body; and there was a substantial detachment of pensioners. The proportion of female deputies, at the same time, fell by about half (to 17.1 per cent), and so too did the percentage of worker deputies (to 17.9 per cent). This

TABLE 3.2

Social composition of the USSR Supreme Soviet (1984) Congress of People's Deputies (1989) and the USSR Supreme Soviet (1989)

	Supreme Soviet 1984 (%)	Congress 1989 (%)	Supreme Soviet 1989 (%)	No.
Top political leadership	1.5	0.7	0.2	1
Top and middle-level managerial personnel	40.0	39.8	32.8	178
Lower echelon managerial personnel	6.6	25.3	35.3	191
Workers, collective farmers, non-professional office employees	45.9	22.1	18.3	99
Highly professional intellectuals	6.0	10.2	12.5	68
Priests	–	0.3	–	0
Pensioners	–	1.6	0.9	5
Total	*100 %*	*100%*	*100%*	*542*

Source: Adapted from *Moskovskie novosti*, 1989, no. 24.

appeared to be the direct result of a competitive choice of deputies on the basis of their political qualities; and regrettably or otherwise, the 1989 elections marked the end of the USSR as a 'workers' state' where policies were at least nominally formulated by ordinary working people rather than by white collar professionals on their behalf.

Perhaps the central aim of the whole exercise, and of the republican and local elections that took place in 1989 and 1990 upon the same basis, was to engage the interest and attention of the Soviet people, and to unlock what Gorbachev referred to as the 'human factor'. The level of turnout, 89.8 per cent, suggested that the March 1989 elections had been reasonably successful in securing at least a high level of formal participation. Survey evidence also indicated a high level of approval for the new arrangements. A poll in urban areas throughout the USSR, for instance, found that 48 per cent were in favour of the new procedures, with only 13 per cent against. A poll in Moscow alone found that 34 per cent of those who were asked in December 1988 thought the new law would make little difference; by the time of the electoral campaign, however, only 10–14 per cent thought there would be no changes, and after the elections had taken place only

8 per cent thought they were no improvement on those that had preceded them. Newspapers reported that complete strangers struck up conversations about their voting intentions, and on polling day itself there were queues in some places to enter the premises and then to enter the voting booth itself, where the final choice had to be made. In one Moscow constituency extra booths had to be constructed on polling day itself, so great was the pressure to make use of them, and reports from other constituencies spoke of the sick and handicapped coming to the polling stations in person, rather than waiting for officials to visit them.

It nevertheless appeared, by the start of the 1990s, that this was an unstable and probably temporary set of arrangements. A number of specific provisions, such as the representation that had been given to social organisations, remained unpopular (this particular provision, in fact, was dropped in December 1989 in respect of future elections), and there was some pressure for the direct election of the chairman of the USSR Supreme Soviet. A much larger issue was raised in late 1989 when the question of the constitutionally guaranteed 'leading role' of the CPSU began to be exposed to public discussion. Why, it was asked, should the party have a guaranteed number of seats, and why as many as 100? And why should the party have the right to dominate the proceedings of state bodies when it represented only a small minority of citizens? The reformed electoral system had based itself upon the 'people's will', expressed, as elsewhere, through a choice of competing candidates at regular and properly conducted elections. But it had left in place a very different principle of government by which the CPSU, on the basis of its 'scientific' ideology, had alone the right and duty to guide Soviet society towards where its real long-term interests lay. The evidence that was available at the outset of the 1990s suggested that the first of these two principles was more likely to be the one that gained ground; the activities of popular fronts in the Baltic and of organised groupings elsewhere, indeed, suggested that the USSR had already acquired the substance of a multiparty system – all that was lacking was its formal acknowledgement. This, in the end, was the argument that appears to have carried most weight when the CPSU Central Committee resolved in February 1990 to propose the removal of its guaranteed leading role from the Soviet Constitution.

Structures of government in Eastern Europe

The transformation of communist systems in 1989 did not take place in a vacuum. The legacy of forty years of having lived under a Soviet-type system influenced the political, economic and social responses of the societies of Central and Eastern Europe in virtually every area of life. This in itself was bound to influence the direction and shape of the new systems, both positively and negatively. The collapse of the old system, of inanition in some cases and because of pressure from below in others, meant that the opportunity for major political innovation did exist and that a far greater fluidity affected these polities in the months of the transformation. On the other hand, the transformation was not limitless, but was bounded by conscious and unconscious factors from the communist period and through memories of what had preceded it.

The central endeavour was twofold – to establish political democracy and to restore the decaying economies that threatened the very fabric of these societies with collapse. This required several distinct steps to be taken, notably the acquiescence of the ruling communist party in its own demise or its defeat; the liquidation of the *nomenklatura* and the party state; the transfer of control of the instruments of coercion from communist party control to some other, democratically constituted agency; the elaboration of a new constitution and move to the rule of law; and the emergence of a new multiparty system.

There can be no doubt that in the late 1980s, Soviet-type systems entered a new phase in their development. They had already shown numerous symptoms of decay for a decade or more and substantial changes in the configuration of the system could hardly be avoided. The advent of Mikhail Gorbachev in the Kremlin made one qualitative difference to the politics of the Soviet Union and its East European allies – he brought the question of change back to the political agenda from where it had been banished by Leonid Brezhnev.

Although this said inherently little about the nature, pace, direction, quality or intensity of change, it recognised that the nexus between politics and economics had reached a state of affairs where qualitative transformation of both was essential if the decay was to be halted. The way in which political reform − the redistribution of power − was an essential precondition for greater economic efficiency had become something new in the history of Soviet-type systems. It implied that political reform now had a new and more cogent incentive. Without political change, the systems faced economic immobility and the longer-term threat of political collapse.

All of this necessitated a redefinition of the system, self-evidently for without a proper understanding of what the system was, it was impossible to launch a reform project with any chance of success. In fact, whatever the rhetorical claims made by these systems about socialism, they are best understood as types of étatism or, indeed, hyper-étatism. In effect, Soviet-type systems were highly centralised systems of redistribution, in which the state (as controlled by the party) claimed the monopoly of rationality and thereby arrogated extensive powers of initiative to itself. All this was legitimated by the varying deployment of socialist, egalitarian, modernising, utopian and nationalist rhetoric. The fact that these different rhetorical discourses were at times in direct contradiction − for example, between nationalism and socialism − was irrelevant, for they had no existence, no authenticity, outside their rhetorical world.

The functioning of the system was vaguely aimed at creating a pseudo-modernisation, at the maintenance of Soviet power over its East European sphere of influence, at the sustaining of élite power within individual states and at the administrative allocation of resources in preference to growth. In a word, this was a static, arbitrary and inefficient system. The modernising aspect of Soviet-type systems was determined by the very particular industrial structure that Marxism−Leninism inherited from Stalin − a concentration on heavy industry of the first generation (coal, steel, heavy construction, heavy metallurgy, energy) relying on relatively straightforward technologies. This may have been appropriate to the Soviet Union in the 1930s, though even this is open to doubt, but for most of Eastern Europe in the 1940s and 1950s, it represented a step backwards.

These countries had to a greater or lesser extent already begun a process of modernisation, involving an extension of the market, a shift from patrimonial to commodity production, urbanisation, social organisation beyond the family or kinship network and the extension of choice. This process may not have been far advanced after the Second World War, and patterns varied from the highly industrial Czechoslovak structure to Middle Eastern Albania, but the various local patterns had their own dynamic in accordance with local conditions. Stalinism swept all these away and homogenised them into a simpler and more backward mode.

The legacy of this pseudo-modernisation still haunts these states today. The destruction of local patterns was compounded by the inappropriateness of the Stalinist patterns imposed. Whatever the arguments against of the Stalinist model of modernisation in the Soviet Union in the 1930s, it had some arguments in its favour. These included the plentiful supplies of raw materials, an enormous amount of space and a large though untrained labour force. For the most part, these were not replicated in Eastern Europe. Furthermore, the concentration of energies required to construct an autarkic heavy industry in each East European country was an expensive luxury, which had no economic rationality. Nor was the East European labour force quite as untrained as the Soviet one had been. In effect, the imposition of the Soviet model of modernity was alien and counterproductive; on the other hand, it determined economic and political patterns thereafter.

The pivot of the system was the party – a misnomer, for ruling communist parties are not the representatives of a 'partial' social interest, but claim to aggregate all interests and to exercise all power and initiatives by virtue of possessing the transcendental ideology of Marxism–Leninism. However, once the ideology had begun to lose its power of attraction in the 1970s, when it became clear that Marxism–Leninism could not be used as a means of transforming political institutions and practice (the meaning of the invasion of Czechoslovakia), the purposiveness of the system underwent a metamorphosis. The power of the élite, the securing of the ruler of the party in effect became the dominant principle of these systems and acquired primacy over all other concerns (like efficiency, justice, equality and so on). This was the significance of the Polish crisis of 1980–1, that rule by some neo-Leninist body was of greater importance than any other consideration.

This was an inherently inefficient system and made more so by its purposiveness, for this made innovation, adaptation or growth secondary or tertiary objectives. It tended to emphasise politico-administrative criteria over all others, with a predictable outcome – potential reductionism. Thus the planning mechanism was ultimately less concerned with the optimal use of resources than with optimalising the administration of those resources. The consequences were only slowly revealed. The countries of Eastern Europe were gradually but inexorably left behind those of the West and their citizens had fewer and fewer reasons for regarding Soviet-type systems as offering them anything for which it was worth making sacrifices. The comparison between Austria and its neighbours is instructive in this respect. Whereas in the 1960s, Austria was only marginally ahead in terms of economic indicators, by the 1980s the gap was unbridgeable.

The system also proved highly detrimental to the development of society as a body capable of responding to initiatives and ready to participate in the projects of its rulers. The aftermath of the takeover was completely destructive of social autonomy, a process with far-reaching consequences for the present. The imposition of a totalising system, legitimated in terms of perfection, managed by convinced utopians and backed up by terror resulted in the elimination of much of what makes a society a society, as distinct from an agglomeration of individuals. Autonomies and solidarities, terms of trust, codes of interpersonal behaviour, the rules governing microlevel transactions were shattered. When Bertolt Brecht wrote that the government should dissolve the people and elect itself a new one, he was being ironical. Yet 'dissolving the people', atomising them, is exactly what the Stalinist revolution aimed at doing and largely succeeded. Figures for Hungary show that whilst in the 1940s there were over 13,000 non-sporting associations, forty years later there were only 3500.

The destruction was not restricted to organisations, but was aimed at values as well. Any system of values not approved of by the party, all rationalities not conforming to Stalin's whims, any attempt by individuals to exercise their judgement autonomously was met with dire punishment. What applied to individuals applied even more to organised groups. Nascent civil society was smothered and then eradicated in the course of the Stalinist project. With it went the alternative value systems, competing currents, differing attempts to give answers to existential or ontological problems and eventually the whole idea of diversity, that decisions were formulated not by one single, overarching, hierarchical set of concepts, but untidily, through diversity and debate.

The elevation of Marxism–Leninism to be the sole source of ideals, values, inspiration and organising principles was highly destructive of patterns of interchange in society, politics and economics. Not only did this severely narrow the range of options and thus potential solutions, but it pushed these systems towards synthetic dynamism veiling stagnation. Intellectually these systems were inert. The insistence on one and only one 'correct' solution was a manifest absurdity. It led ineluctably to dogmatism. At the same time, it also established a sterile Marxist–anti-Marxist dichotomy, which was to characterise these systems until the 1980s.

All these proved to have inflicted lasting damage, making regeneration difficult and leaving these systems vulnerable to normlessness. Centrally, the official ideology was incapable of infusing the bulk of the population with enthusiasm and could not become the source of values for them; and once it was clear that Marxism–Leninism had become frozen, even the minority that sympathised with Marxism began to distance itself from it. The system, its ideology and its rulers had become frozen. In effect, the pre-existing systems had been destroyed and nothing lasting had been put in their place.

The present crisis faced by Soviet-type systems, therefore, had deep-seated causes at many levels. These could be ignored until the 1980s because their symptoms were not immediately manifested at the surface or, where they were, they could be treated as secondary. Attempts could still be made to find remedies from within the system – the various economic reform projects of the 1960s and 1970s fell into this category. However, these added up to trying to reform without reform and by the mid-1980s, to varying degrees, it was increasingly evident that the system had exhausted its capabilities and the resources on which it was drawing. It was no longer possible to maintain the existing standard of living together with the high (and mounting) level of subventions to inefficient industry, even while economic rationality, as determined by supply and demand, could not be applied because of the interlocking of political and economic power. Only a dismantling of the two would help.

This pointed unmistakably towards political reform – reform involving the redistribution of power, something that no ruling communist party had ever willingly contemplated. Yet without some determined moves in this direction, it would be impossible to mobilise the new intellectual, economic and political resources that were regarded as essential to avoid further deterioration. At the same time, only a far-reaching renewal of this kind would allow for a regeneration of legitimacy and élite morale, both crucial if collapse was to be avoided.

It was against this background and with these antecedents that new structures of government were constructed. The new political systems quite clearly required new constitutions, but these needed some time for them to be brought into being. The broad principle behind these new constitutions, or projected constitutions, was the separation of powers and rule of law. One of the driving forces behind the new political order in Central and Eastern Europe was that democracy was one and indivisible and that there was no such thing as 'socialist democracy' which somehow overrode the imperatives of classical democracy as it had evolved in Europe. This immediately implied the elimination of the constitutional guarantee for the leading role of the communist party. Having accepted this, however, there was not much agreement about how the weighting of the powers of the different branches of the political sphere was to be arranged, except that on the whole there was some predisposition to minimise the powers of the state administration in favour of elected organs. This was understandable in the light of the hyper-étatist experience of communism, when by the criteria of its totalising aspirations, all actions and transactions were potentially subjected to the power of the party-state.

Poland and Hungary had more or less completed the formulation and enactment of new constitutional provisions by the beginning of 1990. In the Polish case, these were enshrined in the Round Table Agreement of 5 April 1989, as modified in practice by the election results of 4 June. The Agreement itself was a limited and somewhat one-sided compromise. Essentially, it sought to establish islands of democracy in a sea of authoritarianism. Thus Solidarity, together with Rural Solidarity and the Independent Students' Association, would be relegalised; there would be free elections for all the seats in a new Senate and for 35 per cent of the seats in the Sejm, the lower house of parliament. The Senate would have a suspensatory veto which could be overriden by the Sejm only by a two-thirds majority. This last was a concession of some significance, the only provision that ensured that the Senate would be more than a rubber stamp, for the communist party would not have a two thirds majority on its own, but needed to recruit the support of other forces to this end. Solidarity would have the right to run its own newspaper and to engage in open politics.

However, these concessions were to have been counterbalanced by a very powerful set of reserve powers that the authorities claimed for themselves. There would be a new presidency, with very wide competence and, once elected by it, was no longer subject to the parliament; the *nomenklatura* system would be retained; the repressive legislation of the 1980s would not be repealed; and the authorities would maintain their unchallenged control of the instruments of coercion.

However, as suggested, the Polish voters simply threw this arrangement out. The election results represented a total rout for the party. The official candidates were not just defeated, they were humiliated. The verdict of the population was a devastating rejection of everything that the communist system stood for and a very clear signal that even the minority backing that the system was supposed to have enjoyed had evaporated. The Jaruzelski leadership's legitimacy was zero. The problem with this state of affairs was that authorities were still far from being ready to cede power and it took several weeks before the Solidarity government took office.

These were the results of the first round of voting. The elections in Poland were held on 4 June 1989. There were 100 seats in the newly created Senate at stake of which Solidarity won 92 outright, with a majority of over 50 per cent. Of the 425 seats in the Sejm (lower house), 35 per cent were open to competition; the rest were reserved to the communist party and its allies. Solidarity won 160 out of the 161 that it could contest. A further 35 seats were set aside for the uncontested National List; 33 of these did not receive 50 per cent of the vote so were not elected. Among those rejected were eight Politburo members. The turnout was 62 per cent.

In the second round on the 18 June, Solidarity won the remaining seat in the Sejm and increased its total in the Senate to 99 seats out of 100, giving it a total 260 parliamentary seats out of the 261 that it could contest. The turnout was 25 per cent, though this figure hid major variations, in as much as in districts where Solidarity candidates were competing the turnout was much higher.

Under this dispensation the Polish parliament and government, rather than the party or the Politburo, became the true locus of power. In the event, the restrictive provisions of the Round Table Agreement were largely nullified once the Solidarity-led coalition took office in August, even though the communists insisted on holding on to the interior and defence portfolios. The powers of the presidency, though much more than ceremonial, were not used by Jaruzelski to salvage the privileges of the party, but in a relatively neutral fashion.

By the end of 1989, many of the most anti-democratic features of the old constitution had been eliminated, including the leading role of the party and the provision concerning Poland's alliance with the Soviet Union. The state procuracy had been subjected to the Ministry of Justice, and was thus under parliamentary control; respect for private property, as opposed to the preferential treatment of state property, was a basic principle of the new order; and generally there was a determined move towards the rule of law. Work had been launched on drafting an entirely new constitution, which would incorporate all these provisions, and this was to be subjected to public approval.

Early in 1990, the government extended the process of introducing multiparty pluralism by putting forward a new law on political parties. This would allow any group, rather than any political authority, to register with the Supreme Court; registration would involve a procedure to determine whether the projected group's aims were in conformity with the law and nothing else. Crucially the law envisaged the banning of all political activity from places of work, in other words to prevent communist party cells from continuing to organise in factories and enterprises. This law was aimed at freeing the public sphere from official control and creating the framework for a genuine multiparty system.

In Hungary, the situation was nothing like as clear-cut. The Ministry of Justice began work on formulating a new constitution towards the end of 1988 and this went through several drafts and variations. After some early projects, favouring a quadripartite distribution of powers – parliament, president, constitutional court, communist party – the party began negotiations with the opposition in the spring of 1989 and, largely at the insistence of the Free Democrats and the Young Democrats (FIDESZ), more orthodox variants were accepted. The final draft provided for a weak presidency, a medium-to-weak constitutional court and a very strong unicameral parliament, elected on an extremely complex basis and rounded off by the institution of the referendum.

A law on political parties was adopted by parliament in October 1989. The organisation of political parties at places of work was banned – this move was unexpected, because this particular point had been strenuously contested between the opposition and the communists during the Round Table negotiations, but the *de facto* dissolution of the communist party removed the constraints of party discipline from the Hungarian parliament. The new law also banned political parties from receiving financial support from state bodies, state-owned enterprises and from foreign states. Financial support for parties would come from a fund operated by parliament.

The electoral law adopted at the same session was a most elaborate one. This had its origins in the Round Table talks and the need to balance out the claims of different political forces. The country would have 386 deputies elected in a variety of ways. Just over half, 176, would be elected directly by individual member constituencies; 152 would be elected on the basis of party lists put forward in regional electoral areas (Budapest and the 19 counties); and the final 58 would be elected on a nationwide list. To prevent a proliferation of small parties, before a party could claim the vote cast for it on the party lists it had to receive a minimum of 4 per cent of the vote. In addition, each nomination had to be signed by 750 electors and before a party would appear on the lists, it had to put forward candidates in 25 per cent of individual member constituencies. This meant that 33,000 electors had to be mobilised for a party to appear in the lists, a severe disability for a small party. The individual member constituencies would hold two ballots; the second of these would be a run-off between the leading contenders. In other words, the Hungarians had come up with a system of extraordinary complexity.

Both countries were committed to the restoration of the rule of law, the independence of the judiciary, the creation of proper criminal and civil codes, as well as the appropriate procedures in such cases. There was strong emphasis, as might have been predicted, on depoliticising the criminal law. The basic freedoms – assembly, speech, publication, thought, conscience – were fully guaranteed.

The governments that ran these countries immediately after the disappearance of communism were evidently temporary caretaker administrations, with no mandate to do much more than to govern until elections could bring legitimate governments to power. They tended to include a mixture of communists and non-communists, the latter being important to secure them some legitimacy. Given their caretaker status, their scope for action ought to have been restricted, yet there was surprising variation in their readiness to take new initiatives.

At one end of the spectrum there was the National Salvation Front in Romania, which had been hastily put together in the aftermath of the Christmas revolution. The situation in

Romania resembled nothing so much as a political desert and the Front's moves were greeted with deep suspicion by sections of the country's population and the newly emerging alternative political organisations. The government appointed by the Front was chosen, it claimed, on the basis of competence and it really had no mandate other than to oversee the running of the country until elections could be held, which was in itself a Herculean task. However, the Front saw its role differently. Its leader, the interim president, Ion Iliescu, made it clear that the Front was in a sense the interpreter of the revolution and sought to influence the shape of the political system that was to be constructed. Iliescu's conception was of a one-party pluralistic state, in which a single overarching organisation would encompass and presumably restrict a multiplicity of representative bodies. This was at best a corporatist vision of government and it was rejected by the renascent political parties, which were demanding a Western-style democracy.

In Hungary, the interim government was a remnant of the previous political system. It had been appointed by the communist party and it recognised that it had no mandate to do anything other than oversee the creation of a constitutional framework for its successor. As a result it found itself in difficulty whenever it had problems of major significance to handle, like elaborating a new budget or dealing with a case of illegal phone tapping by the Ministry of Interior.

The Czechoslovak government, on the other hand, proved to be remarkably energetic. It was sworn in on 10 December 1989 as the direct result of the November 'gentle revolution' and was made up of eight communists, nine independents and two each from the two satellite parties. The new prime minister, Marian Calfa, initially a communist who later left the party, saw the government's main task as the preparation of the elections and a radical economic reform. The government's programme was approved by the Czechoslovak parliament, the Federal Assembly. The greatest difficulty in putting together this administration was the ministry of interior. The minister came from one of the satellite parties and the working of the ministry as a whole was placed under a triumvirate including the prime minister. In fact, the new minister moved quickly to curb the secret police and its activities. The elections of 1990, which typically led to the transfer of power from communists to conservatives, in turn consolidated these early moves towards a more fully democratic system.

Overall, the new government structures in Central and Eastern Europe resembled those familiar in the democracies of the West. They were based on the broad principles of popular accountability and separation of power, though their interim quality gave their character a certain fluidity. Their communist antecedents prompted them to look towards the early removal of a variety of activities, especially legal matters and issues of internal order, from the direct influence of party politics and to place them under parliamentary scrutiny instead.

China: constitutions, participants and bureaucrats

The PRC has been governed by four constitutions. The years immediately following the establishment of the régime were a time of radical political, social and economic restructuring and it was not until 20 September 1954 that the first Constitution was adopted. This Constitution detailed the new state structure. Inevitably, it owed much to the Soviet system of government below the centre – the province, the county or municipality, and the town or commune. With minor changes, this structure has remained the same ever since. The first Constitution effectively ceased to operate in 1966–7, when the Cultural Revolution (1966–76) resulted in the disruption of established institutional arrangements and produced new structures and processes which had little, if any, constitutional validity. The second Constitution was adopted on 17 January 1975. This was replaced by the third of 5 March 1978. At the time of writing China is governed under the fourth Constitution, adopted on 4 December 1982.

The 1982 Constitution defines the nature of the state as 'a socialist state under the people's democratic dictatorship', a concept similar to the 1954 definition of China as a 'people's democratic state.' These two Constitutions were adopted during periods when the emphasis in policy-making was on economic development. Clearly, the intention was to use a definition that incorporated as many people as possible thus limiting the number of people to be considered as enemies of the state. This accords with the utilisation of united front tactics by the pro-reform leadership in the 1980s. Vital to this approach was the downgrading of the importance of class struggle in Chinese society – a decision announced at the Third Plenum of the Eleventh Central Committee (December 1978). Thus, the fiercer definition used in the 1975 and 1978 Constitutions of China as 'a socialist state of the dictatorship of the proletariat' was no longer seen as applicable.

As has been noted above, all communist régimes suffer from the problem of party penetration into state affairs. In China this problem has been particularly acute, and during the Cultural Revolution any pretence at distinction between the two was effectively abolished. At the start of the Cultural Revolution, the organs of party and state at the non-central levels were identical. The revolutionary committees, which replaced the pre-1966 party and state organs, initially combined the functions of both in one body. Even after 1969 when the party structure was gradually rebuilt, confusion persisted concerning the correct division of responsibilities between the party and the revolutionary committee. To resolve this problem the post-Mao leadership abolished the revolutionary committees and restored the pre-Cultural Revolution system of local government.

The 1982 State Constitution reflects the attempt to free the state sector from the grip of the party. Unlike the more 'radical' constitutions of 1975 and 1978, the power of the party is played down in the Constitution. Reference to the party as the 'core of leadership' has been dropped, as has the claim that it is the citizens' duty to support the party. Mention of party control now appears only in the preamble, where its leading role is acknowledged in the 'four basic principles' (adherence to the socialist road, the dictatorship of the proletariat, the leadership of the Communist Party, and Marxism–Leninism and Mao Zedong Thought). Yet, in practice, it is clear that the state's freedom for political manoeuvre remains extremely limited.

Unlike the USSR, the PRC has always been a unitary

multinational state. Constitutionally, all nationalities are equal and 'big-nation chauvinism' and 'local-nation chauvinism' are equally opposed. All nationalities are free to use their own languages and there are constitutional arrangements for regional autonomy in areas inhabited by the non-Han minorities. But there is no right to secede: 'All the national autonomous areas are inalienable parts of the PRC.'

Administratively, the PRC is divided into provinces, autonomous regions and municipalities directly under the central government in Beijing. There have been various administrative reorganisations and boundary changes over the years but as of 1990 there were 30 administrative units at this level (3 if one includes Taiwan). Of these 21 are provinces: Liaoning, Jilin, Heilongjiang, Hebei, Shanxi, Shandong, Jiangsu, Anhui, Zhejiang, Jiangxi, Fujian, Henan, Hubei, Hunan, Guangdong, Sichuan, Guizhou, Yunnan, Shaanxi, Gansu, Hainan and Qinghai. Five are autonomous regions: Tibet, Inner Mongolia, Guangxi (home of the Zhuang, China's largest minority), Ningxia (inhabited by the Hui, who are Chinese Muslims), and Xinjiang (where the principal minority is Uighur). The centrally-administered cities are Beijing, Shanghai and Tianjin. The 1982 Constitution contains an article permitting the state to set up 'special administrative regions' which, implicitly, will be different from the rest of China. This is designed to facilitate the return of Hong Kong and, ultimately, Taiwan.

Provinces and autonomous regions are divided into autonomous prefectures, counties, autonomous counties and cities. Counties and autonomous counties are divided into townships, nationality townships and towns. Beijing, Shanghai and other large cities are divided into districts and counties. These divisions are analogous to those in the other communist states. At all levels, state power is vested in people's congresses. The highest organ of state is the National People's Congress (NPC) which is composed of deputies elected by the provinces, autonomous regions and municipalities directly under the central government, and by the armed forces. The NPC is elected for a term of five years and holds one session in each year.

The 1982 Constitution vests in the NPC a wide range of

powers and functions. It has the power to amend the Constitution, to make laws, and to supervise the enforcement of constitutional and legal enactments. It elects the President and the Vice-President and is given some say in determining who the senior officials of the state shall be, although the constitutional formulation used to describe its precise role is somewhat convoluted. Thus it is laid down that the NPC shall 'decide on the choice of the Premier of the State Council upon the nomination of the President'. (In 1978 it was 'upon the recommendation of the Central Committee'.) Similarly it shall 'decide on the choice' of vice-premiers, state councillors and ministers upon nomination by the Premier. Some offices, however, are at the NPC's disposal without such constraints. Thus it is empowered 'to elect' the Chairman of the Central Military Commission, the President of the Supreme People's Court and the Procurator-General. It has the power to remove from office all the persons listed above, from President downwards. The NPC is also entitled to examine and approve the national economic plan, the state budget and report on its implementation, to 'decide on questions of war and peace', and 'to exercise such other functions and powers as the highest organ of state power should exercise'.

The NPC does not, of course, really wield most of these powers. Major decisions and appointments are made by the party usually at a Central Committee meeting before the NPC and are passed on to the NPC for its consideration. Further the NPC has too many delegates (2970 at the Seventh Congress convened in 1988) and meets too infrequently to really exercise its powers. Thus, the NPC elects a Standing Committee to act on its behalf when not in session. Because of its smaller size (approximately 200 members), it can hold regular meetings with comparative ease. This body conducts the election of deputies to the NPC and convenes it. The 1982 Constitution adopted important increases in the powers of the Standing Committee. The Standing Committee has been given legislative power and the right to supervise the enforcement of the Constitution. When the NPC is not in session, its Standing Committee can examine and approve partial adjustments to the state plan and budget. It is hoped that this will provide the state with flexibility and speed when reacting to problems in the economy. The Standing Committee's power of supervision over state organs has also been increased.

The most important body at the central level remains, however, the State Council. The State Council is the executive organ of the NPC, making it the highest organ of state administration. In theory, it is responsible and accountable to the NPC and its Standing Committee and is, in effect, the government of China. The Council is presided over by an executive board comprised of the Premier, Vice-Premiers, State Councillors, and the Secretary General. Formally, the NPC appoints the Premier on the recommendation of the President of the PRC. However, in reality such appointments and major decisions taken will already have party approval.

From 1954 to 1964 the NPC did meet once a year, except in 1961. However, it could not be regarded as a major decision-making body. In 1957, for example, Luo Longji, Minister of the Timber Industry and Vice-Chairman of the China Democratic League (one of the major 'democratic' parties permitted to exist after 1949), took advantage of the 'Hundred Flowers' campaign (discussed in Chapter 7) to observe:

> At the Standing Committee meetings of the NPC ... the democratic parties and groups could not voice any effective opinion on matters under discussion because they were not informed in advance of the matters to be discussed, and they had no time to study them at the moment of discussion.

Although subsequent developments, discussed later in this chapter, gave the NPC a somewhat more important role in Chinese politics from the late 1970s onwards, during the last twelve years of Mao's life the NPC met only once (1975) and on that occasion conformed entirely to the 'rubber stamp' stereotype of communist legislatures.

Mass campaigns

This lack of effective participation in decision-making might appear to contradict Mao's insistence upon bringing 'the masses' into political involvement, which was discussed in Chapter 2. In fact, Mao preferred other channels for participation. The problem with this form of participation was that it could not be regularised and often became random and unstructured. Thus, mass participation in the Great Leap Forward (1958–60) did not lead to the breakthrough in economic development that was expected; planning and coordination, in fact, were rendered a virtual impossibility and widespread famine was experienced. Mass participation in the Cultural Revolution certainly led to the destruction of the old party élite but proved incapable of providing a suitable organisational form that could oversee the process of modernisation.

For Mao, it was not sufficient passively to accept a policy – one must be seen to support it actively. The main instrument for this was the 'mass campaign' and this was used extensively by Mao as a participatory device. Under Mao, numerous campaigns were instituted whereby millions of ordinary Chinese citizens were able to acquire political knowledge and to play a part in implementing policy. Campaigns could be organised for political, social or economic objectives, but all of them tended to display common characteristics which are worthy of mention.

First, each campaign was preceded by a stage in which the leadership gave considerable attention to propaganda matters. Once it had decided that a certain course of action was desirable it would embark on a careful programme to make its views known to the mass of the population. The leadership's views would be spelled out in the greatest detail by the media at all levels. Cadres from central to village level were expected to spend much of their time addressing meetings which varied in size from huge mass rallies to face-to-face contacts with half a dozen people. Organisational support was provided by the publication of massive amounts of relevant literature, much of it in pamphlet form, ranging from relatively sophisticated selections of Marxist writings deemed to be particularly relevant, to material dealing with such *minutiae* as the respective merits of such propaganda tools as blackboards, slogans, cartoons, and wallposters. Even that old standby of politicians everywhere, the 'question-and-answer' book, would be provided, so that cadres would be familiar with the points likely to be raised by members of their audience and would have memorised in advance the 'correct' answers to them. The actual quality of Chinese propaganda was of a relatively high order in that, while the message might be simple and crude, it would be readily comprehensible and would use examples with which 'the masses' were familiar.

The aim of the propaganda barrage which initiated each mass campaign went beyond ensuring that the masses knew what was wanted of them they were also expected to reveal their own feelings on a particular issue. An essential aspect of Chinese propaganda techniques was that they demanded discussion within the organisational context of the 'small group'. Virtually everybody was a member of at least one unit, whether based on factory, school, office, or place of residence, through which they were in regular contact with a cadre. Cadres would see to it that everyone became aware of policy by arranging such activities as collective newspaper-reading or radio-listening; they also had the task of making people declare their opinions in front of their peers. In this way it was possible to identify those individuals who appeared 'progressive' and to carry out 'systematic education' towards those who had doubts, apprehensions, and 'erroneous ideas'. Where a basic-level cadre was faced with widespread opposition to a policy as, say, in the case of the collectivisation campaigns, he could either recommend to his superiors that it be modified or else appeal for moral and practical support from the higher echelons who might, for example, send a high-powered propaganda team to visit an area where local cadres were unable to create the necessary degree of willing support. It should be noted here that it was common practice to try out new policies on a local basis in order to test their efficacy before launching them nationally. This was supposed to ensure that by the time a campaign was launched throughout the country many of its teething troubles had been solved.

The next stage was to 'mobilise the masses' to implement the given policy line. Vast numbers of people who may have had little or no previous involvement in any form of political activity were exhorted to carry out tasks under the guidance of cadres. In many cases special *ad hoc* organisations would be set up to facilitate participation. For example, in the Land Reform of 1950–2, 'peasant associations' and 'tribunals' were established to deal with such matters as conducting investigations in patterns of landownership in a particular village, the implementation of directives on the confiscation and redistribution of land, and the penalties to be meted out to those 'local despots' whose 'exploitation' and 'oppression' had placed them outside the ranks of 'the people'. Similarly, in the 'five-anti' campaign of 1952, hundreds of thousands of workers, shop assistants and students were mobilised to denounce, investigate and punish private businessmen and industrialists allegedly guilty of bribery, theft of state assets, cheating on government cotracts, tax evasion and the theft of state economic secrets. Other campaigns were geared to government-inspired 'self-help' policies, particularly in the field of public health.

Mass campaigns did not give ordinary citizens the opportunity to participate in the formulation of major decisions: this always rested with the senior leadership. But they had important functions nevertheless. One of these was educative. For the first time in China's history 'the masses' were made conscious of what their government's policy was. The unremitting propaganda barrage, and the insistence that 'the masses' involve themselves with political affairs, produced a degree of awareness probably unequalled in the economically under-developed world. Nor was the fact that only one 'correct line' was allowed to flourish entirely without its merits, although repugnant from the Western point of view. After more than two millennia in which the Chinese state had been sustained by the integrative moral code of Confucianism, the disruption and turmoil of the nineteenth and twentieth centuries produced a situation in which Sun Yatsen could describe his country as a 'sheet of loose sand'. After the forty years of violence, warlordism, invasion and civil war which followed the collapse of the Qing dynasty, it was essential to provide a new integrative myth to replace anarchic conditions and to harness the energies of the Chinese people to the tasks of economic reconstruction and industrialisation.

Furthermore, mass campaigns did give ordinary citizens the right to participate in some decisions which, elsewhere, would have been left to the law courts and the central government. For example, peasants had some flexibility in deciding which of the ex-landlords in their villages were to be punished harshly and which to be treated leniently; in some cases they could press for a modification of national policy in the light of local conditions. Some were able to break away from the traditional attitude that 'a poor man has no right to speak'. The campaigns also served a valuable recruitment function in that they were a means by which millions of Chinese could rise to positions where they could take relatively important decisions. With the close of each campaign there would be a recruitment drive to bring into positions of responsibility those activists who had 'bubbled up' during its course.

And, on occasion, the mass campaigns were used to exert control over party and state bureaucrats. In 1951–2, for example, the 'five-anti' was accompanied by a 'three-anti' campaign which used similar methods to attack cadres guilty of 'corruption, waste and bureaucracy'. In the early 1960s a 'socialist education' campaign was waged, partly in an attempt to control rural cadres. Most important of all was the Cultural Revolution. For in 1966 Mao did, in effect, assert that officials must be accountable to the people. In place of the considerable, but in fact largely fictitious, powers enjoyed by the NPC to that date, Mao advocated 'extensive democracy', in which 'the masses' were invited to criticise, dismiss and replace their government (and party) leaders on a scale, and with a degree of violence, that was unprecedented in China or in any of the other communist states. It is not surprising that, under these circumstances, a number of ministries ceased to operate entirely and the NPC did not meet until January 1975 when the leadership tried to re-focus policy once again on economic construction.

Developments in the post-Mao era

This peculiar attempt to control bureaucracy, not by a legislature, but by making it directly accountable to 'the masses', resulted in considerable human misery, grave political instability and economic disruption. It was an astonishing radical experiment but, at the practical level, it created many more problems than it solved and it did not, in fact, survive Mao's death. Since 1976 the PRC has attempted to develop an organisational format and political style which, although it has distinctive features, would be readily recognised by communists from the USSR. Since the late 1970s it has been reiterated on a number of occasions that the age of mass campaigns is definitely over that, while they may have served a valuable purpose especially in the early 1950s, they have long outlived their usefulness and have no part to play in China's present modernisation strategy.

However, more conservative party members still see a continued role for such campaigns in the ideological sphere. While they accept that mass mobilisation techniques are inappropriate for economic development, they are still necessary to combat the influence of 'bourgeois' ideas. Thus, on several occasions in the 1980s, they tried to force through campaigns to combat 'spiritual pollution' and 'bourgeois liberalisation'. While the reformers were able to blunt the earlier campaigns quickly, the purge of Zhao Ziyang in June 1989 meant that it was harder to rein in the latest campaign. Yet, even with Zhao gone, the campaign was still likely to be bogged down by opposition and indifference at the lower levels.

The reformers under Deng Xiaoping have tried to encourage the growth of an efficient state bureaucracy with a managerial ethos, staffed by well-educated and relatively young professionals. The experience of the Cultural Revolution had shown Deng and his colleagues the kind of problems that could arise if the flow of ideas and information from society was cut off or unduly distorted. This has led to attempts to increase freedom of discussion to provide decision-makers with more expert advice. However, Deng's closing down of the Democracy Movement in 1978–9 and the brutal suppression of the student movement in mid-1989 clearly demonstrated that he would not tolerate activity that took place outside of the party's control.

Policy in the 1980s has led to a revitalisation of the state sector with renewed stress not only on the state's economic functions but also its legislative and representative functions. When the NPC met in 1975 there were only 29 ministries operating, a reduction from the 45 before the Cultural Revolution. By 1989, 46 ministries, commissions and similar bodies were in operation. The economic policies followed have affected those ministries and commissions concerned with economic planning, the priority development of agriculture and the increase in foreign economic relations. Thus the combined Ministry of Agriculture and Forestry has been redivided into its two component parts, and a new State Commission for Restructuring the Economy has been set up as has a Ministry for Foreign Economic Relations and Trade. The stress on 'socialist legality' has led to the recreation of the Ministries of Civil Affairs and Justice.

The reformers also made a serious attempt to breathe more life into the National People's Congress. After 1978 it began to meet again annually and has produced a steady stream of legislation. There have been reports in the Chinese press about policy debates conducted during the sessions. Ironically, under the leadership of the orthodox Peng Zhen, the NPC acted to hold up reform legislation on the question of bankruptcy and a new enterprise law that was designed to increase the power of managers at the expense of party committees. It was only when Peng was replaced by reform supporter Wan Li that it ceased to be such a block. This fact shows how important the role of the individual is, despite all the official pronouncements to the contrary.

The clash of views between the orthodox leaders who still see the NPC as only having a 'rubber stamp' function and those who favour genuine debate was highlighted at the NPC session held in Beijing from 20 March to 4 April 1989. The conservative Premier, Li Peng, clearly saw the session as providing the seal of approval to his proposals for economic retrenchment. To ensure his objectives were met, he tried to muzzle both China's domestic press and the delegates to the congress. Indeed, China's most strongly pro-reform newspaper was barred from sending reporters to cover the proceedings. The rest of the Chinese press corps was told not to cover the delegates' complaints but only their positive remarks. Delegates were asked not to raise troublesome issues but to confine themselves to patriotic displays of support for central policy. Such attempts to ensure that only the bright features of socialist life were covered were more reminiscent of the Cultural Revolution years than the 'open door policy' pursued under Deng Xiaoping.

However, these strictures could not prevent some of the discontent coming into public view. Questions raised at the meeting by delegates showed how increasingly difficult it has become to stage manage such events. The biggest success of the dissenting voices was the halting of the project to build a huge dam across the Yangzi River which would have major social, economic and environmental consequences. Some 270 delegates criticised this project during the meeting and consideration of construction was delayed until 1995 at the earliest. Resentment was even displayed at the special treatment that the coastal areas receive. In his report, Li Peng supported the policy of rapidly developing the coastal regions and a special motion was passed that gave Shenzhen, the city and economic zone over the border from Hong Kong, special privileges in terms of drafting its own legislation. Opposition was shown by the fact that 274 delegates voted against the motion while a further 805 abstained – a record in NPC voting. With respect to such criticisms, it is worth noting that the NPC rules of procedure passed by the meeting contained a clause that delegates should enjoy immunity during the debates.

The revitalisation of the state sector has also breathed new life into the Chinese People's Political Consultative Conference (CPPCC). The conference now meets annually, usually around the same time as the NPC. With the recent stress on social harmony rather than class conflict, the CPPCC provides the party with an important link to members of other political parties in China (there are eight apart from the CCP) and to key personnel who have no party affiliation. As the main forum for cooperation with non-CCP intellectuals it provides the party and the NPC with expertise that is helpful for the programme of economic modernisation. For its members, it provides a voice to influence policy-making over a range of economic and social questions. Evidence suggests that proposals from the CPPCC do have some impact, although it should be pointed out that they do not deal with fundamental questions of policy but with rather technical matters, environmental questions, or social issues.

Despite the stress on increasing the state's representative functions, it is clear that the people's congresses and other

bodies are not properly fulfilling these functions. This situation has led to repeated calls to make the system more
democratic by increasing the powers of people's supervision
and curtailing the power of local officials. A number of steps
have been taken to this end, such as abolishing the lifelong
tenure system for officials and extending the scope of competitive direct elections. The commitment to the election of
officials was shown by the abolition of the appointed revolutionary committees and their replacement by directly elected
people's congresses up to, and including, the county level.
Despite this commitment, the process of county-level elections
has not been a success, with the first round of elections begun
in 1980 being more or less abandoned in late 1981. Despite the
stated intent of national leaders, and their willingness to order
fresh elections where evidence of fraud was clearly demonstrated, the campaign became bogged down through a combination of the complexity of the procedures, apathy on the
part of the electorate and abuse of the process by local
officials. This caused a delay in the subsequent elections while
some of the teething problems were dealt with. In September
1986, the Standing Committee of the NPC announced that
new deputies for county and township level people's congresses
were to be elected by the end of 1987 and in December
revisions of both the relevant electoral and organic laws were
adopted.

State organisation below the central level has also undergone a number of changes in an attempt to improve its
functioning. The powers of local people's congresses have
been increased to allow them to adopt local regulations, and
at and above the county level standing committees were
created to carry out the work of the congresses on a more
permanent basis. Also, neighbourhood and villagers' committees have been written into the 1982 State Constitution as 'the
mass organisations of self-management at the basic level'. The
most important change is that the people's communes set up
during the Great Leap Forward (1958–60) no longer function
as both a unit of economic and government administration.
The commune had functioned as both the lowest level of
government in the countryside and as the highest level of
collective economic organisation. Now, the township operates

as a level of government, leaving the commune to operate solely as an economic organisation. This division of powers is designed not only to strengthen the state at the lowest level but also to improve economic performance. Under the old system, it was claimed that the party committees interfered too heavily in the economic life of the countryside. In fact, given the decollectivisation of the Chinese countryside, the commune as an organisation of substance has been seriously reduced.

Whether these tentative steps toward improving the process of decision-making and allowing wider access will continue further depends on the outcome on the power struggle that was taking place in Beijing in the early 1990s. Should the more orthodox leaders be able to tighten their grip on power one would expect to see a return to the more formalistic functioning of bodies such as the NPC and a stricter control over the flow of ideas.

Further reading

The constitutions of the communist states are collected together with brief introductions in Simons (1980a). The role of legislatures on a comparative basis is considered in Nelson and White (1982), which devotes particular attention to Yugoslavia, Poland, Romania, Czechoslovakia, the USSR and China. On electoral arrangements in the communist states, see Pravda (1986). Two useful surveys of the state in communist societies are Holmes (1981a) and Harding (1984). The works of Marxist theory that bear most closely on the state are Karl Marx's *Critique of the Gotha Programme* (1975) and V. I. Lenin's *The State and Revolution* (1917), both of which are available in a variety of modern editions. These and other works of Marxist theory are of course open to a number of interpretations and do not necessarily correspond with, still less justify, all the actions that communist governments have taken in their name.

General treatments of state institutions in the USSR include Vanneman (1977), Friedgut (1976), Hill (1980), White (1982a) and Jacobs (1983). The 1977 Soviet Constitution is widely available in pamphlet form and is reprinted together with extensive introductions in Sharlet (1978), Feldbrugge (1979) and Unger (1981a), which also contains the texts of earlier Soviet constitutions. The electoral process is considered in some detail in Zaslavsky and Brym (1978); the role of the Supreme Soviet in budgetary matters is examined in White (1982b). Gureyev and Segudin (1977) and Krutogolov (1980) provide representative Soviet statements on such matters. The process of political reform in more recent years is considered in Hahn (1989), White (1990a) and Urban (1990).

An assessment of governmental structures in Eastern Europe, as well as in other communist countries, is available in Szajkowski (1981). General surveys of Eastern Europe in this connection include Rakowska-Harmstone (1984) and Volgyes (1986), as well as the contributions on Poland, Czechoslovakia and Romania in Nelson and White (1982). On particular countries, Czechoslovakia up to 1968 is dealt with very fully in Skilling (1976) and also in Golan (1973). In Yugoslavia, Rusinow (1977) is outstanding. Singleton (1976) has a useful chapter on constitutional changes, and Ramet (1984) examines the operation of the federal system, up to 1983. The reform period in Hungary is fully covered in Robinson (1973); an admirable and more recent survey is Heinrich (1986). On the 1985 elections in Hungary, see Heinrich (1986, ch. 2) and Racz (1987). Shafir (1985) provides a well-informed and up-to-date survey of Romania. Polish political developments up to the Solidarity crisis are well covered in Leslie (1980). On the more recent period, see the research reports provided by Radio Free Europe in Munich, West Germany.

A translation of the 1982 State Constitution and an interpretative essay can be found in Saich (1983). O'Brien (1989) provides an interesting review of the evolution of the legislature under the reforms. More generally, Barnett (1967) is an immensely detailed and classic study and Schurmann (1968) is invaluable. An excellent study of the Maoist era is available in Harding (1981). The question of participation is discussed in Saich (1989a). The political decision-making process and policy implementation in more recent years are discussed in Barnett (1985), Lampton (1987) and Liberthal and Oksenberg (1988).

4

The Party Systems

One of the defining characteristics of a communist system, it was suggested in Chapter 1, is the existence of a communist or Marxist–Leninist party exercising dominant political authority within the society in question. Not all the parties we shall consider in this chapter in fact call themselves communist. The Korean party, for instance, is called the Workers' Party of Korea, and the Albanian party is called the Party of Labour of Albania (see Table 4.1). Nor are these parties necessarily the only parties that are permitted to exist in their respective societies: almost half of them, in fact, permit more than one party to exist, with seats in the legislature and a formally independent status (see Table 3.1). Historically, however, none of these states has permitted genuinely alternative parties to exist, and only in the late 1980s did limited forms of pluralistic multiparty politics emerge in Eastern Europe. The dominant role of the communist party within the political system, and within the party of its central leadership, indeed was for many years the essential characteristic of a communist state not just to political scientists but also so far as the communist authorities themselves were concerned; and although many ruling parties relinquished their claim to a constitutionally guaranteed 'leading role' in 1989 and 1990, most of them nonetheless continued to assert the right to guide and direct most aspects of the life of their societies.

The 'leading role of the party', as this dominant role of the party in the society is known, derives from a number of circumstances, including the existence in several of these countries of a tradition of autocratic rule and the establishment of a centralised system of economic management. It derives also from a number of ideological sources, in particular

TABLE 4.1

The communist parties in the late 1980s

Country	Name of Party
Albania	Party of Labour of Albania
Bulgaria	Bulgarian Communist Party
China	Communist Party of China
Cuba	Communist Party of Cuba
Czechoslovakia	Communist Party of Czechoslovakia
GDR	Socialist Unity Party of Germany – Party of Democratic Socialism
Hungary	Hungarian Socialist Party
Kampuchea	People's Revolutionary Party of Kampuchea
Korea	Workers' Party of Korea
Laos	Lao People's Revolutionary Party
Mongolia	Mongolian People's Revolutionary Party
Poland	Social Democracy of the Republic of Poland
Romania*	Romanian Communist Party
USSR	Communist Party of the Soviet Union
Vietnam	Communist Party of Vietnam
Yugoslavia	League of Communists of Yugoslavia

Sources: Richard F. Staar, 'Checklist of Communist Parties in 1988', *Problems of Communism* January–February 1989; *Ezhegodnik Bol'shoi Sovetskoi Entsiklopedii 1988g.* (Moscow, 1989); and current reports. It should be noted that party names, members and leaderships were changing

from the doctrine of the 'vanguard party', formulated most fully by Lenin in works such as *What is to be Done?* (1902). In *What is to be Done?* Lenin argued that socialism would not necessarily come about through the automatic extension of trade union and other forms of economic activity by the working class. Strikes, Lenin argued, represented the class struggle in embryo, but 'only in embryo', because the workers did not as yet have an awareness of the irreconcilable nature of the conflict between their interests and those of the capitalist class. This, Lenin went on, could 'only be brought to them from the outside', by the 'educated representatives of the propertied classes – the intelligentsia'. 'There can be no revolutionary movement without a revolutionary theory,' Lenin insisted, and the role of the vanguard could be fulfilled only by a party which was guided by this advanced theory.

Table 4.1 *cont.*

Membership (c.1989)	% of population	Party leader (in 1990)
147,000	5.1	Ramiz Alia
932,055	9.3	Alexander Lilov
48,000,000	3.6	Jiang Zemin
523,639	4.4	Fidel Castro
1,650,000	10.5	Ladislav Adamec
2,300,000	13.2	Gregor Gysi
870,992	8.0	Renzö Nyers
9,000	0.1	Heng Samrin
3,000,000	15.6	Kim Il Sung
42,000	0.9	Kaysone Phomvihane
88,150	4.2	Gombojavyn Ochirbat
2,126,000	6.0	Alexander Kwasniewski
709,735	15.0	Nicolae Ceauşescu
19,037,946	6.8	Mikhail Gorbachev
2,120,000	3.0	Nguyen Van Linh
2,079,613	3.0	Milan Panchevsky

rapidly in the late 1980s and that (for example) reliable membership statistics were likely to take some time to emerge.
*As of late 1989.

The struggle for socialism, in Lenin's view, must therefore place at least as much emphasis upon raising workers' political consciousness as upon bread-and-butter economic issues, and within this struggle a role of particular importance devolved upon the intellectuals who possessed a knowledge of and commitment to the revolutionary theory by which the wider movement must be guided.

No less important was the question of party structure and organisation, and it was upon this issue that Lenin and the Bolsheviks (majority group) split from the remaining Russian Social Democrats, thereafter called the Mensheviks (minority group), at the Second Congress of the Russian Social Democratic Labour Party in 1903. Lenin argued in *What is to be Done?* that the first and most urgent practical task was to 'create an organisation of revolutionaries able to guarantee the energy, stability and continuity of the political struggle'. Such an organisation, Lenin insisted, must embrace 'primarily and chiefly people whose profession consists of revolutionary activity'; and it must 'inevitably be not very wide and as secret as possible', since it was essential to avoid police penetration. Lenin added that the professional revolutionaries must 'serve' the mass movement, not dominate it or 'think for everyone'; he held that professional revolutionaries would be thrown up by the mass movement itself in 'ever-increasing numbers'; and he insisted that his proposals were intended to be valid for Russian autocratic conditions only, in which an open organisation would simply create a 'paradise for the police'. Lenin's principles have, none the less, been taken as the organisational basis of the ruling communist parties of today, and it is to his concept of a 'vanguard party' – a relatively small group, centrally organised, of professional revolutionaries – that they are still officially committed.

The structure and role of the CPSU

The Communist Party of the Soviet Union (CPSU), in words at least, conforms closely to Lenin's precepts. The party is described, in its revised Rules adopted in 1986, as the 'tried and tested militant vanguard of the Soviet people, which unites, on a voluntary basis, the more advanced, politically more conscious section of the working class, collective farm peasantry and intelligentsia of the USSR'. It is not, in other words, a mass organisation, admitting all those who might wish to join it, but an elite group which, at least in theory, consists of those who have the highest levels of political knowledge and commitment in the society and who have been admitted into the party on that basis by the existing membership. The party is described in the Rules as the 'highest form of socio-political organisation' and as the 'leading and guiding force of Soviet society'. It is based, officially speaking, upon what are called 'Leninist norms of party life', in other words democratic centralism, collective leadership, inner-party democracy, the creative activity of party members, criticism and self-criticism, and broad publicity. The Rules, however, also make clear that the party is committed to 'ideological and organisation unity, monolithic cohesion of its ranks, and a high degree of conscious discipline', and any form of group or factional activity is specifically prohibited. Party activity, finally, is supposed to be based on Marxist–Leninist theory and upon the party Programme, which defines the party's tasks as the 'planned and all-round perfection of socialism' and the 'further progress of Soviet society towards communism'. The party also regards itself as an 'integral part of the international communist movement'.

The Rules lay down the organisational structure of the party, a simplified version of which is set out in Figure 4.1. At the bottom of the structure are the primary party organisations (PPOs), formerly called 'cells', which are formed at workplaces and at a few residential locations throughout the USSR, wherever three or more party members are present. There were over 441,000 of these bodies in 1989. The PPO is the organisational basis of the party; it admits new members, carries out agitation and propaganda work and seeks generally to improve the economic performance of the institution within which it is located. Meetings of members are held at least once a month, and a party secretary and (in all but the smallest PPOs) a party bureau are elected, who hold office for a year. Each PPO elects representatives to the level of the party immediately above it, the district level, which in turn elects to the regional level and then to the republican level of the party. At each of these levels conferences or congresses are held every five years at which party committees, bureaux and secretaries are elected, the latter consisting of full-time officials responsible for various areas of party work. At the apex of this system is the all-union Party Congress which meets every five years, and which elects a Central Committee which in turn elects the party's ruling bodies, the Politburo and the Secretariat.

Membership of the CPSU, according to its Rules, is open to any citizen of the USSR who accepts the party's Programme and Rules, takes an active part in communist construction, works in one of the party organisations, carries out all party decisions and pays his or her membership dues (up to 3 per cent of monthly earnings). Admissions may be made from the

FIGURE 4.1 The structure of the CPSU (simplified)

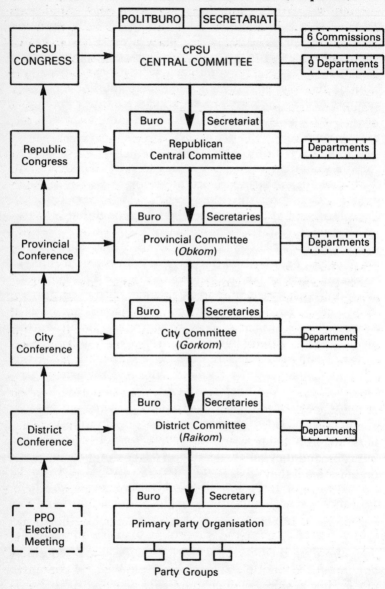

Indicates election (subject to *nomenklatura*)

Indicates lines of authority (subject to democratic centralism)

age of 18, though those aged up to 25 inclusive may join only through the party's youth wing, the Komsomol. Applicants must submit recommendations from three existing members who have been members of the party for not less than five years and who have known the prospective member, professionally and socially, for not less than a year. Membership is initially for a year-long probationary or 'candidate' state, after which a decision on full membership is taken by the members of the primary party organisation to which application has been made. Once admitted, a member gains the right to elect and to be elected to party bodies, to discuss party policies at party meetings and conferences and to uphold his opinions until a decision is taken, to 'criticise any party body and any Communist, irrespective of the position he holds', to address any question, statement or proposal to any party body up to Central Committee level and to demand an answer, and to attend any party meeting at which his conduct is discussed (Party Rules, Art. 3).

Party members are required at the same time to set an example at their place of work, to carry out party policies and explain them to the masses, to take an active part in political life, to master Marxist–Leninist theory, to observe the norms of communist morality, to combat nationalism and chauvinism, to strengthen the party's organisational and ideological unity, to 'wage an unflagging struggle for peace and friendship among nations', and, as if all this were not enough, to 'develop criticism and self-criticism' and 'combat ostentation, conceit, complacency and eyewash' (Party Rules, Art. 2). Party members are also liable to be sent to far-off places on party missions, and they must seek the permission of the local party organisation if they wish to change their place of work or take up residence in another part of the country. Party members, however, are more likely than non-members to be given permission to travel abroad, their sources of political information may be somewhat better than those of non-members, and, above all, their career prospects are likely to be considerably improved since party membership, though no guarantee of a leading position, is often in practice a necessary qualification for such positions and non-members will be at a serious disadvantage in seeking to obtain them. Despite periodic warnings from the leadership that nominal or self-seeking members will not be permitted to remain within the ranks it seems clear that it is the career advantages of party membership that have in the past attracted many applicants, and warnings from the leadership and occasional expulsions are unlikely to alter this situation significantly so long as the party effectively monopolises the leading positions in the society.

The party's total membership has grown steadily in size since the 1950s, both absolutely and as a proportion of the total population, although the central authorities have been attempting to hold down the rate of growth over the last couple of decades in order to preserve the party's élite or vanguard character. The total membership in 1989 was just over 19.4 million, or about 10 per cent of the adult population. Some 45.4 per cent of members were workers by social origin, a proportion which has been increasingly steadily over the past couple of decades as a result of a deliberate decision by the party leadership to maximise recruitment from this section of the population. Collective farm workers accounted for about 11.4 per cent of party members at the same date, a proportion which has been falling slowly over the years, and white-collar workers accounted for the remaining 43.2 per cent. Women are rather under-represented in the party, at 29.9 per cent of all members as against just over half of the total population, but their proportion of total membership has been steadily increasing, and compared with political parties in other countries the present level of female membership may be considered fairly high. Of the nationalities, Russians account for rather more than their share of total party membership, at 58.6 per cent of all members in 1989 as compared with 50.8 per cent of the total population, but Georgians (and Jews) are relatively more heavily over-represented than Russians. The level of party membership is lowest in the Central Asian republics and in Moldavia.

The leading party organs

The 'supreme organ' of the CPSU, according to the Rules, is the Party Congress, which is held every five years. (It is also possible to convene extraordinary Congresses if the circumstances require it.) The Congress hears and approves the reports of the Central Committee and of the other leading party bodies; it reviews and amends the party's Rules and Programme; it elects the Central Committee and the Central Auditing Commission (a largely honorary body which is responsible for overseeing the party's accounts); and it 'determines the line of the party in matters of domestic and foreign policy, and examines and decides the most important questions of party and state life and of communist construction'. The Party Congress is too large and meets for too short a time, however, to serve as a policy-making body of the kind that is implied in the Rules, and in practice it serves mainly as a means of ratifying policies decided in advance as well as a periodic rally and morale-booster, particularly for those, supposedly the 'best of the best', who are sent to the Congress as delegates by their local party organisation. The Central Committee's report, normally presented by the General Secretary, is the most important item of business considered by the Congress; it also receives a report delivered by a government spokesman on the performance of the economy and on the new Five-Year-Plan. These are approved unanimously after a rather perfunctory debate, although individual speakers, as in the Congress of People's Deputies and Supreme Soviet, have increasingly taken this opportunity to press the interests of their own particular institution or area.

Of rather more significance in a policy-making sense is the Central Committee, which is elected by the Party Congress to discharge its responsibilities in the intervals between Congresses. The Central Committee elected by the 27th Party Congress in March 1986 had 477 members, of whom 307 had full membership and 170 had candidate or non-voting status. By January 1990, following a series of resignations, deaths and promotions, there were 249 full and 108 candidate members. The Central Committee is required to meet not less often than once every six months; its responsibilities include the direction of the activity of the party and of its local bodies, the selection and appointment of leading functionaries, and the management of party institutions, the party press, and of the party budget. Its members constitute the closest approximation to the Soviet political élite, including – often, it appears, as of right – the leading party officials from the republican and regional levels as well as leading government ministers, trade union officials, diplomats, generals and heads of academic and scientific institutions, and a small number of 'genuine' workers and peasants. The proceedings of the Central Committee are not normally published, but it seems clear that its periodic meetings serve as sounding-boards for the consideration of policy alternatives as well as occasions for the party leadership to announce new policies or to administer authoritative warnings about shortcomings in various areas of policy. Press reports of its meetings in the Gorbachev period suggested that they could also serve as an opportunity for the regional party leadership to express its misgivings about the course of *perestroika*.

The Central Committee met more frequently under Gorbachev than under his predecessors, and it was the occasion for more vigorous exchanges than at any time since the 1920s. Attempts were also made, as part of the effort to 'democratise' party life, to involve the Central Committee membership more continuously in the process of policy formation. The most important development of this kind was the establishment of six Central Committee commissions in 1988, each of which was chaired by a senior member of the leadership. The commissions dealt with party matters, ideology, social and economic issues, agriculture, international affairs and law reform; each of them had a membership of about 20, and they met two or three times a year. The ideological commission, for instance, dealt in 1989 with the national question and the draft law on the press; the international affairs commission considered the Nazi–Soviet pact and the restructuring of Soviet foreign economic relations. The commissions, it became clear, were the occasion for sometimes vigorous debate, but it was less clear that they could take part in the shaping of party policy rather than its discussion and approval. They nonetheless represented a significant move towards a more open, participatory party of the kind that Gorbachev – and a wide section of party opinion – believed to be necessary.

Gorbachev and the CPSU

The process of 'democratisation', launched by the Central

Committee plenum of January 1987, concerned the CPSU at least as much as other political institutions. The central idea, as the party theoretical journal *Kommunist* put it in early 1988, was that there should be a more restricted understanding of the party's role, involving a kind of 'division of labour' in which the party stood aside from the direct management of public affairs, confining itself to a much more distant coordinating role. The discussion that preceded the 19th Party Conference in 1988 saw very widespread demands for changes of this kind. There were calls, for instance, for party officials to spend more time working 'with the masses' and less time in their offices, and for all party bodies from the Politburo downwards to present annual reports on their work. It was suggested that there should be party congresses every two years and party conferences during the intervals between them, as in Lenin's time, and that the existing membership, recruited to a large extent during the Brezhnev years of stagnation, should be reaccredited and if possible reduced. There was also some concern about the party's own finances, with calls for detailed income and expenditure statements. They knew more about the finances of the British Royal Family and President Reagan, one speaker at the party conference complained, than they knew about the income and expenditure of their own party.

Perhaps the most widely supported proposals, however, were that there should be a choice of candidate at all elections to party office, and that positions of this kind should be held for a limited period. Under the existing system of recommendation from above, wrote one contributor to the discussion, party posts were filled not by election but by appointment, and often for life. Instead of this there should be a 'periodic renewal of elected and nonelected cadres', with maximum periods of tenure. Other contributors to the discussion that took place before the Party Conference called for a normal limit of two five-year terms in the same party position, and some called for the reintroduction of the compulsory turnover rules that had been brought in by Khrushchev but dropped by his successors. Party posts, it was agreed, should also be filled by secret and competitive ballot, and changes were suggested in the manner in which the General Secretary was elected, with some commentators calling for a party-wide ballot on the matter. There might, some thought, be age limits for party positions, such as 65 for Politburo and Secretariat members. And there should be changes in the party's own bureaucracy: it should be smaller, and should less obviously parallel the ministerial hierarchy.

Most of these themes found a place in Gorbachev's address to the Party Conference in June 1988. There had been 'definite deformations in the party itself', Gorbachev told the delegates. Democratic centralism had degenerated into bureaucratic centralism. The rank and file had lost control over the leaderships that spoke in their name; officials had come to believe they were infallible and irreplaceable, and an atmosphere of comradeship and collectivism had been replaced by one of superiors and subordinates. Party and government had lost their distinctive functions, and the party apparatus had become too closely involved in economic and administrative rather than properly political matters. The Conference, in its concluding resolution, agreed with Gorbachev that a 'profound democratisation' of party life was necessary. Towards this end, party primary organisations should be freed from 'petty regimentation' by bodies superior to them. Membership should be determined by the moral and political qualities of applicants, not by their social background or centrally-imposed norms. Party meetings should be more open and constructive; and members must be given a greater role to play than simply attending and 'rubber-stamping lists of candidates and draft resolutions'. More records of party meetings should be published; and – a matter of 'prime importance' – all posts up to Central Committee level should be filled by secret and competitive ballot for a maximum of two five-year terms.

Changes of this kind had already begun to occur: the first contested elections for party office, for instance, had taken place early in 1987, and similar changes had begun in the party's youth movement, the Komsomol, the previous year. The period that followed saw these principles applied still more widely. The party apparatus was restructured at all levels, and generally reduced in size by about 30 per cent. Central Committee commissions were introduced at republican as well as national level. A new journal, *Central Committee News*, began to appear in January 1989: it contained a wealth of biographical, statistical and other material, and came out monthly in a large edition. The party's finances were discussed in its first issue, and also in *Pravda*. Members' dues, it emerged, provided the largest part of the party's income, but 19 per cent of expenditure had to be covered by contributions from party publishing houses and other sources. Most of the party's expenditure was incurred on maintaining the party apparatus at lower levels; the central party bureaucracy alone cost just over 50 million rubles a year to support, which was no more than 3 per cent of the party's total expenditure. Membership statistics were also reported more fully than ever before: among the 19.5 million members on 1 January 1989 were 125 Eskimoes, 7 Englishmen, 3 Americans, 2 'Negroes' and a single Canadian.

There remained some concern, at the start of the 1990s, that the CPSU had restructured itself less fully and swiftly than other institutions in Soviet life. Indeed there was nothing less than a 'democratisation gap' in the USSR, wrote a leading party official in 1989, between the CPSU and the society at large – and it was widening. Relatively few party secretaries, it emerged, were in fact being chosen by a secret competitive ballot; just 1 per cent of the party's regional first secretaries, for example, as compared with 74 per cent of the Congress of People's Deputies that had been elected in March 1989. This was a difference 'hardly in favour of the party'. District party committees, it appeared, still kept their records secret, the rank and file were 'walled off' from their activities, and even members of elected party committees had no access to the meetings of the party bureaux that were nominally accountable to them. The 'vanguard', in short, was 'lagging'.

There was also some evidence, in the late 1980s, that the party was beginning to lose members and more generally experiencing what party officials themselves described as a 'crisis of confidence'. Gorbachev, at the Congress in 1986, had called upon the party to lose its 'infallibility complex'. But it was far from clear what was to take its place. In the absence of a clear and binding conception of their role, some party members, particularly in the Baltic, joined the popular fronts, while others joined the movements that had been set up to oppose them. Some party members went on strike, and even headed the strike committees that emerged in the summer of 1989 in mining areas, while others called for public order to be maintained. Some felt that *glasnost'* had gone too far, and that the party was taking too much of the blame for the Stalin years; and they were concerned that the 1930s were being remembered almost exclusively in terms of repression, and not sufficiently in terms of social and economic achievement. For others, only an honest assessment of the past could prevent the recurrence of similar abuses in the future and establish the party's moral authority. Still others were disheartened by the party's failure to revive the Soviet economy and to overcome social and national tensions. Opinion polls made clear that the party's authority was falling; but without a coherent vision of the kind of society it was attempting to construct it was unlikely that the party's gradual demoralisation, even disintegration, could be avoided.

The 'leading role' of the CPSU

Although its relationship with the society was gradually changing, in the late 1980s the CPSU was still attempting to exercise a 'leading role' in virtually all areas of Soviet life. One of the ways in which the 'leading role' was exercised was through the party's ideological work, covering a wide spectrum of activities from formal political instruction to literature, music and the visual arts. The party's ideological work included *agitprop* (agitation and propaganda), which was conducted through talks and lectures at workplaces and residential areas throughout the USSR. There was also a system of formal political instruction, intended mainly but not exclusively for party members. The subjects of study in this system ranged from the biography of Lenin and party history, at the elementary level, to various aspects of party policy, at more advanced levels. Apart from this there was a considerable political content in the school curriculum, particularly in subjects such as history and civics, and a network of youth movements, ranging from the 'Little Octobrists' (for aged 7 to 9) up to the Komsomol, the party's youth movement, with a membership of about 30 million aged between 14 and 28. The party also sought to exercise more general guidance over literature and the other arts, and it guided the mass media, which were intended not so much to inform the wider population but to 'educate, agitate and organise' (in Lenin's words) on behalf of socialist values and party policies.

A good deal of sociological research has been conducted into the effectiveness of this vast effort. Political classes and lectures, it appears, are often attended unwillingly and as a result of party or trade-union pressure, and they have a very limited effect in changing political values and behaviour, or even in raising levels of political information, since they tend to be attended disproportionately by those who have a better than average level of political knowledge in the first place. International affairs and topical issues are consistently more popular than economic or theoretical questions, and there are frequently complaints about the lack of novelty, excessively abstract character, and lack of convincing argumentation in the political lectures and classes that are provided. There is also some evidence that the party's ideological efforts may not be reaching all sections of the community, particularly those who live in rural areas, young people and pensioners. The improvement of ideological work has been given a good deal of attention in recent years by the party leadership, partly, no doubt, in response to such surveys. There had been too much emphasis upon the customary 'gross' approach, Gorbachev told the 27th Party Congress in 1986. The relevant statistics were indeed impressive: hundreds and thousands of lecturers and propagandists, massive newspaper circulations, and audiences in their millions. And yet real, living people were all too easily forgotten in this 'playing around with figures and with "coverage"'. Party propagandists have been instructed in future years to pay much more attention to work with individuals, and to rebutting the 'psychological warfare' unleashed by the capitalist countries; the mass media have also been urged to respond more promptly and convincingly to current national and international developments. Reforms of this kind have, however, been called for before and it remains to be seen how much difference these latest injunctions will make.

A second and not less important way in which the leading role of the party is exercised is through the party's guidance (*rukovodstvo*) of the soviets and of elected bodies of all kinds. As we have seen in Chapter 3, the party effectively controls the electoral system, by regulating the choice of candidates and in other ways. In addition, the party exercises a leading role within elected bodies of all kinds, wherever there are three or more party members, by means of the formation of party groups or caucuses within them. According to the Party Rules, the CPSU, acting within the framework of the Soviet Constitution, 'exercises political leadership of state and public organisations' and 'directs and coordinates their work'. This leadership role is carried out through the party groups, which are required to promote party policy within the organisation in question and to 'verify the fulfilment of party and government directives', and which are guided in their work by the Central Committee or by a lower level of the party organisation. Party groups meet beforehand to coordinate their tactics, mobilise support for party policies within the body within which they work, and report back upon its activities to the party committee to which they are responsible. Party groups are supposed to develop the activity and initiative of the bodies within which they work, not to command them or attempt to usurp their authority, but at the same time they are supposed to play a leading or guiding role within all such bodies and to ensure that their activities conform to the requirements of party policy. Party groups function, in effect, as means by which the party's authority can be extended to elected state and public bodies of all kinds.

A third and most important form of party control is the party's effective monopoly of appointments to key positions at all levels of society. In the Soviet Union this is usually known as the party's 'cadres policy', or as the 'selection and allocation of cadres'. It is more usually known in the West as the *nomenklatura*, the list of positions at various levels which require the approval of the party before they can be filled (a parallel list or card index of the people who hold these positions, 'nomenklatura workers', is also maintained). The party as such has no authority to make appointments to any positions that are not within its own ranks, but it can exercise a decisive influence over all other appointments through the party committee within the institution in question, which will normally consult with party officials at the appropriate level before making its recommendations in any matters of this kind. The list of positions at the national level includes, for instance, all ministerial appointments, the editors of newspapers, generals and the more important ambassadorships, the heads of the trade union, cultural and scientific bureaucracies, the directors of the largest factories (those of 'all-union significance'), rectors of the major universities and so forth. Parallel lists of positions are maintained by the party apparatus at lower levels of the system, from the republican down to the district level, and all appointments to these positions are similarly regulated. In all it is estimated that about 3 million executive positions throughout the USSR are controlled in this way.

It does not necessarily follow that only party members will be appointed to positions that are on the party *nomenklatura*, or that a purely arbitrary choice will be made and then imposed upon the organisation in question regardless of the wishes of its members. Party approval may in some cases amount to no more than the routine endorsement of the candidate preferred by the institution in question; and account will certainly be taken of the professional as well as party-political credentials of all potential candidates. It has also been known, moreover, usually at the local level, for the party's recommendation of (for instance) a collective farm chairman to be rejected and for a more acceptable alternative candidate to have to be found instead. The Academy of Sciences, the prestigious institution within which most Soviet scientific research is conducted and which admits its members by secret ballot, has also been known to reject particularly unpopular candidates despite the fact that they have party backing. In the last resort, however, the party can exercise decisive influence in all matters of this kind if it decides to do so, and those who hold leading positions at all levels cannot fail to be aware that their continued tenure of their position depends to a very large extent upon the support of party officials at the relevant level in the hierarchy rather than upon the continued favour of those to whom they are nominally responsible. This is not a situation calculated to encourage unorthodoxy, initiative or responsiveness to local needs.

Fourthly and finally, the party apparatus plays a role of key importance in monitoring the performance of government and state bodies at all levels. At the national level this monitoring or supervision – the Russian word is *kontrol'* – is performed by the departments of the Central Committee, under the guidance of the Secretariat. At the republican and lower levels it is performed by the elected officials and full-time party bureaucrats through a comparable but rather smaller network of departments. Following its reorganisation in 1988, the Central Committee apparatus consisted of nine departments: party development and cadres; ideology; social and economic matters; agriculture; defence; state and law; international; general; and administration (for a fuller discussion see below, pp. 182–3). The departments are supposed to refrain from direct interference in the work of the ministries they supervise, but they are expected at the same time to ensure that ministries and other bodies are fulfilling their plan targets, minimising energy losses, introducing new technology and undertaking whatever other tasks the party considers to be of particular importance within the area of policy for which it is responsible.

The Central Committee departments, and the corresponding departments at lower levels in the party hierarchy, carry out this monitoring function in a variety of ways. Of particular importance in this connection is the party committee within the ministry or institution in question, which under the Party Rules has the responsibility of checking upon the fulfilment of party and government decisions by the institution within which it is located and of 'inform[ing] the appropriate party bodies in good time of shortcomings in the work of such institutions and of their individual employees, regardless of what posts the latter may occupy'. Party committees, it appears, may be rather reluctant to undertake duties of this kind, and they may sometimes associate themselves with the interests of the ministries they supervise, if necessary at the expense of other party priorities, since it is upon the performance of the ministries for which they are responsible that they themselves will be judged.

The central party apparatus, however, does have very considerable powers through mechanisms of this kind, ranging from the ability to call an individual minister, as a party member, to account before the party committee in his ministry, to the ability to summon leading party and government personnel from Moscow and the provinces to occasional meetings or conferences in the Central Committee offices at which their performance may be critically scrutinised and at which they may also receive authoritative instructions upon future party policies within the area for which they are responsible. These powers are usually sufficient to ensure that the central party apparatus dominates the policy-making process. Party officials are supposed to refrain from intervening in the day-to-day work of government departments and other bodies, reserving their influence for the selection of leading personnel and general strategic guidance. Often, however, the distinction between a policy and its detailed implementation is a difficult one to draw, and party bodies frequently become involved in routine matters such as the resolution of a transport bottleneck or the procurement of some scarce raw materials, since their authority is often greater than that of the government and economic bodies they supervise and since party bodies are in turn responsible for their satisfactory performance.

The leading role of the party is accordingly a fairly complicated matter, varying a good deal from one policy area to another, from one period of time to another and from one part of the country to another. Party organisations are supposed to guide the work of representative institutions, but not to supplant them (following the reforms of the electoral system and state structure of 1988 and 1989 it was in fact difficult for the party to exercise any decisive influence at all within such bodies). They are expected to make sure that suitable candidates are chosen to fill leading positions, but not to ignore the wishes of those who are nominally responsible for doing so; and they are supposed to refrain from involving themselves in the routine administrative tasks which are the responsibility of governmental and economic institutions, though it will often prove impossible to achieve the party's long-term objectives in the area of policy in question without a good deal of detailed intervention of this kind. The party's exercise of its leading role will, of course, also be influenced by other factors, such as the special interests of various sections of the party bureaucracy itself, the pressures exerted by major institutions such as the trade unions and the military, and by the Soviet public through the various channels that are available to them for this purpose. We shall consider the structures and roles of other ruling parties later in this chapter, and then consider the leaderships in Chapter 5 and the interaction of these various interests and pressures in Chapter 6.

Political parties in Eastern Euorope

In Soviet-type systems, the ruling party is not a political party in the Western sense. Whereas in competitive political systems a political party is, as its name implies, the representative of a partial interest, in Soviet-type systems the communist party is the sole ruling agency of power. This agency has the explicit and exclusive task of aggregating all interests, compressing and absorbing them. The system worked up to a point for several decades, but by the 1980s it was evident that real interests, above all material interests, could not be clearly articulated and were suppressed and distorted by political, i.e. non-economic interests. An illustration of this was the way in which Edward Gierek ignored all the economic arguments against the building and siting of the Katowice steelworks – environmental, transport, supplies of raw materials, steel supplies in the world, etc. – and insisted that they be built largely out of pride in his own local power base and a sense that 'true socialism' meant more steel mills.

The Soviet-type ideal was that the party would not be the victim of such distortions because it was possessed of a superior rationality, based on Marxism–Leninism. In reality, this ideal proved to be unrealisable from the outset, largely because it was applied in a highly contingent, time-bound fashion by Stalin. In any event, as the Soviet-type systems evolved, the aggregation of interests was more and severely distorted as the ruling party's ideology was emptied of content and justification for rule was more and more conceived of in terms of power itself, i.e. 'we rule because we rule'. In practice this meant that ruling parties were increasingly a coterie of cliques, sectional interests and local coalitions which sustained themselves in power by a self-legitimation and by coercion.

However, this system left a particular legacy as far as the relationship of rulers and ruled was concerned. The compression of interests effected under communist party rule meant that both individuals and groups found it extremely difficult to perceive their objectives and, where some kind of a rough and ready calculation was possible, to establish any kind of a hierarchical scale of values between global, group, local or personal interests.

On the other hand, the idea of redistribution of power and the introduction of a market would demand a huge sacrifice from the rulers – no rulers have abandoned monopoly power with any readiness. Ruling Soviet-type systems is not very difficult, above all because there is no concept of individual or collective responsibility for errors. Indeed, there is much to be said for the proposition that one of the central functions of these systems is to protect people from the political consequences of their political decisions and the economic consequences of their economic decisions. In all the Soviet-type states so far the process of redistribution has gone by fits and starts, and this model is unlikely to change in the ones where the transfer has yet to take place. Consequently, many members of the privileged élite have been reluctant to accept the need to move from simple and predictable methods of rule to more complex and competitive ones.

In broad terms, what these polities have needed has been a new set of ideas and principles by which to mobilise society and capture the latent energies that had been held in check by the Soviet-type system. And after 40 years, no society would be satisfied with anything less than a thoroughgoing clean-out of the old. Simply to conceptualise the new political, economic, social and, indeed, moral ideas would mean a radical shift in power relations in the direction of opening up the system to new actors.

The problem of new actors, however, was not as simple as might have appeared on the surface. The functioning of

Soviet-type systems, as already argued, was predicated on the elimination of alternative actors, in whatever sphere. During the Stalinist period, there was a massive uprooting and destruction of the interlocking network of social solidarities that go to making up a civil society. The relationship between what forms of behaviour elicited sanctions and what brought rewards had been completely altered and made arbitrary (see Hankiss, 1990). The reconstruction of social autonomy or new social compacts was not something that could be effected overnight. This made the process of democratising the Soviet-type dictatorships a much harder task than effecting the equivalent with the right-wing authoritarianisms of southern Europe in the 1970s, essentially because in the latter markets and social autonomies had continued to exist and could be used as a basis for later pluralism.

In Western political systems, individual and group interests are primarily identified in material terms and assessed by cost–benefit criteria; and political organisations cluster around these interests. Non-material interests – national, religious, aesthetic, status or gender-related and so on – have a real but secondary function, principally in influencing the way in which material interests have understood at any one time. All this is very different in Soviet-type systems. Crucially, these were utterly destructive of any clarity concerning the perception and articulation of interests, because of the homo-genisation imposed on these societies (see Staniszkis, 1985–6). In effect, because Soviet-type systems look to integrating all interactions into the political sphere, they have constructed an enormously reductionist order. To undo the effects of this and to create conditions for the recognition of interests will take time and will require particular mechanisms.

Arguably it has been this need to escape from the enforced homogenisation that resulted in a striking phenomenon in Central and Eastern Europe – the dominant opposition to the ruling communist party emerged into the political arena with some of the same characteristics. If the communist party was a body that sought to embrace and engulf all political, economic and social interactions and absorb them, it was inevitable that the paramount opposition party would acquire similar features, though without the totalising quality of the former.

In effect, the conversion process in Poland was being effected by Solidarity which was not a political party in the Western sense, but a kind of political conglomeration, in which all political interests were submerged in the name of the higher interest of opposing the PUWP. Once the Solidarity government was in power, the conflicting interests – Solidarity as political party vs. Solidarity as trade union; neo-liberal, christian democratic and social democrat elements – began to come to the fore. Something analogous to this was taking place in Hungary, where the Hungarian Democratic Forum and the Alliance of Free Democrats had increasingly assumed the role of the leading parties by early 1990. The Forum included populist, national radical and christian democratic currents and possibly others all with different, overlapping and conflicting views of the world, while the Free Democrats stood for a centre-left strategy, a commitment to the free market, a rejoining of Europe and an absolute rejection of everything that communism had stood for.

It was not unlikely that some of the newly emergent conglomerate parties might attempt to put forward a 'Third Road' ideology. This has had currency in both Hungary and the GDR and could well appeal to Polish particularism too. The essence of Third Roadism is that the country in question should try to find its own way forward which is neither capitalist nor communist, although it is hard to determine otherwise what Third Roadism actually consists of. Underlying it is a desire to avoid the worst features of capitalism, not just unemployment, drugs and consumerism, but also the perceived soullessness, materialism and the emphasis on the individual over the community that are perceived as the hallmarks of Western modernity. Whatever systems are eventually constructed in Central and Eastern Europe, the chances are strong that they will be relatively more étatist than those in the West and not merely because these polities have lived with hyper-étatism for the last 40 years. In a sense, the Central and East European concept of modernity – or at any rate the dominant elements in the various ways in which modernity is conceptualised – always placed greater stress on community and higher levels of state regulation, state protection and state directed equality than in the West.

As against this, when looking further ahead, it did not seem very plausible that conglomerate parties would remain together for long. Once the market was firmly established and, through its operation, material interests began to transcend non-material ones, political parties would be able to compete for power and the conglomerates would fall apart. Whether this would produce anything like the classical left–right spectrum was hard to predict. On the one hand, after four decades of communism anything that smacked of socialism and planning would be very hard to legitimate in the eyes of public opinion. On the other hand, the need to protect society against the economic consequences of its acts of commission and omission (i.e. the market) is something that is deeply held in both social democracy and christian democracy and it would be likely to inhibit the full operation of free competition. In effect, there was a clear likelihood that non-material interests could continue to play a greater role in former Soviet-type countries than in their Western counterparts.

However, conglomerate parties were not the only feature of the political scene. Paradoxically, as well conglomerates, in some countries there was also a plethora of mini-parties, small or larger groups which called themselves political parties, though some were often no more than ad hoc associations. Their ultimate fate would be settled through the will of the electorate, but their mushrooming was symptomatic of the confusion in societies which had long been repressed by the Soviet-type system and which now looked to reassert themselves. In Czechoslovakia, for example, a scattering of small groups sprang into existence within days of the beginning of the 'gentle revolution'. In the Czech lands, these included the Social Democratic, Green, Agrarian, Christian Democratic, the Czechoslovak Democratic Initiative, which actually constituted itself before the 'gentle revolution', stood for classical liberalism; in addition, there were a number of new parties in Slovakia.

The quality of the new party system and of the new parties themselves was also determined by the way in which democratic opposition movements had functioned before the collapse of communism. The democratic opposition had emerged in the 1970s as one of the responses to the invasion of

Czechoslovakia in 1968, which had signalled that reform of the system was defined exclusively by the Soviet Union and that any ruling party going beyond a certain threshold would find itself in trouble from the Kremlin. The threshold basically started where political pluralism – challenges to the leading role of the party – came up for discussion. This left intellectuals, individuals who generate critiques of the present and formulate alternatives for the future, with the choice of remaining silent or finding an alternative basis from which to act. A minority from inside the Marxist tradition concluded that official Marxism–Leninism was dead as an ideology and moved from this to abandon their previous claim for a monopoly of Marxism. This meant that they could place democracy and human rights on equal footing with Marxism and that, in turn, allowed them to make common cause with non-Marxists for the first time since the communist takeover. Their intellectual need was for a set of values by which they could attack the system from the outside and undermine its totalising quality. Human rights and democracy were ideally suited to this, not least because the régimes themselves had given pro forma recognition to these ideals.

From this basis, the democratic opposition developed a consistent and ultimately demoralising critique of the régimes, by claiming to act in the name of a higher morality than that legitimated by the Marxian utopia. The difficulty with this situation was that while morality was extremely effective as the basis for an opposition to a totalising system, it was worse than useless for open politics. Competitive politics requires not moral purity and clarity, but compromise and bargaining. This reliance on morality led the opposition to adopt positions infused by ideas of moral purity, truth, clarity and transparency. All of this proved an excellent weapon to fight systems claiming the absolute right and power to intervene potentially in all aspects of life.

But at the point when the totalising party state collapsed, the moral basis of the democratic opposition was actually or potentially harmful. The problem was this. While the assault on the legitimacy of the system in the name of a higher morality was essential until the end of communism, in democratic politics the use of moral categories was confusing and destructive. Morality cannot be bargained over, yet politics is about compromises over the allocation of resources, it is muddy rather than clear and does not offer full satisfaction to any of the actors. Indeed, the chances are that a political solution based on the full satisfaction of one actor would result in the deep dissatisfaction of another. The carry-over from the previous state of affairs could not be eliminated overnight. The political discourse of these countries was infused by calls to morality, for moral purity and other categories inimical to political compromise. This trend affected the nascent political parties that were emerging from the democratic opposition movements and would continue to inform politics for the immediate future.

The pulls of different political imperatives – moral purity and compromise – was seen most clearly in Hungary, where the new party system was most developed. However, elements were present in the other newly emerging democracies, notably in the GDR, where part of the weakness of the opposition was that it had acted as a moral pressure group for too long to be able to make the switch easily. In Hungary, the opposition split into two broad groups – the Alliance of Free Democrats and the Hungarian Democratic Forum – each the successor of a current in the old opposition. Neither party could develop readily into organisations with constituencies, but were infused by a propensity to moralise and to spend as much time attacking each other as addressing more pressing political issues. This would undoubtedly colour postcommunist politics for some time to come, and not just in Hungary.

Another group of parties that requires discussion here are those that might be termed the historic parties. These are political parties that existed before the communist takeover, were then suppressed and absorbed by the communists and then reemerged, often led by very elderly survivors from forty years before. The historic parties, precisely because they were from the precommunist past, could claim a degree of historic legitimacy from their potential constituencies. Their continuity could be guaranteed by elderly leaders and they could appeal to their Western counterparts.

Their success varied. In Czechoslovakia, there was little evidence that historic parties were returning to the scene, other than Social Democrats, and in the GDR, the satellite parties represented the tenuous link with the past. In Poland, on the other hand, while the satellite parties could and did play a significant role, the revival of the Peasant Party was a major factor. The Peasant Party had been a considerable force in the countryside and had been a serious antagonist of the communists and thus of the satellite People's Party. In Hungary, the Social Democrats and the Smallholders, both a major force before the takeover and both with a brief flicker of existence during the 1956 revolution, revived fairly quickly, but then their fates diverged. The Social Democrats were largely caught up in their past and seemed unable to make the transition into the 1990s, by coming to terms with Hungarian realities as they had come into being after forty years of communist power. They could still command the allegiance of a smallish constituency among the industrial workers, but not the mass following that might have been theirs. The Smallholders fared better, not least because their rural sup-porters responded more readily than was the case in the towns. In Romania, the historic parties – the Liberals and the National Peasant Party – both sought to reestablish themselves and the Peasants could claim some successes in this regard.

Finally, a brief discussion of the role of satellite parties is called for in this connection. These parties had retained a shadowy existence in several communist countries – Poland, the GDR, Czechoslovakia, Bulgaria – largely as a historical relic. They had no genuine function, with one marginal exception, during periods of normal communist party control. The one exception was that individuals who did not want to join the communist party, but were under pressure to do so for career reasons – their positions in the *nomenklatura* required this – could opt to join one of the satellite parties and this was accepted as a surrogate, though this course would, of course, prevent that individual from rising above a certain hierarchical level. Otherwise, the satellite parties were a ceremonial appendage. On the other hand, in periods of weakened party control, the satellite parties gradually began to act as if they were real organisations, to try and reconnect with their constituencies and to act effectively in the new politics. This was the evidence from Czechoslovakia during the Prague Spring and from Poland during Solidarity.

It was, therefore, not entirely surprising that the satellite parties found themselves endowed with a quite significant role during the transformation. Their existence was helpful as a kind of bridge between pure communist party control and the emergence of a true multiparty system. They smoothed the path in the transfer of power. This was quite evident in the case of Poland in the summer of 1989. In the elections to the Polish parliament on 4 June, Solidarity won all the seats that it could, bar one, under the terms of the 5 April Round Table Agreement; this had allowed it to contest all the seats in the new upper house, the Senate, but only one-third of the seats in the more powerful lower house, the Sejm (see above, pp. 113–15). This meant that the communists, the Polish United Workers' Party, could still rule, but only in combination with the satellites, the People's Party and the Democratic Party. When the satellites began to hesitate after the overwhelming popular support for Solidarity and to consider their own futures separately from the communists, a Solidarity-led coalition moved into the realms of reality and was, in fact, put together by August.

In the GDR, after the destabilisation of the system in October 1989, the ruling Socialist Unity Party (SED) began to try and keep itself in power by relying on the satellite parties, which – it was thought by the SED leadership – were seen by the population as less tainted than the SED itself. Despite these efforts to boost the satellite parties, there was little evidence that the East German population placed much faith in them. Support, rather, tended to go to the fledgling Social Democratic Party, which had been merged with the communists in 1946, precisely because it had no associations with the previous decades of communist rule.

In Czechoslovakia, there were four satellite parties, two of them – the Czechoslovak People's Party (CPP) and the Czechoslovak Socialist Party (CSS) – being significant. Their influence increased as that of the communists declined, notably when the non-communist dominated government was voted in by the National Assembly. The CPP, a historic party associated with Masaryk and Beneš, stood for a

Christian Democrat philosophy, while the CSS was once a liberal party.

These various factors – conglomerate parties, the problems of disaggregating material interests, the role of morality in politics – suggested that for some time to come the shape and tenor of Central and Eastern European politics would be informed by non-material values. The significance of this is that non-material values appeal far more directly to the affective dimension in politics – emotions – than material ones. Non-material factors tend to promote identities and these are much more difficult and painful to bargain away. When deployed in politics, non-material factors, like reference to morality, nationhood, religion and so on, tend to produce instability. Strong emotions block out reason and undermine the stabilising factors that promote democracy. An example of this was the pattern of events in Serbia, where from 1987 onwards the Serbian party leader, Slobodan Milošević, had promoted a brand of demagogic, fiery nationalism, directed against the Albanians of Kosovo (see Chapter 6) in the first place, but generally trying to place the blame for Serbia's economic, social and other problems, in no way connected with nationhood, on non-Serbs. Quiescence was extremely difficult to achieve and without this, the bargaining needed to stabilise Yugoslavia could not take place. The other countries of Central and Eastern Europe could face analogous problems.

The Communist Party of China: role and organisation

The role of the party in the Chinese political system

The Cultural Revolution launched in 1966 witnessed an unprecedented attack on a ruling communist party. This attack was all the more astonishing since it was initiated and led by the leader of the party – Mao Zedong. At a superficial level there are obvious parallels with the CPSU under Stalin. Indeed the conscious attempts to revive party life since Mao's death seem comparable with Khrushchev's efforts following Stalin's death. Certainly, under Stalin the party was emasculated. This is demonstrated by the virtual atrophy of the functioning of the regular party organs. The Party Congress in the USSR did not meet between 1939 and 1952 and the Central Committee did not fare much better. The CCP, comparably, did not hold a Congress between 1958 and 1969. In the Soviet Union under Stalin there was a relative eclipse of the party as the supreme institution of power at the centre. As Stalin's personal power moved into the ascendant that of the party declined. Again one can find a parallel with the party under Mao.

However, there are important differences. Despite Stalin's destruction of his opponents in the party (politically and, invariably, physically), the downgrading of the party's importance and the growth of the personality cult, he always claimed to be acting in the name of the party and invoked its name to sanction its actions. Mao in destroying his opponents and, for a while, the party was willing to invoke his own authority against that of the party. While Stalin turned to the state administration and the public security forces to attain his objectives, Mao appealed to the masses and latterly the army to break down the old system. While Stalin destroyed the old Bolsheviks and began to replace them with a managerial elite, Mao tried to extinguish the 'new class' and inject revolutionary zeal into the merging managerial ethos.

Although differences existed between Mao and his supporters on questions of the nature of the ideal form of the party, his thinking on organisational issues influenced the whole programme of party rebuilding until the late 1970s. Mao's attitude to organisation of any form was ambivalent. While he saw leadership as necessary to guide the revolution forward, he was suspicious of those who occupied leadership positions. He was constantly aware of the possibility of leaders becoming alienated from the masses and adopting bureaucratic postures. In the 1960s, this trend of thought led Mao to believe that the party itself provided part of the basis for the emergence of a new class dedicated to serving themselves rather than the masses and socialism. If the party as an organisation has a tendency towards bureaucratism and if its top leaders could be seduced along the 'capitalist road', purely internal mechanisms of control could not be relied upon. Leaders were exhorted to maintain close contacts with the masses, formalised through programmes such as those for cadre participation in manual labour. The masses, for their part, were expected to exercise supervision over the leadership and offer criticism. The internal party control mechanisms that had operated before the Cultural Revolution were abolished. They were replaced by a faith in a leadership committed to revolutionary values and in the power of the masses to point out problems as they arose. The chapter on organisational principles in the Party Constitutions adopted by the Ninth and Tenth Party Congresses in 1969 and 1973 both referred to the need for 'leading bodies to listen constantly to the opinions of the masses both inside and outside the party and accept their supervision'. The post-Mao stress on the need to re-establish an institutionalised system for maintaining party discipline and the virtual elimination of a mass role in party life meant that such references were dropped in the 1982 Constitution. The organisational principles referred only to the need for higher party organisations to pay constant attention to the views of the lower party organisations and rank-and-file members.

Mao's ambivalence concerning questions of organisation meant that he could not provide his supporters with a clear idea of the precise forms he would prefer. Despite the attempts to separate the party as an organisation from the individuals in the party who were under attack, the effect was to undermine the party's prestige. This brought to the fore the question of legitimacy. With the discrediting of the party as a source of authority and legitimacy the tendency was to resort to the invocation of Mao's name. The fact that the Cultural Revolution did not, or was not allowed to, develop alternative forms of organisation only compounded the problem.

The post-Mao leadership had not only to devise a proper relationship between the party and society but also to deal with the issue of excessive dominance by one person. Hua Guofeng, Mao's successor, was never able to come to terms with this latter problem and continued the Mao cult and set about creating one of his own. Politically, it would have been extremely difficult for Hua to have dismantled the excessively Mao-centred system, as his own right to rule was based on a claim that he was Mao's hand-picked successor. The increasing emphasis from December 1978 onwards on the need to regularise procedures and the mounting criticism of 'feudal work-style' did not augur well for Hua's continued occupation of top party and state posts (he gave up the premiership in July 1980 and his chairmanship of the party in July 1981). The quaint poster that was widely distributed of the aged Mao handing the youthful Hua the piece of paper with the inscription 'With you in charge, I am at ease' written on it by Mao smacked far too much of the Emperor passing on the Mandate of Heaven to his chosen successor.

Although Deng Xiaoping has continually stressed the need to return to 'a conventional way of doing things', he has not been able to break entirely free of this legacy. The stress placed on traditional Leninist notions was intended to come to terms with the problems of over-concentration and hence abuse of power and especially the personality cult. Collective leadership is interpreted as a basic principle of democratic centralism, and the 1982 Party Constitution clearly stipulated that all major decisions should be decided upon by party committees after democratic discussion. Included in the principles of democratic centralism was the express forbidding of all forms of the cult of personality while Article 16 forbade all party members, no matter what their position, from making decisions on major issues by themselves or from placing themselves above the party organisation. However, when the party came under stress in mid-1989, it quickly resorted to its 'unconventional' way of doing things. The events underlined just how far the party was from devising institutional mechanisms capable of dealing with major policy divisions among its élite.

The search for a suitable party form since the death of Mao has divided top leaders. Not surprisingly, suggestions for reform have focussed on the need to reduce the party's influence over day-to-day affairs of other organisations. Since fundamental reform would lead to a diminution of the party's power, it has been strongly resisted. This resistance has led to the dismissal of the last two party secretaries, Hu Yaobang (in 1987) and Zhao Ziyang (in 1989). Since the death of Mao, three major approaches can be discerned among the top leadership. These views are closely related to the question of economic development as clearly the nature of the party depends in large part on the kind of economy over which it presides.

First, there was the view that dominated the initial post-Mao years. The view retained certain features from the Cultural Revolution period along with its ambiguities and was designed to complement the optimistic proposals of the economic development strategy. This approach was represented by Hua Guofeng and the group later denounced as the 'Whateverists'. In January 1977, Hua had put forward the slogan, 'We must resolutely uphold whatever policy decisions Chairman Mao made and unswervingly carry out whatever Chairman Mao instructed'. Essentially, those who took this view proposed the continuance of the party as a vehicle of mobilisation to conduct mass campaigns, both economic and political, to achieve the ambitious targets set. While the party was to be formally in command, the masses were to exercise a monitoring function over abuses by party members. Such a view was liable to allow suspicion of the party to remain while failing to create organisations with legitimacy. It was too dependent on the more 'radical' aspects of Mao's legacy and the creation of a new personality cult around Hua to resist the policy shifts to the new economic programme.

Since the removal of this group from power, two main views have dominated: the pragmatic reformist and the traditional orthodox. These two viewpoints served as points on a continuum along which different opinions clustered at crucial moments. Certainly they were not the only views expressed and some individuals such as Deng Xiaoping moved between the two viewpoints. On occasion, Deng has seemed to give his approval to far-reaching change yet, at crucial moments, he has supported the traditional viewpoint on political issues in order to preserve his economic reforms from attack.

The pragmatic view was presented by Zhao Ziyang at the Thirteenth Party Congress in 1987. The term 'pragmatic' is used as the reforms proposed are designed primarily to improve economic efficiency, and are not seen by this group as having their own intrinsic value. Zhao indicated that future reforms would have to deal with some of the core issues of the party's role and structure as inherited from the Leninist model, developed during the pre-1949 struggle for power and intensified under the centrally planned economy. This role and structure did not suit the demands of a more decentralised, market-influenced economy where flexibility, efficiency and the encouragement of initiative were key values.

Zhao's proposals called for a redistribution of power both horizontally, to state organs at the same level, and vertically, to party and state organs lower down the administrative ladder. To date, the party has so dominated the legislature, the executive and the judiciary as to make their independence a fiction. The intention was for the party to exercise political leadership but not to become directly involved in the routine work of government. Zhao even acknowledged that there existed a limited political pluralism under the leadership of the CCP. Breaking with the monistic view common to CCP thinking and the idea of uniform policy implementation, he acknowledged both that 'specific views and the interests of the masses may differ from each other' and that '[a]s conditions vary in different localities, we should not require unanimity in everything'.

Similarly, the group recognised that experts and intellectuals should be given a greater degree of freedom as a prerequisite for their contribution to policy-making. In turn, they had to be given guarantees that they would not be punished tomorrow for what they said today. This led not only to a greater tolerance of 'dissent' but also to the protection of people's rights by the legal system. Genuine elections are seen as important in this context, not just for allowing mass participation in the decision-making process, but also to ensure that those in leadership positions have the support of their constituencies. Yet this acknowledgement of a limited pluralism was not intended to lead to the accommodation of factions within the party, something which had been suggested by some reform-minded intellectuals. Such reforms were seen as the only way to maintain party leadership in a time of change.

While neither Hu Yaobang in late 1986 nor Zhao Ziyang in mid-1989 saw the student protests as a major threat, the traditionalists in the party saw them as a challenge to the fundamental principles of party rule. Crucially, Deng Xiaoping decided to side with them. Whereas Zhao appeared willing to make concessions to the students' demands, his opponents felt no retreat was possible as it would lead to a collapse of socialism. Their reaction to the events and their brutal repression of the student protest in the summer of 1989 serves to highlight their fear of spontaneous political activity that takes place outside of their direct political control.

Deng has always maintained a traditional view of political activity that occurs outside of party control and has resisted Mao's attempts to open up the party to criticism from outside forces. The general caution derived from his Leninist heritage has been reinforced by his experience of the Hundred Flowers Campaign in 1957, the Cultural Revolution, and the Democracy Movements of the late 1970s and late 1980s. In all these movements, the party as an institution came under attack.

The group Deng sided with oppose wide-ranging political reform because of the consequences of liberalisation for the social fabric of China. This group seek to run the party and its relationship to society on orthodox Leninist lines. Efforts to relax the party's grip over state and society are resisted and they seek continually to institutionalise party dominance. To limit the adverse side-effects of the economic reforms, tight party control backed by ideological education is seen as necessary. In particular, they are concerned about attempts to loosen the control of the party in the workplace. With the decentralisation of limited decision-making powers to the work-units, it is felt important that the party retains a strong role in the enterprises to stop them deviating too much from central party policy. Thus, there is a stress upon the need for party strengthening at the grass-roots level and political and ideological work continues to be taken seriously.

The drive to maintain institutionalised party dominance provides stability and assurance as well as status for party cadres. However, at the same time, this drive does much to explain the stifling of initiative that has been increasingly apparent during the reform period. In combination with the dual-pricing system, it provides the structural basis for corruption that has been heavily criticised not only by student demonstrators but also in the official Chinese press. The concentrated nature of power and the lack of a genuine system of accountability mean that party officials at all levels are in a unique position to turn professional relationships into personal connections for financial gain.

The tendency towards intrusiveness in all spheres of life was increased in the aftermath of the student demonstrations of mid-1989. The Dengist group blamed the disturbances on the emergence of bourgeois ideas in Chinese society along with the economic reforms. To combat the influx of such heterodox ideas, the traditionalists favoured the launching of intensive ideological campaigns. However, at the time of writing these campaigns were already beginning to attack aspects of the market-oriented economic reforms themselves. Traditional leaders recognise full well that certain aspects of the economic reform programme not only create the basis for 'disruptive ideas' but also call into question the traditional ethics of socialism such as equality, solidarity and security.

The strengthening of the party's role throughout the system is signalled by the prominence given to the need to uphold the 'Four Basic Principles'. These vague principles are used by the traditionalists to extend their control over society through party organisations and give them the chance to criticise anything with which they disagree as negating socialism and the party.

This approach to managing the party's role in the political system is clearly outdated in a modern society where economic reform and technological development are creating a more diversified and sophisticated society. Zhao's acknowledgement that a limited pluralism is inevitable is rejected; the traditionalists, rather, think in terms of a single undifferentiated mass of people who work harmoniously for the creation of socialism. The party's role, of course, is to tell the masses what their interests are as they strive to build socialism. Should the current leadership decide to push ahead with the economic reforms, inevitably they will be confronted by precisely the kinds of problems that they so manifestly refused to deal with in April–June 1989. The idea that political problems can be combatted by a large-scale political campaign and sending students down to the countryside before beginning their course is a reflection of just how out of touch the Dengist leadership had become by the early 1990s.

Party organisation

The Party Constitution adopted in September 1982 outlines current thinking about organisational affairs. It describes a party structure more akin to that of the CPSU than those outlined in the more 'radical' Party Constitutions adopted in 1969, 1973 and 1977. The shift of emphasis to economic modernisation caused the party to re-define itself, and the radical political rhetoric of the Cultural Revolution was dropped almost entirely. The 1982 Constitution no longer refers to the party as the 'political party of the proletariat and its vanguard' (as did the Constitutions of 1969, 1973 and 1977), but as the 'vanguard of the Chinese working class'. The term 'working class' is more neutral than that of 'proletariat', the latter conjuring up visions of class struggle. The CCP's current self-description encompasses an even broader appeal than that of 1956. It is described as the 'faithful representative of the interests of all the Chinese people'. This claim does not appear in the 1956 Party Constitution, a Constitution which was also adopted at a time when the main emphasis was placed upon economic development.

Like the CPSU the Chinese Communist Party prides itself on its exclusivity and has never sought to incorporate more than a tiny percentage of the population within its ranks. Its Constitution contains detailed rules governing the admission of members and the duties and behaviour required of them. The actual criteria for membership have changed over the years, reflecting shifts in ideology and recruitment policies. In contrast to a number of its forerunners the 1982 Constitution acknowledges that class background is no longer a significant factor in China and provides an extremely broad definition of eligibility. Thus, membership may be sought by

> any Chinese workers, peasant, member of the armed forces, intellectual or any other revolutionary who has reached the age of eighteen and who accepts the party's programme and constitution and is willing to join and work actively in one of the party's organisations, carry out the party's decisions and pay membership dues regularly.

To become a probationary member an applicant must be

supported by two existing members, accepted by a party branch after 'rigorous examination', and approved by the next highest level of party organisation. Probation normally lasts for one year during which time the candidate's progress is assessed and education is given. If all goes well, full membership will then be granted by the general membership meeting of the party branch and approved by the next highest level. Members who violate party discipline are subject to various sanctions including warnings of varying degrees of severity, removal from party posts, placing on probation and expulsion from the party. The party can also propose to 'the organisations concerned' that an offender should be removed from non-party posts. A member subjected to discipline has the right to be heard in his or her own defence and has a right to appeal to higher levels.

Although the high standards demanded by the Constitution are not necessarily met in practice, membership requires a high degree of commitment and considerable sacrifice of personal time. At times, party members have had the unpleasant task of implementing policies which were widely disliked. During the Cultural Revolution members were particularly vulnerable to the violent oscillations of the Maoist political process and were subject to savage criticism and much worse. Despite the condemnation of factionalism, the party was in practice heavily factionalised and the problem, though reduced, still exists. Many members have suffered simply by backing the losing side in a particular dispute. Over time, the attractiveness of party membership has diminished somewhat as a result of its record of past failures and excesses which has tarnished its image, especially among the young. Recent policies towards agriculture, the emphasis on encouraging and rewarding the professionally competent and the insistence that the party should refrain from interfering in all aspects of day-to-day work have also made it increasingly possible for some sections of the population to pursue relatively well-paid and responsible jobs without joining.

Nevertheless, membership has always conferred great benefits and this remains broadly true. The party is still the locus of political power and few can achieve real political influence without membership and a record of political activism. Membership, moreover, has also always given enhanced access to desirable jobs. In the Maoist era the vast majority of responsible jobs in the state and mass organisations went to party members who, often, had few other qualifications. Deng's insistence on the need for an elite of competent modernisers in all walks of life has meant that political reliability alone is no longer regarded as a sufficient qualification for a senior appointment, but party credentials remain necessary for a wide range of sensitive positions and in a host of others will tip the balance in favour of those possessing them. Moreover, wage scales in China are highly differentiated and those in senior positions enjoying relatively high incomes, commensurate pensions and superior accommodation. There is also a range of 'informal' advantages as elsewhere in the communist world. Although these have differed over time they have always included access to information denied to the general public; an increased ability to obtain 'good' education and to use 'connections' to advance the careers of one's children; opportunities to travel within China and, increasingly, abroad; the right to use cars in a country where private car ownership is extremely rare, and to travel 'soft' class on trains; and the opportunity to enjoy a certain amount of wining and dining at public expense. It may be noted that there have been opportunities for corruption which appear to have increased in scope as a result of the 'Open Door' policy which has brought to China a wider range of foreign luxury goods and foreign businessmen. Since 1982, the Chinese press has published details of scandals similar to those of the Soviet Union.

Although exclusive, party membership has risen steadily since 1949. Then there were only 4 488 000 members. By 1955 membership had more than doubled to 9 393 000 and it rose to 17 million in 1961. By 1973 it had reached 28 million and in 1977 stood at 'more than' 35 million. It increased to 38 million in 1980, in 1986 it was 44 million and by 1989 had reached 48 million. These figures of steady growth, however, disguise certain weaknesses in past recruitment policies which now hinder the party's role as an agent of modernisation. The basic problems are related: the party paid insufficient attention to the recruitment of the educated – especially in the

Cultural Revolution – and the young. In 1984 only 4 per cent of members had received higher education and over 50 per cent were either illiterate or had only been to primary school. Whereas in 1950 nearly 27 per cent of members were under 25, by 1983 this had fallen to less than 3.3 per cent. At the higher levels, the party has had great success in promoting the educated and professionally competent. But at county level and below the problem of elite renewal remains serious despite leadership attacks on anti-intellectual sentiments and lack of interest in recruiting the young.

The structure of the party has been broadly similar to that of the CPSU over the years. Democratic centralism creates a hierarchical pattern of organisation in the party in the shape of a pyramid. At the bottom is the network of some 3 million 'primary party organisations' based on work units or neighbourhoods, wherever there are three or more full party members. Above this is a hierarchy of organisation running upwards through county and provincial levels to the central bodies in Beijing. The National Party Congress is nominally the supreme decision-making body and meets every five years, the last occasion being 1987. However, as in other communist states, it is far too large for effective action and its functions are really to 'represent' the total membership in a symbolic sense.

The Congress elects a Central Committee which takes over its tasks. The last Central Committee (the Thirteenth) was elected in November 1987 and had 175 full members and 110 alternates. In contrast to the situation before the reforms began, the Central Committee consists increasingly of relatively young leaders who have received a higher education. However, in the last decade, institutional power in the party has shifted between the Politburo, its Standing Committee and the Secretariat under the General Secretary (the post of General Secretary replaced that of party Chairman in September 1982). This formal power structure competes with individual patron–client relationships and the Central Advisory Commission, which provides veteran cadres opposed to many aspects of the reform programme with their own institutional power base (for a discussion of the commission see Chapter 6).

The Party Constitution gives no indication about the range of activities of the Politburo and its Standing Committee, simply stating that they are elected by the Central Committee and carry out its functions when it is not in session. Little is known about the actual workings of the Politburo, except for the fact that its meetings are frequent and that discussions at meetings in normal times are said to be unrestrained. The expansion in size of the Politburo meant that the Standing Committee was set up in 1956 and since that time it has been, in theory, the party's highest collective authority.

During the 1980s, as a part of the regularisation of party life, attempts were made to create a clearer division of functional responsibilities between the party's top organs and to regularise the decision-making process. There was an initial attempt to overcome the tendency whereby real power was exercised by individuals and groups operating outside the confines of this organisational framework. As a part of this attempt, membership of the Politburo was to be related more to functional requirements rather than to simple factional loyalties. However, these attempts crumbled as leadership differences among the élite intensified.

At the Thirteenth Party Congress in 1987, Zhao Ziyang announced an important adjustment in the relationship between the Politburo and the Secretariat. The Constitution adopted at the Twelfth Party Congress in 1982 provided that the Politburo, its Standing Committee, and the General Secretary and the Secretariat were all to be elected by the Central Committee. This resulted in the Secretariat and the Politburo acting as competing sources of power. This was not surprising given that one of the reasons for the resurrection of the Secretariat may have been because at the time Deng Xiaoping and his supporters could not gain a natural majority in the Politburo. In fact, there was even talk of the Politburo being abolished.

In theory, the Secretariat was to handle the day-to-day work of the party, becoming its administrative heart. The Politburo and its Standing Committee would be freed to concentrate on taking important decisions on national and international issues. In practice, it placed the Secretariat in an extremely powerful position as it supervised the regional party organs and the functional departments of the party that should, in theory, have been responsible directly to the Central Committee and the Politburo. This access to information and its control functions meant that it could function as an alternative power-base to the Politburo.

Zhao Ziyang announced a clear change in this relationship, downgrading the Secretariat in relation to the Politburo. It was reduced in size from 10 to only four full members (excluding the General Secretary) and one alternate, and was made the working office of the Politburo and its Standing Committee. Instead of being directly elected by the Central Committee, its membership is now nominated by the Standing Committee of the Politburo and approved by the Central Committee. A practical indication of the decline of the power of the Secretariat was the announcement that in the future, agenda items proposed by the State Council for policy-making by the Politburo or its Standing Committee would no longer be 'filtered' by the Central Secretariat. However, in practice, it functioned as Zhao Ziyang's support base in the party headquarters. Zhao and three of his supporters in the Secretariat were removed at the Fourth Plenum of the Thirteenth Central Committee on 24 June 1989.

Despite the stress on the need to institutionalise party life throughout the 1980s, it is clear that formalities can be easily overridden should they prove inconvenient to the senior leaders. This was clearly seen with regard to the Standing Committee of the Politburo elected at the Thirteenth Party Congress. Attempts to institutionalise membership on the basis of functional occupation as stated in the 1982 Party Constitution were abandoned. According to the Constitution, the heads of the Military Affairs Commission (Deng Xiaoping), the Discipline Inspection Commission (Qiao Shi) and the Central Advisory Commission (Chen Yun) must be members of the Standing Committee of the Politburo. Deng presumably felt it was better to face ridicule for yet again ripping up the Party Constitution than to have his strongest opponent, Chen Yun, still in the Standing Committee. Also, given Deng's and Chen's ages it would have made the policy of introducing 'new blood' look ridiculous.

Further reading

The rules or statutes of all ruling communist parties are reprinted together with brief introductions and bibliographies in Simons and White (1984). No other studies are presently available which deal with all the ruling communist parties; Eastern Europe is, however, covered in Fischer-Galati (1979), and political leadership and succession in the USSR, Eastern Europe and China is considered in McCauley and Carter (1986). Lenin's writings on the communist party and its role include *What is to be Done?* (1902), which is available in many modern editions. The most useful general surveys of Leninist theory are Meyer (1957), Harding (1977) and (1981), and Lane (1981).

On the USSR more specifically, there are thorough studies of the CPSU in Hough and Fainsod (1979) and in Hill and Frank (1987). The Rules of the CPSU, as revised by the 27th Party Congress in 1986, are available in White (1989) together with the 1986 edition of the Party Programme. On the party's ideological work, see White (1979, chs 4–6 and 1985). On the party's role in economic management, which is considered further in Chapter 6, see Hough (1969) and more recently Rutland (1985). Two basic studies of party history are Schapiro (1970) and Rigby (1968), which should be supplemented by Rigby (1976). On the *nomenklatura*, see Harasymiw (1969) and (1984) and also Voslensky (1984). On the General Secretary and his role, see Brown (1980) and Gill (1986); on the Politburo more generally, see Löwenhardt (1982). On participation within the party, see Unger (1977–78) and (1981b), which are based upon interviews with emigres.

On the communist parties in Eastern Europe, in addition to the works mentioned at the end of Chapter 3, the following may be consulted: King (1980) on the Romanian Communist Party, Kovrig (1979) on Hungary, Suda (1980) on Czechoslovakia, de Weydenthal (1986) on Poland, and Bell (1986) on Bulgaria, all of which are volumes in the 'Histories of Ruling Communist Parties' series produced by the Hoover Institution. In addition, McCauley (1979) on the GDR and Prifti (1978) on Albania are thorough and well documented. Lowit

(1979) provides a useful theoretical perspective; Fischer-Galati (1979), already mentioned, provides a more general account.

On the CCP, Schurmann (1968) is a classic that is still essential reading. Chang (1978) is a valuable guide to policy-making. Teiwes (1979) is excellent on the period up until the Cultural Revolution. More recent developments are covered in Saich (1984 and 1990). For a perceptive view of Mao's role see Teiwes (1984). The Party Constitution with a short introduction may be found in Simons and White (1984). A useful source on policy changes in the post-Mao era is Deng Xiaoping (1984). For Zhao Ziyang's report to the Thirteenth Party Congress see Zhao (1987). Excellent studies of the Chinese variant of the *nomenklatura* system can be found in Manion (1985) and Burns (1989). On the party's control apparatus see Sullivan (1984).

5

The Leaderships

Communist leaderships have traditionally been powerful ones. Unlike governments in the liberal democracies, they have had little to fear from general elections; and the other agencies by which Western-style governments are held to account, such as the law courts, pressure groups and the mass media, have normally been controlled by the authorities rather than by the society over which they rule. Communist leaderships, despite a verbal commitment to collectivism, have also traditionally been personalist ones. The theorists of totalitarianism took account of this feature when they equated Stalin's rule in Soviet Russia with Hitler's in Nazi Germany and Mussolini's in Fascist Italy. Western parties changed their leaders when they suffered electoral defeat; communist leaders continued for decades, steadily strengthening their grip over Politburos and Secretariats as they marginalised their opponents and coopted their supporters. Communist leaders were normally the most authoritative exponents of the official ideology, and they often combined a number of top-level positions: typically the presidency together with the party leadership. Cuba's Fidel Castro, thirty years in power in 1989, combined both these positions with the prime minister-ship and the leadership of the Revolutionary Armed Forces.

The last two or three decades have nonetheless seen the steady emergence of more oligarchic, consensual patterns of leadership in the communist-ruled nations. To leave almost unrestricted powers in the hands of single leader, it became clear, threatened other members of the leadership as well as ordinary citizens. The demands of running a national government were normally too great to combine with the party leadership, and the additional functions that communist

177

leaders took on were increasingly ceremonial, allowing them to represent the state as a whole and not simply its ruling party. Leaderships at all levels became more 'institutionalised' in character: important interests in the society, from armed forces and industry to the various regions and republics, established an increasingly automatic right to representation in key decision-making bodies. Party leaderships in turn became the institutions within which the most important interests in the society reconciled their competing claims; no longer were they made up simply of the leader's favourite associates. In many cases, if public speeches were any guide, communist leaderships had become almost 'coalitions' whose members favoured very different courses of action within the broad framework of party rule.

The pluralisation of communist politics that took place in the late 1980s introduced still further modifications. A greater emphasis began to be placed, in regimes such as the USSR, upon the representation of women, minority nationalities and (in government) non-party members. In Eastern Europe still more varied practices emerged, including formal rather than *de facto* coalitions in government and combinations of communist presidencies with non-communist prime ministerships. And there was a rapid turnover of party first secretaries, with East Germany's Egon Krenz the recordholder: party leader for just six weeks, he ended the year in disgrace and was expelled from the party's ranks altogether in January 1990. There was a shift, in established communist regimes, from party-based leaderships to more presidential systems; and in Eastern Europe political change brought new elites from non-communist backgrounds into leadership positions. Throughout this pattern of change there was perhaps a single constant: that leadership mattered, as a force for reform or for the maintenance of communist orthodoxy.

The Soviet leadership: Politburo and Secretariat

The Soviet party leadership, like that of most traditional communist systems, was based in the late 1980s upon two key decision-making bodies: the Politburo and the Secretariat.

Both were formally elected (more accurately, approved) by the Central Committee, which also, separately, elected the General Secretary. According to the Party Rules, the Politburo is supposed to 'direct the work of the party' between meetings of the Central Committee. It is, in fact, the functional equivalent of a cabinet in a British-type political system, meeting weekly (usually on a Thursday) and taking key decisions in all areas of policy. The Politburo in January 1990 consisted of 19 members (see Table 5.1): the average age was about 60, rather younger than the Brezhnev Politburo of the late 1970s, and it included the first woman member for more than twenty years, Alexandra Biryukova, who had formerly worked in the central trade union bureaucracy. It was a better educated Politburo than all of its predecessors: three of its members (Medvedev, Yakovlev and Lukyanov) held higher doctorates in economics, history and law respectively, and Yevgenii Primakov, who joined as a candidate in September 1989, was a member of the Academy of Sciences and the former director of its important think-tank, the Institute of the World Economy and International Relations. It was, however, less representative of the party as a whole than the Politburos of earlier years, with only Vladimir Ivashko, the Ukrainian first secretary, heading a major non-Russian party organisation.

Brief reports of Politburo meetings began to appear in the press from November 1982, and still fuller summaries of the discussions from late 1989. There was no typical agenda, but it seemed clear that meetings would normally start with Soviet domestic affairs – plan results, the energy industry, education or whatever – and then move to foreign affairs, more often by way of report than for the purposes of substantive discussion. Meetings normally concluded with 'other matters', almost certainly a reference to appointments to leading positions. The Politburo meeting of 22 January 1990, although on a Monday, was not otherwise untypical. The first and clearly most important item was the draft platform that was to be presented to the Central Committee in early February, covering (it later emerged) the further extension of political reform and the modification if not elimination of the communist party's guaranteed leading role. The Politburo had a

TABLE 5.1

The Soviet leadership, January 1990
(years of birth in parentheses)

Politburo

Full members (12):
Mikhail S. Gorbachev (1931), General Secretary of the CC CPSU
and Chairman of the USSR Supreme Soviet
Vladimir A. Ivashko (1932), First Secretary, Ukrainian party
organisation
Vladimir A. Kryuchkov (1924), Chairman, KGB
Yegor K. Ligachev (1920), CC Secretary
Yuri D. Maslyukov (1937), First Deputy Chairman USSR Council
of Ministers and Chairman, USSR *Gosplan*
Vadim A. Medvedev (1929), CC Secretary
Nikolai I. Ryzhkov (1929), Chairman, USSR Council of Ministers
Eduard A. Shevardnadze (1928), Foreign Minister
Nikolai N. Slyun'kov (1929), CC Secretary
Vitalii A. Vorotnikov (1926), Chairman of the Russian Republic
Supreme Soviet
Alexander N. Yakovlev (1923), CC Secretary
Lev N. Zaikov (1923), CC Secretary

Candidate members (7):
Alexandra P. Biryukova (1929), Deputy Chairman, USSR Council
of Ministers and Chairman, Bureau on Social Development of the
USSR Council of Ministers
Anatolii I. Luk'yanov (1930), First Deputy Chairman of the USSR
Supreme Soviet (or Deputy President)
Yevgenii M. Primakov (1929), Chairman, Council of the Union,
USSR Supreme Soviet
Boris K. Pugo (1937), Chairman, Party Control Committee
Georgii P. Razumovsky (1936), CC Secretary
Alexander V. Vlasov (1932), Chairman, RSFSR Council of
Ministers
Dmitrii T. Yazov (1923), Defence Minister

Secretariat (13 members)

Mikhail S. Gorbachev	Georgii P. Razumovsky
Oleg D. Baklanov (1932)	Nikolai N. Slyun'kov
Andrei N. Girenko (1936)	Yegor S. Stroev (1937)
Yegor K. Ligachev	Gumer I. Usmanov (1932)
Yuri A. Manaenkov (1936)	Alexander N. Yakovlev
Vadim A. Medvedev	Lev N. Zaikov

'thorough' discussion after which it 'on the whole' approved the draft, instructing Gorbachev to prepare a further version taking into account the views that had been expressed. The Politburo also heard about Gorbachev's visit to Lithuania in December 1989 for discussions with its secessionist party organisation, and approved recommendations on this issue for the forthcoming plenum. The other items were concerned with foreign affairs: contacts with the Japanese Liberal Democratic Party, and the discussions that had taken place between Gorbachev, Shevardnadze and the United Nations Secretary General on his recent visit to Moscow.

The Politburo, under Brezhnev, held relatively brief meetings, usually of an hour's duration. Politburo meetings, under Gorbachev, are known to last well into the evening, and an elaborate but changing network of committees attached to the Politburo carries out further work. One of these, for instance, was the commission set up in 1987 to review the sentences that were passed in the 1930s, 1940s and early 1950s and to rehabilitate those who were innocent; it took decisions of considerable political sensitivity and was latterly chaired by a close Gorbachev associate, Alexander Yakovlev. Not all meetings were chaired by Gorbachev in person; nor is the attendance necessarily limited to the formal membership. The editor of *Pravda*, for instance, is normally in attendance; the secretary of the national trade union council has also been present; and ministers and others will normally appear when their attendance is considered appropriate for a particular item on the agenda. Equally, a number of members based outside Moscow may attend less frequently than others. Not all the items on the agenda, it appears, are dealt with at the weekly meetings; in these circumstances the papers are circulated for the equivalent of a postal ballot. Again, Moscow-based members and particularly the full-time members of the Secretariat have a disproportionate influence on these decisions.

The Politburo works closely together with the Secretariat, which is also elected by the Central Committee. In January 1990 there were thirteen Central Committee Secretaries, including the General Secretary, and they normally met weekly as a body (see Table 5.1). The most important members, sometimes called 'super-secretaries', were also

members of the Politburo. The Party Rules say no more than
that the Secretariat 'directs current work, chiefly the selection
of cadres [leading officials] and the verification of the fulfilment of decisions'. This group of top-level officials, together
with its counterparts at lower levels of the system, is in fact an
institution of the utmost importance; it is the instrument
through which the party's decisions are put into practice, it
offers advice and information to the Politburo, and (given the
party's broad conception of its leading role) it functions in
effect as the administrative focus of the whole Soviet system.
Some of the functions of the Secretariat, in the late 1980s,
appeared to have been taken over by the newly-established
Central Committee commissions (see above, p. 142); the
commissions, nonetheless, were headed by individual Central
Committee Secretaries, and they were perhaps better conceptualised as adjuncts to the Secretariat rather than as a
replacement for it.

The Secretariat's main responsibility is to guide the work of
the Departments of the Central Committee, which are the
party's full-time central bureaucracy. Under Gorbachev's
predecessors there had been twenty or more departments,
each of them responsible for a particular area of Soviet life and
many of them responsible for supervising the work of a
particular industrial ministry. In 1988, on Gorbachev's recommendation, the twenty departments that then existed
were reduced to just nine. There was a Department of Party
Development and Cadres, responsible for overseeing the inner
life of the party itself and more general questions of appointments. The Ideological Department was responsible for questions of theory, and also for science and culture. There was a
Socio-Economic Department, responsible for the general (but
not day-to-day) management of social and economic matters,
and an Agricultural Department, with corresponding responsibilities. A Defence Department was to supervise military
industry (again without undermining the position of the
relevant ministries). There was an International Department,
to deal with the party's foreign relations and questions of
foreign policy, and a Department of State and Law, responsible for political and legal reform. A General Department and
Administration of Affairs were also required for day-to-day

matters. The total staffing of the central party apparatus was 1940, with 1275 secretaries and others in addition. Reduced, as intended, by about 30 per cent, this was still a formidable party headquarters.

All of the party's leading bodies are in principle elective and accountable to those that elect them, but in practice, at least until the late 1980s, they largely dominated the congresses and conferences to which they were nominally responsible as well as lower levels of the hierarchy. There were several reasons for this. Perhaps the most important was Article 19 of the Party Rules, which required (in its 1986 formulation) that all party bodies be elective and accountable but also that there be 'strict party discipline and subordination of the minority to the majority', and that the decisions of higher bodies were 'obligatory for lower bodies'. The decisions of leading party bodies could not therefore be openly challenged, at least without the risk of expulsion and other sanctions, and any attempt to form organised groupings or to establish direct links between party bodies at the same level in the hierarchy was explicitly prohibited. The Party Rules also specified various ways in which each level of the party structure supervised the level immediately below it. Of particular importance was the influence that was exerted over the election of leading officials at each level of the party by the level immediately above it. Although there was a secret ballot and although members had the 'unlimited right to challenge candidates and to criticise them', it was normal, until the late 1980s, for a single list of candidates to be 'recommended' by the party level immediately above and for it to be elected without opposition. Each level of the party hierarchy was also supposed to 'direct' and 'inspect the work' of the party bodies immediately subordinate to it, and to hear regular reports on their performance.

Leading officials at each level of the party organisation, accordingly, could usually count upon the support of the party officials immediately superior to them and by whom they had been nominated, and had less need to pay attention to the wishes and opinions of those that nominally elected them. The Party Rules do in fact provide for the 'free and business-like discussion of questions of party policy in individual party organisations or in the party as a whole'; every member has the right to criticise the conduct of any other member or (from 1986) any party body, and special party-wide discussions may be held when the circumstances require them. These are held to be basic principles of inner-party democracy, and severe penalties, even expulsion, are attached to any attempt to suppress criticism or to victimise those who have expressed it. The party press, nonetheless, is full of cases of this kind, with critics being forced to undertake less pleasant work or even to leave their employment for having spoken out of turn at party meetings, and it often requires the intervention of higher-level officials before the injustice can be corrected. Even in Gorbachev's CPSU it was still clear to most members that only 'constructive', that was to say mild and unspecific, criticism would be encouraged, and any more far-reaching criticism could well have adverse consequences for those that had expressed it, including their employment, their families' career prospects and perhaps even their liberty. It was not perhaps surprising, in these circumstances, that the CPSU continued to function in a centralised and hierarchical manner, rather than in the internally democratic manner for which the Party Rules ostensibly provided.

Gorbachev and the politics of leadership

At the outset of his administration Gorbachev's objectives, and indeed his personal background, were still fairly obscure even at leading levels of the party. Gorbachev, unlike his main rivals for the leadership, had not addressed a party congress, and he had still (in March 1985) no published collection of writings to his name. He had made only a couple of important visits abroad, to Canada in 1983 and to Britain in late 1984, on both occasions as the head of a delegation of Soviet parliamentarians. Andrei Gromyko, proposing Gorbachev's candidacy to the Central Committee, explained what had convinced him personally that Gorbachev would be a suitable general secretary: Gorbachev, he indicated, had chaired meetings of the Politburo in Chernenko's absence and had done so 'brilliantly, without any exaggeration' (there was no reference in the published protocol to the remark also attributed to

Gromyko, that Gorbachev had a 'nice smile but teeth of steel'). Gorbachev himself, in his acceptance speech, paid tribute to his immediate predecessor and then pledged himself to continue the policy he had inherited, which he defined as 'acceleration of socio-economic development and the perfection of all aspects of social life'. There were, however, some elements in the new general secretary's biography which suggested that his new administration would be more than a continuation of its predecessors.

One of those elements was Gorbachev's own background, particularly his education and more youthful generation. Gorbachev was born, according to his official biography, in March 1931 to a peasant family in the Stavropol territory of southern Russia. He worked first as a mechanic at a machine-tractor station and then in 1950, with the help of his local party organisation, enrolled in the Law Faculty of Moscow University. Gorbachev was a Komsomol activist while at university, and joined the CPSU itself in 1952. He graduated in 1955, the first Soviet leader since Lenin to receive a formal legal training and the first to graduate from the country's premier university. After graduation Gorbachev returned to Stavropol where he worked in the Komsomol and party apparatus, later completing a correspondence course at the local agricultural institute. In 1966 he became first secretary of the city party committee, in 1970 he was appointed to head the territorial party organisation, and the following year he joined the Central Committee as a full member. In 1978 Gorbachev became a member of the Central Committee Secretariat, taking responsibility for agriculture. In 1979 he became a candidate, and then in 1980 a full member of the ruling Politburo.

It is not customary for a Soviet leader to discuss his personal affairs with the mass media, but Gorbachev did venture some information on this subject when he was interviewed by the Italian communist paper *L'Unità* in May 1987. His main weakness, Gorbachev confided, was that he had too many interests. He had enrolled in the law faculty at university, for instance, but had originally intended to study physics. He liked mathematics, but also history and literature. In later years he had turned more and more to the study of economics, while remaining interested in philosophy (this was not, to put it mildly, the intellectual background of his immediate predecessor, Konstantin Chernenko). Interest in the General Secretary's background was hardly satisfied by such revelations and there were further queries in the press in the spring of 1989. Did Mikhail Sergeevich, for instance, like fishing? And why did *glasnost'* not apply to the man who had invented it? Gorbachev obliged with some further remarks in a Central Committee journal later in the year: he earned 1200 rubles a month, he explained, the same as other members of the Politburo, and the substantial royalties he received for his book *Perestroika* went to party and other charitable purposes. Literature, theatre, music and cinema remained his hobbies, although he had less and less time to devote to them.

Apart from his personal characteristics, there were also some clues in Gorbachev's speeches before his election that gave some indication of the policies he was likely to pursue as General Secretary. Perhaps the clearest indication of this kind was an address to an all-union ideology conference in December 1984. The speech contained positive references to self-management, which Lenin had 'never counterposed to Soviet state power', and drew attention to the need for a greater measure of social justice, in effect an attack on the Brezhnev legacy. There was enormous scope, Gorbachev went on, for the further development of the Soviet political system, and of socialist democracy. This was partly a matter of developing all aspects of the work of the soviets, and of involving workers more fully in the affairs of their own workplace. It was also a matter of securing a greater degree of *glasnost'* or openness in party and state life. Gorbachev's speech at the local elections in February 1985, made at a time when Chernenko's illness was already widely known, repeated some of these themes, combining almost populist references to Soviet power as a form of rule 'of the toilers and for the toilers' and to the need for the party 'again and again to check its political course against the rich experience of the people' with more abrasive remarks about the self-sufficiency of enterprises and labour discipline. These speeches, in effect an election manifesto to the Central Committee 'selectorate', made it clear that Gorbachev would continue Andropov's emphasis upon efficiency and discipline but also that they would be placed within a broader framework involving democratic reform and a re-assertion of the moral values that were, for Gorbachev, implicit in socialism.

The direction of reform became still clearer at the April 1985 Central Committee meeting, the first Gorbachev addressed as party leader. There had been significant achievements in all spheres of Soviet life, Gorbachev told the plenum. The USSR had a powerful, developed economy, a highly skilled workforce and an advanced scientific base. Everyone had the right to work, to social security, to cultural resources of all kinds, and to participation in management. But further changes were needed to achieve a 'qualitatively new state of society', including modernisation of the economy and the extension of socialist self-government. The key issue was the acceleration of economic growth. This was quite feasible if the 'human factor' was called more fully into play, and if the reserves that existed throughout the economy were properly utilised. This in turn required a greater degree of decentralisation of economic management, including cost accounting at enterprise level and a closer connection between the work that people did and their remuneration.

Of all the policies that were promoted by the Gorbachev administration, *glasnost'* was probably the most distinctive. *Glasnost'*, usually translated as 'openness' or 'publicity', did not mean an unqualified freedom of the press or the right to information; nor was it original to Gorbachev. It did, however, reflect the new General Secretary's belief that without a greater awareness of the real state of affairs and of the considerations that had led to particular decisions there would be no willingness on the part of the Soviet people to commit themselves to his programme of reconstruction or *perestroika*. 'The better people are informed', Gorbachev told the Central Committee meeting that elected him, 'the more consciously they act, the more actively they support the party, its plans and programmatic objectives'. This led to more open treatment of Soviet social problems such as drugs, prostitution and crime; it also led to a more honest consideration of the Soviet past, extending to the 'wanton repressive measures' of the 1930s (as Gorbachev put it in a speech in November 1987), and to an attempt to root out the corruption that had become widely established during the Brezhnev years. Brezhnev's son-in-law, sentenced to twelve years' imprisonment in December 1988, was the most prominent casualty of these policies.

The 'democratisation' of Soviet political life, of which *glasnost'* was a part, was also intended to release the human energies that, for Gorbachev, had been choked off by the bureaucratic centralisation that had developed during the Stalin years. The political system established by the October revolution, he told the 19th Party Conference in 1988, had undergone 'serious deformations', leading to the development of a 'command-administrative system' which had extinguished the democratic potential of the elected soviets. The role of party and state officialdom had increased out of all proportion, and this 'bloated administrative apparatus' had begun to dictate its will in political and economic matters. Officials had begun to believe they were beyond criticism; many had become inactive, and some had become corrupt. It was this 'ossified system of government, with its command-and-pressure mechanism', that had become the main obstacle to *perestroika*. The Party Conference duly adopted a resolution on 'radical reform' of the political system, and this led, as we have seen (pp. 95–107), to a whole series of constitutional and other changes in 1988 and 1989. These changes, taken together, were for Gorbachev the most important of their kind to have taken place since the October revolution itself.

Together with these changes, for Gorbachev, there had to be a 'radical reform' of the Soviet economy (for a fuller discussion see below, pp. 223–34). Levels of growth had been declining since at least the 1950s. In the late 1970s they reached the lowest levels in Soviet peacetime history; growth, in the view of Soviet as well as Western commentators, had probably ceased during these years, at least per head of population. Indeed, as Gorbachev explained in early 1988, if the sale of alcoholic drink and of Soviet oil on world markets were excluded, there had been no real growth of the Soviet economy for the previous fifteen years. Radical reform, as Gorbachev explained to the 27th Party Congress in 1986 and to a Central Committee meeting the following year, involved a set of related measures. One of the most important was a greater degree of decentralisation of economic management, leaving broad guidance of the economy in the hands of *Gosplan* but allowing factories and farms throughout the USSR much more freedom to set their own priorities. They were to be guided in making their choices by predominantly 'market' criteria, including the profits they made on their production. Retail and wholesale prices would gradually be adjusted to reflect the cost of production, eliminating food and other subsidies, and enterprises that persistently failed to pay their way might be liquidated. Gorbachev described these changes, which began to be brought into effect from 1987 onwards, as the most significant since the adoption of the New Economic Policy (NEP) in the early 1920s.

Why had difficulties of this kind developed in a socialist society, Gorbachev enquired? In part they had arisen from natural and external factors; but the main reason was deficiencies at the level of political leadership. For years, Gorbachev told the 27th Party Congress, party and state officials had lagged behind the needs of the time. A curious psychology – 'how to improve things without really changing anything' – had taken hold. It was these reasons, 'above all of a subjective character', that had brought the USSR to its present impasse. In January 1987, again, the main reason for the difficulties they confronted was that the party leadership, 'primarily for subjective reasons', had failed to see the dangerous situation that had developed and the need for radical reform. Connected with this was the problem of 'conservatism' in political thinking, both at leading levels and among the society at large. This was the greatest difficulty they confronted in carrying out the restructuring programme, Gorbachev wrote in his book *Perestroika*. Everyone, from General Secretary to ordinary citizen, had been formed in the years of stagnation, and everyone, as a result, had to 'overcome his own conservatism'.

This meant, in the first place, a vigorous shake-up of the existing, mostly Brezhnevite, leadership. Out went elderly associates of the late General Secretary, such as former prime minister Nikolai Tikhonov and the Kazakh first secretary, Dinmukhamed Kunaev (later expelled from the Central Committee itself for 'serious shortcomings' in his tenure of that position). Out went Brezhnev's son Yuri, from the ministry of foreign trade, and his son-in-law Churbanov, from the interior ministry. Out too went the city of Brezhnev, Brezhnev scholarships, Brezhnev square in Moscow and Leningrad and Brezhnev district in the capital. In, to replace them, came a new generation of party leaders: younger, more technically qualified, and untainted by corruption. The 'Gorbachev generation' included people like Nikolai Ryzhkov, formerly the successful director of the Uralmash engineering works in Sverdlovsk. Appointed to the Secretariat by Andropov, Ryzhkov came into the Politburo as a full member at Gorbachev's first Central Committee meeting and became prime minister later the same year. Vitalii Vorotnikov, later president of the Russian Republic, qualified as an aviation engineer and had spent the earlier part of his career in a Kuibyshev factory. Alexander Yakovlev, similarly, held a higher doctorate in history (he had been an exchange student at Columbia University in the late 1950s), and had formerly headed an important institute of the Academy of Sciences.

By January 1990 only two of the 19 members of the Politburo (Gorbachev himself and foreign minister Eduard Shevardnadze) had served in the party leadership during the Brezhnev years, and only three (these two and Vorotnikov) had served in the Politburo or Secretariat before Gorbachev's accession. The Soviet government (as we have noted above, pp. 98–9) was reconstructed still more dramatically: only 22 of the 115 ministers elected in 1984 were still in their posts in 1989, and only ten of them were nominated to the new administration. More than 60 per cent of the Central Committee, by January 1990, had assumed their positions under the Gorbachev leadership, as had all the fourteen republican party secretaries (the Ukrainian and Moldavian first secretaries, in late 1989, were the last to go). Some of the republican party leaderships, indeed, had changed hands several times in Gorbachev's first five years of office. No less than 88 per cent of those elected to the Congress of People's Deputies, in March 1989, were entirely new to representative duties; and about the same proportion of ambassadors were Gorbachev appointees. Overall, this was probably the most extensive reconstruction of the political élite that had ever occurred in Soviet peacetime history.

Changes of this kind showed the use that could be made of one of the General Secretary's most important assets, the ability to influence the selection of leading personnel. They also showed the limitations of an approach to policy formation that confined itself to personnel changes, as national, economic and other difficulties became steadily worse as these changes were made. Moreover, even changes on this scale were insufficient to eliminate some diversity in leadership approaches to the resolution of the Soviet Union's economic and other problems. In the late 1980s at least two distinct 'camps' could be identified. For one, broadly reformist group, the problems the Soviet Union confronted could successfully be resolved only through the development of the market, political pluralism and closer, more cooperative relations between East and West. For Vadim Medvedev, for instance, a Secretariat member from 1986 and a full Politburo member from 1988, socialism was a stage in the development of civilisation that took account of the achievements of other societies, including capitalism. Within the USSR itself there should be a less exclusive emphasis upon state ownership and more scope for cooperative, leasehold and other arrangements. There must also be a place for 'commodity-money relations', in other words the market, which was a 'flexible instrument for reconciling production and consumption' that could be adapted to the needs of a wide variety of social systems.

Another convinced reformist was Alexander Yakovlev, a Secretary and full Politburo member who was probably Gorbachev's closest ally in the leadership. Yakovlev's speeches had three central themes: the necessity of the market, international affairs and, most distinctively, morality. Speaking in Vilnius in August 1988, for instance, Yakovlev devoted particular attention to 'common human interests', such as the conservation of global resources, in which both East and West could cooperate. Speaking to Moscow automobile workers in July 1989, Yakovlev argued that Marx's 'utopia' of non-commodity production had simply not justified itself. Not simply was a market the only effective mechanism for the exchange of goods and services in a largescale modern society; it was also the foundation of democracy, as it provided the economic independence that made it possible to resist any attempt to establish a dictatorship. The larger purposes of *perestroika*, however, were ethical: it must revive moral values like honesty and decency, without which man was 'merely a consumer of material values rather than a bearer and creator of spiritual values'. This, perhaps, was the most fundamental objective of the reformers: to end a system in which the population was seen as no more than an instrument of leadership policies and to create in its place a 'highly moral society of free, creatively thinking, active and independent people'.

A very different, more 'conservative' view was also evident within the leadership, particularly, during the late 1980s, in the speechs of Yegor Ligachev, Lev Zaikov and Viktor Chebrikov. For this section of the leadership the Soviet past was to be seen in a much more favourable light, while a much greater emphasis was laid upon discipline and central control as the solution to economic and other problems. Ligachev, for instance, until 1988 widely regarded as the second-ranking member of the leadership, there had been an unfortunate tendency to see the socialist construction of the 1930s as no more than a series of mistakes. On the contrary, Ligachev argued, it had seen the collectivisation of agriculture, the USSR's emergence as the world's second-largest economy and the defeat of Nazi Germany. Some of their 'class opponents', Ligachev remarked, had been hoping that *perestroika* represented a departure from socialism in favour of a market economy, ideological pluralism and Western-style democracy. On the contrary, he insisted, the USSR would never deviate from the path of Leninism or abandon the achievements of socialism. Interviewed by a weekly paper in 1989, Ligachev added that private property and unemployment would lead to social dislocation and political instability; nor could there be more than a single party in a multinational state like the USSR.

Chebrikov, at this time KGB chairman, made a still more pointed speech in 1987 in which he declared that Western intelligence services were attempting to subvert Soviet youth and to sow the seeds of nationalist discontent, hoping in this way to undermine socialism morally and politically and to inculcate political pluralism (Gorbachev, by contrast, had spoken in favour of 'socialist pluralism' at a meeting with French public figures the same month). Socialist democracy and discipline, Chebrikov went on, were inextricably connected; so too were citizens' rights and their obligations. It must above all be clear that *perestroika* was taking place under the party's auspices and that it would be conducted within the framework of socialism. Chebrikov was particularly hostile towards the informal political associations that were coming into existence in the USSR, accusing them, in a speech in February 1989, of instigating 'anarchy' and in some cases of 'attempting to create political structures opposed to the CPSU'. Another 'conservative', Lev Zaikov, joined the Secretariat in 1985 and the Politburo in 1987. Zaikov, speaking in 1989, was particularly hostile to the idea of a multiparty system, and he attacked 'leftist demagogues and ambitious layabouts' who were really 'saboteurs of *perestroika*'.

The personnel that were associated with positions such as these were obviously subject to change: Ligachev, for instance, was effectively demoted to the agricultural portfolio in 1988, and Chebrikov left the Politburo altogether in 1989. Their views did however serve to indicate that Gorbachev's Politburo, despite five years of often far-reaching changes, remained a broadly based coalition of interest in which the General Secretary had a dominant but clearly not unchallenged voice. This, in turn, related to the manner in which the party leadership had become more representative of the various interests of a complex and heterogeneous society. Stalin, in 1952, had plucked a list of members of the new Politburo out of his pocket. Gorbachev or any other Soviet leader, at the outset of the 1990s, had to recognise that Politburo membership was less exclusively within his gift and that there was probably no alternative to a certain diversity of opinion within the party's leading institutions, reflecting very different approaches throughout the wider society to the problems by which it was confronted. The establishment of a powerful executive presidency in March 1990, elected by the Congress of People's Deputies in the first instance but then by the Soviet people as a whole, suggested the possibility of a further and more fundamental change: a transition from a leadership based within a single ruling party to one that drew its democratic mandate directly from the people through a competitive election.

Leaders in Eastern Europe

The role of leadership in Central and Eastern Europe has long had rather particular characteristics, and some of these pre-date communism. Essentially, these concern the relationship that exists between the personality of the leader and the weight of the office itself. By and large, in the region the political tradition allowed for, even encouraged, the emergence of leaders who transcended politics, the institutional framework and the rules that went with them. In many respects this resembled charismatic leadership or, at any rate, leadership that enjoyed a degree of charismatic legitimation. Regardless of the means that a particular leader used to reach the top, whether it was by election or referendum or coup d'état, once he had consolidated his power and established his authority, he and his strategies tended to be beyond criticism. There is more than one element in this that resembled the legacy of traditional kingship. The leader, once he had moved on to become ruler, was open to questioning only if his power was seriously eroded.

Two examples illustrate this phenomenon. In the precommunist period, Marshal Piłudski in Poland seized power by a coup d'état in 1926 and until his death, his authority was by and large not in question. Piłudski enjoyed enormous prestige, *de facto* as 'Father of the Country' even before he launched his takeover, because of the role he had played in bringing about the liberation of Poland, so that when the Polish parliament, the Sejm, virtually collapsed into warring factions in the 1920s, many were relieved that he had decided to put an end to political chaos and impose a semi-authoritarian régime. Piłudski did not seek to establish a totalitarian system, but civil liberties were curbed, political activity was restricted and the basic freedoms curtailed. No one seriously questioned the

Marshal's authority during his lifetime. His successors, the so-called Colonels, had far greater difficulty in emulating his authority and hence legitimacy.

Piłsudski's position was very largely matched by another Marshal, Josip Broz Tito, who ruled as the unchallenged ruler of Yugoslavia for well over three decades. Like Piłsudski, Tito gained the initial boost to his authority from his success as the wartime leader and then went on to consolidate this power into enormous personal prestige and authority. By the time of his death in 1980, Tito towered over Yugoslavia like a colossus. He was entirely above and outside politics and whatever he said, went. His formal, institutional position was quite irrelevant, for his authority and legitimacy were charismatic. To an extent, of course, they were also traditional, in as much as during his lifetime much of the population of the country looked towards some kind of a traditional authority figure as a focus, just as they had looked to the king before the war.

The political system that Tito put together was very much tailored to his personal requirements. Being a convinced communist, always on the left of the spectrum, Tito believed that nationalism and nationhood were minor issues that could be resolved by giving nations cultural autonomy and the sting would be drawn by ensuring equal economic development. Hence any manifestation of nationalism could be eliminated by his personal intervention. This worked while he was alive, notably in the resolution of the Croatian crisis of 1971-2, but Tito's attempt to pass his authority in this matter to the armed forces, by nominating them to be the guardians of 'brotherhood and unity', i.e. the country's integrity, failed. The armed forces lacked the authority and could not inherit Tito's. That ultimately has always been the problem with the personalised nature of leadership authority in these authoritarian systems – the leader's authority cannot be transmitted to his heirs.

Other leadership styles varied greatly from János Kádár's subdued, almost anti-personality cult to Nicolae Ceauşescu's unbelievable hyperbolic excesses. Kádár developed a very sophisticated form and style of leadership, which reflected his particular concerns and objectives. His two key formative experiences had been Rákosi's Stalinist cult of personality in the 1950s and the 1956 revolution. From the former, he concluded that those hyperbolic styles of leadership served no useful purpose, indeed that they were immoral, for they masked the viciousness and cruelty of the system and reduced the effectiveness of the leader by isolating him from the population.

The revolution taught Kádár a very different lesson, namely that it was dangerous to entrust the people with political power, for they would use it against the interests of communism. Hence he adopted an understated, human style, which emphasised that he had no numinous or charismatic qualities, that there was nothing particularly political about leadership, that he happened to be a man-in-the-street entrusted with running the country as if by accident. Kádár's style was quite effective as long as the rest of the system was functioning. It deflected attention from politics and diffused responsibility. It also made it harder for Hungary to construct leadership styles that were more appropriate to the new conditions after the transformation.

This was perhaps the only factor that was shared between the Ceauşescu and the Kádár styles – their after-effects. Otherwise the purpose and characteristics of the Ceauşescu style could not have been more different. Where Kádár was concerned to project a human, even workaday image, Ceauşescu went in for heightening the superhuman, even godlike effect that he was generating. Indeed, on one occasion he was actually described in public as 'a god'. Ceauşescu made speeches about any and every topic, travelled the world with great panoply, posed as a world leader, had himself depicted with some of the regalia of kingship (sash, sceptre) and generally created an image that signalled that he and he alone was the font of power, authority, knowledge and wisdom. The antecedents of the Ceauşescu cult are to be sought in two sources – the Byzantine court and its reflections in the Wallachian and Moldavian courts in the early modern period and, equally, in Stalin.

The purpose of the Ceauşescu cult was to secure his power and, at the same time, to provide a focus for the Romanian population that had to endure the privations resulting from his overheated industrialisation drive. In his endeavours,

Ceauşescu was flanked by the Ceauşescu dynasty, up to four dozen of his and his wife's extended family, who were placed in various positions of influence and power as, presumably, the most reliable persons. The Ceauşescu style included dynastic ambitions for his wife Elena and for his son Nicu, who was clearly being groomed to succeed Ceauşescu himself. The problem for Ceauşescu was that by concentrating all human activity in himself, he also became accountable for matters when things did not work. However, under the Ceauşescu cult this was impossible – after all, semi-divine leaders are not called to account for their responsibilities. Consequently whenever this difficulty arose, Ceauşescu was forced to rely on a time-honoured device, to put the blame on 'others', subordinates who had failed to carry out his purportedly impeccable directives or foreigners who were conspiring against Romania.

The legacy of the Ceauşescu cult was one of devastation. Whereas in modern political systems, the chains of command include some degree of responsibility for subordinates and measure of routine, this was absent in the completely arbitrary Ceauşescu strategy, where the leader – he used the title 'conducător', which had been used before him by Romania's wartime pro-Nazi leader Marshal Antonescu – would intervene unpredictably and without warning, to disrupt the work of his subordinates. Nor was anybody ever able to acquire knowledge of a particular area of political work. Ceauşescu recognised the potential danger to his power if an individual was left in the same place for too long, where he could build up a coterie of local power, so he employed the device of continuous rotation. Individuals were shifted from post to post after very short spells. This left the Romanian administration bewildered and bred incompetence. The post-Ceauşescu leadership in Romania had severe problems in establishing any kind of authority at all, not surprisingly seeing the widespread suspicion of anyone who claimed to exercise power.

These leadership cults and styles all had a similar purpose – to entrench the leader's authority, to signal that no challenger could possibly hope to succeed and thereby ensure the leader an untroubled period of rule and to provide stability. By placing the leader above politics, these cults were aimed at providing them with a kind of surrogate legitimacy, something that eluded these rulers as long as their power was personal and could not be institutionally anchored. These leaderships were, indeed, reasonably securely grounded after the usual initial period of consolidation, when the new leader removed those loyal to his predecessor from positions of power further down the hierarchy. Thereafter it was only at times of succession that the system was unstable or potentially so.

The legacy of these authoritarian leadership systems was evident in the transition to democracy. In any system, periods of upheaval are made easier to tolerate when the bulk of society can use an individual as a focus for their anxieties. This person, if he has the authority, can play a major role in acting as the symbol of continuity and providing a semblance of meaning during an otherwise chaotic time. The leader, then, becomes the embodiment of people's trust and faith that their interests will be heeded and that the change is in some ways controlled.

This stabilising role is particularly significant during a time when an authoritarian élite is giving way to a new order. The leader in this situation is the guarantee to the representatives of the ancien régime that the new system will not liquidate them, but that they will find a niche in the new system. Hence the leader in question has a highly delicate role – he must be able to satisfy two entirely disparate constituencies, the population which is looking for order and the former members of the élite who are looking for security. To make matters more complicated, in the transition he must play both the roles of charismatic leader and democrat, although the two are barely compatible. He must have legitimation in the eyes of both the old, sinking order and the new rising one, in other words. This implies that he must have come to the fore through the legitimating mechanisms of the ancien régime, but have acquired a degree of popular acceptability in order to secure his authority in the new.

To these factors must also be added the deep-seated suspicions of all politicians and the rejection of politics as such in politically significant sections of the population. The *apparat* will tend to regard any figure of this kind as the liquidator of the system and will give the person only grudging support, as the least bad option, the best chance of salvaging something from the debacle. The hitherto disenfranchised population, on the other hand, will tend to view all politicians as cynical opportunists on the make and concerned solely with lining their own pockets. It is a short step from this to regard all political activity as suspect, as parasitical on the honest endeavours of the people. These populist views, sometimes held very strongly, have deep roots in Central and Eastern Europe. Finally, the transitional leader must also be prepared to give way gracefully once democratically elected personages have emerged through proper institutional procedures.

The experience of Central and Eastern Europe in 1989–90 provided several illustrations of these propositions. In Poland, General Jaruzelski successfully wrote himself a major role in the script, by having provision made under the Round Table Agreement of 1989 for a relatively strong presidency. The parliamentary elections, in which the communists suffered a humiliating rout, nearly undid his calculations and the terms of the Agreement, for he was elected to office only through the joint vote of the two houses of the Polish parliament by the skin of his teeth. Some of the Solidarity representatives were encouraged to vote for him after the satellite party deputies declined to do so. Thereafter, he played his part in controlling the *apparat* and overseeing the transition.

In Czechoslovakia, the new interim president was Václav Havel, who was elected to this post five weeks after the beginning of the country's transformation by the so-called 'gentle revolution'. Havel had played a major role as one of the leading figures in Czechoslovakia's democratic opposition and had been in prison several times. He had built up enormous moral capital as a result and was entirely acceptable to the population. However, he was rather less welcome to the *apparat*, which at first went to considerable lengths to prevent his election and subsequently campaigned against him in order to undermine his strategy. Thus his decision to go to West and East Germany as the first foreign countries to be visited as president and then to offer an apology for the expulsion of the Sudeten German minority after the war was greeted with a clamorous campaign of denunciation by the communists.

In many respects, Havel was the ideal interim leader. He

was elected by a procedure that was acceptable as democratic, by a Federal Assembly that, while no longer reflecting the political situation in the country, was at least the constitutional form that was supposed to elect the president. Equally, he enjoyed universal recognition abroad and was an instantly acceptable negotiating partner throughout the world. This gave him an international authority that no other Central and Eastern European leader could claim.

In Hungary, the attempt by Imre Pozsgay to play the role of transitional leader and have himself elected president was undermined by the Free Democrats. Pozsgay had been pivotal in helping to shift the communist party in the direction of accepting change – indeed, he was accused by many of having been its liquidator – but his unconcealed ambition to become Hungary's first democratically elected president since 1946 aroused the suspicions of a section of the opposition. They argued that Pozsgay, far from being a healer of the wounds of Hungarian society, was in reality seeking to salvage communist power. They collected enough signatures for parliament to be obliged to hold a referendum and in the referendum they gained a small majority for the proposition that the president be elected by parliament, after the general election, rather than directly. There was little chance of the new parliament voting for Pozsgay. In this case, popular suspicions had their part in undermining Pozsgay's campaign.

In general, the issue of leadership was an influential factor both in the communist political structure and in what followed. The results of the particular styles of leadership cults used in the communist system were evidently likely to impact on the way in which leadership was viewed in the new order. In particular, there was unrelenting public pressure that leaders must derive their power from election through orderly procedures and that they should not 'emerge' or 'be parachuted' in from above. Arguably, this was one of the problems faced by the post-Ceauşescu leadership in Romania that claimed legitimation from the revolution, but did not find its claim accepted. In the longer term, however, elected leaders in Central and Eastern Europe were liable to find themselves with the same types of power and authority that were characteristic of Western polities.

The leadership in China

The most striking feature of leadership in the PRC has been the dominance of the system by a paramount individual. From 1949 until his death in 1976, Mao dominated the party and state leadership through a combination of political cunning and ruthlessness when necessary. After a brief interregnum, Deng Xiaoping has dominated the leadership from 1978 until the present. Thus, policies in all spheres bear the hallmark of these two individuals. Despite the CCP's formal emphasis on the norms of democratic centralism and the post-Mao stress on the need for institutionalisation, it is clear that the party has not devised an enduring mechanism for regulating leadership debate or for dealing with leadership succession.

A completely Mao-centred approach to Chinese politics leaves many gaps in one's knowledge of the workings of the political process, but Mao's role cannot be ignored. It is ironic that although Mao played a crucial role in devising the 'rules of the game' in China, it was he who was instrumental in causing a breakdown of these rules when he resorted to alternate channels of communication and a more personalised form of politics. Despite constraints on his leadership, such as objective economic conditions (which in part caused his retreat from the Great Leap Forward) and organisational factors (such as the huge bureaucracy over which he presided) Mao, except for short spells, never lost his ability to initiate policy and break policy deadlock.

While Mao may have invoked the need for party discipline to make opponents follow his line, he saw no such need to submit himself to restrictions of this kind. If he found opposition to his policies within the party, rather than trying to accept the majority point of view he would turn to other forces outside the party for support. While the Cultural Revolution is the most extreme example of this, there have been other occasions when Mao appealed over the heads of his fellow party leaders. For example, in 1955 he appealed to the peasantry to speed up the pace of collectivisation of agriculture after the party had forced him to tone down his original proposals. However, there are examples to be found where the power to initiate policy was out of Mao's hands as, for example, at the Lushan plenum of 1959, when Peng Dehuai's attacks on the disasters brought about by the Great Leap Forward caused Mao to beat a strategic retreat.

Individuals and relations with powerful individuals are decisive throughout the Chinese political system and society. Most Chinese recognise very early on that the best way to survive and flourish is to develop personal relationships (*guanxi*) linking oneself to a powerful political patron. Thus, the Chinese political leadership is riddled with networks of personal relationships and is dominated by patron–client ties. This system of patron–client ties lends itself easily to the formation of factions within the leadership. The basis of such factions are shared trusts and loyalties dating back decades. Obviously the process of faction formation also relates to institutional and regional interests. However, the nature of these personal ties makes it difficult to identify such institutional or regional interests clearly. The venom with which an individual is denounced is often difficult to understand unless one knows that person's history and relationships. Similarly, on occasion an individual may be attacked as a surrogate for a top leader who is the head of one of the rival patronage systems.

This over-dependence on personal relationships makes the Chinese political leadership extremely unstable. Despite the impressive appearance of the CCP as an enduring organisation, it is, in fact, vulnerable to very rapid breakdown. When disputes break out among the leaders of the factions and patron–client networks, this has ramifications throughout the system often leading to large-scale purges of personnel who are deemed to have supported the 'wrong line'. These purges are accompanied by campaigns against particular individuals or groups or individuals who have deceived party members and the masses and led the party away from its correct line. Rather than reasoned debate of policy faults, the most common form of attack is to dole out personal abuse.

The response of the leadership to the student demonstrations of mid-1989 showed how this system of individual power relationships, built up over decades, remained far more important than the rule of law and the formal functions people held. Further, the events highlighted how in the absence of institutional mechanisms for accommodating serious divisions, the system still desperately needs a Mao-like figure to perform the role of final arbiter in policy disputes. Increasingly, Deng Xiaoping has slipped into the same pattern of personalised rule as Mao. This tendency was noticed not only by the democracy wall activists of the late 1970s and the student demonstrators of the late 1980s but also by his opponents at the top of the party. The orthodox economist, Chen Yun, rebuked Deng for abandoning the notion of collective leadership that had been agreed on in the late 1970s. Chen warned Deng not to set himself up as an Emperor by avoiding listening to the views of others. Such criticism notwithstanding, a secret party decision was taken in 1987 that all important matters had to be referred to Deng for his approval.

The pivotal role of Deng explains the resort again to the cult of personality after the crushing of the student movement in mid-1989 in order to restore his shattered prestige and to attempt to extricate him from the party's factional fighting in which he had become too closely embroiled.

Finally, the events highlighted again the incapability of the system to deal with succession. The inability to institutionalise policy debate and succession suggests another debilitating struggle upon Deng's death. There is no-one among the present leadership who has either the prestige or the necessary connections to take over Deng's role.

To date, the method for succession has been anointment by the paramount leader. Deng Xiaoping's attempts to boost the position of current General Secretary, Jiang Zemin, as his successor is merely the latest in a series of attempts to ensure that a successor is in place before the paramount leader dies. In May and June 1989, comments of Deng's were circulated within the party stating that Jiang was to be considered 'the core' of the party's 'third generation of leadership', Mao having led the first and Deng the second. However, so far all attempts to manage succession by transferring legitimacy from the paramount leader to a chosen disciple have failed. For example, Mao's hand-picked successor Lin Biao died in 1971 in an air crash after having supposedly launched a *coup d'état* against Mao. Hua Guofeng's attempts to tie his legitimacy to rule to the view of himself as Mao's hand-chosen successor failed as Mao's legacy came under attack from Deng Xiaoping and his supporters. Deng Xiaoping has proved no more successful than Mao in the process of naming successors. His first two proteges, Hu Yaobang and Zhao Ziyang, were both dismissed from their posts, ostensibly for being too liberal in their reactions to student demonstrations.

Clearly, such legitimacy is not transferable from the paramount leader to his chosen successor. Further, the dependency on the patronage of one individual places constraints on the capacity to develop an independent power base. The successors cannot stray too far from the policies and networks of the patron for fear of being denounced as traitors who have betrayed the trust place in them. Thus, Hua Guofeng, who was catapulted from relative obscurity, did not have the time to construct the kind of power base that his rival Deng Xiaoping had built up during years of pre- and post-liberation struggle. While Hu Yaobang appealed privately to Deng on a number of occasions to retire, thus opening up the way for Hu fully to consolidate his power, Zhao Ziyang pursued his claims by taking Deng's retirement for granted. Yet the attempts to develop their own policy positions and networks of support that would survive Deng's death brought them into conflict with their patron. As discussed below, of vital importance was the inability of either Hu or Zhao to find acceptance with members of the powerful Central Military Affairs Commission. The same problem of establishing an independent power base now faces Deng's third choice, Jiang Zemin.

China's current leadership

Naturally, beyond the supreme leader at anyone time, there are a number of other individuals that make up China's power elite. This power élite comprises about 40 individuals who possess power through individual prestige, their relationship to the top leader or because of the interests they represent within the system. This select group of individuals comprises the membership of the Politburo, its Standing Committee, the Central Secretariat, the Standing Committee of the State Council, the Central Military Affairs Commission and, last but not least, the Standing Committee of the Central Advisory Commission (See Table 5.2).

TABLE 5.2

China's central leadership

(a) Politburo and its Standing Committee

Jiang Zemin	(SC)	Li Peng	(SC)
Qiao Shi	(SC)	Yao Yilin	(SC)
Song Ping	(SC)	Li Ruihan	(SC)
Wan Li		Tian Jiyun	
Li Tieying		Li Ximing	
Yang Rudai		Yang Shangkun	
Wu Xueqian		Qin Qiwei	

Alternate: Ding Guan'gen

((SC) – member of the Standing Committee)

(b) Secretariat

Jiang Zemin (General Secretary)   Ding Guan'gen
Li Ruihan   Qiao Shi
Alternate: Wen Jiabao

(c) Standing Committee of the State Council

Premier: Li Peng
Vice-Premiers: Yao Yilin, Tian Jiyun, Wu Xueqian
Councillors: Li Tieying, Qin Qiwei, Wang Bingqian, Song Jian, Wang Fang, Zou Jiahua, Li Guixian, Chen Xitong, Chen Junsheng (also Secretary General)

(d) Central Military Affairs Committee

Chairman: Deng Xiaoping
Permanent Vice-Chairman and Secretary General: Yang Shangkun
Deputy Secretary Generals: Hong Xuezhi, Liu Huaqing

(e) Standing Committee of the Central Advisory Commission

Chairman: Chen Yun
Vice-Chairman: Bo Yibo, Song Renqiong
Standing Committee:

Wang Ping	Wu Xiuquan	Jiang Hua
Li Desheng	Xiao Ke	Zhang Jingfu
Lu Dingyi	Chen Pixian	Hu Qiaomu
Geng Biao	Huang Hua	Kang Shien
Wang Shoudao	Liu Lantao	Li Yiming
Yang Dezhi	Yu Qiuli	Song Shilun
Zhang Aiping	Chen Xilian	Duan Junyi
Ji Pengfei	Huang Zhen	Cheng Zihua

On 23 and 24 June 1989, the Fourth Plenum of the Thirteenth Central Committee met in Beijing to congratulate the party for crushing a 'counter-revolutionary rebellion' and to make a number of key personnel changes. The meeting was attended by 170 members and 106 alternates. More interesting was the fact that 184 members of the Central Advisory Commission attended as observers. The reformers Zhao Ziyang and Hu Qili were dismissed from their positions in the Standing Committee of the Politburo, the Politburo and the Central Committee. Jiang Zemin was elected to replace Zhao as General Secretary. It should be noted that this was after Deng Xiaoping had already told senior party leaders that Jiang was the core of the third generation of leaders. Together with Jiang, Li Ruihan and Song Ping were also appointed to the Standing Committee to join the orthodox Premier, Li Peng, the conservative economic planner, Yao Yilin, and the head of the security forces Qiao Shi.

The choice of Jiang was a surprise to outsiders. Yet it was important in two respects. First, Jiang was someone not associated with the bloodshed in Beijing and, furthermore, was someone who, as Shanghai party boss, had handled the situation there without loss of life. Secondly, his appointment together with the promotion of Tianjin's Mayor and Party Secretary, Li Ruihan, showed Deng's commitment to salvage something from the economic reforms. The choice of leaders from two of China's major urban centres indicated that Zhao Ziyang's awareness that the future lay with the cities had not been entirely forgotten.

The decision that there had been a counter-revolutionary movement meant that a search had to be launched to find the 'handful of conspirators' who had launched it. They were not hard for the leadership to find – Zhao Ziyang and his coterie of close supporters. While Zhao retained his party membership at the plenum thus suggesting residual support, he was accused of committing the 'mistakes of supporting the disturbances and splitting the party' at a time of 'life-or-death crisis for the party and state'. Zhao was said to bear an 'unshirkable responsibility for the formation and development of the disturbances'. Following the plenum, a major campaign was launched to blame Zhao not only for the disturbances but also for all the problems with the reforms over the past few years.

The balance of power within the Standing Committee has clearly shifted in favour of the orthodox faction in the top leadership. Previously the committee had two mild reformers, Zhao Ziyang and Hu Qili; two orthodox pro-central planners, Li Peng and Yao Yilin; and Qiao Shi, who has tended to follow the prevailing majority without letting any personal opinions become known. The present Standing Committee is dominated by the orthodox viewpoint. Only Li Ruihan could claim to have genuine pro-reform credentials, and even he has been forced to mute his comments. Yao Yilin and Li Peng remain and are joined by Song Ping, a close supporter of Chen Yun. Song runs the organisation department of the party, thus ensuring that the party's power of appointment through the *nomenklatura* system remains in safe hands. Jiang Zemin, although favouring limited economic reform while running Shanghai, has shown himself to be a vehement opponent of any consequent political change. Indeed, it is rumoured that when Jiang was appointed to run Shanghai in 1985, it was at the request of Chen Yun. This fact helps explain why the more radical economic reforms were slow to get off the ground in Shanghai.

Yet, all the members of the Standing Committee have very little room for manoeuvre because of their dependence on the patronage of the veteran revolutionaries. The only member who is not so directly tied to this group is Li Ruihan, who as Mayor of Tianjin has established better credentials in the eyes of the reformers. Their ties to the patronage of the veterans makes it difficult for them to establish their own power base which could be used to support them in any forthcoming power struggle. This suggests very strongly that this current formal leadership is a transitional one. The real struggle for succession will begin when the veterans die. Further, their dependence on the patronage of the veteran revolutionaries means that the current leadership has become frozen. Those concerned are unwilling to take risks or launch new initiatives to deal with China's problems; policy, accordingly, has tended to fluctuate between a general drift and periods of tightening up to reassert conformity.

Beyond their patron–client relationships, the party veterans have an institutional base of support in the Central Advisory Commission. Through this body they have been able to wield major influence behind the scenes. The Commission was originally set up in 1982 in an attempt to relieve aged officials of their posts. It was referred to as a 'temporary expedient' until a proper system of retirement for cadres was introduced. However, the Commission has shown no signs of fading away and its Standing Committee has become an alternative power centre to the Politburo's Standing Committee. Members of this Commission played the key role in the ouster of both Hu Yaobang and Zhao Ziyang from the post of General Secretary. Having experienced the taste of political battle once again in 1989, Song Renqiong, the Deputy Chairman of the Advisory Commission, clearly showed the intention of these veterans to become more involved in the daily work of deciding policy when he re-emphasised the fact that members of the Commission's Standing Committee had the right to attend Politburo meetings.

The events of June 1989 showed that control of the People's Liberation Army is still the vital factor in Chinese politics. Its institutional support, in particular, is crucial for any aspiring leader. It showed that, despite the attempts to shift the army's focus to acting as a professional standing army, senior party leaders still depend on party members in the army to use it as a coercive force in political power struggles and over questions of succession.

Indeed, the question of succession to Deng Xiaoping will first become evident in the struggle over who should succeed him as chairman of the Central Military Affairs Commission, the only formal leadership post which Deng retains. The Commission has existed under one name or the other since 1931 when it was established on the instructions of the First All-China Congress of Soviets. Deng has recognised that control of this commission through its Chairmanship is a vital pawn in the game of consolidating power. In fact, Deng tried to ensure that Hu Yaobang would succeed him, and after Hu's fall Deng tried to force Zhao Ziyang on the Commission. Zhao was duly appointed first vice-Chairman in May 1988 but Deng's attempts to have him take over the Chairmanship were resisted by other members of the Commission such as China's President, Yang Shangkun, who serves on the Commission as permanent vice-Chairman. Despite the cutback in political influence of the military during the last decade, senior army leaders refused to let the military come under genuine civilian control. They blocked the attempt to bring it under a new commission that would be responsible to the National People's Congress, leaving it in the farcical situation of being run by two identical commissions, one under the state and the other under the party. Similarly, by refusing to accept either Hu or Zhao the Commission forced a change in the Party Constitution in October 1987 when Deng retired from the Politburo to enable him to keep his position as Chairman of the Military Commission.

If Deng really wishes Jiang Zemin to become the core of the third generation of leaders, he must try to ensure that Jiang takes over the Chairmanship of the Military Commission. However, this attempt will meet considerable resistance not the least because it is a post which Yang Shangkun seems to covet for himself. Further, Jiang has not been involved in military work in the past and thus suffers from the same weakness as Hu and Zhao before him. The genuine military members of the Commission are unlikely to accept him.

Despite the power that the orthodox leaders wield through their patronage of spokesmen in the Standing Committee of the Politburo, their capacity for action is limited by passive reaction further down the party system. While they can still use their prestige for short-range activities such as the ouster of a General Secretary, it has yet to be shown whether they can sustain the momentum over a longer-term campaign. The events of mid-1989 have shown not only that the party has lost the trust of large sectors of the urban population, but also that it is seriously divided internally. It should not be forgotten that many of the students who demonstrated were children of well-placed party members. Some party members will have lost family members or will know of friends who have lost relatives. The brutality of the repression must have shocked even some of the current leadership's supporters and it seems many of them were kept deliberately in the dark. Further, it must be remembered that when Beijing's citizens came out on to the streets to support the students, many of them were party members. This suggests that over the longer term there may be support for further experimentation with reform.

There have already emerged differences about the scale of the purge that is necessary to weed out the influence of Zhao Ziyang in the party. It appears that Deng Xiaoping has called for a two-year moratorium on the political issues while the party tries to restore its battered image by giving China's citizens a taste of economic success. By contrast, others have called for a full-scale purge of Zhao's supporters throughout the system. Clearly, they fear that the strong residual support for Zhao within the party might be used to support a comeback after Deng and other key veteran leaders die. Comments in August 1989 by Li Peng, Jiang Zemin and Song Ping on the 'shocking' state of affairs within the party ranks attest to the level of opposition that remains. The fact that the veterans have seen previous campaigns in the 1980s to weed out 'bourgeois elements' from the party fade away seems to have made them all the more committed to one last fling. The calls of Li, Jiang and others have an air of desperation to them and, despite the fearsome rhetoric, there are clear signs that their effects were being blunted at the lower levels of the party.

As one moves down the hierarchy it is unclear how firmly party organs stand behind the campaigns. Both the remaining Politburo and the Central Committee have a clearer pro-reform profile. Although the Politburo has lost three reformers (Hu Yaobang, Zhao Ziyang and Hu Qili), five of the remaining eight members seem to have a more pro-reform orientation. These are the Chairman of the National People's Congress, Wan Li; the Minister of National Defence, Qin Qiwei; the former Foreign Minister and current vice-Premier, Wu Xue-qian; the vice-Premier, Tian Jiyun; and the party secretary of Sichuan province, Yang Rudai. They are opposed by the head of the Education Commission, Li Tieying; the party secretary of the Beijing Municipality, Li Ximing; and State President, Yang Shangkun.

The Central Committee elected at the Thirteenth Party Congress in 1987 was thought of as Zhao's committee. A number of orthodox leaders who had been associated with previous campaigns against 'bourgeois liberalism' failed to gain election or suffered an embarrassingly low vote. The most notable victim was the orthodox ideologue, Deng Liqun. In deals struck before the congress met it had been decided that he would take the Politburo place vacated by his ally, Hu Qiaomu. However, in the elections there were 5 per cent more candidates than places to be filled. Delegates could indicate their preferences by striking out the names of those they did not wish to see elected. For the veterans to ensure that their policy preferences continue after their death they will have to orchestrate the election of a new Central Committee within a short period of time.

Future challenges to the leadership

The current Chinese leadership is extremely unstable, internally divided and has to try to rule the country without the support of key elements of its urban population and with growing problems among the peasantry. The leadership seems unable to offer any new visions of the future and its policy line can be best summed as 'back to the future'. China's orthodox leaders would like to turn the clock back to the 1950s when there was social stability, greater trust in the party as an infallible leadership organisation, solid economic growth under an essentially Soviet-style economic plan and when it was clear who were enemies and who were friends.

Importantly, the social compacts which the party had tried to conclude with society when they initiated reforms have broken down, perhaps beyond recovery. The agreement with intellectuals and students that offered them a wider freedom for intellectual debate and a greater stake in China's future began to crumble when the pro-reform General Secretary, Hu Yaobang, was dismissed in January 1987. It broke down irretrievably in June 1989, when the troops were ordered into the centre of Beijing to put down the student demonstrations. Secondly, the promises to provide the urban population with a better standard of living and a more efficient economy have foundered on the high inflation and the economic stagnation that struck in 1988 and 1989. Even if inflation can be brought under control, it is questionable to what extent the party leadership can revive the enthusiasm of the working class.

Finally, relations with the peasantry have begun to break down. Since 1985, the agricultural reforms have begun to go awry with the result that many policy practices which the peasants had been promised they had seen the back of were revived (see Chapter 6).

The party, having based its legitimacy to rule on its capability to provide a better economic future, is in severe trouble. The present attempts to revert to old-style ideological campaigns extolling the superiority of socialism over capitalism are no answer for a population that had been promised a better economic future and which was getting used to its greater political freedoms. In this atmosphere of uncertainty, a number of possibilities suggest themselves for the future of China's leadership. The most likely outcome over the coming two or three years is the continuation of the current policy line, a form of Chinese Brezhnevism with lower economic growth rates accompanied by increasing (partially hidden) inflationary tendencies and endemic corruption brought about by the distorted economic system. On the occasion of the fortieth anniversary of the founding of the PRC (October 1989), the Chinese leadership refused the chance to offer an olive branch to its own society and the international community. In his keynote speech, Jiang Zemin reaffirmed the hardline approach. He called for vigilance against what he termed the efforts by the West to subvert the Chinese government and institute capitalism. He proposed vigorous repression of any sign of dissent, economic retrenchment and increased central planning.

However, it is unlikely that such a grim picture will exist for all of China. First, despite attempts to reassert central control, the question is whether the central leadership has the capacity to do so. It is clear that the austerity measures that were introduced late in 1988 did not have the same effect in all areas and met with stiff opposition. Leaders from inland provinces asked why they should suffer from austerity when they had been under effective austerity measures for decades. They argued that the coastal regions and provinces such as Guangdong in South China should be forced to tighten their belts. Similarly, the leaders of the coastal areas and Guangdong province did not seem over-enthusiastic about the idea of retrenchment for their relatively booming economies. In this kind of situation, even if the centre can sort itself out, it will be very difficult to force policy through in all the provinces. The more relaxed economic spheres in these areas may also lead to less stringent political and ideological controls.

The pending death of the veteran revolutionaries, especially of Deng Xiaoping, seems certain to set off another round of political struggle contributing further to instability. The likelihood of a crisis arising with future succession struggles might suggest a greater role for the People's Liberation Army, and indeed some observers have sketched a scenario of a military coup. Yet, the military as an institution has shown a reluctance to become too involved again in government. Many of the military commanders remember being dragged into the political arena during the Cultural Revolution and the subsequent criticism of their role. A straightforward coup seems unlikely despite the fact that the Third World is littered with examples of the military taking power in the name of law, order and economic development.

However, the army will clearly play an important role in any succession struggle and its support will be crucial for any aspiring Secretary General. At present, the People's Liberation Army is riven by the same divides that run through the party, and this makes it difficult to act in political unison. Should it act, there is no guarantee it would be to support the orthodox party leaders. The new-style army had begun to do rather well from the reforms after the problems of adjustment and it may be concerned by too great an economic reversal. In fact, it has been the first victim of the West's economic sanctions against China. The last few years had seen a booming arms trade and the idea of China as a bulwark against Soviet aggression in the Far East meant that it acquired the kind of high-level military technology denied to other socialist countries. Thus, the military might push for a return to some, if not all, of the aspects of Zhao's reform programme.

The problems for the leadership are further compounded by Deng's desire to continue with the economic reforms. Here a dilemma arises. Continued reforms in the economic sphere will bring with them the same political problems that the current leadership has refused to come to terms with. China's current leaders share the views of the nineteenth century reformers. Both groups see technology as essentially neutral and as something that can be grafted on to any socio-economic system. They refuse to see the link between technology and the socio-economic matrix that has produced it. Ironically, they have the un-Marxist view that change in the economic base does not imply change in the political super-structure. Their idea that the social and political implications of the economic programme can be stopped by launching campaigns of ideological education is in fact a non-starter. Sooner or later, the party will have to come to terms with the implications of its own desire for economic growth. Unless it can come to terms with this swiftly and in a manner that creates a real forum for dialogue between the different interests in Chinese society, the party risks being swept away by a further round of social unrest. Its only alternative would be further warfare on its own people.

The final possibility, which seems the most unlikely over the short term but the most probable over the longer term, is a return to wider-ranging reforms under a new General Secretary or even under a restored Zhao Ziyang. This would lead China further down the path pursued by Gorbachev in the Soviet Union and in Eastern Europe where a serious attempt is being made to negotiate with civil society rather than to deny its existence and repress any manifestations of it as signs of 'counter-revolutionary' activity. As has been noted above, considerable residual support remains in the party for further experimentation with reform and clearly China's urban society is pitted against the current policy direction. Even powerful sections of the military might support the return to Zhao. We know that Defence Minister, Qin Qiwei, was sympathetic to what Zhao was trying to do. Such figures might see the return of Zhao as the best way to restore the army's shattered reputation among the people. Support of Zhao's return would almost certainly be accompanied by the denunciation of Li Peng's and Yang Shangkun's 'wicked use' of the military to pursue their own ends when suppressing the student movement in June 1989.

Further reading

There are several general studies of communist political
leadership, among them Rush (1975), which focuses on
leadership succession, and McCauley and Carter (1986),
which deals with leadership turnover and policy formation in
the Soviet Union, Eastern Europe and China. A more recent
symposium on leadership change in communist systems has
been edited by Ray Taras (1989).

On the Soviet Union particularly, the process of leadership
change has been examined in a symposium edited by Archie
Brown (1989). Biographies of Gorbachev include Medvedev
(1988); see also Schmidt-Hauer (1986). There are several
useful symposia on the process of change under Gorbachev,
including McCauley (1987) and (1990), Hill and Dellenbrant
(1989), Bloomfield (1989) and Joyce *et al.* (1989). The fullest
available study of the Gorbachev administration to date is
White (1990a), from which some of the material in this
chapter has been drawn. Gorbachev's articles and speeches
are available in several convenient editions; his bestselling
book *Perestroika* (1987) is available in most languages. On the
Politburo more particularly, see Shevchenko (1985), an in-
sider's account, and Löwenhardt (1982), an academic study.
On Eastern Europe see the more general works listed earlier.

For an excellent study of the factional basis of Chinese
politics see Pye (1981). Teiwes (1984) provides an interesting
view of questions of leadership and legitimacy. For an assessment of Mao's role in the political system see Wilson (1977).
For Jiang Zemin's fortieth anniversary review of policy see
Jiang Zemin (1989). Christiansen (1989) looks at the events of
1989 in terms of the political bargaining machine.

6

The Policy Process

Until relatively recently it was not generally believed that the communist states possessed anything that could properly be called a 'policy process'. The ruling communist parties, it was believed, simply issued decisions which were then handed over for implementation to the various subordinate bureaucracies – governmental, social and cultural, and economic. Party decisions were binding in all matters of this kind, and they were held to reflect the influence of ideology or of power politics within the leadership, but not, as in a Western country, of individuals or groups outside the leadership or of the institutions responsible for implementing the policies on which the leadership had decided. These institutions, after all, were staffed by communist party members, usually on the advice of the relevant party committee, and there was no shortage of sanctions, from the secret police to the threat of loss of employment, to make sure that they complied with the party's directives. Policies, moreover, were believed to be relatively simple, the overriding priority being the highest possible rate of economic growth and more particularly of heavy industry. This was clearly close to the view of communist politics held by those who adhered to the totalitarian approach, with its emphasis on party dominance. Modernisation theorists and many others, however, also accepted most of the assumptions of this 'directed society' image of the communist states, the central element in which was a small, monolithic and monopolistic party directing all aspects of society with little reference to the views and wishes of its members.

Most writers on communist politics would probably accept that there is still a substantial amount of truth in such a characterisation, and that there are important distinctions to be drawn between authoritarian forms of politics, such as those that exist in the communist and postcommunist states, and the forms of politics that are to be found in the Western liberal democracies. It has become apparent in recent years, however, that the 'directed society' image is, and perhaps always was, too simple. The leadership, it emerged, was often unsure of its priorities, or even divided into rival factions. The government and other bureaucracies, moreover, were certainly staffed by party nominees, but it turned out that they often argued with the party in the interests of their own area or institution and did not simply implement whatever the party might propose. Party policies, in any case, were becoming increasingly complex and difficult to reconcile with each other, leaving a good deal of scope for the *de facto* selection of priorities by lower-level officials and various other forms of evasion of central control, and for specialist advice and influence. Major social institutions, such as the trade unions and the military, also turned out to have particular interests to defend, and even the public at large was not powerless – it could refuse to buy what was produced or to go where labour was required, and if its wishes were ignored it could engage in various forms of protest or direct action.

Even in the USSR in the Stalin period, it has become clear, economic and other policies were not unaffected by the special pleading of ministries and other bodies and by personal factions and followings. In the post-Stalin period the role of group and bureaucratic politics has become increasingly apparent, and few would now accept the adequacy of a view of the policy process in the communist states which failed to take account of the numerous and conflicting pressures upon the central leadership as well as of the considerable resources available to the central leadership in its efforts to ensure the implementation of its own priorities. A good deal of debate has taken place about the applicability of terms such as 'interest group' to the forms in which political pressures of this kind are exerted in the communist states, and about the extent to which terms such as 'bureaucratic' or 'institutional plural-ism' can be applied to their political systems more generally. Clearly, potential interest groups have far less ability to organise and to take action than their counterparts in the liberal democracies, and a few scholars would go so far as to suggest that terms such as 'pluralism' can usefully be applied to a political system in which the authority of the communist party is ultimately unchallengeable and in which individuals and groups lack most of the means by which governments elsewhere can (at least theoretically) be held in check, such as an independent judiciary, a free press and competitive elections. And yet a view of the policy process in the communist states which left out the role of bureaucratic and group interests and of popular pressures would, at least in the early 1990s, be seriously incomplete and misleading. In this chapter we shall look at three different examples of the ways in which interests and policies interact in the communist and postcommunist states, devoting particular attention to the process of economic management and reform which, in virtually all the states concerned, was the most important item on the policy agenda.

The USSR: the politics of the command economy

The management and performance of the economy is a central issue in any political system, particularly so in the case of a communist political system in which there are as a rule no private entrepreneurs and in which most of the economic activity of the society takes place in publicly-owned enterprises under the direct supervision of the government. The economy, moreover, is perhaps for most writers the sphere of communist politics to which the 'directed society' image most obviously applies. Unlike Western societies, in which individual firms more or less autonomously decide what to produce, how to produce it, to whom to sell their produce and at what price, in the communist world it is commonly supposed that all matters of this kind are decided by the government by means of a comprehensive economic plan drawn up by the centre and then undeviatingly implemented. An economy of this kind is often described as a 'command', or at least as an 'administered' or 'managed economy'; it is an economy, in other words, in which the government directs most areas of economic life in accordance with its political priorities, rather than leaving them, as Western governments supposedly do, to be determined by the free play of self-regulating market forces. The management of economic activity is therefore not only a central area of policy-making in the communist states; it is also a particularly promising arena in which to consider the extent to which central directives are influenced, resisted, modified or even challenged by individuals, groups and institutions within and outside government and the implications that this has for the 'directed society' image of the policy process in these states more generally.

The Soviet planning process

It should first of all be noted that there is no necessary connection between communist rule and a centrally-planned economy. In the Soviet Union after the revolution a variety of forms of economic management were adopted, the most long-lasting of which, the NEP or New Economic Policy (1921–28), kept large-scale industry, foreign trade and finance in the hands of the state but allowed private entrepreneurs to run enterprises employing fewer than twenty workers and for the most part left agriculture and retail trade in private hands. This form of mixed economy, however, soon led to a number of social strains and tensions. The richer peasants, called *kulaks*, were believed to be getting richer, to be employing large numbers of their colleagues and to be threatening to withhold the supply of grain to the towns. A social group known as 'NEPmen' also sprang up, consisting of speculators, money-lenders and petty criminals as well as those who had lost their possessions and civil rights as a result of the revolution. Above all, the authority of the communist party itself was in question, as it was weakly represented in the countryside and vulnerable to political pressure both from its domestic political opponents and from the outside capitalist powers, which had invaded militarily after the revolution and were believed likely to attempt to do so again. An extended debate took place throughout the 1920s, in which the supporters of Trotsky, who wished to continue the revolution throughout Europe and to develop heavy industry, were ranged against those of Stalin, who were more sceptical of the possibility of a European revolution and initially more inclined to stress the needs of agriculture. A decision was eventually made, at the end of the 1920s, to resolve these various difficulties by adopting a centrally-directed economic plan. It is probably fair to say that there has been no more significant decision in Soviet post-revolutionary history.

The first Five-Year Plan was introduced on 1 October 1928, and pronounced achieved ahead of time at the end of 1932. It was followed by a second Five-Year Plan (1933–37) and then by a third Five-Year Plan, which lasted from 1937 until the Soviet Union entered the Second World War in the summer of 1941. For the first time anywhere in the world, at any rate in peacetime, the direct management of the economic affairs of the nation was taken into the hands of government, on a compulsory and centralised basis. Priority was given to industrialisation, with the lion's share of investment being allocated to heavy industry, producer goods, transport and military production; less attention was paid to quality, variety or waste or to the consumer goods sector generally. A quasi-military atmosphere prevailed: targets were 'stormed', areas of policy became 'fronts', and critics or doubters became 'spies' or 'wreckers'. In the countryside a parallel extension of state control was taking place, as more or less all private peasant households were moved 'voluntarily' – in fact with great violence and loss of life – into collective farms. Some 93 per cent of the rural population had been resettled in this way by 1939. The first five-year plans saw some heroic achievements, such as the construction of the Magnitigorsk iron and steel works, the Dnieper hydro-electric scheme and the Ural-Kuznetsk coal-mining complex. In overall terms the Soviet Union moved from a level of 7 per cent of American industrial production in 1928 to 45 per cent of the American level in 1938, at a time when most Western economies were experiencing slumps and mass unemployment. To many Soviet leaders the achievements of these years, followed by the Soviet victories in the Second World War, must have seemed to vindicate the planning apparatus they had created, and it has survived, in modified but recognisable form, down to the present day.

The central institution in the Soviet planning system is *Gosplan*, the State Planning Committee, a body of union-republican status whose chairman is a member of the USSR Council of Ministers. It is Gosplan which is responsible for the preparation of draft proposals for each new five-year plan and annual plan, based upon the reports on plan fulfilment and requests for inputs for the following year that it has received from ministries and enterprises. Gosplan's proposals are submitted to and approved by the Council of Ministers and by the Central Committee of the CPSU, and are then submitted to the Supreme Soviet, together with the state budget of the USSR and a report on plan fulfilment for the current year. A number of relatively minor changes are made at this stage; the final draft, incorporating these amendments, is then adopted as a formal law and is thenceforth binding upon all ministries, enterprises and any other bodies to which it makes reference. Gosplan is assisted in its work by *Gossnab*, the State Committee on Material-Technical Supplies, which is responsible for ensuring that the inputs and outputs of producing units, so far as possible, match up throughout the economy. The State Committee on Prices, which sets wholesale and retail prices, and the State Committee on Labour and Social Questions, which determines wage rates and job gradings throughout the economy, also have important roles to play. A simplified version of the planning process as a whole is set out in Figure 6.1.

The plan, as approved, is then passed for implementation to the ministries, which are responsible for ensuring that the targets in the plan are met by the factories, farms and other

FIGURE 6.1 The Soviet planning process (simplified)

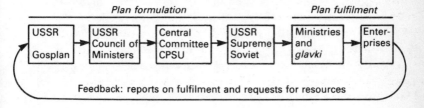

productive units that they supervise. The overriding aim of
ministries, and of the enterprises themselves, is to fulfil the
plan within the period allotted, and if possible to over-fulfil it
by a small margin. Targets for each subsequent year are in
turn based upon the levels previously achieved, with a few
percentage points added on (the so-called 'ratchet principle').
The ministry entrusts its task of guidance to its chief administrations (*glavki*) which undertake the day-to-day management
of productive units, appointing their key personnel in consultation with the party authorities and keeping a detailed watch
over their activities. State farms (*sovkhozy*) are run by the
central government in much the same way as other industrial
enterprises; their managers are appointed by state officials
and their employees have the same rights and duties as
workers in other sectors of the economy. In addition to the
state sector of agriculture there is also a co-operative sector,
consisting essentially of the collective farms (*kolkhozy*). Collective farms are theoretically run by the collective farmers
themselves with land that has been leased to them in perpe-
tuity by the state, and they nominally elect their own chairmen. Collective farmers are also allowed to sell the produce of
their private plots upon the open market, and collective farm
markets, where this is done, account for a considerable
proportion of the Soviet Union's agricultural production. The
collective farms, however, are subject to the provisions of the
national economic plan, and they must make certain compulsory deliveries to the state at prices that the state can fix. In
general their independence is more nominal than real.

The plan that was sent to individual enterprises was
formerly very detailed, specifying precisely what was to be
produced, in what quantities, and with what inputs. This led
to a number of problems. Enterprises might fulfil their plans,
for instance, but with produce for which there was only a
limited demand (such as pairs of right-footed or left-footed
shoes). Enterprises might also attempt to fulfil their plans,
which were usually specified in quantitative terms, in the
easiest way possible: for instance, by producing excessively
heavy steel or unduly heavy chandeliers. (A cartoon of this
period, quoted by Alec Nove in his *Soviet Economic System*,
showed an enormous nail hanging in a workshop. 'The

month's plan fulfilled', said the director, pointing to the nail. And many other examples of this kind could be quoted.) As a result of these difficulties a series of reforms were introduced from the mid-1960s onwards. The first of these, the 'Kosygin reforms' of 1965, reduced the number of targets that enterprises had to meet and placed more emphasis upon output which was actually sold to consumers or other producers ('realised output') than upon gross output (*val*). Enterprises were also encouraged to earn a 'profit' or surplus upon their operations, part of which could be retained to finance additional investment and to provide a material incentive fund for employees. Further reforms in 1973 encouraged the formation of larger productive units, associations or *ob"edineniya*, in order to reduce the number of intermediate steps in the planning process, and in 1979 another round of reforms extended these principles further and attempted to make it easier for enterprises to innovate without jeopardising their plan fulfilment targets. The Soviet planning system, however, for all these modifications (most of which have in any case been implemented incompletely), has remained essentially a command or administered one: the plan is a law, management is responsible to the government for its fulfilment rather than to shareholders or private owners, and capital and other inputs are allocated by the planners rather than obtained upon the market.

Gorbachev and economic reform

Despite its current difficulties there is little doubt that Soviet economic performance, over the longer term, has been one of impressive achievement. Russia in 1913 was a backward country by the standards of the time, the 'poorest of the civilised nations' in the words of a contemporary but still authoritative account (Prokopovich, 1918). There was a small but active manufacturing sector, and levels of production in some areas, such as oil and textiles, were high by world standards. The overwhelming majority of the population, however, were engaged in agriculture, only a quarter of them could read and write, levels of infant mortality and other forms of morbidity were high, and living standards were very low by the standards of the time. National income in pre-revolutionary Russia is estimated to have been about 15 per cent of that in the USA and 22 per cent of that of the United Kingdom; labour productivity in industry, according to Soviet sources, was no more than a tenth of the level achieved in the United States. And although living standards were improving in late Tsarist Russia, they appear to have been improving less rapidly than was the case elsewhere in Europe.

Seventy years later, the contrast could hardly have been greater. The USSR was one of the world's economic super-powers, with a level of industrial production that was exceeded only by that of the United States (and possibly Japan). In many areas – oil, gas, cast iron, steel and tractors, for instance – Soviet levels of production were the highest in the world. The USSR had pioneered the exploration of outer space, and led the world in the number of its scientific personnel. Soviet national income, 58 per cent of that of the USA in 1960, had increased to 67 per cent by 1980. Soviet industrial production, about 3 per cent of the world total in 1917, had increased to 20 per cent by 1987; by this date, indeed, the USSR produced more than the whole world had done in 1950. These achievements, moreover, had taken place in historical circumstances that could hardly have been more difficult. As Gorbachev told interviewers from *Time* magazine in 1985, the old regime had left Soviet Russia a 'grim legacy: a backward economy, strong vestiges of feudalism, millions of illiterate people'. To this had to be added two devastating world wars, in the second of which more than 20 million had been killed and many more maimed and wounded. The arms race, after the Second World War, had placed a further burden on the domestic economy, pre-empting resources that could otherwise have been devoted to the improvement of living standards.

Yet if the economic achievements of the USSR over the longer term were clear, particularly when war and other factors were taken into account, it was equally apparent by the late 1970s that there were deep-seated difficulties that still had to be resolved. The most striking indicator of these difficulties was the rate of economic growth, which fell consistently from the 1950s to the early 1980s with only a slight reversal in the late 1960s (see Table 6.1). Levels of economic

TABLE 6.1

Soviet economic growth, 1951–85
(average annual rate of growth, official data, %)

	Produced national income	Gross industrial output	Gross agricultural output	Real incomes per head
1951–5	11.4	13.2	4.2	7.3
1956–60	9.2	10.4	6.0	5.7
1961–5	6.5	8.6	7.2	3.6
1966–70	7.8	8.5	3.9	5.9
1971–5	5.7	7.4	2.5	4.4
1976–80	4.3	4.4	1.7	3.4
1981–5	3.2	3.6	1.0	2.1

growth in the late 1970s and early 1980s, in fact, were the lowest ever recorded in Soviet peacetime history. In 1979, for instance, national income (in the Soviet definition) rose just 2.2 per cent, and living standards per head of population a bare 1.9 per cent. Some Soviet as well as Western scholars were prepared to argue that, in real terms, growth had altogether ceased during these years. The 11th Five Year Plan, covering the first half of the 1980s, was in turn substantially underfulfilled; the 26th Party Congress, in 1981, had approved directives providing that national income should increase 18–20 per cent by 1985, but the actual increase was 16.5 per cent. And each extra unit of output had been bought at the cost of an increasing consumption of energy, raw material and investment funds, unlike the experience of other industrialised nations. If this was the legacy of Brezhnev it was not a happy one.

Even these figures, moreover, overstated the real level of Soviet economic achievement. They normally left out the rate of growth of population – about 0.9 per cent annually in the 1970s and 1980s. They also concealed a steady increase in over-reporting, amounting to 3 per cent or more of total production in the 1980s and up to a third or more in certain sectors (the Central Asian cotton crop, in particular, became increasingly fictitious). Nor did the figures allow adequately for price increases and changes in specification. According to a highly controversial reassessment of official figures published in 1987 (Selyunin and Khanin, 1987), taking such factors into account Soviet national income from 1928 to 1985 had increased six or seven times – a highly creditable performance, in comparative terms, but well short of the ninetyfold increase recorded in official sources. Much of Soviet economic output was in any case hardly a contribution to real wealth. More tractors and combine harvesters were produced, for instance, than people were available to operate them. And more than twice as many pairs of shoes were produced as in the USA, but the quality was so poor that millions more had to be imported. Even on the official figures some alarming developments were occurring. Soviet national income, for instance, 67 per cent of that of the USA in 1980, had slipped to 64 per cent by 1988, and labour productivity in agriculture, 'about 20 per cent' of that of the United States in the 1970s, had fallen to 16 per cent by the late 1980s.

The broad framework of Gorbachev's approach to economic reform was set out in his speech to the 27th Party Congress in 1986. The top priority, in his view, was to overcome the factors that had been holding back the country's socio-economic development as quickly as possible and to resume the growth, based upon scientific and technical progress, structural change and new forms of management and labour incentives. A change of this kind – from extensive growth, based upon the use of additional resources, to intensive growth, based upon the better use of existing resources – was not simply desirable: for Gorbachev, there was 'no other way'. In the light of these requirements the revised Party Programme and the Guidelines for the new 12th Five Year Plan, both of which were adopted at the Congress, set out as their central objective the doubling of national income by the year 2000, based upon scientific progress, decentralised management, more 'flexible' prices and greater opportunities to participate in the running of enterprises.

More detailed guidelines for economic reform were approved by a Central Committee meeting in June 1987, at which Gorbachev delivered the key address. There had been outstanding successes, in the years after the revolution,

Gorbachev suggested, but the centralised and detailed forms of management that had been established at that time had now outlived their usefulness. Attempts at reform, from the 1950s onwards, had been unsuccessful. Now, in the 1980s, the Soviet economy was in not just a difficult but a 'pre-crisis' situation. The rate of economic growth had dropped to a level which 'virtually signified the onset of economic stagnation'. Resources were being wastefully used, and technological levels were lagging increasingly behind those of the rest of the developed world. Budget deficits were being covered by the sale of oil and other raw materials on world markets and by tax returns on the sale of alcohol, which had more than doubled over the previous fifteen years. Spending on wages had systematically exceeded plan targets, while increases on output and productivity had been less than predicted. This meant that money incomes were increasingly outstripping the supply of goods and services. Shortages, inevitably, had become worse: indeed there was a shortage of 'everything', from metal and cement to consumer goods and manpower. Nothing less than a 'radical reform' in the whole system of economic management was needed to reverse these alarming trends.

In agriculture, Gorbachev suggested, greater use should be made of the 'collective' or 'family contract', by which a small group of workers obtained the use of an area of land for a fixed price and received in return the right to sell their surplus produce for whatever it would fetch on the open market. Storage and processing facilities should be modernised (up to 30 per cent of agricultural output was being lost in this way); and more generally, the management of agriculture should be shifted away from officials at the central and local levels and into the hands of the workers themselves on a long-term basis. Comparable changes were needed in the housing and construction industries, which were operating well below their capacity. Still more important, the output of consumer goods should be given a higher priority, and so should services. Was it really normal, Gorbachev asked, when having household appliances repaired or items of footwear or clothing made up became a 'big problem'? Gorbachev quoted an official estimate which suggested that the size of the 'shadow' or black economy was at least 1.5 billion rubles a year; this arose because the individuals concerned had been unable to obtain the services they wanted in the state sector. Local officials could not escape their responsibility for such matters; nor could national-level ministers, a number of whom were directly named.

Above all, an attempt must be made to establish an 'integrated, efficient and flexible system of economic management', relying much less on administrative or 'command' forms of direction and rather more on market-based or 'economic' methods. Enterprises should be more autonomous, with more responsibility for their own production and finances, leaving *Gosplan* and other bodies with the responsibility for setting out the broad strategy of economic development, but not for detailed intervention in the operation of enterprises themselves. Plans would continue to be produced, but they would be concerned with long-term objectives and major state programmes, not with the day-to-day functioning of industries and enterprises. Economic management at this level would in future be based to a much greater extent upon commercial 'state orders' (*goszakazy*), which would be allocated on a competitive basis by the central planners, and upon the orders of other enterprises. Equipment and raw materials would similarly be obtained to a much greater extent through wholesale trade between enterprises, rather than from the central authorities. In extreme cases, if an enterprise failed to pay its way it might be liquidated. There should also be a much closer relationship between the Soviet and the world economy, including joint ventures and other forms of cooperation. These principles were embodied in a set of 'Guidelines for the radical restructuring of economic management', adopted by the plenum, and were carried further by a Law on the State Enterprise, which was adopted by the Supreme Soviet later in the year.

Other elements to the programme of economic reform were added over the months that followed. Under legislation approved in November 1986, for instance, a wide variety of forms of 'individual labour activity' was specifically legalised. The main aims, as set out by the chairman of the State Committee on Labour and Social Questions, were that the activities concerned should not detract from production in the state sector, and that the income obtained should correspond to the work that had been performed. Those who were eligible to engage in activities of this kind included housewives, students, invalids and ordinary employees on their days off; the kinds of work they could undertake included car repairs, translation, photography, typing and handicrafts (but not pornography or the manufacture of armaments). A further, potentially more significant, change was the adoption in May 1988 of a new Law on Cooperatives which was widely seen as the most radical of all the changes that had so far been introduced by the Gorbachev leadership. The new cooperatives were, in principle, exempted from obligatory state plans and state orders, although they were required at least to inform the relevant authorities of their intentions. Cooperatives could fix their own prices, except when they were producing for state orders or using state-supplied materials (in practice, a very considerable limitation). They were entitled to conduct foreign trade operations, and to keep a significant part of the hard currency they earned, and they could form joint ventures with foreign companies. By January 1990 the new cooperatives employed 4.5 million workers on a full-time or part-time basis and were increasing rapidly in number, although they still accounted for no more than 1.5 per cent of retail trade and services.

If the central objective of the Gorbachev reform strategy was to recover the economy's growth dynamic, it was clear it had fallen far short of success in its early years. The Five Year Plan adopted in 1986 called for a 4.2 per cent annual rate of growth in produced national income, as compared with the rate of 3.6 per cent achieved in the first half of the decade. The Guidelines adopted by the 27th Party Congress stipulated a still higher rate of growth in the 1990s, 5 per cent annually, in order to double national income by the year 2000 (see Table 6.2). The rate of growth achieved in 1986, 1987 and 1988 in fact averaged a modest 3.6 per cent, which was exactly as had been achieved in the late Brezhnev, Andropov and Chernenko years. The 1988 plan results, compared with the others, were relatively more satisfactory: national income rose by 4.4 per cent, and gross national product (GNP) (which was much

TABLE 6.2

Soviet economic growth, 1981–9 (official data, %)

	1981–5 average	1986–90 average (plan)	1986	1987	1988	1989
National income produced	3.2	4.2	2.3	1.6	4.4	2.4
Industrial output	3.6	4.6	4.4	3.8	3.9	1.7
Agricultural output	1.0	2.7	5.3	−0.6	1.7	1.0

closer to the definitions of economic activity used in the West) rose by 5 per cent. The figure for national income, however impressive, still left economic growth for the first three full Gorbachev years below the Five Year Plan target; grain production was particularly poor (substantial foreign purchases had to be made), and wages were still increasing much more rapidly than the output of goods and services. The 1989 results, reported in the central press in January 1990, showed a lower rate of growth of GNP, just 3 per cent, and there were falls in housing, transportation, oil and coal. In the view of reform-minded economists the economic performance of the late 1980s, taken as a whole, represented a stagnation or even decline in the level of economic performance, not the resumption of growth that the leadership had intended.

Many of the difficulties the economy had experienced, admittedly, were the result of exogenous factors of various kinds. One of these was a change in the terms of trade, particularly a fall in the value of Soviet oil exports. Further heavy losses were incurred by a series of natural disasters of various kinds, of which the most important were the Chernobyl nuclear explosion of April 1986 and the Armenian earthquake of December 1988. The reforms, in any case, often made relatively little difference to the realities of economic management. Perhaps the most conspicuous example of this kind was the state orders which were supposed to replace ministerial directives under the Law on the State Enterprise. It soon became apparent that the Law was largely a dead letter; ministries continued to issue directives but simply renamed them state orders, and these directives in turn continued to account for the overwhelming share of output. Enterprises, for their part, often sought to obtain a high level of state orders so that their sources of supply could be secured. As a result, *val* or gross output, rather than market-related success criteria, continued to determine the pattern of production in much the same way as it had done ever since the command economy had been established. In the absence of a comprehensive price reform and in conditions of shortage and monopoly, the profitability of enterprises was in any case a poor guide to their efficiency.

More fundamentally, the reform programme led to tensions between the traditional mechanism of central planning, which still defined the framework of economic activity, and market criteria of various kinds. Giving greater autonomy to enterprises, for instance, allowed them more freedom to choose their output mix in a way that met their obligations in the easiest possible way. One general response was to reduce or discontinue the production of cheaper and less profitable items and to concentrate on other products. This led to shortages of children's goods and many other necessities. The lack of soap and washing powder, in the late 1980s, was a source of particular indignation. 'What kind of regime is it if we can't even get washed?', asked an angry group of workers in the Vladimir region. Quality was a related concern. An increasing proportion of sausage, for instance, included fat or additives of various kinds. The weekly paper *Literaturnaya gazeta* tried it out on thirty cats who knew 'nothing of chemistry, bureaucracy or economies of scale'; 24 of them refused all the varieties of sausage they were offered, and five more refused most of them.

One result of shortages was queues, sometimes of wartime proportions, and the widespread use of coupons for rationing purposes. Another was a rapid increase in prices as producers took advantage of their new ability to make use of market conditions. Inflation, according to the State Statistics Committee, reached a level of 7.5 per cent in 1989; unofficial estimates suggested a level of up to 20 per cent. The greater the shortages, the more shoppers had to make use of collective farm markets and cooperatives where prices were still higher.

The prices that were charged by cooperatives, often for goods that had originally been bought in the state sector, and the huge incomes they were able to pay their workers, aroused particular resentment. There were cases of cooperatives paying their members a hundred times more than a minister, or twice as much in a day as an ordinary worker was able to make in a month. There was also some concern that cooperatives were simply a convenient way of legalising stolen money, and the large sums of money that were involved in any case encouraged protection rackets and crime of various kinds. There was strong public support for the restrictions upon the activity of cooperatives that were imposed at the end of 1988, and which were taken further in 1989 and 1990.

Greater enterprise autonomy led to increasing difficulties of a different but related kind: it made it easier for management to put up wages more rapidly than would otherwise have been possible, covering their costs by higher prices. The result was a rapid increase in inflationary pressures, as rising incomes chased a much less rapidly increasing supply of commodities. In 1988 as a whole the average monthly income of workers and white collar staff in the state sector rose by 7 per cent, but productivity in the economy as a whole by just 5.1 per cent. In 1989 the same tendencies were even more apparent: money wages rose by 9.5 per cent, but labour productivity by a much more modest 2.3 per cent. As a regional party first secretary told the Central Committee in April 1989, wages were increasing ahead of production at such a rate that soon the whole of the economy would be devoted to printing paper. If individuals and enterprises had financial difficulties, so too did the state itself. With increasing levels of consumption and unchanged prices, the subsidies that were paid particularly for foodstuffs shot up. Heavy costs fell directly upon the state budget from the Chernobyl explosion and the Armenian earthquake. Meanwhile, income was reduced with the fall in the world price of oil, and the vigorous campaign against alcohol abuse, launched in 1985, led to a massive loss of revenue without significantly affecting the consumption of alcohol itself (black marketeers pocketed the difference).

The problem of economic reform in the USSR was in the end a political one at least as much as it was a technical or organisational one. In the late 1980s two distinct approaches were acquiring coherent form. For one group of commentators, including most economists, the continuing problems of the Soviet economy stemmed from too little reform, not too much. Like the 'radical right' in other countries, they called for cuts in public spending, the elimination of indiscriminate subsidies, privatisation of state assets, wider inequalities of income and, if necessary, limited forms of unemployment. For Nikolai Shmelev, for instance, an economist who was also a member of the Congress of People's Deputies, better living standards would come about only through satisfying the market. The way forward in agriculture was through the private and cooperative sector. In industry, enterprises should be compelled to operate in free market conditions. Fears that this would result in massive unemployment were 'greatly exaggerated'; people were continually changing jobs as it was, nor could they close their eyes to the 'great harm being done by our parasitic reliance on guaranteed employment'. If disorderliness, drunkenness and poor workmanship were really to be eliminated, there was probably no alternative to the establishment of a 'comparatively small reserve army of labour'. Foreign firms should be given greater access to the Soviet market so as to force Soviet enterprise to become competitive, the role of *Gosplan* and the ministries should be reduced drastically, and prices should be brought into line with those that prevailed internationally.

There was however another view, more directly linked with the industrial working class and articulated with considerable force by politicians such as the former Moscow party leader Boris Yeltsin. Seen from this perspective, the source of the country's economic difficulties lay much more in the distribution of benefits and the relations between social groups on which that distribution was based. The Soviet working class, they pointed out, was poorly remunerated, even in relative terms. Spending on the health service, once at a high level, had dropped to 3 or 4 per cent of national income as compared with 8–12 per cent in most other developed nations. Public spending on education, housing and other programmes had also fallen steadily to levels that were often far below those of comparable nations. Subsidies, it was argued, were not necessarily regressive. In some cases, such as housing and meat, those with higher incomes also had a higher level of consumption, and thus of public support; but in other cases, such as bread and potatoes, the better-off did not on the whole consume more than the poor and the subsidy which kept the price down was in effect a form of income redistribution in their favour.

For many radicals, in fact, the monetarist diagnosis was not simply on shaky ground empirically: it was actually an attempt to solve the nation's economic difficulties at the expense of ordinary workers. Yeltsin, for instance, speaking to the Congress of People's Deputies in 1989, argued that there had been no real advance in social justice in the 70 years of Soviet rule, and that there was every reason to speak of an 'élite stratum' in the society, 'wallowing in luxury' while tens of millions lived in abject poverty. The radical sociologist Tatiana Zaslavskaya, also a people's deputy, spoke in a newspaper interview of 'indirect exploitation' of the working class by the full-time party and state bureaucracy. Indeed for some Soviet writers in the late 1980s, social relations in the USSR were best understood in straightforwardly Marxist terms, with a bureaucratic 'class' exploiting the labour of ordinary workers.

Gorbachev and the party leadership as a whole distanced themselves from the more extreme monetarist prescriptions, but also from a class analysis of this kind. For Gorbachev personally, speaking in 1989, there could be no talk of private property – did they really want to work for the capitalists, he asked a group of Leningrad workers? – and price increases, where they occurred, would be discussed widely and introduced in a form that would protect the living standards of the least affluent. There was much that could be done, in any case, within the existing framework, such as reductions in military expenditure and obvious forms of waste. It was likely to be difficult in the longer run, however, to avoid a choice: either a revolution 'from above', made in the name of working people but without their participation and possibly against their interests, or a popular movement 'from below', in a form that was likely to challenge the power and not simply the (often fairly modest) privileges of Soviet officials at all levels of the system.

The policy process in Eastern Europe: nationalities in Yugoslavia

The national question in Yugoslavia under communist rule was subject to a complex and at times successful policy, but in the long term – from the founding of the communist system during the Second World War and its expected demise in the 1990s – it proved to be a failure. This section explores the factors affecting the formulation of the policy and offers an explanation of why it failed.

The factual background was one of an immensely complex patchwork of different ethno-national groups that inhabited the areas that came to make up the state. Territorial borders satisfactory to all were impossible to draw and a number of ethnic groups had no clearly developed national consciousness at all. The markers differentiating the various groups were cultural, religious, linguistic and historical. Serbs, Montenegrins and Macedonians are Orthodox; Croats and Slovenes are Roman Catholic. Slovenes and Macedonians speak languages of their own. Serbs and Croats speak different variants of the same languages, but write it in the Cyrillic and Latin alphabets respectively. The Moslems of Bosnia also speak this Serbo–Croat language; between the wars, their national allegiance was contested by Serbs and Croats. The Macedonians were denied any separate nationhood by the Serbs and they were also claimed by the Bulgarians, to whom they are close linguistically.

Slovenes and Macedonians live in relatively compact blocks, in the republics that were set up after the Second World War. Serbia proper is inhabited overwhelmingly by Serbs, but there are also sizeable Serbian minorities in Croatia, in Bosnia–Hercegovina, in the Vojvodina and in the Kosovo. Croats live in Croatia, in Bosnia–Hercegovina and in the Vojvodina (see Table 6.3).

The basics of the national question in Yugoslavia begin from the very foundation of the state. Yugoslavia came into being on 1 December 1918 as an amalgamation of lands that had been ruled by Serbia, the Ottoman Empire, the independent state of Montenegro, Austria and Hungary. Not only did these lands and the people who inhabit them have very

TABLE 6.3

Regional distribution of Yugoslavia's ethnic communities

Republic/ Autonomous Province	Population (m) (1985)	Albanians	Croats	Macedonians	Montenegrins	Muslims	Serbs	Slovenes
		(As % of Republic and Autonomous Province populations)						
Bosnia-Herzegovina (R)	4.280	0.1	18.4	0.1	0.3	39.5	32.0	0.1
Croatia (R)	4.760	0.1	75.1	0.1	0.2	0.5	11.6	0.6
Macedonia (R)	1.920	19.8	0.2	67.0	0.2	2.1	2.3	0.0
Montenegro (R)	0.610	6.5	1.2	0.0	68.5	13.4	3.3	0.0
Serbia (R)*	5.890	1.3	0.6	0.5	1.4	2.7	85.4	0.1
Slovenia (R)	1.980	0.1	2.9	0.2	0.2	0.7	2.2	90.5
Kosovo (AP)	1.645	77.4	0.6	1.7	1.7	3.7	13.2	0.0
Vojvodina (AP)	2.115	0.2	5.4	2.1	2.1	0.2	54.4	0.2
Yugoslavia	23.200	7.7	19.7	6.0	2.6	8.9	36.3	7.8

*Excluding Kosovo and Vjvodina 'autonomous provinces'.
Source: Calculated from Yugoslav official data.

different histories and traditions, but the very basis on which the state was put together was obscure. During the First World War, Serbian and Croatian leaders negotiated about the future Yugoslav state and believed that they had come to an agreement (the Corfu Declaration of 1917) satisfactory to both sides.

In fact, this was proved to be an error. While the Croats, and to a much lesser extent the Slovenes, believed that a democratic and constitutional monarchy, as agreed at Corfu, would permit them a good deal of autonomy, the Serbs were committed to a unitary state as the best bulwark against the new country's enemies, Italy foremost among them. It was to forestall Italian annexation of sizeable areas of Slovenia and Croatia that the Serbian army occupied these areas, thereby creating the impression of a conquest. The Serbian experience before the war had been of a steady expansion of the territory of the state through war and this was not seen as a significant exception.

Both the Croats and Slovenes, on the other hand, had had some experience of legal and constitutional rule and expected that this would be taken into consideration under the new order. This was not to be. In effect, the various nations comprising the Yugoslav state were never in agreement on the form of the state, on the powers of the central government, extent of devolution, so that disagreement split along national lines from the outset. This bedevilled the interwar monarchy to such an extent that when the restraints were removed in 1941, when the Second World War reached Yugoslavia, Serbs, Croats, Bosnian Moslems and other nationalities fought a devastating civil war of their own, in which more Yugoslavs were killed by other Yugoslavs than by enemy action.

This was the situation into which Tito's communist-led partisans entered. Large numbers of Serbs in Croatia were being massacred by the wartime Croatian Ustasa Fascist state, the boundaries of which included Bosnia. In other areas, Moslems were killed by Serbs, and so on. It was a Hobbesian war of all against all. The partisans then launched a policy designed to take advantage of the revulsion against the killings. They proclaimed that when they were in power, all national groups would enjoy full equality. This was an understandably attractive policy, which gained them much support, though the Serbs of Serbia proper were the least enthusiastic.

After the war, Tito, now in control, was as good as his word. The 1946 constitution established Yugoslavia as a federal state and all the nations and national groups were granted the same degree of autonomy – none to speak of in real terms (see Map 6.1). The communist party ran the country on a very tight leash and all manifestations of national autonomy were ruthlessly suppressed for many years. Under the slogan of 'brotherhood and unity', the national question was supposed to have been solved. However, there was an important result of creating a federal system, with which the communists did not reckon. By establishing republican institutions on a more or less ethno-cultural basis, they set up the political frame-work which could later be filled by national sentiments, that is once the party's control over them weakened.

The concept underlying Tito's strategy was straightforward and ultimately not capable of meeting the demands of the situation. For the Yugoslav communists, nationhood was an entirely secondary matter, strictly subordinate to class and born of economic oppression. Consequently, if the economic bases of national inequality were removed, they argued, the national question itself would be solved. On their assumption a Serbian worker could not have an interest or a consciousness different from a Croatian, once he was brought to full awareness of his true class identity.

In effect, they followed Lenin's dictum of 'national in form, socialist in content' very closely. This meant that it did not really matter in what language and through what cultural forms ideas were expressed as long as these were socialist. The difficulty with this strategy was that class (economic interest) has a quite different function from nation (cultural identity). The idea of placing one above the other and proceeding as if this were really so simply led to sweeping national issues under the carpet and keeping them there by force, if need be.

For a while, the communists were well served by their strategy of relying on 'brotherhood and unity'. The memory of the wartime killings and the role claimed by partisans in

MAP 6.1 Yugoslavia:
boundaries of republics and autonomous provinces

stopping them was deployed as an instrument of legitimation by the party (the League of Communists of Yugoslavia after 1952). This was used to resolve two further issues that had been major headaches before the war – the Macedonian and Moslem problems.

The Macedonians were quite evidently not 'Southern Serbs' as the royal régime had claimed, but at the same time Belgrade also had cause for concern that they might turn towards Bulgaria. Some individual Macedonians had, in fact, opted to become Bulgars. To preclude any further such claims, the communists encouraged the Macedonians to develop their nationhood as far as they could. A new Macedonian language was developed, Macedonian cultural institutions were set up and the republic was, of course, given the full panoply of rights. In 1967, the Belgrade government gave tacit encouragement to the three bishops of the Orthodox church in Macedonia to declare themselves independent of the Serbian patriarchate, under whose jurisdiction they had lived until then. In the Orthodox world, autonomous nationhood is generally accompanied by autocephaly and the communists of Macedonia gave a good deal of support to the church in this endeavour, despite the apparent contradiction of communists backing religion.

As a matter of fact, this strategy has worked on the whole. Macedonian nationhood appears to be a going concern and the overwhelming majority of Macedonians accept it. This also secures their loyalty to the Yugoslav state, for they know perfectly well that under Bulgaria they would lose their independence and the benefits that flow from it.

The Moslems presented a different kind of problem. It was clear that the Moslems of Bosnia were neither Serbs nor Croats, though many individuals had opted for one or other nationality, but that as long as both Serbs and Croats claimed them, tension could be generated as a result. Hence, as with the Macedonians, the Moslems were encouraged to set themselves up as a separate nation, which they duly did. This was even more paradoxical than the relationship between Macedonian communists and the hierarchy, for the dominant differentiating marker for Moslems is their religion. The idea of an avowedly communist régime encouraging Islam is decidedly contradictory. In fact, the Moslems have assiduously constructed a separate national history for themselves and have used the customary devices for nation-building – history, culture and symbolic markers, which in this case are overwhelmingly Moslem. On the other hand, the differentiation has worked. The Moslems effectively control the Bosnian republic, where they have a plurality of the population and neither Serbs nor Croats raise any serious claims to incorporate them.

If these devices can be said to have worked, other aspects of the communists' nationalities policy were less effective. The central difficulty in Yugoslavia has always been the Serb–Croat relationship. This has never been a simple matter of the Serbs of Serbia being engaged in visceral antagonism with the Croats. Rather, it was the problem of the *prećani* Serbs, the Serbs outside Serbia, the victims of the wartime massacres and whose future was always seen as being at risk by the Serbs, that envenomed relations.

To overcome this, the communists decided to move towards

the construction of an entire new identity, that of 'Yugoslav'. The content of Yugoslavism was supposed to transcend separate Serbian and Croatian identities and was promoted strongly. Tito himself always gave his nationality as 'Yugoslav'. But in addition to this, a concerted attempt was made to create a new, Yugoslav culture, history and language. The history that Serbs and Croats were taught in the 1950s and 1960s emphasised the elements of unity and ignored events that each regarded as constitutive of its national identity. This effectively produced an a-national history, which neither found satisfactory, the hidden agenda of which was that Serbs and Croats would have lived together in happy amity had they not been separated by the exploiting classes. Thus the end goal of South Slav history was Yugoslavia and Yugoslavism.

In 1954, Serbian and Croatian intellectuals were encouraged by the party to sign the Novi Sad agreement on language. This stated that Serbian and Croatian were one language, Serbo–Croat, spoken in two variants. In effect, the underlying idea was to create a single 'Yugoslav' language and thereby gradually move towards the elimination of the ethno-cultural differences between Serbs and Croats. In fact, the Novi Sad agreement was accepted at a time when Croatian self-regard was at a very low ebb and as the years passed, Croatian intellectuals began to feel that they had for all practical purposes abandoned their national language. The issue came to a head over the editing of a dictionary of the Serbo–Croat language, which the Croats felt relegated literary Croatian to the status of a dialect and, after a good deal of acrimony in the 1960s, they withdrew from the project. Thereafter, they returned to the idea and goal of a separate standard and literary Croatian acquired a separate vocabulary making it as distinct from Serbian as possible.

The failure of Yugoslavism on the language question was the clearest illustration of the unrealistic nature of the entire project. Yet even the re-emergence of the national question in the 1960s, Yugoslavism was never entirely abandoned. It resurfaced occasionally in the 1970s, whenever the party sought to offset the decentralising trends in the country. And there remained on important stronghold where Yugoslavism never died – the armed forces. The army saw itself as the repository of the unity and integrity of the country, indeed they were formally entrusted with this role by Tito, and promoted Yugoslavism wherever it could.

Other aspects of Tito's nationalities policy were the attempts to settle relations with the two large non-Slavonic minorities – the Hungarians of the Vojvodina and the Albanians of Kosovo. Neither could be termed a great success. The Hungarians, who make up about a quarter of the population of the Vojvodina, which was a part of Serbia but enjoyed considerable autonomy, were granted limited cultural rights on paper. But these were severely restricted in practice and any attempt by the Hungarians to develop their own projects was slapped down as nationalism. Officially, the Hungarian minority was supposed to be a bridge between Yugoslavia and Hungary; the Hungarians of Hungary never showed the kind of interest in their co-nationals in Yugoslavia that they did with Romania. In this sense, the bridge function worked.

But the idea of the Albanian minority being a bridge towards Albania was much less successful for the Yugoslavs. The Albanian minority in Yugoslavia is Moslem, economically still very backward in Yugoslav terms and with a long memory of Slavonic repression. They live concentrated in Kosovo and in the western third of Macedonia, basically the areas bordering in Albania.

Until 1966, Kosovo was run by the Serbian-dominated secret police, the UDBA, as a Serbian colony, but after the fall of Alexander Ranković, the secret police chief, the Albanians began to start demanding the rights which they felt were theirs. These were focused on the establishment of an Albanian-language university in Priština, which was conceded. From this, a young Albanian élite emerged, which regarded itself as committed to Yugoslavia and hence wanted an Albanian republic. For many Slavs in Yugoslavia this was quite unacceptable. For a start, it went way beyond the bridge function and, at a deeper level, it was felt that making Kosovo a republic would undermine the Slavonic character of the Yugoslav project. Besides, an Albanian republic in Kosovo would have been a magnet for the Albanians of Macedonia, which would then have had a strongly destabilising result.

At the same time, the Albanians turned not only towards

Belgrade, which to an extent they did, but also towards Tirana, as well as the West. In this sense, the bridge between Kosovo and Tirana definitely existed, but the traffic across it was somewhat onesided. Albania had greater influence on Kosovo than vice versa, as could have been expected, given the very tight control exercised over Albanian culture by Enver Hoxha's régime.

In fact, the remaining results of the project of Yugoslavism were even more meagre. Not only did Serbian and Croatian identities remain separate, but these grew stronger with the years and acquired new political functions in the 1980s. The fact that between 5 and 10 per cent of the population returned its national allegiance in the various censuses as 'Yugoslav' did not significantly alter this picture. The hard political reality was that a single Yugoslav identity did not arise to transcend the pre-existing ones.

The first major conflict over nationalism with which the communists had to deal was the Croatian crisis of 1971. The origins of this lay in the non-national question of economics. Some of the leaders of the Croatian republic in the 1960s felt that they were providing too much to the rest of the country through various equalisation projects and not receiving enough in return. Gradually, they began to press their demands through the federal institutions and, at the same time, to generate support at home by permitting, some would say even encouraging, a rediscovery of Croatian identity. The return of the Croatian national identity to Yugoslav politics was unwelcome to most people outside Croatia and was particularly attacked by the Serbs, sensitive as they were to the fate of the *prečani*. However, developments in Croatia remained within barely acceptable limits until late 1971, when Croatian intellectuals began to challenge the party itself. It was when the leading role of the party was threatened that Tito decided to intervene and use the armed forces to achieve this. The Croatian autonomy movement collapsed and the years that followed saw a harsh campaign of arrests and imprisonments of those involved. This imposed quiescence on Croatia for the best part of 20 years. It was, in that sense, a solution.

The Serbian problem, however, was of a different order.

The Serbian tradition had been an integrative one, where the Serbs had played the role of Piedmont, the land which dominates and unifies the rest. Consequently, the Serbs had tended to see themselves as the embodiment of Yugoslavia. That, in a way, was the problem. Given their numerical weight (around two-fifths of the population) and their geographical distribution (they lived in some numbers in every republic except Slovenia and Macedonia), it was not surprising that their belief in themselves as the repository of Yugoslav values alarmed the non-Serbs. Their response was to complain of 'unitarism' and 'hegemonism', which became code-words in the official jargon for Serbian nationalism.

In the mid-1970s, there was a new mood in Serbia. The pro-Yugoslav attitude was fading to be replaced by a kind of Serbian separatism. The gist of the argument was that the Serbs had suffered more than any other nation in Yugoslavia, had made greater sacrifices and had yet ended up as the losers. Serbs were divided up over three republics (Serbia, Croatia and Bosnia) and in the two provinces that were supposedly parts of Serbia – the Vojvodina and Kosovo – Serbian control was weakening. Even Montenegro, which was supposedly the most Serbian land, was being encouraged to see itself as a separate nation. To this grievance was added the economic one, that the north-western republics (Croatian and Slovenia) were richer.

These currents were never dealt with in Tito's lifetime, and they could not have been in the paradigm that he constructed. He tried to re-establish party centralism after the Croatian crisis, but this was only partly effective, as the republics were loth to cede power to the centre. The outcome was a stand-off. In most matters, the republican parties were left alone to deal with matters as they wanted, but if there was any really major difficulty Tito would knock heads together and impose a solution. In other words, the Croatian solution of 1971–2 was institutionalised. The 1974 constitution reflected this, in that it gave rise to the republican veto. In government matters, each republic and later province too had the power to veto decisions which it disliked. This was a recipe for paralysis once Tito was gone, in 1980. As long as he was alive, he controlled the system, but he could not bequeath it to a successor, so that the eight republics had to define strategies by agreement. In practice this proved impossible.

By the mid-1980s, the federal system was in a shambles. Federal legislation was freely flouted by the republics and Yugoslavia was in reality eight separate polities rather than a single country. For a few years, the tacit agreement that the republican parties would run their republics as they chose, but would keep a one-party system in being, held. But by 1986, Slovenia was beginning to move towards one-party pluralism. The local party leader, Milan Kucan, argued that it was preferable to rule with the consent of the people rather than against it and he permitted the emergence of various officially unsanctioned organisations. By 1989, and only partly under the impact of what was happening elsewhere in Central and Eastern Europe, Slovenia was preparing to institute a multiparty system; in 1990, after competitive elections, it elected Yugoslavia's first postwar non-communist government.

In the meantime, there were major changes in Serbia too, though in a very different direction. The issue that transformed the situation was Kosovo. The Serbian minority in the province was gradually but inexorably finding that its future was becoming bleaker and bleaker. The problem was very simple – demography. The Albanian birthrate was three to four times higher than the Serbian, so that by the late 1980s, the Serbs and Montenegrins were outnumbered nine to one. In situations of this kind, where a minority concludes collectively that it will not survive in that area because its cultural and ethnic needs cannot be met, then it will emigrate and/or assimilate. This is what happened to the Serbs of Kosovo in the 1980s.

The Serbs of Serbia, however, saw the entire situation in very different terms. To understand this, one has to have some empathy with the Serbian view of the world. This was constituted out of a variety of elements, but these included the central factors of strict demarcation against Islam and glorification of a heroic past from which the Serbs' present corpus of values is drawn. Kosovo in this context has been a sacred land, the site of the battle where the mediaeval Serbian empire was defeated by the Moslem Ottoman Empire. When seen in this perspective, Albanian habitation of the Kosovo – and arguing the Albanian case on the basis of elementary human rights – is offensive and irrelevant. It can be likened to sacrilege in Serbian eyes. In the panoply of Serbian sentiments, the emotional argument has far more force than mere considerations of demography or legal rights or even the constellation of political forces that derives from the overwhelming Albanian presence.

Hence after Tito's death, the pressure from the Serbs was directed at being able to discuss the Kosovo situation openly – this had not been possible under Tito, who regarded all such manifestations as nationalism. By 1987, when Slobodan Milošević successfully captured control of the Serbian party, popular sentiments were well prepared for the kind of demagogic strategy that he pursued. It was not, however, by any manner of means the sole option. A pluralistic or democratic alternative existed, but was defeated very largely because the Serbian apparat refused to consider it for fear of undermining its power. Indeed, by acceding to the Milošević initiative, it concluded that it could actually conserve its power.

Milošević's strategy was simple, to call upon Serbian nationalism and to insist that all of Serbia's problems, economic, political, social, would be resolved if Serbs took their destinies into their own hands. He was enormously successful in mobilising massive demonstrations and putting the republican administrations in the Vojvodina and Montenegro under such pressure that they caved in. Subsequently, he reestablished the power of the Serbian republic over Kosovo as well, thereby removing the institutional barriers between Serbs and Albanians. The overall consequence was not what Milošević expected. His wider strategy was to remake Serbia the centre of Yugoslavia and to impose his ideas and policies on it. In reality, he generated so much opposition in the non-Serbian republics that the country was brought several steps closer to disintegration.

Essentially two broad lines of approach were formulated to the Serbian challenge. The Slovenes concluded that the Serbs were beyond all reason and that there was less and less to keep them in the Yugoslav federation. This lay behind their determination to institute multiparty democracy, regardless of what the federal party said, and explained their decision to walk out of the League of Yugoslav Communists' extraordinary congress in January 1990. By taking this step the Slovenes signalled that they were not interested in the party, but would deal only with state institutions. The Croats, on the other hand, were far more hesitant about taking the Slovene road. Perhaps mindful of their post-1971 experience, they still looked to some kind of a tolerable solution within a Yugoslav framework, though by the early months of 1990 this looked less and less feasible. Croatia too was committed to multiparty elections, in which it was hard to see the communists doing well.

Looked at in a long-term perspective, Tito's policy of dealing with a multinational state proved to be a failure. Essentially, the reason was the same as elsewhere in Central and Eastern Europe. Communism could not provide the constitutive cement and the corpus of values by which a community could organise itself and around which it could cohere. Indeed, by attaching the solution of the national question in Yugoslavia so intimately to the success of communism, Tito and the Yugoslav communists ensured that both would be discredited together.

The economy and the policy process in China

In December 1978, the Central Committee of the Chinese Communist Party decided that the focus of future work would be economic modernisation and that all other work must be subordinated to meeting this objective. Legitimacy was shifting effectively to the capacity of the leadership to deliver the economic goods. This approach resulted in significant changes in the relationship between the plan and the market and the party and the economic decision-making apparatus, with previous regime practice being significantly liberalised. This focus on the economy and the attempts at systemic transformation did not go unchallenged and, as the events of late 1989 have shown, it continues to be challenged by orthodox party members who see little role for the market in the economic sphere. Having moved to the point of transition in 1988, China's leaders retreated to reassert the old central administrative mechanisms when confronted by major problems of overheating of the economy and rising inflation. This resort to the bunker mentality at the first signs of economic problems has been a recurrent feature of attempted reforms not just in China but also throughout the communist-ruled world.

The break with the Soviet Union in the late 1950s has meant that China's leaders possessed a greater capacity to pursue their own domestic policies without worrying about Soviet reaction. This meant that even before Gorbachev came on to the political scene they were able to pursue radical economic reform that would have been unthinkable in Eastern Europe, and later after Gorbachev had come to power they began to roll back many of the reforms which Gorbachev was anxious to promote both at home and in Eastern Europe.

The stress placed on economic modernisation by Deng Xiaoping and his supporters had specific causes in the recent past. First, living standards in the late 1970s had barely risen from those in the late 1950s for much of the population. The government's over-concentration on accumulation at the expense of consumption meant that rationing, queueing and hours spent on laborious household chores were the daily fare for most. The Chinese population had had enough of tightening their belts today in return for promises of a bright future tomorrow.

Secondly, the failure of the initial post-Mao strategy to improve economic performance significantly caused the leadership to focus more sharply on the need for fundamental economic reform. The ascription of blame to the policies of the 'Gang of Four' with the associated policy of returning to a 'golden age' before they existed was seen to lead to a dead end. It was increasingly recognised that the main problems were deep-seated structural ones. Also, the ambitious pursuit of 'Maoism without Mao' under Hua Guofeng's leadership had led to serious short-term problems such as a towering budget deficit and increasing inflationary pressures. The politically inspired measure of offering the urban labour force increased wages and bonuses to win their confidence and allegiance was exhausted.

Thirdly, the party was faced with a serious problem of legitimacy. The continual twists and turns of policy since the mid-1950s left the party's claim to be the sole body in society capable of mapping out the correct path to socialism looking a little thin to say the least. Nor could Mao's name be invoked any longer to legitimise policy. Thus, the party began to promise a bright economic future for all within a relatively short space of time. More than any other post-1949 leadership, Deng Xiaoping and his supporters tied their legitimacy to their ability to deliver the economic goods.

The new policies revolved around the promotion of market mechanisms to deal with the inefficiencies of allocation and distribution that occur within the central state planning system. Awareness of the 'new technological revolution' increased the Chinese leaders' desire to make their system more flexible and thus more amenable to change. To take advantage of market opportunities, more power of decision-making was to be given to the localities, and in particular to the units of production themselves. Production units now have more autonomy to decide what to produce, how much and where to market the products. At the core of this system lie the ubiquitous contracts that are expected to govern economic activity. Correspondingly material incentives are seen as the major mechanism for causing people to work harder, and the socialist principle of 'to each according to his work' is to be firmly applied. Egalitarianism is attacked as a dangerous notion that retards economic growth. These reforms of the domestic economy have been accompanied by an unprecedented opening to the outside world in search of export markets and the necessary foreign investments, technology and higher quality consumer goods.

However, considerable opposition to this programme has persisted. Two main groups have been critical of the reforms. First, there are those grouped around veteran economic planner, Chen Yun, who object on economic grounds. While Chen is not opposed to the introduction of limited market reforms, he does oppose too great a role for the market and a corresponding weakening of the central planning apparatus. Institutionally, he is supported by representatives of the large, formerly privileged state sector. This sector has proved resistant to change, particularly with respect to the key areas of prices and property relationships.

Secondly, there are those such as Wang Zhen and Peng Zhen who are opposed to the refoms because of their adverse social and political effects. They recognise that the greater contacts with the outside world have exposed Chinese society to all kinds of thought patterns which they denounce as 'bourgeois'. Similarly, they realise that the domestic economic reforms provide a structural basis for the emergence of new groups, such as entrepreneurs. These groups are less amenable to control by the party.

These opponents were able to use the economic crisis of 1988 and the political crisis of 1989 first to blunt the thrust of the reforms and then to remove General Secretary Zhao Ziyang and launch a more wide-ranging critique of the economic reform programme.

Agricultural policy

The economic reforms began, and have proceeded furthest, in the agricultural sector. Indeed, while the industrial reforms present very little that has not been tried in the Soviet Union and Eastern Europe, the agricultural reforms represent a radical new departure, throwing up the question of whether there is still a socialist agricultural system in China. However, the sweet success of the early 1980s had soured by the end of the decade and threatened to become the policy headache of the 1990s.

At the time of Mao's death, the Chinese countryside was organised on the basis of communes (set up during the Great Leap Forward, 1958–60). These communes functioned as the highest level of economic organisation in the countryside and as the basic level of government in the countryside. Below the commune were production brigades and teams. For most peasants, the teams were the most important unit as they made the final decisions concerning both the production of goods and the distribution of income in accordance with the work-points accumulated. While the radicals of the Cultural Revolution tried to force this level of accounting upwards, the reforms of the 1980s have placed many of the functions in the hands of the individual household. Further, the commune has been relieved of its government functions. Townships have been resurrected as a level of government. With the de-collectivisation of the countryside, the economic functions of the commune have also been considerably weakened. The old commune system lent itself to central planning, large-scale production and unified distribution. It is precisely these aspects of rural policy that the reforms set out to undermine.

Initial post-Mao policy sought to encourage growth in agricultural production by raising substantially procurement prices and by modernising agriculture through brigade and team financing. At the same time, policy was relaxed to let different regions make use of the 'law of comparative advantage'. Also, private plots of land and sideline production were stressed as playing an important role in agricultural growth. To allow the peasants to sell their products – for example, their above-quota grain – private markets were again tolerated. This policy was firmly based on the collective and represented nothing radically new.

In December 1978, it was decided that the procurement price of grain deliveries would be increased by an average of 20 per cent, above-quota grain by 50 per cent, and cotton by 30 per cent. However, the result of this policy was to increase massively state expenditures on agriculture. In addition, the policy of agricultural modernisation did not bear fruit. A new strategy had to be found that would raise agricultural incomes, permitting modernisation but without significantly increasing state investment.

The most important subsequent reform was the introduction of the responsibility system. Although this was introduced in December 1978, it did not entail any significant undermining of the collective. However, by 1980 the more radical reforms of contracting various activities to the household were becoming commonplace despite official denials. The household was clearly becoming the key economic unit in the countryside. This household contracting system makes the peasant household the nucleus of agricultural production, working on a clearly stipulated piece of land for a specific period of time. It includes all raw materials and means of production except land-use rights and access rights to irrigation facilities; the latter rights are made available by the collective. Later legislation confirmed this situation and extended the cropping contracts to over 15 years; it also encouraged the concentration of land with the most productive households, facilitated the flow of capital across regions for investment and reduced the funds that the collective could demand from the peasantry.

In January 1985, in a further radical move, the state announced its intention to abolish its monopoly over purchasing and marketing of major farm products. Instead of the state assigning fixed quotas of farm products to be purchased from farmers, a system of contract purchasing was to be introduced. All products not purchased in this way could be disposed of on the market. Clearly, the aim of this reform was to improve the distribution of commodities and further reward efficient producers. It was hoped that this would encourage wealthier peasants to re-invest capital and labour in the land. Essentially, the contract procurement system was intended to establish a market relationship between the state and the peasantry and between the urban and rural areas.

However, this new measure came as a massive shock to the agricultural system and challenged the old economic assumptions on which it was built. It led to the breakdown of the unequal terms of trade between the rural and urban areas under which an estimated 600–800 billion *yuan* was extracted from the peasantry over a 30 year period. New channels opened for the circulation and marketing of surplus grain and other agricultural products. However, the state could not increase the price of grain to the urban dwellers and thus returns on grain production began to decline and in some instances money could even be lost on grain production. For example, between 1983 and 1985, average prices paid for chemical fertilisers rose by 43 per cent and those for pesticides by 83 per cent, reducing net income gained from one hectare of grain by about 30–40 per cent. In comparison with cash crops, grain production was no longer a lucrative activity.

The initial agricultural reforms had thus provided a major boost to the rural sector, but by 1985 they were beginning to falter. Grain production increased from 305 million tons in 1978 to 407 million tons in 1984 only to fall back to 379 million tons the following year. This was the second largest fall in grain production in the history of the PRC. Further the growth in rural incomes began to slow from 17.6 per cent per annum from 1978 to 1984 to only 5.5 per cent by 1987. Finally, the income gap between rural and urban areas which had been coming down began to widen again and by 1986 it was 2.33:1, worse than it had been at the beginning of the reforms.

The cause of these problems lies in major part with poor policy implementation and by the central authorities not taking their policies through to their logical conclusion. This has left Chinese agriculture, as with industry, in a never-never land that is governed neither by the market nor the central plan. First, during the reform period, the state cut its investment in the agricultural sector from 10 per cent of the capital construction budget in the period 1976–80 to 3.9 per cent for 1986–90. In part, this cut was to make up for the massive subsidies that were necessary to cover the increased price of grain. Its fear of urban unrest made it impossible to pass on the price rises to residents. The expectation was that the collectives and/or individuals would take up the investment, thus off-setting the reduction in state funds. The effective collapse of the collectives as powerful economic entities sealed off one of the alternative sources of funds. Initially, individual households were wary of reinvesting profits because of their uncertainty about how long it would be before policy would change yet again. When they did begin to invest, it was not in grain production but in more lucrative cash crop or sideline production.

Secondly, the contract procurement system was effectively abandoned before the reform had been properly carried out. Under the system there was dual pricing, with the state buying the grain needed for urban consumption and state industry at artificially low prices while allowing surplus grain to be sold at free market prices. Eventually, the difference between the two price systems was to be eliminated. Unfortunately this system had been introduced following the bumper harvest of 1984 when the market price of grain was below the state purchase price. But by 1985, it was already back above this price and continued rising. The level of exploitation that had always been disguised thus became clear to the peasantry. Further, this system meant that when grain was scarce market prices would go up further, thus making the 'exploitation' even greater.

Not surprisingly, the peasantry reacted angrily to the policy and began to hold back grain from the state whenever possible. The state, on the other hand, did not pursue the logic of its policy and began to resort to old administrative measures to force the peasantry to produce more grain. This was exacerbated by the fact that grain production was already a political issue in China and the Maoist obsession with self-sufficiency in grain still strongly influences many leaders.

The policies adopted have alienated the peasantry still further. Old administrative controls were revamped to force the peasantry to deliver more grain to the state, thus abandoning the newly emerging market relationship between the state and peasantry. In practice, this meant that the peasantry was being forced to sell more grain at below market prices. The extra purchases are increasing the state's fiscal problems and it was reported that the Agricultural Bank of China was some US$ 3 billion short of the purchase loans needed for the July to August 1989 harvest. As a result, many peasants are being paid with letters of credit. Of course, when these can be redeemed the actual value of payment will be considerably below that of the time of issue. As a result, riots and outbursts of anger have become features of rural life.

After an initial period of success that released the pent-up resources and energies of the rural sector, the agricultural reforms have run into trouble. They have slipped into the same oscillation between administrative mechanisms and new market-based measures that have been a permanent feature of the urban industrial reforms.

Industrial policy

Just as the reforms of the agricultural sector began to run out of steam in 1984, the leadership turned its attentions to reform of the urban industrial sector. In contrast with the rural reforms, industrial reforms have followed a stop-go pattern from the beginning. However, by 1984 pressure increased for further reform of the industrial sector, as it was clear that the industrial system was unable properly to meet the needs of the increasingly commercialised decentralised agricultural system. Indeed, the reformers were using the successes to date of the rural sector to argue for the implementation of similar measures in the industrial sector. However, it was much harder to transfer these experiences to the urban environment where production was more socialised and bureaucratised.

The need for reform, and the reform experiments to date, were recognised in the Central Committee 'Decision on Reform of the Economic Structure' of October 1984. This decision chronicles the problems of the industrial economy, noting that 'defects in the urban economic sector ... seriously hinder the development of the forces of production'. The measures proposed offered a more thoroughgoing reform than the piecemeal experimentation that had previously taken place. However, in 1985–6 and again in 1988, when problems became apparent, orthodox leaders have tried to bring the reforms to a halt by reasserting the levers of administrative controls at the expense of market forces.

The key to the industrial reform programme was to make enterprises more economically responsible. Most important has been the introduction of enterprise profit retention. In 1983 a system of tax profits was introduced, and this was adopted in the 1984 Decision as a policy for all enterprises. This new system replaced the old system of requisition of profits or covering losses and the initial reform experiments of profit contracting. The intention was that the tax system would stabilise state revenues and force enterprises to become more fiscally responsible.

To ensure that enterprises could take proper advantage of their limited market opportunities, managers of factories and other enterprises were to be given greater powers of decision-making with respect to production plans and marketing, sources of supply, distribution of profits within the enterprise and the hiring and firing of workers. While this was to provide the carrot, it was recognised by some that there should be a stick with which to beat inefficient enterprises. Thus, a draft bankruptcy law was drafted, and in August and September 1986 an enterprise in Shenyang won fame by becoming the first enterprise to be declared bankrupt since the founding of the PRC. However, this measure provoked a strong reaction from opponents and reformers alike. A decision on the law was postponed and in December 1986 the Standing Committee of the National People's Congress reached a compromise by adopting a 'trial law' to come into effect three months after a general enterprise law had been adopted. The final adoption of the law may have more to do with trying to deal with the scarcity of funds than with the desire to introduce 'capitalist' mechanisms into the Chinese economy. Bankruptcy would put an end to enterprises that wasted scarce resources and materials.

As with the peasantry, the main incentive to make workers work harder and raise labour productivity was to be a material one. Wage rises, bonuses and piece-rate systems have all been tried to increase worker productivity, although to date the results have not been remarkable. Here, also, along with the carrot comes a stick: the 'iron rice bowl', the name given to the system under which it was impossible to fire workers, is to be abolished. Lifelong tenure is to be replaced by a system of fixed-term labour contracts. In October 1986, a new labour contract law and supplementary regulations were introduced to cover the recruitment and dismissal of undisciplined employees. This new system was intended to reward those who work well, provide the basis for dismissal of bad workers and, at the same time, cut down the costs of social security and welfare.

Not surprisingly, such a programme affected the vested interests of the old centrally planned system and resistance consolidated. At the Thirteenth Party Congress in October 1987, Zhao Ziyang tried to rebuff this resistance and to give the reforms a new impetus. To refute criticisms along ideological lines Zhao announced that China was in the 'initial stage of socialism', a stage that would last for approximately 100 years. Because this was taking China into uncharted waters, theory was to be defined as policy developed, thus freeing China's decision-makers from Maoist dogma. The major task of this period was defined as improvement of standards of living rather than the waging of class struggle. The theory was used to justify different forms of ownership and the use of what had previously been denounced as capitalist economic mechanisms for regulating the economy.

At the Congress, Zhao outlined a reduced role for central planning and a greater variety in ownership forms. Further, he broke with the principle that the only source of income was 'distribution according to work'. In the future, Zhao envisaged a situation wherein 'buyers of bonds will earn interest, [and] shareholders dividends, enterprise managers will receive additional income to compensate for bearing risks, and owners of private enterprises who employ workers will receive some income that does not come from their own labour'. Zhao brushed aside possible accusations that this was making use of capitalist economic mechanisms with the simple statement that devices of this kind were 'not peculiar to capitalism'.

However, Zhao was forced to compromise on key issues such as grain production and price reform, and the economic problems of 1988 enabled his opponents to push him aside and restore more orthodox economic policies. The student demonstrations of 1989 gave them the chance to remove him altogether and to launch a major attack on the reform programme.

While the central administrative controls were being weakened, they were not being replaced by adequate market mechanisms. In 1988, this led to major economic problems of overheating and attendant inflationary tendencies. In 1988 industrial production increased 17.7 per cent, well above the proposed 8 per cent. While looking good on paper, this economic growth put an enormous strain on the energy and transport sectors, where growth rates hovered around the 5 per cent mark. These problems of imbalance aggravated the inflation rate. Official figures show an inflation rate of 21 per cent for 1988 but most reliable, unofficial estimates for urban areas placed it at around 35 per cent.

This perceived economic crisis gave the orthodox leaders a chance to slow down the process of economic change. While the reformers were perplexed by their inability to control the adverse phenomena through the market mechanisms that they had put in place, orthodox leaders were scandalised at what they saw as the unravelling of the Leninist foundations of the regime. However, it is important to point out that all the features that made up the crisis of 1988 were always apparent. What had changed was that whereas under the old administrative system features such as inflation, unemployment and low quality products could be hidden, under the reforms they had been exposed for all to see.

In September 1988, an austerity programme combined with reassertion of central control was launched. This was tightened up at the meeting of the National People's Congress meeting of March–April 1989. This austerity programme initially concealed an attack on Zhao's reforms and the attack became obvious after Zhao's fall (June 1989). Market mechanisms are again relegated to a secondary role with the primacy of the plan being reasserted. The reassertion of the plan's role will preserve the vested interests of the central bureaucrats who felt their privileged position threatened by a more open economic system. In addition, new ownership forms that challenge traditional notions of socialism are being criticised.

A major point of disagreement has been how far to move with price reform. The major problem with the increased use of market levers in China's economy is that the market, such as it exists, is an imperfect one and is quite capable of distorting policy intentions. The irrational price structure was recognised in the 1984 Decision as the 'key to reform of the entire economic structure'. However, recognising the problem and dealing with it are two quite separate matters. While China's leaders recognised the necessity for some form of price reform, many fear the potential unrest caused by a major overhaul.

At the session of the National People's Congress, Li Peng announced that the government had restored price controls on some 32 commodities and that this was merely a beginning. This strengthens China's dual-pricing system which the reforms were intended to undermine. Under this system some prices for a product are set by planners, while others are supposedly determined by market forces. This provides the structural basis for the corruption against which the students were demonstrating in mid-1989. Officials with good connections can purchase goods at state regulated prices and then sell them on to other enterprises at higher market prices.

Unlike Western governments, China will not increase interest rates as a way of calming growth and bringing down inflation. The reason for this is quite simple – such a rise would cause thousands of inefficient enterprises to become bankrupt, throwing even more people out of work. Instead in March 1989, new controls and taxes for the private business sector, rural enterprises and farming were proposed. To date, these have been the most buoyant sectors of the economy. In detail, investment loans to the collective sector were to be cut; factories that produced shoddy products or that used up scarce raw materials needed by the state sector would have to close down; and a new government levy of 10 per cent on private and collective enterprises was introduced.

As a result of such measures the number of small private businesses dropped by 15 per cent in the first half of 1989 to almost 12.5 million. The transport sector was particularly badly hit with some 26 per cent of the businesses going under. If the present policies continue for any length of time, entrepreneurs will become much more cautious and will be exposed much more readily to charges of corruption or of engaging in 'bourgeois liberalisation'.

These measures may well succeed in bringing a temporary solution to the problems of too rapid economic growth and inflation that occurred in 1988 and 1989. Over the long term this policy of 'back to the future' offers no solution other than to lead China into its own form of Brezhnevism. Having come to the point of crossing the Rubicon from one economic system to another, the current Chinese leadership decided to pull back. In the absence of anyone who can chart a way forward, China now faces the same problem as the partially reformed economies of Eastern Europe. To date no socialist country has shown itself capable of devising policies that can manage an economy partly run by the market mechanism and partly by the old central administrative mechanisms. Although the situation may be changing in Hungary and Poland, no country has been capable of putting together a coalition of interests strong enough to break through the constraints of the old system. The tendency is for policy to oscillate between a slight loosening of control followed by quick withdrawal once prices begin to rise and potential unrest emerges. During the 1980s Chinese economic policy-making has followed this same stop-go pattern. China now faces the risk of slipping into dangerous oscillation between central control and attempts at relaxation.

If this is so, it will finish up with the worst aspects of a centrally planned system and the worst features of a market economy.

Further reading

A considerable literature is now available on groups and the policy-making process in the communist states. The pioneering contributions are those of Gordon Skilling; see particularly Skilling (1966) and (1973). A symposium on the utility of the group approach, 'Pluralism in communist societies: is the emperor naked?', appeared in *Studies in Comparative Communism*, vol. 12 (1979). Two sceptical contributions are Janos (1970) and Odom (1976); see also Skilling's reflections upon the debate (1983) and the discussions on pluralism and the role of groups in policy-making in Solomon (1983). The opportunities for political participation by the mass public and considered on a comparative basis in Schulz and Adams (1981) and Nelson (1988). Holmes (1981b) considers the policy process in communist states with particular reference to industrial policy in the USSR and the GDR.

On the USSR more specifically the most helpful single work, which has considerable relevance for the other communist states, is Skilling and Griffiths (1971). Also useful are Juviler and Morton (1967), for the Khrushchev period, and Smith (1980), for the Brezhnev period. On the development of the Soviet economy see Ellman (1989), Nove (1989), Gregory and Stuart (1986) and Aslund (1989). On the politics of economic reform, see the chapters on the *apparatchiki*, industrial managers and economists in Skilling and Griffiths (1971); see also Lewin (1975), Hough (1969), Azrael (1966), Andrle (1976) and Rutland (1985). On the role of the military, see particularly Colton (1979), Jones (1986) and the International Institute of Strategic Studies' *Military Balance* (London, annual). On the politics of labour, see Lane and O'Dell (1978), Ruble (1981) and Schapiro and Godson (1984). The role of letters from the mass public is considered in White (1983b), and 'covert political participation' is considered in a stimulating article by DiFranceisco and Gitelman (1985). See also Hahn (1988).

Most of the books mentioned in earlier sections on Eastern Europe deal with policy formation; there is at present no single study specifically devoted to this theme. On nationality and related issues in Yugoslavia, several fairly general studies are useful including Singleton (1985), Rusinow (1977), Wilson (1980), Lydall (1984 and 1989), and McFarlane (1988). A longer-term historical background is provided in Jelavich (1983), which deals with the Balkans as a whole. On the national question more specifically see Burg (1983) and Ramet (1984).

An interesting collection of essays comparing China with Eastern Europe can be found in Nee and Stark (1989), while Prybyla (1987) provides a stimulating analysis of the relationship between plan and market. The radical approach to Chinese rural policy is covered in Zweig (1989). A good series of essays on the earlier phase of economic reform can be found in Perry and Wong (1985) and these can be supplemented by those in Feuchtwang and Hussain (1988). The most recent developments can be followed in Fewsmith (1988), Prybyla (1989) and Solinger (1989). The important area of science and technology and its relationship to economic reform is covered in Saich (1989b).

7

Democracy and Citizen Politics

Communist states, for many years, were able to claim an impressive record of social and economic achievement. They had high rates of economic growth, but low levels of inflation and unemployment. They had high educational enrolments and comprehensive welfare programmes; they had low cost housing and comprehensive health services. There were few, however, who argued that they had made a comparable contribution to the field of politics, or to the enlargement of human liberty in particular. It had been supposed by Marx that, broadly speaking, once capitalism – the last of the class-divided and exploitative societies – had been abolished, there would be no more need for a separate sphere of political administration and the state would (in Engels's celebrated phrase) 'die out'. In the communist states, however, there was little sign of a process of this kind (some unkindly suggested that the only thing that had withered away was the *idea* that the state should wither away). The communist states, on the contrary, were large, powerful and authoritarian institutions throughout the 1980s, in which the rights and liberties of the citizen, at least in Western terms, were systematically repressed. They were generally regarded, not as having inaugurated a new era of freedom, but as having added a new chapter to the history of dictatorship.

The communist states, however, did not claim to have constructed a form of democracy that conformed to the precepts of Western liberal theory. On the contrary, they had, and still have, a democratic theory of their own which, in line with Marxist and indeed with some earlier theories of democracy, places more emphasis upon the content of democracy than upon its form, and upon the socio-economic rights of citizens rather than upon their formal independence of state power. In terms of this theory, which cannot simply be ignored, the communist states have constructed a society far more democratic than that of their major Western counterparts. To describe the communist states as uniformly repressive, moreover, is unduly gross, even in terms of Western liberal theory. The degree to which individual rights have been respected has varied from country to country, from period to period and from area to area, and general statements of this kind also obscure the gradual but perceptible development in the communist states of, if not a rule of law, then at least an increased tendency on the part of the authorities to avoid the routine perversion of judicial procedures and the denial of what is called 'socialist legality'. For all the limitations and imperfections of such developments, they deserve at least to be taken into account in any assessment of democracy and citizen politics in the communist (and now postcommunist) states.

The USSR: democracy, law and civil rights

Soviet democratic theory is based upon classical Marxist theory, in terms of which there can be no 'democracy' in the abstract but only particular forms of class democracy depending upon which social group owns the means of production and thereby, it is thought, holds political power in the society. In the Soviet Union, as in the other communist states, the means of production – factories, farms and so forth – belong to the people as a whole, and it is the people, rather than a narrow exploiting group, who control the national resources and supposedly ensure that they are used for the benefit of all members of the society. As the current edition of the *Great Soviet Encyclopedia* puts it, bourgeois democracy, such as exists in Western countries, is a 'form of dictatorship of capitalists over proletarians and other semi-proletarian and non-proletarian toiling classes and strata of the population. It is characterised by a blatant contradiction between the declared "power of the people" and the actual domination of the exploiters'. In a socialist democracy, on the other hand, as in the communist states, there is a 'complete accord between the form and content of democratic institutions, laws, etc. and the power of the toilers'. These societies, it is argued, are characterised by real and not fictitious rights for the people as a whole, by an absence of inequalities based upon race, class, religion or sex, and by the broadest possible participation of ordinary people in the administration of cultural and economic as well as political affairs. A democracy of this kind is held to be the 'historically highest type of political democracy' and the 'only possible form of socialist state'.

These principles of socialist democracy, it is argued, are fully applied in the contemporary USSR, as in the other communist-ruled states. All power belongs, according to the Constitution, to the people, who exercise it through the soviets of people's deputies which they elect and which alone have law-making powers. The people, it is pointed out, are themselves well represented in these bodies, in line with the Soviet principle that the people should administer the state directly rather than leave it to a professional class of politicians. The soviets at all levels of the system are indeed representative of all sections of the nation, of all its nationalities, age groups, genders and classes (although much less so after 1989 than under the earlier arrangements which ensured that patterns of representation of this kind were maintained from election to election). It is of course accepted that the communist party, a small minority of the total population, plays a 'leading' or at least dominant role in the work of such institutions and in political life generally. But, it is pointed out, ordinary workers and peasants constitute a majority of the party's membership, and for them it is an instrument of rule, a means of ensuring that their preferences are reflected in the policies that are pursued by the Soviet government. What, it might be asked, could be more 'democratic' than that?

The Soviet Constitution, it is argued, extends these principles further. Unlike the constitutions of capitalist states, it is pointed out, which do no more than proclaim the rights of citizens in purely abstract terms (the 'right of anyone to dine at the Savoy [a luxury London hotel]' though very few will in practice be able to afford to do so), the Soviet Constitution actually provides the means by which the rights that it proclaims can be enjoyed. The right to education, for instance (Article 45), is 'guaranteed' by the free provision of all forms of education, by the payment of scholarships and grants to students, and in other ways. Similar means are provided by which the other rights mentioned in the Constitution, such as the right to work, to housing, to social security and to health care, can at least ostensibly be made available to all citizens. The Constitution also provides and again nominally guarantees a wide range of civil liberties, such as the right to freedom of scientific, technical and artistic work, the right to take part in the management of state and public affairs, the right to associate in public organisations and the rights of freedom of speech, of the press and of assembly. The last of these, for instance (Article 50), is supposedly guaranteed by 'putting public buildings, streets and squares at the disposal of the working people and their organisations, by broad dissemination of information, and by the opportunity to use the press, television and radio'.

Most of these rights, however, are qualified in various ways. The right of freedom of speech, of the press and of assembly, for instance, is guaranteed only in so far as it is 'in accordance with the interests of the people and in order to strengthen and develop the socialist system'. The rights of freedom of scientific, technical and artistic work and to associate in public organisations (Articles 47 and 51), similarly, are granted only in so far as they are 'in accordance with the aims of building communism'. This means that it is in fact the Communist Party, as the only legitimate interpreter of the people's best interests and of the requirements of the building of communism, which decides whether these rights are to be enjoyed or not, and they are in practice extended only to approved individuals and organisations such as the trade unions, the Komsomol and the co-operatives. Further more general restrictions are contained in Article 39, which states that citizens' enjoyment of their rights must 'not be to the detriment of the interests of society or of the state', and in Article 59, which states that citizens' performance of their duties and freedoms is 'inseparable from the performance of their duties and obligations', which include the duty to engage in socially useful labour, to protect state property and to bring up their children to be 'worthy members of socialist society'. In any conflict of interpretation, moreover, it will be the party's wishes that prevail, as there are no means of challenging its decisions in the courts or of enforcing the observance of some of the other provisions in the Constitution, such as the right to inviolability of the home and of postal and telegraphic communications (Articles 55 and 56).

Official sources claim, as we have noted, that in making such decisions the party is guided by the interests of the majority of the population, and more particularly of the workers and peasants who make up a majority of its members. This claim would be more convincing were it not for the fact that the party, as we have seen, is a highly centralised, hierarchical institution, and that workers and peasants account for a steadily diminishing proportion of the total as one moves upwards in the hierarchy. Workers and peasants, for instance, accounted for 56.8 per cent of the party's total membership in 1989 (and this figure is itself somewhat suspect because of the continued tendency to report such statistics in terms of social origin or occupation at the time of entry rather than in terms of current occupation, which may often be white-collar). In the Central Committee that had been elected three years earlier, however, there were only twenty-three workers or peasants, no more than 7 per cent of the total, and in the Politburo itself there were none at all (though most of its members were admittedly from modest backgrounds). Much the same is true of representation in the soviets as one moves from the local to the national level. The party and state leadership may, for various reasons, promote policies which are in the interests of the mass of the population, or at least enjoy majority support. But there is little guarantee, in terms of social origin, that they will do so, and there are few means of compelling them to do so should they decide otherwise.

Law and the courts

This situation results largely from the fact that in the USSR, unlike the Western liberal democracies, the courts are not independent of the government but form part of the same integrated state system. The Western doctrine of the separation of powers was regarded by Soviet official theorists, at any rate until recently, as a smokescreen for the defence of capitalist interests. In the USSR, on the other hand, the court system is seen as one which represents and promotes the interests of the majority of the population, and which like all the other parts of the state system is directly or indirectly responsible to the people. All judges in the USSR, for instance, are elected, accountable to their electors, and can be recalled in the same manner as deputies to the soviets. The Soviet court system is organised at three levels: at the local level, where people's courts (the judges in which are elected by higher-level soviets) deal with minor criminal and a large number of civil cases; at the regional level, where regional courts deal with appeals from the people's courts and with more serious criminal and civil matters; and at the republican level, where supreme courts deal with appeals from the regional courts and with civil and criminal cases of some gravity. At the apex of the system is the Supreme Court of the USSR, elected by the USSR Supreme Soviet, which supervises the administration of justice at lower levels and in addition exercises original jurisdiction over cases of exceptional gravity.

The Constitution prescribes that court proceedings shall be open to the public in all but exceptional circumstances, that the defendant in a criminal trial shall have a right to legal assistance, and that judges and the people's assessors who assist them in their work shall be 'independent and subject only to the law' (Article 155). In practice these guarantees are subject to a number of serious qualifications. In the first place, the election of judges and of people's assessors is controlled by the party through the *nomenklatura* in the same way that elections to all other positions of importance are controlled, and no candidate is likely to be considered, whatever his technical competence, unless he or she is willing to accept the principle of party dominance. Judges are also subject to the authority of higher court officials and of the Procuracy (a mainly supervisory body) in their work, and their decisions may be set aside if they fail to accord with the wishes of those at higher levels of the system. It is clear, moreover, that the party keeps a close watch on the work of the courts and intervenes in detail whenever it considers it necessary to do so, particularly when matters of a politically sensitive nature are involved. The work of the courts is supervised at the highest levels by the State and Law Department, one of the sections of the Central Committee apparatus, and according to emigre testimony it is normal practice for legal judgements in particularly controversial cases to be drawn up in this department. In the ordinary run of cases, however, most of which are civil and of little state significance, detailed party intervention of this kind is neither common nor even necessary.

It would be wrong, moreover, to imply that there had been no significant improvement in the administration of Soviet justice over the years. In the Stalin period, for instance, the most elementary legal norms were routinely disregarded. The criminal code of the time, adopted in 1926 and subsequently much amended, contained the notorious Article 58 on 'counter-revolutionary crimes', whose various sections provided severe penalties for any form of real or imagined dissidence. People were arrested and imprisoned, according to Solzhenitsyn, for the most preposterous of 'crimes':

> A tailor laying aside his needle stuck it into a newspaper on the wall so it wouldn't get lost and happened to stick it in the eye of a portrait of Kaganovich [at that time a prominent member of the Politburo]. A customer observed this: Article 58 – ten years (terrorism) ...
>
> A tractor driver of the Znamenka Machinery and Tractor Station lined his thin shoes for warmth with a pamphlet about the candidate for elections to the Supreme Soviet, but a charwoman noticed it was missing (she was responsible for the leaflets) and found out who had it. Counter-revolutionary agitation – ten years ...
>
> A *deaf and dumb* carpenter got a term for counter-revolutionary *agitation*. How? He was laying floors in a club. Everything had been removed from the big hall, and there was no nail or hook anywhere. While he was working, he hung his jacket and his service cap on a bust of Lenin. Someone came in and saw it. Article 58 – ten years.

If the court could find no specific offence that the defendant had committed it could sentence him 'by analogy' with some other crime, and sentences could also be passed retrospectively. In addition the NKVD (People's Commissiariat of Internal Affairs or security police) administered a separate court system, the Special Boards, set up in 1934, which could try a suspect in his absence and impose whatever sentence it wished, including the death penalty. In the later 1930s it appears to have handled hundreds of cases daily.

Following the death of Stalin in 1953 a new emphasis began to be placed upon 'socialist legality', or the proper observance of judicial procedures. The NKVD Special Boards were abolished in the same year; large numbers of people were released from prison camps and their sentences investigated and quashed if they were found to lack a proper foundation in law; some of the leading officials of the security police were tried and executed; and most important of all, a new criminal code was adopted which outlawed many of the abuses of legality of the previous period. The new code, adopted in the form of general principles for the USSR as a whole in 1958 and then in the form of more specific codes for each of the union republics in 1960 and 1961, prohibited trial by analogy or retrospective justice; only actions specifically designated as criminal at the time of their commission could be used as the basis of judicial proceedings. An associated Code of Criminal Procedure prohibited night-time interrogation and torture, which had previously been widely practised. The security police (now called the KGB) retained certain powers of arrest and investigation, particularly in the case of 'especially dangerous crimes against the state' such as espionage and treason, but their powers were greatly reduced and their investigations were placed under the supervision of a department in the Procurator General's office. From this time forward, at least in theory, no trial could take place other than in a properly constituted court of law and in accordance with established court procedures.

The present position is that it is unusual (as well as illegal) for people to be arrested simply for their beliefs or their expressions of opinion. They must, as a rule, engage in actions which are specifically designated as criminal at the time of their commission if they are to fall foul of the authorities, and they will be properly tried in open court, with the right to employ a defence counsel, if they do so. Far fewer people, also, are in detention than was the case under Stalin: between 1 and 2 million altogether, it is estimated, of whom about a hundred could reasonably be classified as political prisoners, as against the 10 to 15 million who were languishing in the prison camps at the time of Stalin's death in 1953. The individual citizen, however, has still no firm guarantee of equitable treatment if the authorities decide to persecute him, and there have been frequent reports of deviations from the established norms in such cases. Some critics were expelled from the USSR against their wishes, others were tried in proceedings which were effectively closed to the public by filling the courtroom with specially invited audiences (often secret policemen), and in a small but disturbing number of cases apparently sane dissidents were accused of having 'delusions of reforming society' and diagnosed as schizophrenics (this disturbing practice was apparently discontinued in the 1980s).

The law as it stands, moreover, is unusually comprehensive and rather ambiguous in its formulation, lending itself easily to abuse if the authorities decide accordingly. The article under which political dissenters were most frequently sentenced, for instance, was Article 70 of the RSFSR Criminal Code, which dealt with 'anti-Soviet agitation and propaganda'. In effect until the Criminal Code was revised again in 1989–90, it read as follows:

> Agitation or propaganda carried on for the purpose of subverting or wakening the Soviet regime or of committing particular, especially dangerous crimes against the state, or the circulation, for the same purposes, of slanderous fabrications which defame the Soviet state and social system, or the circulation and preparation and keeping for the same purposes, of literature of such a content, shall be punished by deprivation of liberty for a term of six months to seven years, with or without additional exile for a term of two to five years, or by exile for a term of two to five years.

In addition Article 190, which dealt with 'crimes against the system of administration', prohibited the 'systematic circulation in an oral form of fabrications known to be false which defame the Soviet state and social system' and the 'preparation or circulation in written, printed or other forms of works of such content', and provided for a prison term of between three and five years for those who were found guilty of having violated it. The result was that the authorities had a good deal of scope in which they could, if they wished, deprive critics of their liberty or otherwise inconvenience them without necessarily stepping outside the strict letter of the law.

Civil rights and citizen politics under Gorbachev

The process of reform under Gorbachev has involved a reassertion of the role of law in Soviet society and a broadening of the scope for independent citizens' politics as well as economic and other changes. Gorbachev, a lawyer by academic training, told interviewers in 1988 that *perestroika* was as much a 'legal revolution' as a reform of the political system as such. He set out the main elements of his thinking on this point in his book *Perestroika*, published in 1987. Democracy, he argued, could not exist and develop without the rule of law, because law 'is designed to protect society from abuses of power and guarantee citizens and their organisations and work collectives their rights and freedoms'. This was why the party leadership had taken such a firm stand on the matter; and they knew from their own experience what could happen if there were deviations from such principles. The law, equally, should not be overprescriptive: it was better to follow the principle 'Everything which is not permitted by law is allowed'. Important steps in this direction had already been taken, in Gorbachev's view: legislation of 1987, for instance, permitted appeals against the actions of officials and established a procedure for submitting important public issues to a process of national discussion. Much more, however, remained to be done, including the adoption of measures that would guarantee the independence of judges and secure the 'most strictly democratic principles' in the work of the courts.

These principles found expression during 1988 in an entirely new concept, the 'socialist law-based state'. First mentioned at a meeting between Gorbachev and media workers in May

1988, it became the centrepiece of a resolution on legal reform that was adopted at the 19th Party Conference the following July. The resolution called for 'large-scale legal reform' over the coming years, including a review of existing codes of law, greater safeguards for the independence of judges, and an extensive programme of legal education for the population at large. The process of reform was carried further in the constitutional amendments that were approved in December 1988. In the most notable of these changes, a 23-member Committee of Constitutional Supervision was established, elected by the Congress of People's Deputies for a ten-year term, with responsibility for ensuring that government decisions and draft legislation were in full conformity with the constitution. Judges, in addition, were to be elected by soviets at the level immediately above them, in order to free them from dependence upon those whose behaviour they were supposed to monitor, and they were to hold office, for the same reason, for ten rather than five years at a time. All of this, in Gorbachev's view, represented a distinctive 'socialist system of checks and balances', protecting society at large from the abuse of office by those who held the highest executive positions of state.

Legal reform was carried further in a number of other changes, among them the adoption of a new criminal code, the first for thirty years. The code was intended to contribute to the 'humanisation' as well as modernisation of the law: the number of crimes for which custodial sentences were mandatory was reduced very considerably, better conditions were instituted for the great mass of prisoners, and the scope of the death penalty was greatly restricted. Legislation on the courts, introduced in 1989, established for the first time the principle of the presumption of the innocence of the accused. Another law enforcement agency, the KGB (Committee of State Security), sought to bring its work into line with the requirements of *glasnost'* by publishing regular bulletins on its work and allowing its leading officials to be interviewed in the mass media. Welcoming these and other changes, a report produced by Amnesty International in late 1989 nonetheless found the general picture 'very confusing'. Significant extensions of human rights were under discussion and many were being implemented; but at the same time a series of decrees had reduced the right of unofficial groups to hold meetings, and armed police units set up to combat 'public disorders' had been used against peaceful crowds in a way that had alarmed a wide section of official and independent opinion.

One of the most notable respects in which the civil rights of ordinary citizens were extended in the late 1980s was through the policy of *glasnost'* or openness in the official media. Gorbachev, for whom the change was a personal priority, appears to have believed that *glasnost'* would help to bring about a more energetic and constructive atmosphere in the Soviet workplace and to reverse the economic stagnation of the later Brezhnev years. 'The better people are informed', he told the Central Committee that elected him, 'the more consciously they act, the more actively they support the party, its plans and programmatic objectives'. The monotony and other inadequacies of the official media had in any case attracted a lot of popular criticism. One of the newspapers that had pressed most actively for a change of policy, the Moscow daily *Sovetskaya Rossiya*, printed a letter from a reader in Kaluga in late 1985 who complained that he knew in detail what the situation was in various African countries, but had only a very rough idea what was happening in his own town. The delays and silences of the official media were often counterproductive: people listened to foreign radio broadcasts and gossip, and sometimes believed things were worse than they really were.

Influenced by these and other considerations, the Soviet media, with Gorbachev's evident encouragement, began to respond to the new call for openness in ways that often astonished their readers at home and abroad. Newspapers and television, for instance, began to report the 'dark sides' of Soviet life much more fully, many of which were formerly all but totally taboo. For instance, prostitution – previously held to be a phenomenon peculiar to capitalism – was reluctantly acknowledged as a feature of Soviet life as well. One of the earliest reports in *Sovetskaya Rossiya* in 1987 concentrated upon Komsomol Square in Moscow, site of three important railway stations, where the local police chief had made a special study of the 3500 or so prostitutes that had come to the attention of his department. The typical case, he explained, was a 'dynasty' of a mother, daughter and grandmother, all of them working the same beat, and all displaying the same physical attributes, 'the vacant look, the puffy and unwashed faces and tousled hair'. Another social issue that began to surface was the drugs problem. It was, it emerged, a serious problem in the USSR and not just in capitalist societies. The number of registered addicts, about 30,000 when the first reports appeared in 1987, was admittedly very small when compared with the numbers in the West. But the number of addicts was growing, many were very young, and some of them were obtaining their supplies, despite the Hippocratic oath, from doctors and hospitals.

Another change was in the area of official statistics. As problems mounted in the Brezhnev period, they were simply swept under the carpet by discontinuing the publication of any information about them. The official statistical yearbook, for instance, which had been published regularly since 1956, became progressively slimmer throughout the 1970s as more and more kinds of information became politically embarrassing. Life expectancy was one such case. After a steady rise since the revolution, the average life expectation for both men and women began to fall in the 1970s. The official response was to publish the data for 1971–2 year after year, not those for later years that showed the disturbing decline. Under Gorbachev a very different policy has been followed, with more and more information being made public whether or not it flattered the authorities. The 1986 statistical yearbook, the first 'Gorbachev' issue, made a start by restoring some series that had not been seen for a decade or more. The figure for infant mortality was back, although it was tucked away on p. 547. At 26 per thousand live births (though with very wide regional variations), it was nearly three times as high as the British and more than twice as high as the American level. Life expectancy figures also returned, at 64 for men and 73 for women. Again, these were low by comparison with other industrialised nations.

A third important change was the opportunity that became available for Soviet readers and viewers to obtain a genuinely alternative viewpoint on current world issues from Western and non-communist politicians, journalists and scholars. *Pravda*, for instance, began a new series in 1987 called 'From different positions' in which a variety of Western public figures were able to set out their position, in full and without any kind of editing. The first such article, in February 1987, featured Robert Dole, at this time the Republican leader of the US Senate. The weekly *Moscow News*, published in Russian as well as in foreign languages, featured interviews with Zbigniew Brzezinski and Richard Pipes, as well as the complete translation of a manifesto written by Vladimir Bukovsky and a number of other prominent emigres. Soviet television began to feature interviews with Western politicians and others, and visiting leaders such as George Schultz and Margaret Thatcher were allowed to present their views for the first time to a mass audience. A related innovation was the 'spacebridge', linking studio audiences in the Soviet Union and foreign countries. One of the first of these linked studio audiences in Leningrad and Seattle; transmitted on Soviet TV's First Programme, it was seen by an estimated 270 million people (virtually the entire population) on its two showings.

A greater openness to domestic and international developments went hand in hand with an increasing politicisation of Soviet society. Gorbachev, in his address to the 27th Party Congress in 1986, had called for the establishment of women's councils (bodies of this kind had existed in the 1920s) and a veterans' association. Both of these organisations were duly established in 1986 and 1987; so too were a Children's Fund, a Designers' Union, a Cultural Fund and many others. In 1988 an all-union Environmental Fund was established, and in 1989 the first consumers' associations. Some of the organisations concerned were granted electoral rights under the 1988 constitutional amendments and they were part of a wider attempt to develop a 'civil society' in the USSR, based for the most part upon citizen initiative rather than state action. Raisa Gorbachev was personally associated with the Cultural Fund, and the General Secretary himself donated some of his foreign earnings to charitable associations as well as to party funds. The existence of charitable associations, and the revival of the philanthropic traditions with which they were associated, was in itself a sign of 'new thinking' on such matters.

The gradual formation of a network of 'informal associations', so called because of their indefinite status under the law and their lack of a regular structure, was a still more significant development. The new movements were in part a response to the overly formalised nature of official youth and other organisations, one of the most important of which, the Komsomol, was acknowledged to be in a 'critical' condition in the late 1980s. Equally, they represented a response to the lack of provision of any kind for a wide range of minority interests – environmental, dietetic, or philosophical. Although it was difficult to establish the number and, still more, the membership of such groups, *Pravda* estimated in 1989 that there were about 60,000 of them throughout the USSR and about 2000 in Moscow alone. A large proportion were concerned with sporting and other leisure pursuits (three-quarters of those established in Moscow, for instance), but among the others there were many that had a directly political purpose. A number based themselves upon the principles of *perestroika* but wished to push it forward more quickly. 'Memorial', for instance, established in 1988, sought to advance the critique of Stalinism by collecting oral and other testimony from survivors. The popular fronts, in the Baltic and other republics, had environmental and other objectives as well as purely nationalist ones.

More controversial, in the late 1980s, were a number of other political associations: a liberal, anti-socialist group centred around the Democratic Union, and an openly chauvinist organisation, *Pamyat'* (Memory). The Democratic Union, founded in 1988, argued that the October revolution had established a 'system of stagnant totalitarianism' and openly advocated the overthrow of party rule and the socialist order. *Pamyat'* also rejected socialism but held it to a Jewish rather than a Marxist plot, and its meetings became increasingly intolerant of dissenting opinion. The process of 'democratisation', launched in early 1987, had evidently extended much more rapidly than the party authorities had originally intended; the old pattern of centrally-dominated 'transmission belts' had clearly gone for good, but it was too soon to say that a stable, legimate pattern of citizen-based politics had replaced it.

The emergence of citizen politics in Eastern Europe

The collapse of communism and the transformation of the political systems of the countries of Central and Eastern Europe was a surprisingly rapid process. It was equally surprising that the Soviet-type systems, which had previously seemed so well established and firmly grounded, should have caved in as easily as they did. The course of the events in this process was, first, the transformation of Hungary, Poland and then, more rapidly, East Germany, Czechoslovakia, Bulgaria into nascent democracies, as symbolised most spectacularly by the chipping away at the Berlin Wall after the announcement on 9 November 1989 from East Berlin that all GDR citizens were free to travel to the West. The divided halves of Europe could now begin the slow movement towards reintegration. And this was then followed by the most dramatic of all transformations, the Romanian revolution.

It is important to be clear as to what it was that decayed and was replaced in the countries of Central and Eastern Europe. Thus, in terms of the rhetoric of legitimation, it should be understood that Soviet-type systems have next to nothing in common with socialism as this was defined in the West. Socialism has traditionally involved a commitment to equality, social justice, respect for the individual, widening choice and access to the decision-making processes that govern the life of a community.

Soviet-type systems have had nothing in common with any of these ideals, but used the slogans of socialism as one of their legitimating myths. Their connection with the socialist agenda has been twofold. First, they have used the state as an instrument of social engineering, which has been an acceptable device to Western socialism as well, but have done this without regard to society. Second, they have used the language of socialism entirely devoid of its content as a means of legitimation at home and abroad. Whereas at home this attracted very little support, essentially after the 1968 invasion of Czechoslovakia had signalled that the Soviet road was mere form without real content, in the West many regarded the verbal commitment to socialism in the communist world as real and gave these slogans some credence, even while deploring some of the failures of the Soviet-type systems. This credulousness effectively prevented much of the Western left from undertaking a much needed analysis of these systems and thereby contributed to the survival of these systems for a while.

In reality the pivot of the Soviet-type system was that it enforced the construction of a wholly politically determined future, in which all spheres – economic, social, legal, aesthetic and religious – were subordinated to political criteria regardless of appropriateness in the name of an ideologically derived goal – socialism. The rulers of these systems, essentially because of their one-sided distribution of power, could never accept any significant degree of social autonomy and, indeed, consistently destroyed all manifestations of uncontrolled social thought and action particularly in any organised form.

The initial commitment to an ideologically derived concept of the future gave these systems a degree of cohesiveness and consistency, although these were firmly directed against the wishes of the majority. However, once the shift towards the decomposition of ideology began in the 1970s, as seen in Gierek's Poland or Husák's Czechoslovakia for example, the systems became increasingly arbitrary and discretionary. The language of the ideology was still deployed in public, but decisions were taken by other criteria, ranging from the pragmatic to the opportunistic, which undermined consistency and made it easier for individuals to deflect public policy to personal gain.

In the short term, this pattern of development was useful for disorientating criticism from below and relativising it. But in the medium to longer term it led the rulers into an intellectual and eventually a moral morass from which they found it impossible to escape. However, the damage inflicted on these societies during the forty years of Soviet-type rule was far-reaching and profound, often in ways that have yet to be fully understood. Crucially, the Soviet-type revolution destroyed the civil societies that were coming into being after the

Second World War. Before the communist takeovers, these countries were at best semi-developed – even the Czechoslovak experiment in democracy between the wars had its shortcomings – but they were not the homogenised, simple polities that they became as a result of the Stalinist revolution. The countries of the region had embarked on their own, often rather fitful roads towards modernity, which recognised the existence of the market and the move towards greater complexity. These processes were cut short and all subsequent development took place under the aegis of the state.

In the process of collapse, seven factors can be isolated as having played a role in all the countries, although in some of them the events were so telescoped that their role might have been marginal. The seven factors are (1) economic decay, (2) the loss of support from pro-régime intellectuals, (3) the break in the surface unanimity of the system, (4) the growing division in the leadership, (5) the level of élite morale, (6) the international dimension and (7) the role of the crowd.

Economic decay

The political system introduced by Stalinism was in many respects simple and unstructured and depended heavily on the potential or actual politicisation of all transactions. Its centre was the *nomenklatura*, the arrangement by which all significant appointments were made with the acquiescence of the party and relying on political criteria. This proved to be particularly damaging in the running of the economy. Soviet-type economies were, in the final analysis, concerned not with matching supply and demand, but with administering inputs and outputs; in other words the economy was detached from the consumer and producer and non-economic criteria were frequently used to distort economic rationality. The much vaunted central planning system tended towards conserving a simplified industrial structure that was less and less capable of meeting the challenge of the world market. And once the Stalinist model of autarky diminished in its significance, the imperatives of the world market could no longer be fully ignored.

The unproductive and uncreative nature of the Soviet-type

system was masked for a long time. It could survive by, in effect, pursuing a kind of slash-and-burn policy, in that it used up existing resources without adding enough to replace them. In the first stage, it lived off the surplus labour in the countryside and the capital resources that had been amassed before communism. These were largely exhausted by the early 1960s and, indeed, the states of the area experienced a general downturn at that point, with Czechoslovakia becoming the first communist country to register a negative growth rate. In the second stage, the running of the system, which was concentrated on first generation heavy industry (coal, steel, energy generation and heavy metallurgical manufactures), was supported by the release of additional energies derived from the economic restructuring of the 1960s and the neglect of infrastructure, as well as to some extent of agriculture. In the third stage, the running and expansion of heavy industry – to an extent the area underwent a second heavy industrialisation in the 1970s – was financed by borrowing from the West, a resource that ran out with the Polish fiasco of 1980–1.

At this stage, the pressure to return to economic rationality became hard to fend off, but it took the best part of a decade before the rulers concluded that the political equation was in danger of coming apart. The situation was most clearly visible in Poland, where the reconstruction of a neo-Leninist, politically determined system after 1981 may have brought the semblance of a temporary and highly conditional stability, but the growing gulf between rulers and ruled was threatening to become explosive. A particular danger point was the steady loss of authority by the rulers, which was replaced by a kind of normlessness. In essence, although the economic deterioration was the proximate cause of the crisis, this was no more than its most salient manifestation. For all practical purposes, by the end of the 1980s Soviet-type systems were no longer capable of self-reproduction.

Loss of support from intellectuals

Not surprisingly in the light of the foregoing, the Soviet-type systems that were imposed on these countries after the Second World War never gained genuine popular legitimacy. At best they were tolerated in periods when the going was good by the bulk of the population, as, say, in Poland in Gierek's heyday or Hungary when Kádár's régime was at its zenith. But these systems never really sought legitimacy in the Western sense, of seeking continuing popular approval expressed through open elections. Rather they claimed to derive their legitimacy from the multitiered proposition that the party ruled because it was the legatee of a communist revolution, that it was the repository of history, that it was the most rational and efficient force in the state, that it represented the best and most progressive elements of the national tradition and, when all these claims were exposed as threadbare and no longer creditworthy, the party insisted on its monopoly rule because it held power and there was no alternative.

What is fascinating about the unravelling that was witnessed in 1989 was, in the first place, the fact that it took so little to launch the process and, second, that once started, it happened at breathtaking speed. The reserves of the system were exhausted – reserves in this connection meaning not just the economic and material benefits that it was supposed to deliver, but its political reserves as well. This raises the problem of self-legitimation. An authoritarian élite sustains itself in power not just through force and the threat of force, but more importantly because it has some vision of the future by which it can justify itself to itself. No régime can survive long without some concept of purposiveness to project its existence forward in time.

In both Poland and Hungary, the vital nexus in the process of delegitimation was the loss of the support of the significant sections of the critical intellectuals and the intelligentsia. Other than in periods of high revolutionary mobilisation, that is to say after routinisation has overcome the initial impulsion to power, the supporting intellectuals sustain authoritarian régimes by acting as a mirror in which the rulers see themselves reflected. It is vital that this mirror reflects a picture that is positive for the rulers, hence censorship, because at the moment when some other, much more realistic picture is visible in the public sphere – and the intellectuals control the public sphere through their hegemonial control of language – the rulers become confused. This confusion is then trans-

mitted through the hierarchy, upwards and downwards, until
the ruling party loses its cohesion and becomes prey to self-
doubt. Something like this was experienced in all the major
crises of communism in the post-war period – in Poland and
Hungary in 1956, in Czechoslovakia in 1968 and in Poland in
1980.

The next likely stage is the radicalisation of at least a
section of the party membership and moves towards self-
preservation by the middle and upper levels of the élite. The
membership is likely to demand a return to some kind of
idealised vision of socialism; the upper echelons, on the other
hand, will try to limit changes to the minimum in order to
preserve as much of their power as is compatible with the new
situation and possibly more. The pace and extent of change
then depends on resistance to change by leadership, the
effectiveness of control over the media and the perception of
threat from a popular upheaval.

One near standard feature of change in Soviet-type polities
is their propensity to try and avoid paying the high political
price that goes with the redistribution of power and to change
leaders rather than policies. This was tried in Hungary with
the dropping of Kádár in May 1988, in the GDR with the
purging of Honecker in October 1989 and with rather greater
success with the replacement of Husák by Jakeš in December
1988. The temporary success of the Czechoslovak switch was
attributable to a variety of factors, of which its timeliness was
the most salient. As of early 1990, it was uncertain how effective
the retirement of Zhivkov in favour of Petur Mladenov in
Bulgaria was likely to be.

Cracks in the surface unanimity

Soviet-type systems rely heavily for the maintenance of power
on the party's control of the language of public discourse. All
ideologically derived systems place great emphasis on ideological conformity, because any deviation from that threatens
one of the central legitimating myths of the system as a
whole. In this context, public unanimity has a multiple purpose.
It serves as a means of reassurance to the élite that the system
is in place and is not under threat, that the party remains in

control and that opposition is being kept out of sight. Second, the continued use of the ideologically derived language, i.e. Marxist–Leninist jargon, is a constant reaffirmation that the party is still relying for some of its legitimation on the claim that it rules by virtue of having seized power in the name of a Marxist–Leninist revolution. Third, the insistence on the use of this language has a simple censorship function. It keeps unsanctioned ideas away from public opinion and prevents alternative and thus challenging ideas from being articulated. That, in turn, helps to sustain the atomisation of society on which stability and social peace are predicated.

The loss of control over the public sphere, therefore, is a serious stage for Soviet-type systems. It implies that an important aspect of power has begun to fray and that the loss of support from the supporting intellectuals is gaining public notice. By the same token, it means that alternative ideas are likely to gain wider currency, radicalising the population and the party membership and giving an option to reconstitute themselves as a society, as subjects, rather than as mere objects of power. This is the moment at which the now dissident intellectuals will start to give wider currency to their ideas, to generate public support for them and to signal that, maybe, the system is after all vulnerable.

This stage was reached in Hungary in late 1986–early 1987, when several key groups of previous loyal intellectuals concluded that the Kádár régime was neither ready nor willing to engage in the far-reaching reforms that they regarded as necessary and, hence, that they would have to go public with their critiques. Inevitably, this involved a struggle, but by this stage the contest was more even than it had been before, as the party's self-confidence was beginning to erode. In Poland, this stage came less dramatically. Under Martial Law censorship was never as rigidly enforced as in the other countries and, in any case, it was under constant challenge from the enormous amount of samizdat that was being produced. In a very real sense, the public sphere was circumscribed by secondary public opinion, or the parallel polity, to give it the name that some commentators have used.

In Czechoslovakia, on the other hand, the whole process was much more telescoped – both the second and third stages.

The loss of support from sections of previously supportive
intellectuals could be observed from late 1988–early 1989 and
the public sphere was increasingly witnessing bolder deviations from officially sanctioned norms, though the surface
unanimity never cracked in the sense suggested above. That
took place during the 'gentle revolution' itself, after the
formation of Civic Forum on 19 November 1989, when
television and some of the press began to report fully on the
demonstrations of the week beginning 20 November. In both
East Germany and Bulgaria the process was equally abbre-
viated and tended to emerge together, rather than as separate
stages. In Romania, there was no strong indication that either
process was seriously under way, though there had been a
few signs that some groups of intellectuals were dissatisfied
and that they were prepared to voice this publicly through
samizdat.

Leadership divisions

Once the system came under challenge, the communist party
leaderships also began to lose their way. Essentially, they had
no answers to the dilemmas in their storehouse of ideas. In
simple terms, they could either try to contain the processes of
systemic disintegration by force or they could give way more
or less gracefully. The implications of such divisions were
highly serious, however, for hierarchically organised polities,
because it meant that at every level the bureaucracy would be
at a loss for instructions and the decay of the system would
accelerate as a result.

   This paralysis began to affect Hungary with the removal of
Kádár in May 1988, after which the Politburo was deeply
divided between the adherents of those who essentially took
the view that Kádárism without Kádár was a viable option
and those who recognised, however tentatively, that new
departures were needed if the communist party was to retain
any role at all. In Poland, General Jaruzelski found himself
under severe pressure from public opinion in 1988, through
the strikes of that spring and summer, and was able to shed
the sceptics from the leadership – the sceptics, in this case,
being the opponents of a dialogue with Solidarity.

In Czechoslovakia, the division was not perceptible until after the demonstrations had begun. At the Central Committee meeting of 24 November 1989 the party élite was told that the Ministry of Interior had forces at its disposal sufficient to deal with demonstrations of up to 50,000, but could not cope with the 200,000–300,000 people who were crowding into Wenceslas Square every day. The Central Committee was then asked if it would accept the use of the armed forces, which it refused. Essentially, there was a division in the leadership over whether it was prepared to employ such a high level of force that could well result in a bloodbath. It refused, possibly mindful of the outcome of Tienanmen Square earlier that year. In Bulgaria, a group of reformers in the Politburo, who had been scandalised by Zhivkov's earlier move to expel the Turkish minority, decided that they would seek to topple him, which they did successfully. And in the GDR, after Honecker's fall, the leadership remained profoundly divided and weak, beset as it was by the repeated hammer-blows of demonstrations and pressure for emigration.

Level of élite morale

The process and pattern of decay impacted significantly on the later fate of the communist party itself. Where the process was thorough and the loss of morale affected leadership and rank-and-file alike, the ability of the party to regroup was much diminished. That in turn affected the political scene as a whole, in as much as it came to constitute a political vacuum. Some of this had been preconditioned by the deideologisation of the previous period. Where leaders and members had overwhelmingly abandoned their belief in Marxism–Leninism and ruled by some other set of beliefs, mostly the ideology of power itself ('we rule because we rule'), morale collapsed very rapidly and the party itself disintegrated.

Hungary led the way. The MSZMP (Hungarian Socialist Workers' Party) had long previously lost its ideological élan and had ruled by a mixture of pragmatic ideas and some vague sense of a better future that it alone could guarantee. When it was challenged in the course of 1989, it essentially had no real response. Step by step, it abandoned its Leninist organisation, its control over the *nomenklatura*, its monopoly over the media and its attempt to control the past and future. In political terms, the moderates and the hardliners were under severe pressure from the reformers to transform the party into a social democratic grouping or face defeat at the polls – by the spring of 1989 it was evident that the coming elections in Hungary would no longer be controlled by the communists. The reformers hoped to effect the transformation at an extraordinary congress of the party in October 1989. In the event, they mustered only about two-fifths of the delegates and the other factions could not be stampeded. The outcome was a messy compromise, satisfying nobody, but leading to the rapid disintegration of the last remnants of party control. The subsequent outcome was that a section of the membership opted out entirely, the reformers constituted themselves into the Hungarian Socialist Party, and the hardliners reassembled the Hungarian Socialist Workers' Party.

In Poland, the ruling party, the PZPR, had already suffered a major defeat in 1980, when it was forced to accept Solidarity as a contender irreconcilable with its political monopoly. Jaruzelski's takeover was not a simple military putsch, but the victory of the Main Political Administration – the branch of the party charged with supervising the armed forces – over the civilian part of the party. The PZPR never properly recovered from this and throughout the 1980s it was only one of the political actors in the Polish constellation, jostling for power with the military establishment, the state administration and the economic bureaucracies. Nevertheless, the PZPR had begun to recover some of its self-confidence, sufficient to put up a considerable resistance to the idea of a non-communist government even after its shattering defeat in the 4 June 1989 elections. It gave way in the end only after it was forced to do so by electoral arithmetic – it could no longer command a majority in the Sejm, the more powerful of the two houses of parliament. But the eventual fate of the party was a complete three-way split in January 1990, between radicals who sought to transform it into a social democratic party, hardliners (the 'concrete' in Polish political terminology) and the pragmatists, who looked only for moderate changes.

Only in Bulgaria did the communist party manage to

maintain itself reasonably intact. There were several explanations to account for this. Some of them are to do with the leadership and the relatively smooth way in which the removal of Zhivkov was engineered, which precluded any major demoralisation and division on that issue. But equally important was that the Bulgarian party had not suffered the kind of loss of self-confidence that had affected its Polish or Hungarian counterparts, not least because the level of popular dissatisfaction was not articulated to anything like the same extent. The consequence was that on the whole, the Bulgarian party was successful in keeping itself together and holding off the challenge from a relatively weak opposition. Divisions inside the party did exist, so for example the Alternative Socialist Alliance, a radical faction, threatened to leave the party entirely, but these were not, in the first instance, serious enough to cause the communist party any heart-searching.

External factors

The international situation had a major impact on the changes. In both the slow and the rapid transformations, the process was clearly affected by the international demonstration process. This had several aspects. In the first place the fact that the Soviet Union was no longer a force for the status quo but in the vanguard of reform was significant in making it more difficult for conservatives to rely on the pretext of Soviet disapproval to keep change off the agenda. This was undoubtedly effective in Poland and Hungary from about 1987 onwards, in widening the potential agenda of change and making it possible to sketch scenarios of democratisation which would have been dismissed as absurd beforehand.

Equally, there is reason to suppose that the Kremlin accepted the strategies of the reform communists in both these countries and encouraged them to persevere. It has been suggested that at some stage in the autumn of 1988, Gorbachev discussed the legalisation of Solidarity with Jaruzelski and indicated that there was no Soviet objection. Presumably the Soviet reasoning was that without such an opening, which would however be controlled, the situation in Poland might shift towards ungovernability and thereby store up far greater trouble for the Soviet Union in the long run. In Hungary, the reformers likewise received some backing, probably at the time when Alexander Yakovlev, a senior Soviet Politburo member close to Gorbachev, visited Budapest in November 1988. It was shortly after that visit that the beginnings of a multi-party system could be discerned.

Soviet intervention was much more direct in the other three countries, though not in Romania, where Moscow had little leverage anyway. When Gorbachev visited the GDR on the 40th anniversary of the founding of the state in October 1989 it was quite evident that he voiced his disapproval of Honecker's refusal to consider change, despite the mounting evidence of dissatisfaction, notably through the great wave of emigrations to the West. Equally, the Soviet Union appeared to raise no objections to Honecker's removal two weeks later and to the succession by Egon Krenz. In both Bulgaria and Czechoslovakia, in November 1989, it was reported that the respective leaders, Zhivkov and Jakeš, appealed for Soviet backing and were refused it. The Warsaw Pact summit in early November in effect denied the justifiability of the 1968 invasion of Czechoslovakia, thereby undermining the Brezhnev doctrine and one of the main planks of the Jakeš régime's legitimacy.

The Kremlin's reasoning, arguably, was based on the analogy of Poland and Hungary, where the party reformers seemed to be adequately placed in the political constellation. In Poland, the communists retained the key portfolios of the interior and defence, despite the installation of the Solidarity government. It would seem, therefore, that the crumbling of the East German and Czechoslovak régimes was not a part of Soviet calculations; on the other hand, the gamble paid off in Bulgaria.

Equally important, events in the other Central and Eastern European countries became more difficult to ignore when they were no longer isolated to one country or another. It is hard to avoid the conclusion that the sight of demonstrating crowds in the GDR influenced those in Prague – accessible through West German, Austrian, Polish and Hungarian television – and that the changes in Poland, Hungary and the GDR affected events in Bulgaria. And at least some of the explanation for the Romanian revolution lay in the fact that Bulgarian television was accessible to Romanians in Bucharest, so that they were aware of what was happening in the rest of Central and Eastern Europe.

The role of the crowd

Soviet-type régimes spent a great deal of time and effort in keeping societies atomised and preventing them from integrating themselves. Consequently, unauthorised and unsupervised demonstrations are a major threat to these systems, in as much as they call into question the power and authority of the rulers. When authoritarian régimes are faced by mass action which they can no longer control, they tend to disintegrate very rapidly. This has been especially true of Soviet-type systems, which still hark back to the concept of revolution and proletarian action and which, therefore, find it even more difficult to come to terms with mass action directed against them. The eroded self-legitimation of Soviet-type leaderships simply could not withstand the massive symbolic acting out of popular disapprobation.

Although the most spectacular such case was that of the crowds demonstrating night after night in Wenceslas Square in the centre of Prague, it was not the only one. The earlier demonstrations in various East German towns, especially the regular Monday evening rally in Leipzig, which for all practical purposes assumed the function of a kind of alternative mass assembly, made an analogous impact on the East German leadership, which suddenly saw its authority and self-legitimation vanish. The removal of Zhivkov in Bulgaria was given an added fillip by the largest demonstration in Sofia since the war at a time when the anti-Zhivkov faction was ready to move. The crowds in Bucharest, which suddenly turned on Ceauşescu, who was visibly disconcerted by this, were playing the role of the trigger in a revolution which had already been launched by the events in Timişoara earlier that week. In Timişoara, a crowd had gathered to prevent the Securitate, the secret police, from evicting the ethnic Hungarian pastor, László Tökés; this seemed to have been the signal for others, including ethnic Romanians, to join in the demonstration. When the secret police fired on the crowd, this did not have the expected reaction of dispersing them, but of spurring them to further action. In all these instances, then, mass action proved to be a key factor in the transformation.

However, these were not the first. In October 1988, under the influence of the Serbian demagogue Slobodan Milošević, crowds chased away the provincial government in the Vojvodina and, a little later, in the republic of Montenegro. Milošević was acting to strengthen Serbian positions, but the precedent was set and, no doubt, was not lost on others. In Poland, the strikes of 1988 were the functional equivalent. Only in Hungary was there no serious public action at all. In all probability, the Hungarian leadership felt deeply threatened by the memory of the revolution of 1956, when the demonstrating crowds chased away the communist leadership overnight.

The impact of these factors was not, of course, identical in each and every country, but to an extent they all played a role, at times explicitly, at others barely visibly. The interrelationship between the different factors likewise varied from state to state. At the end of the day, the collapse of the communist systems is best understood as the outcome of a series of factors, among which the sense of failure by communism as a system must be seen as the most influential.

Socialist legality, dissent and human rights in China

Like the other communist states discussed in this chapter, the People's Republic of China has conceived of human rights in collective rather than individual terms. In so far as the four state constitutions promulgated since 1949 have enshrined the rights enjoyed in 'bourgeois' democracies, these have regularly been negated by other constitutional provisions, by actual practice or, in some instances, by subsequent constitutional amendment. Thus in 1954 the Constitution stated that capitalists were entitled to own the means of production but subsequently asserted that capitalist ownership would 'gradually' be replaced by ownership by the whole people. Two years later the private sector of industry and commerce was nationalised. The 1975 Constitution guaranteed freedom of the press at a time when the leftist 'Gang of Four' had encased the media in an ideological straitjacket that was exceptional even by communist standards. In 1978 a new Constitution gave the Chinese masses the 'four big freedoms': 'speaking out freely, airing views fully, holding great debates and writing big-character posters'. Two years later, as a result of the 'Democracy Wall' phenomenon, it was decreed that this clause should be deleted. The present Constitution, introduced in 1982, stipulates that it is an offence to attempt to 'sabotage' socialism. The definition of 'socialism', however, varies in accordance with whichever group is in power at the time. In 1989 the student demonstrators were accused of being anti-party and against the socialist system, thus opening up the possibility of the severest penalties for 'offenders'.

The PRC has, in fact, gone to great lengths to restrict personal choice and it was only after Mao's death that attempts were made to bring about liberalisation and to establish a reasonably effective system of 'socialist legality'. The frailty of these attempts was shown by the authorities' response to protests from the Democracy Movement (1978) onwards. As long as one was prepared to function within the guidelines laid down there was a greater degree of predictability to the system, but this did not extend to guaranteeing genuine freedoms of speech and assembly. Those who overstepped the guidelines were treated with great severity.

One method of enforcing conformity has been through ideological control. In common with communist states the PRC created a massive system of censorship and propaganda. The management of news (with the provision of a variety of 'restricted' bulletins and journals for the elite); the re-writing of history; and the doctoring of photographs to remove all evidence that a disgraced leader was even present on a particular occasion are all too reminiscent of George Orwell's *1984*. Much attention has also been devoted to 'ideological reform' and to 'criticism' and 'self-criticism' in group sessions, where psychological techniques are used to break down a transgressor's resistance and so compel him or her to affirm or renew commitment to the party's goals.

The state has also used a considerable amount of coercion.

In the early 1950s a series of mass campaigns were used to destroy the power of 'counter-revolutionaries', 'rural despots' and other enemies of society, many of whom were executed. Those who survived were sentenced to 'reform through labour' and, along with their families, were classified as 'bad elements'. Even after their release such individuals were deprived of political rights, confined to menial occupations, remained under what was in effect a system of permanent probation and, at times of mass mobilisation, w¬re likely to be harassed and humiliated as 'negative examples'.

The pro-independence demonstrations in Tibet in the late 1980s were met with huge police and military force and martial law was declared there in March 1989. While such violence could be ignored by claiming that this was just a traditional conflict between the Han Chinese and one of its minorities, the use of the People's Liberation Army to crush the student protests of mid-1989 could not. This was the first time since 1949 that the army had been given direct orders to shoot its own people.

From 1954 to 1966 a legal system of sorts developed and over 1100 statutes and decrees were promulgated to add to the handful of very wide-ranging, vague, and highly politicised directives of the early years. But, despite valiant attempts by a few party leaders and legal specialists to establish a modicum of 'socialist legality' in the mid-1950s, it was the public security (police) organs which dominated the legal system. They were responsible for the maintenance of public order; the investigation, arrest and detention of suspects; and the administration of the prisons and 'Reform Through Labour' camps. Although prosecution was supposedly the function of separate procuratorial organs, these tended to be subordinate to the police. Similarly the courts were not so much concerned with determining guilt or innocence, but rather 'educational' institutions which publicised the crimes of the guilty as a warning to others. Indeed, the police possessed legal powers in some instances to imprison offenders without the formality of a trial. Moreover, as sentences were virtually open-ended in that they could be shortened or lengthened in the light of a prisoner's willingness to 'reform', the police had considerable discretion to recommend parole or an extension of the sentence.

Furthermore, the police had considerable powers to control the lives of ordinary citizens. Every household was required to keep a registration book of those domiciled within it, travel was difficult without police permission, and itinerants had to register with the local police on arrival at their destination. And while the size of the public security forces was not exceptionally large, they were assisted by a network of semi-official 'informers'. In imperial China there had been an ancient tradition of mutual surveillance and this reappeared in the form of residents' committees, Youth League branches and other mass organisations which, *inter alia*, made it their business to keep a watchful eye on unlawful or unseemly behaviour. The right to privacy was certainly not one which Chinese citizens enjoyed.

Thus Chinese society before the Cultural Revolution was well-policed in the sense that 'deviant' behaviour could be quickly identified and dealt with. Chinese justice was not, however, as arbitrary as this account might suggest, for the system did contain a measure of predictability. For example, people of 'bad' class background like ex-landlords and counter-revolutionaries' were well aware that they would suffer more for making 'political' criticisms than would poor peasants or workers. Conversely, party cadres knew that their sins would be punished more leniently if they made a full confession, 'achieved merit' by implicating others, or manifested 'repentance'. There is evidence that many policemen took their job seriously, went to considerable pains to collect and sift evidence, and usually only arrested someone after they had built up a solid case.

The Cultural Revolution, however, destroyed these developing conventions. The legal organs themselves were early victims of the Left's determination to drag out 'capitalist roaders'. In 1967 especially Leftist factions 'seized power' by invading and ransacking police stations and court buildings, and by beating, torturing and imprisoning police and legal officials who, by their training, were assumed to be on the side of established authority and were therefore easy targets for the 'rebels'. In one province alone it was later claimed that 281 police stations were sacked, over 100 000 dossiers were stolen, and large quantities of guns and ammunition were seized.

Throughout 1967 and 1968 legal institutions virtually ceased to function and mob rule was the order of the day throughout much of urban China. Rival factions battled for supremacy, sought revenge for real or imagined grievances, and acted with massive violence. Hundreds of thousands of cadres, ranging from Liu Shaoqi, Chairman of the People's Republic, down to minor officials, were attacked and many were paraded before kangaroo courts of Red Guard activists where they were abused, tormented and sometimes tortured as a prelude to being thrown into prison or labour camp. There many of them were to remain until the late 1970s. And, for a considerable number, their eventual rehabilitation had to be posthumous.

In some areas factions even set up their own private prisons. At the Tianjin Soda Works, for example, a prison was set up where, it was later claimed, 'ruffians' used torture to extract confessions from 'leading cadres and the broad masses' who were held in illegal custody for long periods. In 1970, when outrage was mounting, the person responsible found a simple but effective means of suppressing it. He issued a directive making it an offence to comment on the prison's existence. In Beijing 56 children of senior government officials were arrested and put in what was euphemistically called a 'study class' but was, in fact, an unofficial prison. Seventy per cent of them were 20, one was only 14, and some were held there for five years. They were worked hard, ill-treated and forced to write lengthy reports on their parents' alleged crimes.

The attempt to reaffirm socialist legality

Following the death of Mao and the arrest of the 'Gang of Four', China experienced a massive display of revulsion against the anarchism and brutality of the Cultural Revolution period. From the beginning of 1977 the leadership began a lengthy process of investigation which resulted in the reversal of verdicts on literally hundreds of thousands of people who had suffered unjust punishments ranging from death to demotion in that movement. As the horrifying evidence of lawlessness mounted, the leadership began to stress that such injustices must never happen again. Although primarily motivated by a recognition of the human costs of the Cultural Revolution, the leadership was also conscious of the enormous damage it had done to the economy.

This process was covered by the phrase 'socialist legality'. Thus a system of rules and regulations, known by and applicable to all citizens, was to be created to replace the more arbitrary and uncertain situation of the Cultural Revolution. The fact that it was *socialist* legality set certain constraints and retained for the party the major role in deciding what was, and what was not, a crime.

In 1978, a Commission for Legal Affairs was established and it produced a stream of legislation. Drafts of seven laws were presented to the Second Session of the Fifth National People's Congress (summer 1979), including the organic laws for the people's courts and people's procuratorate and, most importantly, the first criminal code and law of criminal procedure. These laws came into effect on 1 January 1980 to serve as the basis for the new socialist legality.

The code of criminal law and the law of criminal procedure were designed to promote the idea of equality of all before the law. The criminal law brought together in one relatively short document the major categories of criminal offence and the range of penalties they were likely to attract. An offence was broadly defined as 'any action which endangers state sovereignty and territorial integrity, jeopardises the dictatorship of the proletariat, sabotages socialist revolution and socialist property of the whole people, collective or legitimate private property, infringes upon the personal, democratic and other rights of citizens, or any other action which endangers society and is punishable by law'. Punishment could be given to anyone of sixteen or over and of sound mind.

The law paid attention to the need for stability, rejecting various legacies of the Cultural Revolution. Thus penalties were laid down for extracting confessions by torture; gathering a crowd for 'beating, smashing and looting'; bringing false charges; unlawfully incarcerating a person; and 'seriously insulting' a person by any means, including the use of wall-posters to spread libels.

Further, the law paid great attention to what it termed

'counter-revolutionary' crimes. Twenty-four articles dealt with this problem. Included were not only predictable activities such as plotting to overthrow the government or leading armed rebellions but also using 'counter revolutionary slogans ... to spread propaganda inciting the overthrow of the political power of the dictatorship of the proletariat and the socialist system'. These were the first official definitions of 'counter-revolutionary' behaviour, thus making it formally a crime to work against communism. In September 1989, the mere fact that six nuns shouted the slogan 'Independence for Tibet' was enough to have them arrested and five of them sentenced to three years of 'reform through labour'.

The Law on Criminal Procedure made meticulous arrangements for the handling of criminal cases, and carefully defined the rights and responsibilities of the legal organs and those accused. The role of the procuratorate is to exercise authority to ensure the observance of the Constitution and the laws of the state and to protect the rights of citizens. It decides whether to approve a request for arrest by a public security department, and also whether the person, if arrested, should be held criminally responsible. This was a marked change from Cultural Revolution practice. Indeed the 1975 State Constitution had a new article that gave the Public Security Bureau the right to make arrests without authorisation from the people's court which, to an extent, enshrined the power of the police in the Constitution. The continued role of the party is shown by the fact that all key appointments in both the procuratorate and court system fall under the *nomenklatura* system.

In all cases the appropriate punishments were stipulated. In order of ascending degrees of unpleasantness these were:
Surveillance – essentially a form of probation, not to exceed two years.
Detention – imprisonment by the local police force for not more than six months, during which time the offender was allowed to return home for two days a month, and was to be paid for work done under police supervision.
Fixed term or life imprisonment – to be served in prison or labour camps.
Death penalty – by firing squad. However, the law followed

earlier statutes in insisting that this was only to be used for the most heinous offences and, moreover, that the penalty should often be deferred for two years, during which time the offender would be imprisoned and given the opportunity to show if he or she had 'reformed'. In this case the sentence might be commuted to imprisonment for life or for a shorter period. Jiang Qing, Mao's widow and leader of the 'Gang of Four', was the most notable beneficiary of this two-year reprieve.

The Law also provided for 'supplementary' penalties, the most notable of which were confiscation of property, fines, and deprivation of political rights. It also echoed earlier enactments (and, indeed, ancient Chinese ideas on legal matters) by stressing that mercy should be shown to those who showed contrition. Voluntary surrender, confession and the achievement of merit by implicating fellow offenders were to be rewarded by reduced punishment. And even in gaol not all was lost – 'good behaviour' could result in early parole.

The Law on Criminal Procedure emphasised that the accused was entitled to defence by him or herself, by a lawyer, by someone appointed by a mass organisation or work unit, by a relative or by a guardian. The court might appoint an advocate for someone who had failed to do so himself. The accused or his advocate had the right to see the material pertaining to the case, witnesses had to be available for examination, and no one could be convicted on the basis of a statement unsupported by other evidence. The Law also made careful provision for those who might help the police with their enquiries. Criminals caught in, before or immediately after the act, together with 'major suspects', could be arrested by anyone, as could escaped prisoners and those on 'wanted' lists. Otherwise the police were required to produce a warrant from the Procuratorate. After arrest, a detainee's family was normally to be informed within twenty-four hours. Moreover, the police were to ask the Procuratorate to examine and approve the arrest within three days. The Law stipulated the time in which the accused should normally be brought to trial, and laid down detailed regulations governing delays in so doing. It also specified that trials should be public (except where state secrets were involved or where the innocent might suffer unnecessary embarrassment), and that there were to be proper appeal procedures.

In the 1980s, the Chinese leadership has continued to insist on the maintenance and extension of the legal system, including the provision of legal education programmes for those who work in it and the general populace also. However, as the 1980s progressed, there has been a move back away from what were, by Chinese standards, the remarkably liberal laws outlined above. The reason for this is two-fold. First, there was a considerable rise in 'white collar' crime as a result of the new economic and 'open-door' policies. In 1983 a major crackdown was introduced and the laws were amended to increase the penalties for serious crime (including the extension of the list of offences meriting capital punishment) and to weaken somewhat the rights of the accused in order to speed up procedures for handling and disposing of serious cases. In the same year policing was reorganised with the creation of a separate Ministry of State Security. A notable consequence of this harsher attitude has been a significant rise in the number of executions. Some estimates calculate that 10,000 were executed in 1983 alone.

Secondly, there was a rise in political activity that took place outside of the party's direct control. The party's inability to come to grips with the issue of political reform meant that more people took to the streets to vent their grievances, and such protests became increasingly anti-systemic. Orthodox party members were quick to seize on these actions as 'counter-revolutionary' movements in order to crush them and reassert strict party control.

Political dissidence in China

Criticisms of the political system in China have come from the left as well as the right. In the Cultural Revolution various groups of Red Guards and others produced radical critiques of an extreme nature and called for such changes as reorganising China along the lines of the famous Paris Commune of 1871. Although subsequently branded as 'ultra-leftists' it is difficult to characterise such people as 'dissidents' because they were operating in conditions of near-anarchy when leaders and policies changed with dramatic suddenness, and often believed themselves to be 'faithful followers of Chairman Mao' and of those close to him. Here the focus is on the occasions when ordinary citizens have pressed for the introduction of freedoms similar to those enjoyed in 'bourgeois' democracies.

The first major outburst of dissent in the PRC occurred in 1956–7 during the 'Hundred Flowers' campaign. Initially, this was a movement launched by Mao Zedong as a response to de-Stalinisation in the Soviet Union and the Hungarian uprising of 1956. Although Mao considered the reaction in Hungary to be 'rightist' in nature, he was concerned that the mechanical copying of the Soviet Union might also lead to problems in China. The solution to this problem, Mao felt, was to operate the mass line properly. What was needed was not the repression of complaints, but the encouragement of open criticism of the party apparatus.

Launched in May 1956, the campaign tried to generate greater discussion and debate by widening the forum of those who could criticise the party. As a result writers were encouraged to produce works containing more than received stereotypes. The campaign was opposed by those in the leadership who favoured a more guided and limited form of criticism. For a while the movement was scaled down, but in February 1957 Mao gave it renewed impetus with his speech 'On the Correct Handling of Contradictions Among the People'. This speech invited intellectuals to raise criticisms and suggested that the party was not above criticism from those outside. Such criticisms, Mao suggested, could help prevent leaders from becoming divorced from the led.

The harshness of the criticisms was unexpected. The range of criticism was wide, from the airing pf personal grievances to indictments of the whole political system. Such indictments came not only from opponents of the communist regime but also from people who assessed the system on its own terms and found it wanting. At a series of forums, intellectuals and members of the 'democratic parties' that had been allowed to exist in a 'united front' with the CCP after 1949 savagely attacked the party's monopoly of power. They demanded, among other things, such major ingredients of 'bourgeois' democracy as competitive elections, a free press, effective trade unions, academic freedom and an independent judiciary. Badly shocked by this, the party declared that the 'Hundred Flowers' had become 'poisonous weeds' opposed to socialism, and an anti-Rightist campaign was launched that consigned hundreds of thousands to labour camps. Many remained there for ten or more years and, even when released, were badly treated because of their 'bad element' status. It was not until 1978–9 that it was officially admitted that there had been countless miscarriages of justice at this time.

The criticisms unleashed caused Mao Zedong to lose faith in his intellectual elite. Shocked by their criticisms, he felt that they were no longer trustworthy to be the main contributors to building socialism in China. As a result, Mao turned to the peasant masses to become the main driving force in this development strategy by launching the Great Leap Forward.

In November 1978, many of the ideas expressed during the 'Hundred Flowers' campaign received a second airing. The major difference was that this time the movement began spontaneously and was not sponsored by China's top leadership even though it did prove tactically useful to Deng Xiaoping in his inner-party struggles. The movement took its name from 'Democracy Wall' in central Beijing where people congregated to put up wall-posters and to express their grievances. The use of wall-posters had, of course, long been common in China and had been particularly prevalent during the Cultural Revolution. In 1978, the writing of wall-posters had been enshrined as a constitutional right. What really inspired the protesters, however, was the decision taken in November 1978 to 'rehabilitate' the Tienanmen incident of 5 April 1976. On that day a massive and largely spontaneous riot had taken place in Tienanmen Square in the centre of Beijing. It was sparked off by widespread resentment at the 'Gang of Four's' crude attempts to suppress demonstrations of mourning for Zhou Enlai, and the campaign of vilification they were then directing against Deng Xiaoping. The demonstrations were used as an excuse to remove Deng Xiaoping from all his posts for instigating a 'counter-revolutionary' incident.

By November 1978, however, the 'Gang of Four' were in prison, Deng was back in power, and it was decreed that the

Tienanmen incident (and similar ones which had occurred in other cities) had been 'completely revolutionary'. This was of great symbolic importance for it implied that 'the masses' had the right to make their views known, and to criticise their leaders. 'Democracy Walls' appeared in major cities, meetings were organised at what were actually referred to as 'Speakers' Corners', and various groups began to publish their own journals. Unlike *samizdat* literature these were openly sold and, in some cases, it was actually possible to take out subscriptions.

This phase of dissent differed significantly from dissident movements in the other communist states in that it did not have the support of leading intellectuals. China's greatest scientists and writers had already been recompensed for their suffering in the Cultural Revolution and were being given exceptional freedom and responsibility in the interests of 'elite modernisation' policies. Nor was there any significant religious or ethnic element in the protests. It was, rather, a movement of 'little people' who had suffered in the Maoist era and who had not had their grievances redressed. A majority of those participating were concerned with single issues. Thus many people sought justice for wrongs done to themselves or their relatives. Groups of peasants travelled to Beijing and other cities to publicise their poverty. 'Educated youths' came to town to demand that they be allowed to return permanently to the cities; some of these 'youths' had actually been in the countryside for twenty years. In Shanghai, in February 1979, they organised a spectacular sit-in at the railway station, bringing the rail system to a halt until forcibly removed by the police.

The most detailed and serious criticisms were to be found in the unofficial journals which were generally produced by young people of 'middle class' families whose education had stopped during the Cultural Revolution and who were too old to resume it after Mao's death. Many had participated in the Red Guard movement and had eventually come to realise that their naive idealism had been simply manipulated by the elite. Their cynicism and sense of betrayal was heightened by the fact that they had tended to end up in relatively menial urban jobs with no great prospects for improvement.

Most of the activists who edited and wrote for unofficial journals wanted democratisation within a framework of socialism. They were not opposed to the party as such. Sometimes the activists were simply ahead of their time in that they demanded changes the leadership was later to introduce. For example, the call for the party to reassess the role of Mao and admit his mistakes was answered in June 1981 when the sixth plenum of the Central Committee adopted a lengthy resolution doing just this. Demands for the dismissal of unpopular leaders like Wang Dongxing also found official favour, as did requests that Liu Shaoqi and other victims of the Central Revolution be rehabilitated. The numerous articles on the need for 'socialist legality' were also broadly in keeping with the way official thinking was moving.

But some 'Democracy Wall' writers were critical of Deng as well, and found little to praise in the communist system. The most famous of these was Wei Jingsheng. He came to the attention of the Western world as early as December 1978, and was promptly hailed as a 'leader' of the 'democracy movement', an image which probably exaggerated his importance and also suggested that the 'movement' was far more united than was in fact the case. A thirty-year-old electrician at Beijing Zoo, Wei was the son of a party cadre but had made the mistake of joining a Red Guard faction opposed to Jiang Qing, Mao's wife, and had suffered as a result.

His major statement, however, was a long essay which argued that 'Democracy is the Fifth Modernisation'. In this he scathingly attacked Mao and those people who refused to admit his mistakes and, instead, kept 'running to Democracy Wall to pat Mao on the arse'. He was no more sparing of the new leadership who had replaced faith in Mao with the equally superstitious catchphrase of the 'Four Modernisations' as a panacea for China's problems. He attacked Deng Xiaoping for having thanked Mao for restoring him to office in 1973, but for failing to thank the Chinese people whose efforts had brought him back again in 1977. The attention of his readers was drawn to their own poverty and their lack of rights, both of which were contrasted unfavourably with the situation in capitalist countries. He pointed out, for example, that in the latter it was possible to get rid of leaders the people disliked, mentioning former US president Nixon and former Japanese premier Tanaka as examples. He also challenged the official argument that, under socialism, respect for human rights was directed at the elimination of such social evils as poverty, prostitution and unemployment, affirming that all these existed in the PRC. His readers were urged to ignore the blandishments of the 'despots' who simply replaced Mao, telling them to 'take control of their own lives' and 'ignore the lords in authority'. This, he implied, would mean struggle: 'Democracy has never developed by itself. It will require sacrifice.'

By March 1979 even Deng had become concerned that 'Democracy Wall' was getting out of hand, not least because participants were sometimes only too willing to share their grievances and criticisms with foreign journalists. In that month Wei was arrested and a general crackdown on dissent was instituted. As one directive put it, 'all slogans, posters, books, journals ... and other representations which oppose socialism, the dictatorship of the proletariat, the leadership of the CCP, Marxism–Leninism–Mao Zedong Thought ... are prohibited'. Steps were taken to curb contacts with foreigners. In October 1979, Wei was put on trial and was found guilty of passing 'military secrets' to foreigners (he had talked to journalists about China's invasion of Vietnam) and of spreading 'counter-revolutionary propaganda and agitation'. He defended himself stubbornly and was sentenced to fifteen years' imprisonment with a further three years' deprivation of political rights. It was widely believed that his failure to show contrition was the principal reason for his severe punishment. Thereafter the unofficial journals were suppressed, Beijing's 'Democracy Wall' was scrubbed clean and a small alternative was provided in an enclosed park where poster-pasters could put up their *signed* offerings under the watchful eye of the police. Finally, in February 1980, a party plenum gravely decreed that experience had shown that the 'four big freedoms' had 'never played a positive role in safeguarding the people's democratic rights' and that 'to help eliminate factors causing instability' the relevant article should be deleted from the Constitution.

At its height the 'Democracy Wall' movement probably

embraced only two or three hundred activists. In the early 1980s, dissent was sporadic and often directed against specific policies rather than the political system itself. However, in 1986 and more particularly 1989, major demonstrations broke out in Beijing and a number of other cities that provided a more fundamental challenge to the leadership. Yet neither of these movements produced the kind of well thought out critiques as presented, for example, by Wei Jingsheng.

Both rounds of demonstrations have to be seen in the light of the unfulfilled promises for political reform that had been presented by Deng Xiaoping as an important part of the reform programme: a part of the reform programme he was prepared to sacrifice to more orthodox party leaders to keep his economic reforms on track. The December 1986 demonstrations followed a summer of extraordinary debate in the official press on the need for a major shake-up of the political system. In the summer, when China's top leaders withdrew to their summer retreat of Beidaihe, it was expected that they would draft a document on political reform. Instead a document was published on the need to combat 'spiritual pollution', a war-cry of the orthodox party leaders.

It seems that the students who came onto the streets in December 1986 did so with the intention of supporting Deng Xiaoping's faction by giving renewed impetus to the need for more political reform. While there were a few calls for an end to 'one-party autocracy' and the establishment of a 'multiparty system', the overwhelming majority wanted to support the official moves towards political reform. There were a number of personal grievances expressed about living and study conditions on the campuses but generally the calls were for greater democracy, freedom of the press and freedom of speech. These demonstrators were different from those of the earlier Democracy Movement. They were not the victims of the Cultural Revolution but those who stood to gain most from the newly emerging system. As a consequence they wanted to place their concerns for a better future on the agenda.

The passion and the numbers of demonstrators shook the orthodox party leaders. They together with Deng Xiaoping could not cope with this public display of protest. Not only do they share the natural Leninist tendency to fear activity that takes place outside of their direct control, they are also haunted by visions of the Cultural Revolution when 'extensive democracy' led to chaos. Deng condemned the demonstrations as 'counter-revolutionary' led by a 'few people' who sought to overthrow the socialist system. This was essentially the same verdict as he was to deliver on the movement of 1989. For the students, the movement backfired and the reform-minded General Secretary, Hu Yaobang, was dismissed from his post for having allowed the political situation to get out of hand. However, it provided a basis on which the demonstrations of 1989 could build.

The student-led democracy movement of 1989 was one of unprecedented scale that rocked the party to its foundations and came within a few days of bringing the leadership down. Unlike the previous movements, shortly before it was crushed it began to bring together students, intellectuals and workers into one movement. Ever since 1981, orthodox elements in the Chinese leadership had been frightened of a Solidarity-type phenomenon in China. The coming together of workers with students and the creation of an autonomous workers' federation was more than the leadership was willing to tolerate. The fact that the federation and the students had taken over Tiananmen Square, the political heart of China and the symbol of communist power, caused them to retaliate with massive force to try to crush once and for all the growing demands for greater democracy.

Since 1986, student political activity had continued on the campuses through the organisation of lectures, discussions and the convening of 'democratic salons'. On 3 April 1989, students at Beijing University had put up a wall-poster proposing that the university be turned into a special zone for promoting democratic politics. Across Beijing's campuses independent student federations had been created, and this provided the basis for the organisation to expand quickly once the movement was launched.

As in 1986, the demonstrations took place against the background of a defeat for the reformers in the party. The March–April 1989 meeting of the National People's Congress made it clear that the then General Secretary, Zhao Ziyang, and his pro-reform allies had lost the policy debate. Premier Li Peng put forward a programme of tight economic austerity combined with attempts to curtail political liberalisation.

The immediate catalyst for the student demonstrations was the death of Hu Yaobang on 15 April 1989. As with the demonstrations of 1986, the demands were simple and were not articulated in an elaborate, systematic way. Essentially, the students called for a significant relaxation of régime practice with greater freedom of speech and the press and the curtailing of the corrupt practices of the leadership and their children. The simplicity of the demands perhaps partly explains why they found such a massive following: a following that included many party members themselves. The students portrayed themselves as patriots who simply wanted to enter into a dialogue with their own leadership. For the most part, the movement began with the idea of reform from within. It was only later that more radical demands were made. Some of the students began to call for the formation of a nation-wide citizens' organisation like Solidarity that could deal openly and directly with the government. In this respect, it is clear that much of the inspiration for the students derived from reforms in Poland and Hungary and from the reform programme launched by Gorbachev in the Soviet Union. Indeed Gorbachev's visit in mid-May gave the protests further impetus.

This does not explain why the students received such massive support by mid-May from the citizens of Beijing. This is explained by the fact that both the political atmosphere and the economic situation had declined noticeably since 1986 and the reservoir of discontent in the urban areas had risen greatly. Indeed, the manner of Hu Yaobang's dismissal caused many intellectuals who had previously been willing to set aside their doubts and accept their new found prestige to become disillusioned with the top party leadership. Further, it was clear to many that the party had no real clear idea any more over the future direction of the reforms. The economic problems in the urban areas, particularly inflation, caused further erosion of acquiescence to party rule particularly among those government employees on fixed incomes and the industrial working class.

Despite such factors, it is important to note that the students had been demonstrating a full month before the intellectuals and workers actively supported them. In particular, the hunger strike of mid-May brought the students enormous support. This, combined with the feeling that the movement had reached a crucial phase, encouraged many ordinary citizens to take to the streets. Also, by now the student movement had unwittingly become part of the power struggle within the top party leadership between Zhao Ziyang and his opponents. The massive increase in the size of the demonstrations and particularly the appearance of workers and government employees on the streets between 15 and 18 May prompted the orthodox party members to take harsh action, culminating in the massacre of the night of 3–4 June.

The suppression of the movement revealed in brutal fashion just how far the orthodox party leaders were from allowing any significant political activity to take place outside of their control. The fact that the events took place in front of the world's press and that pictures were beamed into people's living-rooms all over the world has created a human rights problem for the PRC. In comparison with other communist-ruled countries, the PRC had always been handled lightly by Western governments. In the future, human rights will play a more prominent role in the PRC's relations with the West. Its denunciations of foreign interference in its domestic affairs plus broad hints that 'foreign powers' helped instigate the demonstrations indicate that the West and China are on a collision course on this issue similar to that between the West and the Soviet Union in the 1970s.

Finally, for the first time in the history of the PRC, the authorities are confronted by an organisation abroad, the Federation for a Democratic China, that possesses a moral force to allow it to speak up against the party's official interpretation of events. The federation has denounced the one-party system and called for extensive democratisation of the PRC's political life. The federation, made up of a mix of refugees from the movement and Chinese living abroad, may eventually come to form a government-in-exile.

Further reading

There is a substantial literature on the questions of democracy
and human rights with which this chapter is concerned: see
for instance Macpherson (1972), Miliband (1977), Lively
(1975), Pennock (1979), Macfarlane (1985) and Sartori
(1986). On the Soviet theory of democracy more particularly,
see Churchward (1975, ch. 17) and Krutogolov (1980). On
the Soviet legal system, see Butler (1983a) and also Barry and
Berman, 'The jurists', in Skilling and Griffiths (1971), and
Barry *et al.* (1977–79). The RSFSR Criminal Code is translated in Berman and Spindler (1972) and is reprinted together
with other legal codes and documents in Simons (1980b) and
Butler (1983b). On changes in the media see Mickiewicz
(1988), Remington (1988) and Benn (1989). On informal
movements, see Brovkin (forthcoming).

On human rights in Eastern Europe, two works edited by
Rudolf Tökés are useful general surveys (Tökés 1978 and
1979). See also Curry (1983), a more recent overview. Opposition movements in the various countries are analysed in Kusin
(1978), Riese (1979) and Havel *et al.* (1985), which deal with
Czechoslovakia; Woods (1986), which deals with the GDR;
Ostoja-Ostaszewski *et al.* (1977) and Lipski (1985), which
deal with Poland; and Sher (1977), which deals with Yugoslavia. On Solidarity in Poland, see Staniszkis (1984), an
interpretive work by a Polish sociologist, Ash (1985), an
account by a well-informed Western journalist, and Ruane
(1982), a good general introduction with extensive quotations
from contemporary sources. Mason (1985) considers the
movement of Polish public opinion during this period. Up to
date information may be found in the journals *Labour Focus
on Eastern Europe* and *Index on Censorship*, both published in
London; the latter is an invaluable source on all questions of
censorship, unofficial literature and *samizdat*. See also *East
European Reporter* (London), which deals with Poland,
Hungary and Czechoslovakia, and *Poland Watch* (Washington, DC), which gives detailed attention to the largest of these
countries. On the media and censorship, see Lendvai (1981)
and Schöpflin (1983); see also Robinson (1977) on Yugoslavia
and Curry (1984), which gives a detailed inside picture of the

operation of censorship in Poland. On religion, see Bociurkiw and Strong (1975) and Ramet (1984), and also the periodical *Religion on Communist Lands* (London). Adelman (1984) provides a general study of the role of coercion. The demonstration process in 1989–90 has yet to generate a substantial scholarly literature and is best followed through the newspapers and periodicals, although Ash (1990) is helpful.

A massive study covering major aspects of the legal system in China is Cohen (1968), which may be supplemented by Li (1970). Dreyer (1980) and Leng (1981) deal with criminal justice in the post-Mao period. Moody (1977) is interesting for dissent in the Maoist period while MacFarquhar (1960) covers the views of the 1957 critics. MacFarquhar (1974) provides a detailed study of the background to the 'Hundred Flowers'. The uncertain development of human rights and 'socialist democracy' is covered in Henkin *et al.* (1986) and Nathan (1986). The 'Democracy Movement' is covered in Seymour (1980) Goodman (1981), and Chen Erjin (1984). The movement of 1986 is covered in Munro (1988). The question of political 'crime' is considered in Amnesty International (1984) and the same organisation has provided a detailed analysis of the events of June 1989 (1989). An excellent collection of writings by critics of the system can be found in Barmé and Minford (1988).

8

Communist and Postcommunist States in Comparative Perspective

So far in this book we have been concerned with politics in the sixteen communist and postcommunist states, and not to any significant extent with politics in the world outside them. As we suggested in the first chapter, however, comparative communism should properly be thought of as a subfield of comparative politics rather than as a substitute for that method of inquiry, and if we are interested in examining the performance of the communist states in relation to that of similar but non-communist states, in other words in the significance of communist rule as such, then it is clearly the comparative approach that we require. When dealing with the communist states we can normally take for granted a good deal in terms of institutional and other similarities, and the group of states to be considered is fairly easily determined. In dealing with a wider range of political systems, however, the choice of units of comparison becomes somewhat more arbitrary. Should we compare the communist (and now post-communist) states, for instance, with the major capitalist states, which the communist states have pledged themselves to overtake but which are still, by and large, at a more advanced stage of social and economic development? Or should we compare the communist states with states at a similar level of social and economic development, given the very similar constraints that this is likely to impose upon the political leaderships of such countries? Or should we compare the communist states with all of the world's 150 or so states, irrespective of their ideologies and their levels of socio-economic development?

Even when we have chosen the units of comparison, further problems remain. What, for instance, about the factors which are unique or distinctive to a state, such as its historical experience or religion, and which in turn may have a considerable impact upon its politics quite independent of its form of government and level of socio-economic development? Unlike the natural sciences we cannot isolate these various factors and test them separately for their effects, and yet there are good reasons for thinking that each of them – and perhaps others – may provide at least a part of the explanation that we require. To some extent it is possible to allow for unique cultural or historical factors of this kind by taking 'matched pairs' of stakes which share a common background, such as West and East Germany or North and South Korea, on the assumption that the differences between them must be due to factors other than those they share in common. Even here, however, it is impossible to be certain that cultural or historical differences have been excluded entirely, or that there are no other differences, for instance in natural resources, which may render such comparisons invalid. It is an extremely complicated matter, in other words, to isolate the effects of 'communism as such' upon a country's politics, and it is difficult to be sure that the differences we observe are not caused by factors we have not considered or of which we cannot easily take account.

The choice of criteria by which to compare political systems is also a difficult and somewhat arbitrary one, for there are many ways in which such comparisons could be made and little agreement as to which are the most important. Perhaps the most obvious of such disagreements is the different priorities accorded by different people to the value of political liberty, which is arguably better protected in the Western democracies, as compared with that of social equality, in terms of which the communist states could reasonably be said to have made more progress. But what, for instance about the relative priorities to be attached to political and social values, such as liberty and social equality, as compared with economic values, such as full employment, stable prices and a high standard of living, which most of these states have also sought to achieve? And even in the case of a single value, such as social welfare, how should we compare the performance of the communist states, which typically devote a disproportionate share of their resources to the care and upbringing of the young, with that of the liberal democracies, which are relatively more generous towards their aged, and not just because they tend to have more elderly populations? There is in fact no single agreed order of merit in terms of which political systems can be ranked and classified, and in what follows we shall accordingly examine the performance of the communist states in relation to their non-communist counterparts under a number of different headings: their level of political democracy, their economic performance and their level of social welfare. The relative weight to be attached to performance in each of these fields must necessarily remain a matter for individual judgement.

Communist and non-communist states: levels of political democracy

If there is little agreement about the way in which political systems in general are to be ranked, there is even less about the manner in which their level of political democracy should be assessed. The communist states, as we have seen, have their own criteria; and there are many Western scholars who, while not going so far as to say that democracy is simply a matter of socio-economic rights, would none the less accept that inequalities of wealth and social standing must at least be taken into account in any assessment of such matters. It would probably be fair, however, to say that the majority of scholars, at least in the non-communist world, are agreed that a useful definition of democracy, broadly speaking, must relate to the relative degrees of power enjoyed by the mass of the population and by the governing authorities in a society. Power, in this sense, may derive from the ownership of wealth, as the orthodox communist view maintains; but it may also derive from factors such as control of information, the ability to set agendas, the degree of group cohesion and access to skills, to policy-makers or to a natural resource, factors which were generally unforeseen by Marx. There is again no way in which relative degrees of power can be unambiguously quantified. A number of political scientists, however, have attempted to devise measures of this kind which can be applied to the communist and non-communist nations, and we shall consider some of their efforts in what follows. All exercises of this kind, as the authors of these studies have themselves pointed out, are to various degrees arbitrary and approximate, but they help to clarify at least some aspects of the question, and the alternative, to rely entirely upon impression and assertion, is hardly an improvement.

One of the earliest attempts to measure levels of democracy in communist and non-communist nations in this way was by Robert Dahl in his book *Polyarchy*, published in 1971. Dahl defines democracy as 'a political system one of the characteristics of which is the quality of being completely or almost completely responsive to citizens', a state of affairs not necessarily attained in any of the world's existing political systems but at least a yardstick in relation to which they can all be measured. A political system of this kind, Dahl suggests, requires, as a necessary but not sufficient condition, that all citizens have the opportunity to formulate their preferences, to signify their preferences to their fellow citizens and to the government by individual and collective action, and to have their preferences weighed equally in the conduct of the government. The institutional guarantees of democracy, Dahl argues, can be reduced to two principal dimensions, available to a greater or less extent in different regimes at different times: the extent to which public opposition or contestation is permitted, and the extent to which the population as a whole is permitted to engage in such activities. It is these two dimensions, public contestation and the right to participate, which form the basis of Dahl's classification of regimes. In 'polarchies' (in effect, liberal democracies) both are maximised; in 'closed hegemonies' (in effect, dictatorships) both are minimised; while in 'inclusive hegemonies' (in effect, the communist states) the right to participate is high but the level of contestation is low.

In the remainder of the volume Dahl is primarily concerned

with the conditions that favour or hinder polyarchy, such as the dispersion of economic resources and a relatively high level of GNP per head. Dahl himself points out that many of these factors cannot be measured (or at any rate the necessary data are not available), and that no weighting can readily be assigned to them. In an appendix, however, 114 countries are classified by Dahl and two collaborators according to the extent to which they permit popular participation in elections and, somewhat more arbitrarily, the extent to which they permit public contestation, defined as the freedom to form and join organisations, access to alternative sources of information, free and fair elections and so forth (these are in effect the two dimensions of democracy already mentioned). The results obtained, converted into percentage terms, are set out in Table 8.1 (in all of the states considered electoral participation is close to universal and the results therefore represent the relative extent to which public contestation is permitted). For all the reservations that must necessarily attach to precise measurement of such matters, on which Dahl's methodological discussion must be read in full, one result is immediately apparent: the very low levels of political democracy, measured in this way, of the communist states, and the very much higher levels attained by the major Western states, and even by a developing but liberal democratic state such as India.

A more recent analysis along similar lines has been

TABLE 8.1

Communist and non-communist states: some indicators of political and human rights (percentages)

	UK	USA	India	USSR	China	GDR	Poland	Yugo-slavia
Dahl, c.1969	87	90	77	13	6	6	16	13
Bollen, c.1965	99	92	91	18	16	18	22	51
Humana, c.1986	94	90	60	20	23	33	41	50

Sources: Robert A. Dahl, *Polyarchy* (New Haven, 1971), app. I, adapted; Kenneth A. Bollen, 'Issues in the Comparative Measurement of Political Democracy', *American Sociological Review*, vl (1980), pp. 370–90; Charles Humana (comp.), *The Economist World Human Rights Guide* (London, 1986), various pages.

conducted by Kenneth Bollen. Bollen presents a political democracy index based upon separate indicators of political liberties and of popular sovereignty. The indicators of political liberties included in Bollen's calculations are press freedom, the scope for group opposition and governmental sanctions (actions taken by the government which curtail the political activities of one or more groups of the population, such as the banning of a political party). The three measures of popular sovereignty incorporated in the index are the fairness of elections, executive selection (whether the chief executive is elected or not) and legislative selection (whether the legislature is elected and effective). Each of these indicators was given a score for each country considered; these were then converted into percentages and averaged to obtain the final political democracy rating. Bollen points out that the observed scores are not necessarily 'true' scores, and that minor differences should not be overinterpreted. The results, none the less, are again extremely clear in the respect with which we are concerned: all the liberal democracies, even those in developing countries, record high levels of political democracy, while all the communist states, with the partial exception of Yugoslavia, perform very poorly. The same impression emerges from the *World Human Rights Guide*, also reported in Table 8.1, which attempts to assess regimes around the world in terms of their observance of the Universal Declaration of Human Rights and the International Covenants on Civil and Political and on Economic, Social and Cultural Rights, adopted by the United Nations in 1948 and 1976 respectively. In the fourteen NATO countries included in the survey human rights performance was assessed at an average of 90 per cent (Turkey was by far the lowest, at 40 per cent); in the eleven communist-ruled countries included, however, human rights performance was assessed at no more than 29 per cent, well below the world average of 55 per cent.

A further international survey of this kind is the *Comparative Survey of Freedom*, which is published annually by Freedom House of New York. The Survey incorporates separate measures of political rights, such as the right to participate in the political process through competitive elections and in other ways, and of civil liberties, such as the right to take part in demonstrations and to a degree of personal autonomy in such matters as religion, education and travel. Countries are then ranked in terms of their performance on these two dimensions from 1 (the highest level) to 7 (the lowest). There is again a considerable variation in the level of performance, even among the individual communist states. Yugoslavia, for instance, receives credit for its effective federal system, and Hungary, while it remained a 'Communist state under the control of the party hierarchy' in the late 1980s, receives recognition for having organised parliamentary elections in 1985 in which competition for most posts was required. The candidate selection process was open, and some independent candidates were successfully returned to the national legislature. The liberalisation that had taken place in the USSR was 'perhaps the most significant gain for freedom' in the 1989 *Survey*, including a 'partial opening up of the decision-making process within the Communist party' and 'more effective and lively legislative bodies at all levels of the formal government'. Poland and Hungary both qualified as 'partly free' in terms of the *Survey* in the late 1980s. All the other communist-ruled states, however, are classified as 'not free' with very low scores for both political rights and civil liberties, while all of the member countries of NATO (except Turkey) are classified as 'free' and receive maximum or near-maximum marks on both dimensions.

Quantitative surveys of this kind can hardly be taken as conclusive, given the difficulty of attaching unambiguous scores to many of the indicators concerned and the possibility that the choice of indicators in the first place may have reflected the liberal or other biases of those who have proposed them. The *World Human Rights Guide*, for instance, deliberately takes more of its indicators from the International Covenant on Civil and Political Rights than from the International Covenant on Economic, Social and Cultural Rights, on the grounds that the rights embodied in the latter (such as the right to adequate employment, health and education) are 'concerned with broader social and economic questions' and cannot be allowed to take precedence over classic 'individual' rights such as those to freedom of movement, behaviour and self-expression. This is clearly a choice which, however legitimate, largely determines the outcome of the inquiry. The *Comparative Survey of Freedom*, similarly, acknowledges that many of the criteria on which it is based cannot be quantified satisfactorily and necessarily involve an element of personal judgement. Although the Survey claims not to be a 'capitalist undertaking' and takes account of socio-economic circumstances such as infant mortality and GNP per capita, it none the less assumes that political rights are maximised under conditions of multiparty democracy and it regards thoroughgoing socialism, in practice, as incompatible with basic freedoms. For all their individual shortcomings, however, there is a considerable measure of agreement between these various indices, and they largely agree also with more 'qualitative' assessments of democracy and human rights such as those produced annually by the London-based organisation Amnesty International.

Amnesty, a worldwide organisation which claims to be independent of all governments, political groupings, economic interests and religious creeds, deliberately eschews quantitative or more general comparative assessments of human rights in the various countries with which it deals. Its concern is rather to monitor the extent to which, in each of them, the provisions of the Universal Declaration of Human Rights and other international conventions have been observed, particularly the provisions that relate to the treatment of 'prisoners of conscience' (those imprisoned because of their beliefs, colour, sex, ethnic origin, language or religion who have not used or advocated violence). Its reports make clear that the performance of Western governments is by no means beyond reproach in this connection. In the United Kingdom, for instance, recent Amnesty reports have expressed concern about the judicial procedures employed in political cases in Northern Ireland, particularly the 'Diplock courts', which operate without a jury. There were also complaints about the alleged planting of evidence by the police and about the arrest of peaceful or intending picketers during the miners' strike of 1984–85, some of whom had reportedly been ill-treated in police custody and restricted in their subsequent freedom of movement. In the United States Amnesty expressed particular concern about an increase in the number of judicial executions and about allegations of politically or racially motivated prosecutions. In India, a non-communist but developing country, there were complaints about the detention of prisoners of conscience and about large numbers of political detainees (mostly Sikhs) who were being held without trial or who were awaiting trial under special legislation permitting trial *in camera*.

Reported violations of human rights, however, were on the whole much graver in the communist-ruled countries (as well, of course, as in many others). In relatively liberal Yugoslavia, for instance, there were criticisms of the ill-treatment of prisoners in custody and of political proceedings in which the accused had not received a fair trial. Citizens had also been convicted of 'hostile propaganda' for no more than the peaceful expression of dissenting (often nationalist) opinions. In Poland, Amnesty expressed concern about the arrest and detention of hundreds of prisoners of conscience and about allegations of ill-treatment and torture of prisoners while in official custody. In a small but disturbing number of cases political activists had died in unexplained circumstances during or shortly after police interrogation. Among the larger communist countries, China was criticised for the large number of public and often summary executions that had taken place in connection with that country's anti-crime campaign, as well as for the arrest of people who had been peacefully exercising their human rights and for trials of political detainees in which (for instance) the accused had been presumed guilty beforehand in the official press. Amnesty found that at least a thousand peaceful demonstrators had been killed in the Tienanmen Square massacre of June 1989. In the USSR, Amnesty welcomed the reform of legal codes and procedures, but continued to express concern about a hundred or more prisoners of conscience who were believed to be imprisoned, in internal exile, or confined in psychiatric hospitals against their will.

More detailed, qualitative assessments such as these evidently agree closely with the results of more quantitative and directly comparative investigations. Both, moreover, agree closely with the historical record. As Dahl points out, for instance, there have been many cases of mass coercion in

hegemonic or communist regimes, such as the forced collectivisation of agriculture in the USSR in the 1930s, the Cultural
Revolution in China (in which, according to the Chinese
authorities themselves, nearly three-quarters of a million
citizens were unjustly persecuted and nearly 35,000 lost their
lives), and in more recent years the forced deurbanisation
policies followed with great loss of life by Pol Pot in Kampuchea. No repression on a comparable scale has ever
occurred in the liberal democracies. Whatever reservations
there might be about individual indices or assessments,
findings such as those we have considered do at least point to
differences in the extent to which communist and non-
communist regimes provide formal democratic rights to their
respective populations such as electoral choice, the ability to
form interest groups and a relatively unconstrained press.
And while there is some point in the orthodox communist
response that socio-economic as well as formal democratic
rights must be considered, it is clear from the number of cases
of the abuse of power in the communist states, many of which
have been acknowledged by the authorities themselves, that the
content of democracy may prove a rather vulnerable commodity
so long as its form has not been assured. In these respects the
onus of proof must remain, as it has done until now, upon the
communist rather than the liberal-democratic states.

Communist and non-communist states: comparative economic performance

We are concerned in this volume with the politics of the
communist states, not with their economic performance as
such. None the less, as we have pointed out, the interpenetra-
tion of politics and economics in a communist-ruled country is
such that the distinction between them is rather less meaning-
ful than it would be in a Western liberal democracy; and even
in a Western liberal democracy the state often plays a central
role in economic life and political parties base their appeals to
the electorate upon the superior economic performance they
claim to be able to achieve. The attitudes of mass publics
towards their respective regimes, also, may depend to a

considerable extent upon their economic performance. The liberal democracies, unlike the communist states, provide a means of legitimating the actions of government through competitive elections in which the people's will is notionally expressed. Even in the liberal democracies, however, some doubts have been expressed as to the extent to which the regimes concerned will be able to survive a prolonged period of relatively poor economic performance, and in the communist states the need to justify the actions of government in terms of what it provides for its population is rather greater. The performance of the economy is therefore a central aspect of politics in both communist and non-communist systems, and the performance of one compared with the other has considerable implications for politicians as well as for economic statisticians in both cases.

Comparisons of communist and non-communist economic performance are unfortunately fraught with a number of serious and intractable difficulties. In the first place, the concepts employed for economic measurements in East and West are often different. The most important of these, gross national product, is normally defined in the West as the total value of all goods and services made available in the economy within a specified period. In the communist countries, however, a different concept, 'net material product', is generally employed; this is similar to gross national product but excludes 'nonproductive' activities such as governmental administration, finance, education, medicine and other professional services, and also capital construction or depreciation. Economic performance in the communist states is not normally reported in sufficient detail to allow an equivalent of GNP in these countries to be reconstructed with total accuracy. Further problems arise when a common expression of value is required. Conversions by means of official exchange rates are generally unsuitable for this purpose because exchange rates in the communist countries are centrally administered and often artificial (as the thriving black market testifies). Prices which reflect the real resource costs of each product must therefore be calculated in order to derive theoretically accurate measures of the real growth and distribution of GNP, an exercise which is difficult and highly imperfect.

Calculations of this kind may be expressed in either Western prices or in those of the communist countries. Some goods, such as foodstuffs and public transport, are cheaper and account for a higher proportion of total output in the communist countries than in the West; conversely, goods such as motor-cars and computers are much cheaper and account for a larger share of total output in the West than in the communist countries. Expressed in Western prices, the GNP of communist countries will appear to be larger; expressed in the prices of the communist countries, on the other hand, it will appear to be smaller. In neither case has 'real' GNP been altered in the slightest. Comparisons of military spending in East and West are particularly susceptible to distortion of this kind depending upon whether 'dollar costing' or 'rouble costing' is employed. Valuing the military effort of the communist countries in terms of what it would cost to provide the same resources in Western countries tends to inflate the apparent level of communist military expenditure, because the communist countries use relatively large quantities of military manpower which is poorly remunerated and relatively low quantities of advanced technology which tends to be very expensive in local prices. Valuations in terms of the prices of the communist countries themselves has the opposite effect. Comparisons of growth rates in communist and Western countries, although not without shortcomings, may avoid some of these difficulties, but the result can at best convey an impression of relative levels of performance and not of absolute differences in living standards. Comparisons in terms of physical units, such as hospital beds, washing machines or potatoes, avoid the distorting effects of comparisons in terms of monetary equivalents but for their part cannot be converted into a single measure of relative levels of prosperity.

In an effort to achieve greater comparability in such matters the United Nations has initiated an International Comparison Project which seeks to develop measures of GNP in various countries using purchasing power parities rather than exchange rates. So far the project covers only a limited number of countries, and serious methodological difficulties remain to be resolved (the World Bank's *World Development Report* acknowledges that perfect cross-country comparability of GNP per capita may in fact be unattainable). At present, recalculated estimates of GNP per capita are available for only four of the sixteen communist nations considered in this volume: China, Hungary, Poland and Yugoslavia. In 1987 GNP per capita in these countries was assessed at US $290, 2240, 1930 and 2480 respectively, as compared with India, the United Kingdom and the United States at US $300, 10420 and 18530 respectively. More comprehensive data have, however, been developed by two of the authors associated with the International Comparison Project, Robert Summers and Alan Heston. According to their figures, based upon a measure of world average relative prices, differences in GNP per capita between a number of communist and non-communist countries between 1950 and 1980 were as set out in Table 8.2 (their calculations in full are reported in Summers and Heston, 1984).

Whatever figures are employed, there is little doubt that the communist nations, taken as a whole, are less prosperous than the major industrialised countries of the capitalist West.

TABLE 8.2

Communist and non-communist states: comparative economic performance (real per capita GNP in US dollars)

	1950	1960	1970	1980
India	333	428	450	498
United Kingdom	2700	3388	4216	4990
USA	4550	5195	6629	8089
China	300	505	711	1135
USSR	1373	2084	3142	3943
GDR	1480	3006	4100	5532
Poland	1516	1996	2731	3509
Czechoslovakia	2182	3189	4027	4908
Yugoslavia	769	1256	2027	3318
Communist non-communist average (%)	50	67	74	82

Source: Compiled from Robert Summers and Alan Heston, 'Improved International Comparisons of Real Product and its Composition, 1950–80', *Review of Income and Wealth*, xxx (1984), pp. 207–62.

There is considerable variation within both groups, however, and on Summers and Heston's figures, at least, some of the more advanced communist nations such as the GDR and Czechoslovakia may now have drawn ahead of major capitalist nations such as the United Kingdom and Italy respectively in their GNP per capita. The communist states, moreover, have by and large been expanding their economies at a more rapid rate than the major capitalist countries (see Table 8.2), although in both cases rates of growth have been showing a tendency to fall in recent years and there have been some spectacular reverses in the communist-ruled world in the late 1980s. There is no communist state whose rate of growth since the Second World War has exceeded that of a capitalist state such as Japan, but their rate of growth as a group has exceeded that of the major Western countries as a group, and the fluctuations in their annual rates of growth have also been much less. This relatively rapid rate of economic growth has been in part a product of the fact that the communist states have started their growth from a lower point than that of the major Western countries – the phenomenon known as 'catching up' – but it has also been in part the result of the deliberate selection of economic growth as a priority by their political leaderships, and in the case of at least some of the most developed communist states it has continued after they have overtaken some of their capitalist competitors.

It is also worthy of note that the communist states, by and large, have achieved their levels of economic performance without the levels of inflation and unemployment that have become an increasingly prominent feature of the major capitalist economies in the 1970s and 1980s. Unemployment and inflation have not been entirely eliminated in the communist countries, particularly in those whose economies are not centrally planned in the orthodox manner, such as China and Yugoslavia. In Yugoslavia, for instance, the annual rate of inflation was officially reported to have exceeded 1000 per cent in the late 1980s, and its level of unemployment has also been considerable, despite the fact that many Yugoslavs have left the country and found employment in Western Europe. The more conventionally centrally planned economies which exist in the other communist states also permit a measure of inflation, usually by replacing older and cheaper goods by newer and more expensive ones of much the same quality, but also by making increases in the prices set by the state in order to prevent the prices of goods getting too far out of line with their production costs. There is also a certain amount of unemployment in these states as a result of people changing jobs, although officially no unemployment exists and none is recorded in government statistics. Most estimates of the degree of inflation and unemployment that result from such factors, however, are extremely low, usually in the 2–3 per cent range, and in general it is fair to say that the centrally planned communist economies have achieved their relatively high levels of economic performance without sacrificing their other objectives of virtually full employment and low levels of inflation. It is not surprising that this model of economic development has been popular in many other countries, particularly in the Third World.

It is also fair to say that the benefits of economic growth have as a rule been distributed more equitably in the communist states than in the majority of non-communist states. Calculations of this kind must inevitably rely upon published data on monetary earnings, which may be difficult to compare across systems and may be to various degrees misleading. The existence of the 'second economy' in most of the communist states, for instance, is an important source of bias, as is the existence of administered privilege – the allocation of superior housing, transport and health care facilities to party and government officials, for instance, as well as the opportunity to shop at special closed stores to which the majority of the population are not admitted but in which prices are lower and the range of goods much better than in the ordinary state retail sector. In Western economies, however, a variety of benefits are also extended to senior employees, such as assistance with school fees and rehousing, car allowances, private health insurance and subsidised meals, and in the Western countries there is also a substantial black economy where monetary transactions take place which are not recorded by the income tax authorities. There may be some rough comparability between these two; in any case neither extends over a sufficient number of people to make a significant difference to the national averages in terms of which such comparisons are usually made. At this level it is clear that the communist states, as a rule, distribute their incomes in a more egalitarian manner than most Western countries.

Comparisons of this kind may be expressed in various ways. The ratio between the earnings of the best-paid and worst-paid tenths of the labour force (the 'decile ratio') is one of the most common such summary statistics. The relevant figures for various countries in the late 1960s and early 1970s, according to the best Western estimates, were as follows (these figures are taken from Peter Wiles's *Economic Institutions Compared*, published in 1977): the USA, the least egalitarian, 6.7; Canada, 6.0; Italy, 5.9; Sweden and the USSR 3.5; United Kingdom, 3.4; Czechoslovakia, 3.1; Hungary, 3.0; and Bulgaria, the most egalitarian, 2.7. It was not the case that all the communist states were more egalitarian in their income distribution than all of the capitalist states considered; but as a group, their distribution of incomes was certainly more egalitarian than that of the capitalist countries also considered as a group. These findings are supported by a comparative study of income distribution in Poland, the USSR, the United Kingdom and the USA, undertaken by Peter Wiles and Stefan Markowski, which found that in all these countries the distribution of income had become more equal over time, but that it was more equal in the two communist states, taken together, than in the two capitalist states, and that there was no equivalent in the communist states of the rich private capitalists that existed in the United Kingdom and the USA. This, the authors found, was the 'most striking difference between the two systems'. Several other studies, although by no means all (see for instance Bergson, 1984 and Morrisson, 1984), have come to similar conclusions.

Communist and non-communist states: comparative social welfare

We turn finally to the area of comparative social welfare, that is to say of the social purposes upon which governments spend their revenues in different systems. A variety of indicators could be chosen to illustrate such comparisons. In what follows we have taken what are widely regarded as among the most important areas of social policy, such as housing, education, health care and social security, and looked at the different patterns of spending of different states and at some of the outcomes, such as infant mortality and life expectancy, that are associated with them. Again, there are many problems associated with comparisons of this kind. The data are often unavailable or of doubtful quality; national averages may conceal substantial within-nation differences, particularly in heterogeneous and multi-ethnic states such as the USSR and Yugoslavia; and allowances must be made for factors such as the different levels of socio-economic development of the countries involved in the comparison as these will tend to have a considerable influence upon the countries' levels of performance in such matters quite independent of the efforts of their governments. Social indicators of the kind that have been mentioned, however, in many ways provide a better basis upon which to compare the performance of different political regimes than the purely economic statistics considered in the previous section, since they reveal more clearly the various purposes to which different governments attach the most importance. They are, in other words, one of the best ways in which we can examine the difference that is made to national policies if a country is ruled by communists rather than non-communists.

Some of the evidence relevant to a comparison of this kind is set out in Table 8.3. These statistics record the performance of individual nations irrespective of differences in their total economic resources, although clearly more prosperous nations, by and large, will be better able to finance generous social welfare programmes than their less prosperous communist counterparts. The performance of the communist states, taken as a group, none the less compares not unfavourably in many respects with that of the major capitalist countries, particularly in the fields of housing and health care. Indeed in many respects the performance of at least some of the communist states is as good as or better than that of the United Kingdom and the USA, an impressive performance

TABLE 8.3

Communist and non-communist states: selected indicators of social welfare

	Housing units completed per 10,000 population, 1988	Doctors per 10,000 population, c.1987	Infant mortality rate per 1000 births, 1988	Life expectancy at birth, 1987	Daily calorie supply, 1986	Students in education per 10,000 population 1988
	(1)	(2)	(3)	(4)	(5)	(6)
United Kingdom	43	18.2	9	75	3256	112
USA	60	25.7	10	75	3645	257
India	n.a.	n.a.	99	58	2238	58
USSR	78	43.3	25	69	3399	177
China	n.a.	13.6	32	69	2630	18
GDR	66	31.9	9	73	3814	79
Poland	51	25.1	16	71	3336	91
Yugoslavia	51	21.2	26	71	3563	150
Hungary	48	32.9	16	70	3569	93
Czechoslovakia	52	36.5	13	71	3448	109
Vietnam	n.a.	3.2	46	66	2297	21
Cuba	n.a.	30.5	13	75	3124	250

n.a.: not available.

Source: Cols 1–3 and 6: *Narodnoe khozyaistvo SSSR v 1988 g.* (Moscow, 1989); Cols 4, 5, *World Development Report 1989* (New York, 1989).

when it is remembered that their levels of GNP per head are generally much lower.

Controlling so far as we can for variations in levels of prosperity (or GNP per head), some interesting comparisons are revealed. In a close analysis of such matters, for instance, A.J. Groth has found that the communist nations, despite their relative poverty, have been distinctive in the proportion of public spending they have devoted to education. Poorer communist states have in fact provided a better educational service than many wealthier but non-communist nations. Albania, for example, has expanded its educational system much faster and enrolled a higher proportion of the relevant age-groups within it than economically comparable nations such as Spain, Portugal and Greece, and the more developed communist nations have also out-performed wealthier non-communist nations such as France, West Germany and the United Kingdom. Educational enrolment ratios in East Germany have also exceeded those in West Germany and those in North Korea have exceeded those in South Korea, although their respective economic resources would have suggested the reverse (Groth, 1971; see also Wade and Groth, 1989). In terms of social security benefits, similarly, such as old age, injury and sickness allowances, Groth (1982) found that the communist states, as a rule, provided a range and level of assistance that was generally high and in excess of that provided by non-communist states at a similar level of socio-economic development. Groth and Hunt (1985) also found that communist regimes were distinctive in the share of their resources that they devoted to culture and mass communications, such as theatre performances, museums, books published, public library volumes and circulation of daily newspapers per head of population.

Issues of this kind may be explored further on the basis of internationally comparable data such as those published annually in the World Bank's *World Development Report*. India and China, for instance, are both low income economies in terms of the Bank's classification, with very similar levels of GNP per capita. China, however, has a substantially higher life expectancy at birth, much lower rates of infant mortality and child death, more doctors and nurses per head of population, and enrols a greater proportion of its population in full-time education at primary and secondary (although not at tertiary) levels. Yugoslavia, according to the World Bank an 'upper middle-income economy', is above the average for all states in this category in its life expectancy and has much lower levels of infant and child mortality, many more doctors and nurses per head of population and substantially better standards of nutrition. In educational terms Yugoslavia's performance is also better than the average for its income group, and comparable with or better than that of more prosperous nations such as Greece, Italy and the United Kingdom. Hungary, another communist nation in the 'upper middle-income' category in World Bank terms, has a better level of health and educational provision than other economically comparable nations and indeed improves upon many of the advanced capitalist countries in its provision of medical and nursing care.

There has been a long and fairly inconclusive debate among political scientists about the extent to which 'politics matters' in variations in spending patterns of this kind. Comparisons between American states and between Western liberal democracies, for instance, have frequently concluded that factors such as the level of social and economic development of the state or nation concerned may be a better predictor of spending patterns than the political orientation of their governments. These findings have not been universally accepted, however, and certainly when comparisons are made between states at approximately the same level of socio-economic development some significant contrasts emerge. We have seen this to be true of communist and non-communist nations at approximately the same stage of development; and it is also true of comparisons between 'matched pairs' of states, such as West and East Germany or North and South Korea, the differences between which appear to be largely attributable to their different political regimes. We have already mentioned Groth's findings, which deal in part with these two pairs of states. Jaroslav Krejci (1976), in a more extended study of the two Germanys, found many similarities between them in their economic and social structures despite their political differences. The opportunities for social mobility through education, however, were greater in the GDR than in the Federal Republic, as both higher and secondary education were more accessible to ordinary workers, and opportunities for political mobility for ordinary workers were also greater in the GDR than in the Federal Republic. These findings are borne out in the *World Development Report*, which indicates that the Federal Republic has a slightly higher life expectancy and level of medical provision than the GDR but that the GDR, although less prosperous, has almost exactly the same levels of infant and child mortality and a higher level of enrolment in post-primary education. Again, these are differences which appear to be largely attributable to the different political regimes of the two countries concerned.

It does not necessarily follow that the basic social welfare needs are satisfactorily met in all the communist-ruled countries, still less that their performance is always superior to that of states at a similar level of social and economic development. The slowdown in economic growth experienced by most the communist countries in the 1970s and 1980s has in fact exposed a number of serious shortcomings in social welfare provision in these countries and has contributed to the emergence or re-emergence of social problems of a kind for which there was supposedly no basis under socialist conditions. One of the most striking indicators of this kind is life expectancy. Unlike the major Western countries, where life expectancy has steadily been increasing, in most of the communist countries it has been tending to decline over the past decade or so, quite against the experience of industrially developed nations. This fall has been attributed to a variety of causes including alcohol abuse, poor nutrition and unhealthy patterns of living, especially in urban areas. Still more remarkably, poverty and other forms of social deprivation have re-emerged, particularly in some of the East European countries which have been engaged in the process of economic reform (which usually means higher prices). In Hungary, for instance, at least 10–15 per cent of the population were estimated to suffer in the mid-1980s from 'multiple disadvantages' (the official euphemism for poverty). The poorest of these had a monthly income of less than half the national average, and had a diet seriously deficient in meat, fish, fruit

and vegetables. The individuals concerned were disproportionately pensioners, the elderly and those with large families,
whose benefits from the state had lagged behind rising prices
and who had little opportunity to increase their earnings in
the 'second economy'. In Poland in the late 1970s the
'Experience and Future' study group reported similarly that
large sections of the population, particularly the working
class, lower-level office employees and pensioners, suffered
from serious poverty and even malnutrition.

Quantitative data, moreover, however impressive, may
often give a misleading impression of the quality of the
services that communist states make available to their citizens. Czechoslovakia, for instance, according to official statistics, had the third highest proportion of doctors to population
in the world in the mid-1980s, and the fifth highest proportion
of hospital beds per head of population. Czech health services,
according to press reports, were none the less suffering from
serious problems. A high proportion of equipment is obsolete;
there is a shortage of hard currency to buy equipment and
medication from abroad; doctors are poorly paid, and bribes
and gratuities are often necessary if urgent or specialist
treatment is to be obtained. In Hungary, similarly, free health
care is available, as a legal entitlement, to every citizen.
Hospital buildings, however, are often antiquated; much of
the equipment is obsolete or in poor working order; many
basic medications are unavailable because of a lack of hard
currency to buy them in the West; and overcrowding in
hospital wards is commonplace. In Poland, at least 30 per
cent of hospitals are reckoned to be unsuitable for use (it is
popularly held that one needs to be extremely healthy to dare
to register in a Polish hospital). As elsewhere, there are serious
shortages of modern equipment and medicines, and shortcomings even in basic hygiene (between 5 and 20 per cent of
patients are reported to contract a serious infection during
their stay, prolonging their treatment and contributing further
to already overcrowded conditions). In Romania, similarly,
there are acknowledged to be serious gaps in medical provision in rural areas, and hospital patients are sometimes placed
two in a bed because of overcrowding.

Many of these problems, admittedly, are not unknown in

more prosperous Western countries, and in general it is still true to say that it is in their medical services, as well as their educational and other welfare facilities, that communist regimes compare most favourably with their non-communist counterparts and indeed for which they appear to be most highly valued by their own domestic populations. In a detailed analysis of health care provision in Germany, Britain and Japan as well as the Soviet Union, for instance, Leichter (1979) found that the USSR had been 'enormously successful in providing all [its] citizens with professionally competent, comprehensive, free medical care', and that the health care system had contributed to a substantial improvement in popular health standards despite the existence of a number of distributional problems, themselves 'by no means unique to the Soviet Union'. The main reason for the health care policies promoted in the USSR appeared to be the regime's ideology: in other words, the provision of a highly centralised, free, comprehensive and universal state-run medical care system, with priority given to the proletariat, was essentially an attempt to 'spell out the humanitarian, egalitarian, and collective implications of socialist ideology'. Communist countries were not unique in introducing a comprehensive national system of health care; they were distinctive, however, in the share of spending that they devoted to education and health care as compared with their non-communist counterparts, and in the content, operation and evolution of the health care systems that they maintained. If communist regimes must generally be accounted authoritarian, as we have suggested earlier in this chapter, they may reasonably be regarded also as broadly egalitarian and welfarist in the social and economic policies that they pursue.

Variations of this kind do not necessarily occur without compensating costs in other areas, and a number of writers have pointed out the extent to which a greater degree of social equality of this kind may be obtainable only by sacrificing a degree of personal liberty. Upward political mobility in the GDR, for instance, is greater than in the Federal Republic because of a policy for political recruitment which deliberately discriminates in favour of the lower strata of the population and against white-collar workers. Income differentials in the communist states, similarly, are generally lower than in the major capitalist states at least in part because middle-class pressure groups, such as those formed by doctors and lawyers in the West, are dominated by the communist party authorities and given very little opportunity to organise on behalf of their members. Levels of economic growth are typically somewhat higher than in the capitalist countries because the political authorities maintain a rate of investment in industry at the expense of popular consumption which the population at large might not ordinarily be expected to favour. And levels of crime are relatively low because it is not easy to escape from the country with the proceeds of one's crime or to find anything of value in the shops on which to spend them. In all of these matters a trade-off is apparently occurring, by which a social or economic value is being realised but at the expense of a political value such as individual liberty or the ability to form or join an organisation.

Several writers have suggested that these combinations may not be accidental, that there is, in other words, a logical connection between a relatively egalitarian society whose political system is authoritarian, on the one hand, and a more unequal society whose political system is liberal-democratic, on the other. Frank Parkin, for instance, has argued that the combination of a market economy and political pluralism is 'one which makes the redistribution of advantages between social classes difficult to bring about'. The government in the pluralist system, he suggests, is simply one power among many; any attempt it might make to bring about a relative improvement in the position of the less privileged is likely to be frustrated by the greater organisational and ideological influence of the dominant class. In a command economy, on the other hand, it is much easier for the government to achieve a redistribution of resources of this kind, because privileged groups have no access to a market to sustain their position and little opportunity to organise in defence of their interests. It follows that 'socialist egalitarianism is not readily compatible with a pluralist political order of the classic western type'; egalitarianism seems, on the contrary, to 'require a political system in which the state is able continually to hold in check those social and occupational groups which, by virtue of their skills or education or personal attributes, might otherwise attempt to stake claims to a disproportionate share of society's rewards' (this quotation comes from Parkin's *Class Inequality and Political Order*, published in 1971).

It would be too much to say that the experience of the communist states considered in this volume unambiguously supports such a proposition, and unduly pessimistic to suggest that the future holds out no other potential. It is, however, by and large the case that the periods of communist rule which have permitted the greatest degree of personal liberty, such as the New Economic Policy period in Russia or the Dubček period in Czechoslovakia, have generally been associated with a relative widening of social and economic differentials, and that periods of particularly authoritarian rule, such as in the 1950s in Czechoslovakia or the period of the Cultural Revolution in China, have generally been associated with a narrowing of differentials and a general hostility towards material rather than moral incentives. It is, of course, also possible for a particularly authoritarian communist regime to increase differentials, such as during Stalin's campaign against 'petty bourgeois equalitarianism' in the USSR in the 1930s. The experience of the communist states, however, does suggest that both liberty and equality may be more difficult to combine than had originally been supposed, and none of these states has yet managed to maximise both for an extended period of time any more successfully than any of the major liberal democracies (though there are considerable variations between individual countries in both cases). If politics is about choice, this, it would appear, is one of the most fundamental that rulers and peoples in both East and West have so far had to make about the system of government under which they live.

Further reading

The comparative analysis of political systems in terms of their outputs is considered further in Almond and Powell (1978, part IV); see also Groth (1971) and Pryor (1968), a pioneering study. Related issues of comparative political analysis are considered in Dogan and Pelassy (1984). Useful sources of cross-national data are the *United Nations Statistical Yearbook* (New York, annual), the *UNESCO Statistical Yearbook* (Paris, annual), the World Bank's *World Development Report* (New York, annual), and Ruth Sivard, *World Military and Social Expenditures* (Washington, DC, annual). The need to relate the communist states to broader comparative perspectives of this kind is argued in Kautsky (1973) and in Bunce and Echols (1979).

On comparative levels of political democracy, see Dahl (1971), Bollen (1980) Humana (1986), and the Comparative Survey of Freedom reported in Gastril (1986). Amnesty International publishes an *Annual Report* on the observance of human rights on a global basis, and has also produced more detailed surveys of human rights and the treatment of prisoners of conscience in the USSR (1980), China (1984) and Yugoslavia (1985). A somewhat more partisan report is produced by the United States Department of State: *Country Reports on Human Rights* (Washington, DC, annually since 1977). Wider comparative issues of human rights in East and West are considered in Lane (1984) and Szymanski (1984).

Comparative economic performance is reviewed in Wiles (1977), Ellman (1989, ch. 10), Gregory and Stuart (1985) and Zimbalist *et al.* (1989). The difficulties of comparing performance and measuring living standards in East and West are considered in US Congress Joint Economic Committee (1982), Summers and Heston (1984) and Marer (1985). On income differentials, see Wiles and Markowski (1971), Bergson (1984) and Morrisson (1984). Comparative surveys of social welfare include Groth (1971) and (1982), Krejci (1976), Connor (1979), Leichter (1979), Madison (1980) and Echols (1981). The research reports produced regularly by Radio Free Europe and Radio Liberty provide abundant and up-to-date information on social conditions in the USSR and Eastern Europe.

On the association between socio-economic and political systems more generally, see Parkin (1971), Brus (1975), Lindblom (1977) and Selucky (1979). On the rather wider question of socialism and the experience of the communist states, see Kolakowski and Hampshire (1974), Bellis (1979),

Bahro (1981), Lane (1982), Nove (1982), and Fehér, Heller and Márkus (1983). Matters of this kind are also reviewed in periodicals such as *Monthly Review* (New York, monthly), *New Left Review* (London, bimonthly) and *Critique* (Glasgow, bi-annually). *World Marxist Review* (Prague, monthly), the English edition of *Problems of Peace and Socialism*, gives the point of view of the communist regimes themselves.

Bibliography

Adelman, Jonathan (ed.) (1984) *Terror and Communist Politics* (Boulder, Col.: Westview).

Akiner, Shirin (1985) *The Islamic Peoples of the Soviet Union* (London: Kogan Paul International).

Almond, Gabriel and Powell, G. Bingham, Jr. (1978) *Comparative Politics: System, Process and Policy*, 2nd ed. (Boston: Little, Brown).

Amnesty International (1980) *Prisoners of Conscience in the USSR*, 2nd ed. (London: Quatermaine House).

Amnesty International (1984) *China: Violations of Human Rights* (London: Amnesty International).

Amnesty International (1985) *Yugoslavia: Prisoners of Conscience* (London: Amnesty International).

Amnesty International (1989) *People's Republic of China: Preliminary Findings on Killings of Unarmed Civilians, Arbitrary Arrests and Summary Executions since 3 June 1989* (London: Amnesty International).

Andrle, Vladimir (1976) *Managerial Power in the Soviet Union* (Aldershot: Saxon House).

Armstrong, John A. (1965) 'Sources of Administrative Behavior: some Soviet and Western European Comparisons', *American Political Science Review*, vol. 59, no. 3 (September), pp. 643–55.

Ash, Timothy Garton (1985) *The Polish Revolution: Solidarity* (London: Coronet).

Ash, Timothy Garton (1990) *We the People* (Harmondsworth: Penguin).

Aslund, Anders (1989) *Gorbachev's Struggle for Economic Reform* (London: Pinter).

Azrael, Jeremy (1966) *Managerial Power and Soviet Politics* (Cambridge, Mass.: Harvard University Press).

Bahro, Rudolf (1981) *The Alternative in Eastern Europe* (London: Verso).

Banac, Ivo (1984) *The National Question in Yugoslavia: Origins, History, Politics* (Ithaca, NY: Cornell University Press).

Barmé, Geremie and Minford, John (1988) *Seeds of Fire. Chinese Voices of Conscience* (New York: Hill and Wang).

Barnett, A. Doak (1967) *Cadres, Bureaucracy and Political Power in Communist China* (New York: Columbia University Press).

Barnett, A. Doak (1985) *The Making of Foreign Policy in China* (London: I. B. Tauris).

Barry, Donald D. *et al.* (eds) (1977–79) *Soviet Law since Stalin*, 3 vols (Leyden: Sijthoff).

Beaufort, Simon de (1978) *Yellow Earth, Green Jade. Constants in Chinese Political Mores* (Cambridge, MA: Harvard Studies in International Affairs).

Bell, John D. (1986) *The Bulgarian Communist Party from Blagoev to Zhivkov* (Stanford, Calif.: Hoover Institution Press).

Bellis, Paul (1979) *Marxism and the USSR* (London: Macmillan).

Benewick, Robert and Wingrove, Paul (eds) (1988) *Reforming the Revolution. China in Transition* (London: Macmillan).

Benn, David Wedgwood (1989) *Persuasion and Soviet Politics* (Oxford: Blackwell).

Bergson, Abram (1984) 'Income Inequality under Soviet Socialism', *Journal of Economic Literature*, vol. 22 (September), pp. 1052–99.

Berman, Harold J. and Spindler, John W. (eds) (1972) *Soviet Criminal Laws and Procedures: the RSFR Codes*, 2nd ed. (Cambridge, Mass.: Harvard University Press).

Beyme, Klaus von (1982) *Economics and Politics within Socialist Systems* (New York: Praeger).

Bialer, Seweryn (1980) *Stalin's Successors* (New York: Cambridge University Press).

Bloomfield, Jon (ed.) (1989) *The Soviet Revolution* (London: Lawrence and Wishart).

Bociurkiw, Bohdan and Strong, John W. (eds) (1975) *Religion and Atheism in the USSR and Eastern Europe* (London: Macmillan).

Bollen, Kenneth (1980) 'Issues in the Comparative Analysis of Political Democracy', *American Sociological Review*, vol. 45, no. 3 (June), pp. 370–90.

Brovkin, Vladimir (forthcoming) 'Informal Political Associations in Russia, 1988–1989', *Soviet Studies*.

Brown, A. H. (1974) *Soviet Politics and Political Science* (London: Macmillan).

Brown, Archie (1980) 'The Power of the General Secretary of the CPSU'. In Rigby (1980), pp. 135–57.

Brown, Archie (1985) 'Gorbachev: New Man in the Kremlin', *Problems of Communism*, vol. 34, no. 3 (May–June), pp. 1–23.

Brown, Archie (ed.) (1985) *Political Culture and Communist Studies* (London: Macmillan).

Brown, Archie (ed.) (1989) *Political Leadership in the Soviet Union* (London: Macmillan).

Brown, Archie and Gray, Jack (eds) (1979) *Political Culture and Political Change in Communist States*, 2nd ed. (London: Macmillan).

Brugger, Bill (ed.) *Chinese Marxism in Flux, 1978–1984* (London: Croom Helm).

Brus, Wlodzimierz (1975) *Social Ownership and Political Systems* (London: Routledge).

Brzezinski, Zbigniew K. (1967) *The Soviet Bloc: Unity and Conflict*, rev. ed. (Cambridge, Mass.: Harvard University Press).

Bunce, Valerie and Echols, John M. (1979) 'From Soviet Studies to Comparative Politics: the Unfinished Revolution', *Soviet Studies*, vol 31, no. 1 (January), pp. 43–55.

Bunce, Valerie and Echols, John M. (1980) 'Soviet Politics in the Brezhnev Era: "Pluralism" or "Corporatism"?'. In Kelley (1980), pp. 1–26.

Burg, S. L. (1983) *Conflict and Cohesion in Socialist Yugoslavia* (Princeton NJ: Princeton University Press).

Burns, John F. (ed.) (1989) *The Chinese Communist Party's Nomenklatura System* (Armonk, NY: Sharpe).

Butler, W. E. (1983a) *Soviet Law* (London: Butterworths).

Butler, W. E. (ed.) (1983b) *Basic Documents on the Soviet Legal System* (New York: Oceana).

Carrère d'Encausse, Hélène (1979) *An Empire in Decline* (New York: Newsweek).

Chang, Parris H. (1978) *Power and Policy in China* (University Park: Pennyslvania University Press).

Chen Erjin (1984) *China: Crossroads Socialism* (London: Verso).

Chen, Jerome (1968) *The Criminal Process in Contemporary China* (Cambridge, Mass.: Harvard University Press).

Christiansen, Flemming (1989) 'The 1989 Student Demonstrations and the Limits of the Chinese Political Bargaining Machine: An Essay', *China Information* vol. 4, no. 1 (Summer), p. 17–28.

Churchward, Lloyd G. (1975) *Contemporary Soviet Government*, 2nd ed. (London: Routledge).

Cohen, Jerome (1968) *The Criminal Process in Communist China* (Cambridge, Mass.: Harvard University Press).

Cohen, Lenard and Shapiro, Jane (eds) (1974) *Communist Systems in Comparative Perspective* (New York: Anchor).

Cohen, Stephen F. (1985) *Rethinking the Soviet Experience* (New York: Oxford University Press).

Colton, Timothy J. (1979) *Commissars, Commanders and Civilian Authority* (Cambridge, Mass.: Harvard University Press).

Connor, Walker (1984) *The National Question in Marxist–Leninist Theory and Strategy* (Princeton, NJ: Princeton University Press).

Connor, Walter D. (1979) *Socialism, Politics, and Equality* (New York: Columbia University Press).

Copper, John *et al.* (1985) *Human Rights in Post-Mao China* (Boulder, Col.: Westview).

Curry, Jane L. (ed.) (1984) *The Black Book of Polish Censorship* (New York: Random House).

Curtis, Michael (ed.) (1979) *Totalitarianism* (New Brunswick, NJ: Transaction Books).

Dahl, Robert A. (1971) *Polyarchy* (New Haven, Conn.: Yale University Press).

Dahl, Robert A. (ed.) (1973) *Regimes and Oppositions* (New Haven: Yale University Press).

Dawisha, Karen L. (1980) 'The Limits of the Bureaucratic Politics Model: some Observations on the Soviet Case', *Studies in Comparative Communism*, vol. 13, no. 4 (Winter), pp. 300–26.

Deakin, William, Shukman, Harry and Willetts, Harry (1975) *A History of World Communism* (London: Weidenfeld & Nicolson.

Deng Xiaoping (1984) *Speeches and Writings*, ed. Robert Maxwell (Oxford: Pergamon Press).

Dennis, Mike (1988) *The GDR: Politics, Economics and Society* (London: Pinter).

DiFranceisco, Wayne and Gitelman, Zvi (1985) 'Soviet Political Culture and "Covert Participation" in Policy Implementation', *American Political Science Review*, vol. 78, no. 3 (September), pp. 603–21.

Doder, Dusko (1978) *The Yugoslavs* (New York: Random House).

Dogan, Mattei and Pelassy, Dominique (1984) *How to Compare Nations. Strategies in Comparative Politics* (Chatham, NJ: Chatham House).

Dreyer, June (1986) 'The Limits of the Permissible in China', *Problems of Communism*, vol. 29, no. 6 (November–December), pp. 48–65.

Dunlop, John B. (1983) *The Faces of Contemporary Russian Nationalism* (Princeton, NJ: Princeton University Press).

Dunlop, John B. (1985) *The New Russian Nationalism* (New York: Praeger).

Echols, John M. (1981) 'Does Socialism Mean Greater Equality? A Comparison of East and West Along Several Major Dimensions', *American Journal of Political Science*, vol. 25, no. 1 (February), pp. 1–31.

Ellis, Jane (1986) *The Russian Orthodox Church* (London: Croom Helm).

Ellman, Michael (1989) *Socialist Planning*. 2nd ed. (Cambridge: Cambridge University Press).

Etkind, Efim (1978) *Notes of a Non-Conspirator* (Oxford: Oxford University Press).

Fehér, Ferenc, Heller, Agnes and Márkus, György (1983) *Dictatorship over Needs. An Analysis of Soviet Societies* (Oxford: Blackwell).

Feldbrugge, F. J. M. (ed.) (1979) *The Constitution of the USSR and the Union Republics* (Alphen aan den Rijn: Sijthoff and Noordhoff).

Fetjö, Francois (1974) *A History of the People's Democracies*, rev. ed. (Harmondsworth, Middx.: Penguin Books).

Feuchtwang, Stefan and Hussain, Athar (1988) *Directions in Development: The Chinese Economy in the 1980s* (London: Zed).

Fewsmith, Joseph (1988) 'Agricultural Crisis in China', *Problems of Communism*, vol. 38, no. 6 (November–December), pp. 78–93.

Fischer-Galati, Stephen (ed.) (1979) *The Communist Parties of Eastern Central Europe* (New York: Columbia University Press).

Fleron, Frederick J., Jr. (ed.) (1969) *Communist Studies and the Social Sciences* (Chicago: Rand McNally).

Friedgut, Theodore H. (1979) *Political Participation in the USSR* (Princeton, NJ: Princeton University Press).

Friedrich, Carl J. (ed.) (1969) *Totalitarianism in Perspective* (New York: Praeger).

Friedrich, Carl J. and Brzezinski, Zbigniew K. (1965) *Totalitarian Dictatorship and Autocracy*, 2nd ed. (Cambridge, Mass.: Harvard University Press).

Furtak, Robert K. (1986) *The Political systems of the Socialist States: An Introduction to Marxist-Leninist Regimes* (Brighton: Wheatsheaf).

Gastril, Raymond D. (1986) 'The Comparative Survey of Freedom 1986', *Freedom at Issue*, no. 88 (January–February), pp. 3–17.

Gill, Graeme (1986) 'The Future of the General Secretary', *Political Studies*, vol. 34, no. 2 (June), pp. 223–35.

Ginzburg, Evgeniya (1967) *Into the Whirlwind* (London: Collins).

Ginzburg, Evgeniya (1981) *Within the Whirlwind* (London: Collins).

Gitelman, Zvi (1977) 'Soviet Political Culture: Insights from Jewish Emigrés', *Soviet Studies*, vol. 29, no. 4 (October), pp. 543–64.

Glazov, Yuri (1985) *The Russian Mind since Stalin's Death* (Dordrecht: Reidel).

Golan, Galia (1973) *Reform Rule in Czechoslovakia, 1968–1969* (Cambridge: Cambridge University Press).

Gold, Thomas B. (1985) 'After Comradeship: Personal Relations in China since the Cultural Revolution', *China Quarterly*, no. 104 (December), pp. 656–75.

Goodman, David S. G. (1981) *Beijing Street Voices* (London: Boyars).

Goodman, David S. G. (ed.) (1984) *Groups and Politics in the People's Republic of China* (Cardiff: University College of Cardiff Press).

Gorbachev, Mikhail (1987) *Perestroika: New Thinking for Our Country and the World* (London: Collins).

Gregory, Paul R. and Stuart, Robert C. (1985) *Comparative Economic Systems*, 2nd ed. (Boston: Houghton Mifflin).

Gregory, Paul R. and Stuart, Robert C. (1986) *Soviet Economic Structure and Performance*, 3rd ed. (New York: Harper and Row).

Groth, Alexander J. (1971) *Comparative Politics: A Distributive Approach* (New York: Macmillan).

Groth, Alexander J. (1982) 'Worker Welfare Systems in Marxist-Leninist States: a Comparative Analysis', *Coexistence*, vol. 19, no. 1 (April), pp. 33–50.

Groth, Alexander J. and Hunt, William R. (1985) 'Marxist-Leninist Communication Systems in Comparative Perspective', *Coexistence*, vol. 22, no. 2 (July), pp. 123–38.

Gureyev, P. P. and Segudin, P. I. (1977) *Legislation in the USSR* (Moscow: Progress).

Hahn, Jeffrey, W. (1988) *Soviet Grassroots: Citizen Participation in Local Soviet Government* (Princeton, NJ: Princeton University Press).

Hahn, Jeffrey W. (1989) 'Power to the Soviets?', *Problems of Communism*, vol. 38, no. 1 (January–February), pp. 34–46.

Hammond, Thomas T. (ed.) (1975) *The Anatomy of Communist Takeovers* (New Haven, Conn.: Yale University Press).

Hankiss, Elemer (1990) *East European Alternatives: Are There Any?* (Oxford: Oxford University Press).

Harasymiw, Bohdan (1969) '*Nomenklatura*: the Soviet Communist Party's Leadership Recruitment System', *Canadian Journal of Political Science*, vol. 2, no. 4 (December), pp. 493–512.

Harding, Harry (1981) *Organising China: the Problem of Bureaucracy, 1949–1976* (Stanford, Calif.: Stanford University Press).

Harding, Harry (1987) *China's Second Revolution. Reform after Mao* (Washington DC: Brookings).

Harding, Neil (1977, 1981) *Lenin's Political Thought*, 2 Vols. (London: Macmillan).

Harding Neil (ed.) (1984) *The State in Socialist Society* (London: Macmillan).

Havel, Václav *et al.* (1985) *Power of the Powerless* (London: Hutchinson).

Heinrich, Hans-Georg (1986) *Hungary: Politics, Economics and Society* (London: Pinter).

Henkin, Louis *et al.* (1986) *Human Rights in Contemporary China* (New York: Columbia University Press).

Hill, Ronald J. (1980) *Soviet Politics, Political Science and Reform* (Oxford: Martin Robertson).

Hill, Ronald J. and Dellenbrant, Jan A. (eds) (1989) *Gorbachev and Perestroika* (Aldershot, Hants.: Edward Elgar).

Hill, Ronald J. and Frank, Peter (1987) *The Soviet Communist Party*, 3rd ed. (London: Allen & Unwin).

Hirszowicz, Maria (1986) *Coercion and Control in Communist Societies* (Brighton: Harvester).

Holmes, Leslie T. (ed.) (1981a) *The Withering Away of the State?* (London: Sage).

Holmes, Leslie T. (1981b) *The Policy Process in Communist States* (London: Sage).

Holmes, Leslie T. (1986) *Politics in the Communist World* (Oxford: Oxford University Press).

Hosking, Geoffrey (1985) *A History of the Soviet Union* (London: Fontana).

Hough, Jerry F. (1969) *The Soviet Prefects* (Cambridge, Mass.: Harvard University Press).

Hough, Jerry F. (1977) *The Soviet Union and Social Science Theory* (Cambridge, Mass.: Harvard University Press).

Hough, Jerry, F. and Fainsod, Merle (1979) *How the Soviet Union is Governed* (Cambridge, Mass.: Harvard University Press).

Humana, Charles (comp.) (1986) *The Economist World Human Rights Guide* (London: Hodder & Stoughton).

Hunt, Michael H. (1984) 'Chinese Foreign Relations in Historical Perspective', in Harry Harding (ed.) *China's Foreign Relations in the 1980s* (New Haven: Yale University Press).

Huntington, Samuel P. and Moore, Clement H. (eds) (1970) *Authoritarian Politics in Modern Society* (New York: Basic Books).

Inkeles, Alex and Bauer, Raymond A. (1969) *The Soviet Citizen* (Cambridge, Mass.: Harvard University Press).

Ionescu, Ghita (1972) *Comparative Communist Politics* (London: Macmillan).

Jacobs, Everett M. (ed.) (1983) *Soviet Local Politics and Government* (London: Allen & Unwin).

Janos, Andrew (1970) 'Group Politics in Communist Societies: a Second Look at the Pluralistic Model'. In Huntington and Moore (1970), pp. 437–50.

Jelavich, Barbara (1983) *A History of the Balkans*, 2 vols. (Cambridge: Cambridge University Press).

Jiang Zemin (1989) 'Speech at the Meeting in Celebration of the 40th Anniversary of the Founding of the People's Republic of China', *Beijing Review*, vol. 32, no. 41 (9–15 October), pp. 11–24.

Johnson, Chalmers (ed.) (1970) *Change in Communist Systems* (Stanford, Calif.: Stanford University Press).

Jones, Ellen (1986) *Red Army and Society. A Sociology of the Soviet Military*, paperback ed. (London: Allen & Unwin).

Jowitt, Kenneth (1971) *Revolutionary Breakthroughs and National Development: the Case of Romania 1944–1965* (Berkeley: University of California Press).

Joyce, Walter *et al.* (eds) (1989) *Gorbachev and Gorbachevism* (London: Cass).

Juviler, Peter H. and Morton, Henry W. (eds) (1967) *Soviet Policy-Making* (London: Pall Mall).

Kanet, Roger (ed.) (1971) *The Behavioural Revolution and Communist Studies* (New York: Free Press).

Karklins, Rasma (1986) *Ethnic Relations in the USSR* (London: Allen & Unwin).

Katz, Zev (ed.) (1975) *A Handbook of Major Soviet Nationalities* (New York: Free Press).

Kautsky, John H. (1973) 'Comparative Communism versus Comparative Politics', *Studies in Comparative Communism*, vol. 6, nos. 1–2 (Spring–Summer), pp. 135–70.

Kavanagh, Dennis (1972) *Political Culture* (London: Macmillan).

Kelley, Donald R. (ed.) (1980) *Soviet Politics in the Brezhnev Era* (New York: Praeger).

Khrushchev, N. K. (1971) 1974) *Khrushchev Remembers*, 2 vols. (London: Deutsch).

King, Robert R. (1980) *A History of the Romanian Communist Party* (Stanford, Calif.: Hoover Institution Press).

Kohout, Pavel (1972) *From the Diary of a Counter-Revolutionary* (New York: McGraw-Hill).

Kolakowski, Lezlek (1978) *Main Currents of Marxism*, 3 vols. (Oxford: Oxford University Press).

Kolakowski, Lezlek and Hampshire, Stuart (eds) (1974) *The Socialist Idea* (London: Weidenfeld & Nicolson).

Kolankiewicz, George and Lewis, Paul G. (1988) *Poland: Politics, Economics and Society* (London: Pinter).

Kovrig, Bennet (1979) *Communism in Hungary* (Stanford, Calif.: Hoover Institution Press).

Krejci, Jaroslav (1976) *Social Structure in Divided Germany* (London: Croom Helm).

Krutoglov, M. A. (1980) *Talks on Soviet Democracy* (Moscow: Progress).

Kusin, Vladimir V. (1978) *From Dubcek to Charter 77* (Edinburgh: Q Press).

Lampton, David M. (ed.) (1987) *Policy Implementation in Post-Mao China* (Berkeley: University of California Press).

Lane, David (1981) *Leninism: A Sociological Interpretation* (Cambridge: Cambridge University Press).

Lane, David (1982) *The End of Social Inequality? Class, Status and Power under State Socialism* (London: Allen & Unwin).

Lane, David (1984) 'Human Rights under State Socialism', *Political Studies*, vol. 32, no. 3 (September), pp. 349–68.

Lane, David (1985) *Soviet Economy and Society* (Oxford: Blackwell).

Lane, David and Kolankiewicz, George (eds) (1973) *Social Groups in Polish Society* (London: Macmillan).

Lane, David and O'Dell, Felicity (1978) *The Soviet Industrial Worker* (Oxford: Martin Robertson).

Lapidus, Gail W. (1984) 'Ethnonationalism and Political Stability: the Soviet Case', *World Politics*, vol. 36, no. 4 (July), pp. 555–80.

Leichter, Howard M. (1979) *A Comparative Approach to Policy Analysis: Health Care in Four Nations* (New York: Cambridge University Press).

Lendvai, Paul (1981) *The Bureaucracy of Truth: How Communist Governments Manage the News* (London: Burnett Books).

Leng, Shao-chuan (1981) 'Criminal Justice in Post-Mao China', *China Quarterly*, no. 87 (September), pp. 440–69.

Leslie, R. F. *et al.* (1980) *A History of Poland since 1863* (Cambridge: Cambridge University Press).

Lewin, Moshe (1975) *Political Undercurrents in Soviet Economic Debates* (London: Pluto).

Lewis, John W. (ed.) (1970) *Party Leadership and Revolutionary Power in China* (London: Cambridge University Press).

Lewis, Paul G. (1989) *Political Authority and Party Secretaries in Poland 1975–1986* (Cambridge: Cambridge University Press).

Li, Victor (1970) 'The Role of Law in Contemporary China', *China Quarterly*, no. 44 (October–December), pp. 66–111.

Lieberthal, Kenneth and Oksenberg, Michel (1988) *Policy-Making in China: Leaders, Structures, and Processes* (Princeton NJ: Princeton University Press).

Lindblom, Charles E. (1977) *Politics and Markets* (New York: Basic Books).

Lipski, Jan J. (1985) *KOR: Workers' Defense Committee in Poland, 1976–81* (Berkeley: University of California Press).

Lively, Jack (1975) *Democracy* (Oxford: Blackwell).

Löwenhardt, John (1982) *The Soviet Politburo* (Edinburgh: Canongate).

Lydall, Harold (1984) *Yugoslav Socialism: Theory and Practice* (Oxford: Clarendon Press).

Lydall, Harold (1989) *Yugoslavia in Crisis* (Oxford: Clarendon Press).

McCauley, Martin (ed.) (1977) *Communist Power in Europe, 1944–49* (London: Macmillan).

McCauley, Martin (ed.) (1979) *Marxism-Leninism in the GDR* (London: Macmillan).

McCauley, Martin and Carter, Stephen (eds) (1986) *Leadership and Succession in the Soviet Union, Eastern Europe and China* (London: Macmillan).

McCauley, Martin (ed.) (1987) *The Soviet Union under Gorbachev* (London: Macmillan).

McCauley, Martin (ed.) (1990) *Gorbachev and Perestroika* (London: Macmillan).

McFarlane, Bruce (1988) *Yugoslavia: Politics, Economics and Society* (London: Pinter).

Macfarlane, L. J. (1985) *The Theory and Practice of Human Rights* (London: Gower).

MacFarquhar, Roderick (1960) *The Hundred Flowers* (London: Stevens).

MacFarquhar, Roderick (1974) *The Origins of the Cultural Revolution* (London: Oxford University Press).

McIntyre, Robert J. (1988) *Bulgaria: Politics, Economics and Society* (London: Pinter).

McLellan, David (1979) *Marxism after Marx* (London: Macmillan).

McLellan, David (ed.) (1983) *Marx: The First Hundred Years* (Glasgow: Collins).

Macpherson, C. B. (1972) *The Real World of Democracy* (New York: Oxford University Press).

Madison, Bernice Q. (1980) *The Meaning of Social Policy* (London: Croom Helm).

Manion, Melanie (1985) 'The Cadre Management System, Post-Mao: the Appointment, Promotion, Transfer and Removal of Party and State Leaders', *China Quarterly*, no. 102 (June), pp. 203–33.

Marer, Paul (1985) *Dollar GNPs of the USSR and Eastern Europe* (Baltimore, Md.: Johns Hopkins University Press).

Mason, David S. (1985) *Public Opinion and Political Change in Poland, 1980–1982* (Cambridge: Cambridge University Press).

Medvedev, Zhores (1988) *Gorbachev*, rev. ed. (Oxford: Blackwell).

Meyer, Alfred G. (1957) *Leninism* (Cambridge, Mass.: Harvard University Press).

Meyer, Alfred G. (1961) 'USSR, Incorporated', *Slavic Review*, vol. 20, no. 3 (October), pp. 369–76.

Meyer, Alfred G. (1965) *The Soviet Political System: An Interpretation* (New York: Random House).

Mickiewicz, Ellen (1988) *Split Signals. Television and Politics in the Soviet Union* (New York: Oxford University Press).

Miliband, Ralph (1977) *Marxism and Politics* (Oxford: Oxford University Press).

Millar, James R. (ed.) (1987) *Politics, Work, and Daily Life in the USSR. A Survey of Former Citizens* (New York: Cambridge University Press).

Minority Rights Group (1984) *Religious Minorities in the Soviet Union*, 4th ed. (London: Minority Rights Group).

Mlynář, Zdeněk (1980) *Night Frost in Prague* (London: Hurst).

Moody, Peter R. (1977) *Opposition and Dissent in Contemporary China* (Stanford, Cal.: Hoover Institution).

Morrisson, Christian (1984) 'Income Distribution in East European and Western Countries', *Journal of Comparative Economics* vol. 8, no. 2 (June), pp. 121–38.

Munro, Robin (1988) 'Political Reform, Student Demonstrations and the Conservative Backlash', in Benewick and Wingrove (eds) (1988).

Nathan, Andrew (1986) *Chinese Democracy* (London: I. B. Tauris).

Nee, Victor and Stark, David (eds.) (1989) *Remaking the Economic Institutions of Socialism: China and Eastern Europe* (Stanford: Stanford University Press).

Nelson, Daniel N. (1978) 'Political Convergence: an Empirical Assessment', *World Politics*, vol. 30, no. 3 (April), pp. 411–32.

Nelson, Daniel N. (1988) *Elite–Mass Relations in Communist Systems* (London: Macmillan).

Nelson, Daniel N. and White, Stephen (eds) (1982) *Communist Legislatures in Comparative Perspective* (London: Macmillan and New York: SUNY at Albany Press).

Nove, Alec (1982) *The Economics of Feasible Socialism* (London: Allen & Unwin).

Nove, Alex (1983) 'The Class Nature of the Soviet Union Revisited', *Soviet Studies*, vol. 35, no. 3 (July), pp. 298–312.

Nove, Alec (1986) *The Soviet Economic System*, 3rd ed. (London: Allen & Unwin).

Nove, Alec (1989) *An Economic History of the USSR*, 2nd ed. (Harmondsworth, Middx.: Penguin).

Nuti, Domenico Mario (1979) 'The Contradictions of Socialist Economies: a Marxian Interpretation', *The Socialist Register 1979* (London: Merlin Press), pp. 228–73.

O'Brien, Kevin J. (1989) 'Legislative Development and Chinese Political Change', *Studies in Comparative Communism*, vol. 22, no. 1 (Spring), pp. 57–75.

Odom, William (1976) 'A Dissenting View on the Group Approach to Soviet Politics', *World Politics*, vol. 28, no. 4 (July), pp. 542–67.

Oren, Nissan (1973) *Revolution Administered: Agrarianism and Communism in Bulgaria* (Baltimore, Md.: Johns Hopkins University Press).

Ostoja-Ostaszewski, A. *et al.* (1977) *Dissent in Poland* (London: Association of Polish Students and Graduates in Exile).

Parkin, Frank (1971) *Class Inequality and Political Order* (New York: Praeger).

Pavlowitch, Stefan (1971) *Yugoslavia* (London: Benn).

Pennock, J. Roland (1979) *Democratic Political Theory* (Princeton, NJ: Princeton University Press).

Perry, Elizabeth J. and Wong Christine (eds) (1985) *The Political Economy of Reform in Post-Mao China* (Cambridge, MA: Council on East Asian Studies).

Pravda, Alex (1986) 'Elections in Communist Party States'. In White and Nelson (1986), pp. 27–54.

Prifti, Peter (1978) *Socialist Albania since 1944* (Cambridge, Mass.: MIT Press).

Prokopovich, S. N. (1918) *Opty ischisleniya narodnogo dokhoda 50 gubernii Evropeiskoi Rossii*, as cited in Peter Gatrell, *The Tsarist Economy 1850–1917* (1986) (London: Batsford).

Prybyla, Jan S. (1987) *Market and Plan under Socialism: The Bird in the Cage* (Stanford: Hoover Institution Press).

Prybyla, Jan S. (1989) 'China's Economic Experiment: Back from the Market?', *Problems of Communism*, vol. 39, no. 1 (January–February), pp. 1–18.

Pryor, Frederick L. (1968) *Public Expenditures in Communist and Capitalist Nations* (London: Allen & Unwin).

Pye, Lucian W. (1981) *The Dynamics of Chinese Politics* (Cambridge, MA: Oelschlager, Gunn and Hain).

Pye, Lucian W. (1985) *Asian Power and Politics. The Cultural Dimensions of Authority* (Cambridge, MA: Harvard University Press).

Pye, Lucian and Verba, Sydney (eds) (1965) *Political Culture and Political Development* (Princeton, NJ: Princeton University Press).

Racz, Barnabas (1987) 'Political Participation and Developed Socialism: the Hungarian Elections of 1985', *Soviet Studies*, vol. 39, no. 1 (January), pp. 40–62.

Rakowska-Harmstone, Teresa (ed.) (1984) *Communism in Eastern Europe*, 2nd ed. (Bloomington: Indiana University Press).

Ramet, Pedro (1984) *Nationalism and Federalism in Yugoslavia, 1963–1983* (Bloomington: Indiana University Press).

Ramet, Pedro (ed.) (1984) *Religion and Nationalism in Soviet and East European Politics* (Durham, NC: Duke University Press).

Remington, Thomas F. (1988) *The Truth of Authority. Ideology and Communication in the Soviet Union* (Pittsburgh, PA: University of Pittsburgh Press).

Rigby, T. H. (1968) *Communist Party Membership in the USSR, 1917–1967* (Princeton, NJ: Princeton University Press).

Rigby, T. H. (1976) 'Soviet Communist Party Membership under Brezhnev', *Soviet Studies*, vol. 28, no. 3 (July), pp. 317–37.

Rigby, T. H. *et al.* (eds) (1980) *Authority, Power and Policy in the USSR. Essays dedicated to Leonard Schapiro* (London: Macmillan).

Robinson, Gertrude J. (1977) *Tito's Maverick Media: the Politics of Mass Communication in Yugoslavia* (Urbana: University of Illinois Press).

Robinson, W. F. (1973) *The Pattern of Reform in Hungary* (New York: Praeger).

Rosenbaum, Walter A. (1975) *Political Culture* (London: Nelson).

Rothschild, Joseph (1974) *East Central Europe between the Two World Wars* (Seattle and London: University of Washington Press).

Rothschild, Joseph (1989) *Return to Diversity: A Political History of East Central Europe since World War II* (New York: Columbia University Press).

Ruane, Kevin (1982) *The Polish Challenge* (London: British Broadcasting Corporation).

Ruble, Blair A. (1981) *Soviet Trade Unions: Their Development in the 1970s* (Cambridge: Cambridge University Press).

Rush, Myron (1975) *How Communist States Change their Rulers* (Ithaca, NY: Cornell University Press).

Rusinow, Dennison (1977) *The Yugoslav Experiment, 1948–1974* (London: Hurst).

Rutland, Peter (1985) *The Myth of the Plan* (London: Hutchinson).

Saich, Tony (1983) 'The Fourth Constitution of the People's Republic of China', *Review of Socialist Law*, vol. 9, no. 2, pp. 113–24 and 183–208.

Saich, Tony (1984) 'Party-building Since Mao: a Question of Style?' In Maxwell and McFarlane (1984), pp. 149–67.

Saich, Tony (1989a) 'Modernization and Participation in the People's Republic of China', in Joseph Y. S. Cheng (ed.) *China: Modernisation in the 1980s* (Hong Kong: Chinese University Press).

Saich, Tony (1989b) *China's Science Policy in the 1980s* (Manchester: Manchester University Press).

Saich, Tony (1990) 'Much Ado about Nothing: Party Reform in the Eighties', in Gordon White (ed.) *From Crisis to Crisis: The Chinese State in the Era of Economic Reform* (London: Macmillan).

Sartori, Giovanni (1986) *Theories of Democracy Revisited*, 2 vols. (Chatham, NJ: Chatham House).

Schapiro, Leonard B. (1970) *The Communist Party of the Soviet Union*, 2nd ed. (London: Eyre & Spottiswoode).

Schapiro, Leonard B. (1972) *Totalitarianism* (London: Pall Mall).

Schapiro, Leonard and Godson, Joseph (eds) *The Soviet Worker: From Lenin to Andropov*, 2nd ed. (London: Macmillan).

Schell, Orville (1988) *Discos and Democracy. China in the Throes of Reform* (New York: Pantheon).

Schmidt-Hauer, Christian (1986) *Gorbachev: The Road to Power* (London: Tauris).

Schöpflin, George (1983) *Censorship and Political Communication in Eastern Europe* (London: Pinter and New York: St Martin's).

Schöpflin, George (ed.) (1986) *The Soviet Union and Eastern Europe: A Handbook* (New York: Facts on File).

Schram, Stuart R. (1970) *Mao Tse-Tung* (Harmondsworth, Middx.: Penguin Books).

Schram, Stuart R. (ed.) (1973) *Authority, Participation and Cultural Change in China* (London: Cambridge University Press).

Schram, Stuart R. (ed.) (1974) *Mao Tse-Tung Unrehearsed* (Harmondsworth, Middx.: Penguin Books).

Schram, Stuart R. (1981) 'To Utopia and Back: a Cycle in the History of the Chinese Communist Party', *China Quarterly*, no. 87 (September), pp. 407–39.

Schram, Stuart R. (1984) *Ideology and Policy in China since the Third Plenum, 1978–84* (London: School of Oriental and African Studies).

Schram, Stuart R. (1986) 'Mao Tse-Tung Thought to 1949', in John K. Fairbank and Albert Feuerwerker (eds) *Republican China 1912–1949* Part 2 (Cambridge: Cambridge University Press).

Schulz, Donald E. and Adams, Jan S. (eds) (1981) *Political Participation in Communist Systems* (New York: Pergamon).

Schurmann, Franz (1968) *Ideology and Organisation in Communist China*, 2nd ed. (Berkeley: University of California Press).

Selucky, Radoslav (1979) *Marxism, Socialism, Freedom* (London: Macmillan).

Selyunin, V. and Khanin, G. (1987) 'Lukavaya tsifra', *Novy mir*, no. 2, pp. 181–210.

Seton-Watson, Hugh (1960) *The Pattern of Communist Revolution*, rev. ed. (London: Methuen).

Seton-Watson, Hugh (1967) *The Russian Empire 1801–1917* (Oxford: Clarendon Press).

Seton-Watson, Hugh (1980) *The Imperialist Revolutionaries: World Communism in the 1960s and 1970s*, rev. ed. (London: Hutchinson).

Seton-Watson, Hugh (1985) *The East European Revolution*, rev. ed. (Boulder, Col.: Westview).

Seton-Watson, Hugh (1986) *Eastern Europe between the Wars, 1918–1941*, new ed. (Boulder, Col.: Westview).

Seymour, James D. (1980) *The Fifth Modernization* (New York: E. M. Coleman).

Shafir, Michael (1985) *Romania: Politics, Economics and Society* (London: Pinter).

Sharlet, Robert (1978) *The New Soviet Constitution of 1977* (Brunswick, Ohio: King's Court).

Shatz, Marshall S. (1981) *Soviet Dissent in Historical Perspective* (Cambridge: Cambridge University Press).

Sher, Gerson (1977) *Praxis: Marxist Criticism and Dissent in Socialist Yugoslavia* (Bloomington: Indiana University Press).

Shevchenko, Arkady (1985) *Breaking with Moscow* (New York: Knopf).

Shoup, Paul S. (1968) *Communism and the Yugoslav National Question* (New York: Columbia University Press).

Shoup, Paul S. (comp.) (1981) *The Eastern European and Soviet Data Handbook: Political, Social and Developmental Indicators, 1945–1975* (New York: Columbia University Press).

Simes, Dmitri K. (1975) 'The Soviet Invasion of Czechoslovakia and the Limits of Kremlinology', *Studies in Comparative Communism*, vol. 8, nos. 1–2 (Spring–Summer), pp. 174–80.

Simons, William B. (ed.) (1980a) *The Constitutions of the Communist World* (Alphen aan den Rijn: Sijhoff and Noordhoff).

Simons, William B. (ed.) (1980b) *The Soviet Codes of Law* (Alphen aan den Rijn: Sijthoff and Noordhoff).

Simons, William B. and White, Stephen (eds) (1984) *The Party Statutes of the Communist World* (The Hague: Martinus Nijhoff).

Singleton, Fred (1976) *Twentieth Century Yugoslavia* (London: Macmillan).

Singleton, Fred (1985) *A Short History of the Yugoslav Peoples* (Cambridge: Cambridge University Press).

Skilling, H. Gordon (1966) 'Interest Groups and Communist Politics', *World Politics*, vol. 18, no. 3 (April), pp. 435–51.

Skilling, H. Gordon (1973) 'Opposition in Communist East Europe'. In Dahl (1973), pp. 89–120.

Skilling, H. Gordon (1976) *Czechoslovakia's Interrupted Revolution* (Princeton, NJ: Princeton University Press).

Skilling, H. Gordon (1983) 'Interest Groups and Communist Politics Revisited', *World Politics*, vol. 36, no. 1 (October), pp. 1–27.

Skilling, H. Gordon and Griffiths, Franklyn (eds) (1971) *Interest Groups in Soviet Politics* (Princeton, NJ: Princeton University Press).

Smith, Gordon B. (ed.) (1980) *Public Policy and Administration in the Soviet Union* (New York: Praeger).

Solinger, Dorothy J. (1989) 'Capitalist Measures with Chinese Characteristics', *Problems of Communism*, vol. 39, no. 1 (January–February), pp. 19–33.

Solomon, Richard H. (1971) *Mao's Revolution and the Chinese Political Culture* (Berkeley: University of California Press).

Solomon, Susan G. (ed.) (1983) *Pluralism in the Soviet Union. Essays in Honour of H. Gordon Skilling* (London: Macmillan).

Staniszkis, Jadwiga (1984) *Poland's Self-Limiting Revolution* (Princeton, NJ: Princeton University Press).

Staniszkis, Jadwiga (1985–6) 'Forms of Reasoning as Ideology', *Telos*, no. 66, pp. 67–80.

Starr, John B. (1979) *Continuing the Revolution: the Political Thought of Mao Tse-Tung* (Princeton, NJ: Princeton University Press).

Suda, Zdenek L. (1980) *Zealots and Rebels: A History of the Communist Party of Czechoslovakia* (Stanford, Calif.: Hoover Institution Press).

Sullivan, Lawrence R. (1984) 'The Role of the Control Organs in the Chinese Communist Party, 1977–1983' *Asian Survey*, vol. 24, no. 6, pp. 597–617.

Summers, Robert and Heston, Alan (1984) 'Improved International Comparisons of Real Product and its Composition, 1950–1980', *Review of Income and Wealth*, vol. 30, no. 2 (June), pp. 207–62.

Swain, Geoffrey (1985) *Collective Farms which Work?* (Cambridge: Cambridge University Press).

Szajkowski, Bogdan (ed.) (1981) *Marxist Governments: A World Survey*, 3 vols (London: Macmillan).

Szajkowski, Bogdan (1982) *The Evolution of Communist Regimes* (London: Butterworths).

Szajkowski, Bogdan (ed.) (1985ff) *Marxist Regimes*, 36 vols (London: Pinter).

Szymanski, Albert (1984) *Human Rights in the Soviet Union* (London: Zed Press).

Taras, Ray, (ed.) (1989) *Leadership Change in Communist States* (Boston: Unwin Hyman).

Tarschys, Daniel (1977) 'The Soviet Political System: Three Models', *European Journal of Political Research*, vol. 5, no. 3 (September), pp. 287–320.

Teiwes, Frederick C. (1979) *Politics and Purges in China: Rectification and the Decline of Party Norms, 1950–1965* (White Plains, NY: M. E. Sharpe).

Tökés, Rudolf, L. (ed.) (1979) *Opposition in Eastern Europe* (London: Macmillan).

Toma, Peter and Volgyes, Ivan (1977) *Politics in Hungary* (San Francisco: W. H. Freeman)

Tucker, Robert C. (1972) *The Soviet Political Mind*, 2nd ed. (London: Allen and Unwin).

Tucker, Robert C. (ed.) (1977) *Stalinism* (New York: Norton).

Ulč, Otto (1974) *Politics in Czechoslovakia* (San Francisco: W. H. Freeman).

Unger, Aryeh L. (1977–78) 'Images of the CPSU', *Survey*, vol. 23, no. 4 (Autumn), pp. 23–34.

Unger, Aryeh L. (1981a) *Constitutional Development in the USSR* (London: Methuen).

Unger, Aryeh L. (1981b) 'Political Participation in the USSR: YCL and CPSU', *Soviet Studies*, vol. 33, no. 1 (January), pp. 107–24.

Urban, Michael E. (1990) *More Power to the Soviets* (Aldershot: Edward Elgar).

US Congress Economic Committee (1982) *USSR: Measures of Economic Growth and Development, 1950–1980* (Washington, DC: US Government Publishing Office).

Vanneman, Peter (1977) *The Supreme Soviet* (Durham, NC.: Duke University Press).

Volgyes, Ivan (ed.) (1979) *The Peasantry of Eastern Europe*. 2 vols (New York: Pergamon).

Volgyes, Ivan (1986) *Politics in Eastern Europe* (Homewood, Ill.: Dorsey).

Voslensky, Michael (1984) *Nomenklatura. Anatomy of the Soviet Ruling Class* (London: Bodley Head).

Wade, Larry L. and Groth, Alexander J. (1989) 'Predicting Regime Educational Outcomes by Political Regime: A Global Comparison', *Coexistence*, vol. 26, no. 2, pp. 147–60.

Walder, Andrew G. (1986) *Communist Neo-Traditionalism. Work and Authority in Chinese Industry* (Berkeley, Cal.: University of California Press).

Waller, Michael and Szajkowski, Bogdan (1981) 'The Communist Movement: from Monolith to Polymorph'. In Szajkowski (1981), vol. 1, pp. 1–19.

Watson, James L. (ed.) (1984) *Class and Stratification in Post-Revolutionary China* (Cambridge: Cambridge University Press).

Westoby, Adam (1989) *The Evolution of Communism* (Cambridge: Polity).

Weydenthal, Jan de (1986) *The Communists of Poland*, rev. ed. (Stanford, Calif.: Hoover Institution Press).

White, Stephen (1978a) 'Communist Systems and the "Iron Law of Pluralism"', *British Journal of Political Science*, vol. 8, no. 1 (January), pp. 101–17.

White, Stephen (1978b) 'Continuity and Change in Soviet Political Culture: an Emigré Study', *Comparative Political Studies*, vol. 11, no. 3 (October), pp. 381–95.

White, Stephen (1979) *Political Culture and Soviet Politics* (London: Macmillan).

White, Stephen (1982a) 'The USSR Supreme Soviet: a Developmental Perspective', In Nelson and White (1982), pp. 125–59.

White, Stephen (1982b) 'The Supreme Soviet and Budgetary Politics in the USSR', *British Journal of Political Science*, vol. 12, no. 1 (January), pp. 75–94.

White, Stephen (1983a) 'What is a Communist System?', *Studies in Comparative Communism*, vol. 16, no. 4 (Winter), pp. 247–63.

White, Stephen (1983b) 'Political Communications in the USSR: Letters to Party, State and the Press', *Political Studies*, vol. 31, no. 1 (January), pp. 43–60.

White, Stephen (1985) 'Propagating Communist Values in the USSR', *Problems of Communism*, vol. 34, no. 6 (November–December), pp. 1–17.

White, Stephen (1989) *Soviet Communism: Programme and Rules* (London: Routledge).

White, Stephen (1990a) *Gorbachev in Power* (Cambridge: Cambridge University Press).

White, Stephen (1990b) '"Democratisation" in the USSR', *Soviet Studies*, vol. 42, no. 1 (January), pp. 3–24.

White, Stephen and Nelson, Daniel N. (eds) (1986) *Communist Politics: A Reader* (London: Macmillan and New York: New York University Press).

White, Stephen and Pravda, Alex (eds) (1988) *Ideology and Soviet Politics* (London: Macmillan).

Wiles, Peter (1977) *Economic Institutions Compared* (Oxford: Blackwell).

Wiles, Peter (ed.) (1983) *The New Communist Third World* (London: Croom Helm).

Wiles, Peter and Markowski, Stefan (1971) 'Income Distribution under Communism and Capitalism', *Soviet Studies*, vol. 22, nos. 3 and 4 (January and April), pp. 344–69 and 487–511.

Wilson, Dick, (ed.) (1977) *Mao Tse-Tung in the Scales of History* (Cambridge: Cambridge University Press).

Wilson, Duncan (1980) *Tito's Yugoslavia* (Cambridge: Cambridge University Press).

Woods, Roger (1986) *Opposition in the GDR under Honecker* (London: Macmillan).

Yevtushenko, Yevgeny (1963) *A Precocious Autobiography* (London: Collins).

Zaslavsky, Victor and Brym, Robert J. (1978) 'The Functions of Elections in the USSR', *Soviet Studies*, vol. 30, no. 3 (July), pp. 362–71.

Zhao Ziyang (1987) 'Advance along the Road of Socialism with Chinese Characteristics', *Beijing Review*, vol. 30, no. 45, supplement.

Zimbalist, Andrew *et al.* (1987) *Comparing Economic Systems: A Politico-Economic Approach*, 2nd ed. (New York: Harcourt, Brace, Jovanovich).

Zukin, Sharon (1975) *Beyond Marx and Tito* (New York: Cambridge University Press).

Zweig, David (1989) *Agrarian Radicalism in China, 1968–1981* (Cambridge, MA: Harvard University Press).

Index